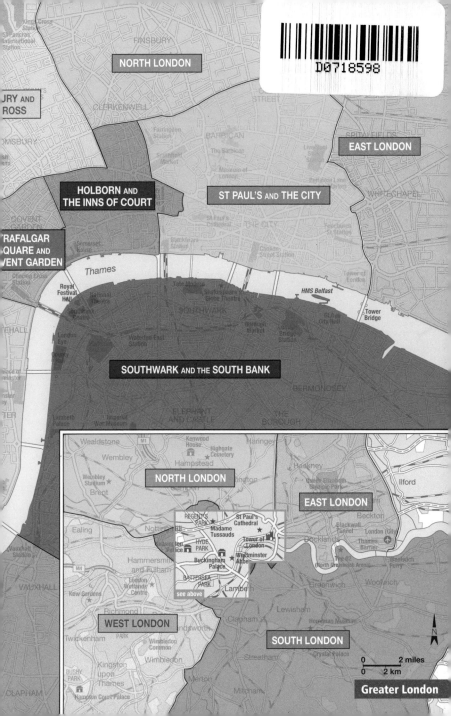

INSIGHT GUIDES
LONDON

2

HOW TO USE THIS BOOK

This book is carefully structured both to convey an understanding of the city and its culture and to guide readers through its attractions and activities:

◆ The Best Of section at the front of the book helps you to prioritize. The first spread contains all the Top Sights, while the Editor's Choice details unique experiences, the best buys or other recommendations.

◆ To understand London, you need to know something of its past. The city's history and culture are described in authoritative essays written by specialists in their fields who have lived in and documented the city for many years.

◆ The Places section details all the attractions worth seeing. The main places of interest are coordinated by number with the maps.

◆ Each chapter includes lists of recommended shops, restaurants, bars and cafes.

◆ Photographs throughout the book are chosen not only to illustrate geography and buildings, but also to convey the moods of the city and the life of its people.

◆ The Travel Tips section includes all the practical information you will need, divided into four key sections: transport, accommodation, activities (including nightlife, events, shopping, sports and tours) and an A–Z of practical tips.

◆ A detailed street atlas is included at the back of the book, with all hotels, restaurants, bars and cafes plotted for your convenience.

PLACES AND SIGHTS

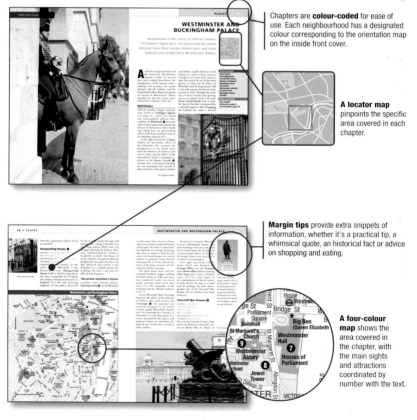

Chapters are **colour-coded** for ease of use. Each neighbourhood has a designated colour corresponding to the orientation map on the inside front cover.

A locator map pinpoints the specific area covered in each chapter.

Margin tips provide extra snippets of information, whether it's a practical tip, a whimsical quote, an historical fact or advice on shopping and eating.

A four-colour map shows the area covered in the chapter, with the main sights and attractions coordinated by number with the text.

PHOTO FEATURES

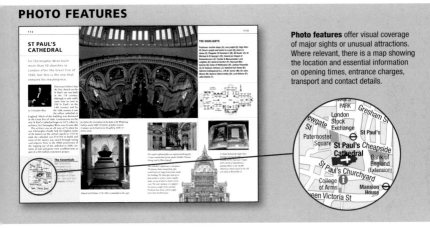

Photo features offer visual coverage of major sights or unusual attractions. Where relevant, there is a map showing the location and essential information on opening times, entrance charges, transport and contact details.

SHOPPING AND RESTAURANT LISTINGS

Shopping listings provide details of the best shops in each area. **Restaurant listings** give the establishment's contact details, opening times and price category, followed by a useful review. Bars and cafés are also covered here. The coloured dot and grid reference refers to the atlas section at the back of the book.

French

L'Atelier de Joel Robuchon
13–15 West St, WC2. Tel: 7010 8600.
www.joelrobuchon.co.uk Open: L & D daily.
£££–££££ (pre-theatre menu available)
(③ p306, C2)
French food with Spanish influences at this two Michelin-starred restaurant. Foie gras ravioli, free range quail, Scottish scallops, lobster and steak are just some of the offerings. Diners sit at a counter surrounding the kitchen so you can

TRAVEL TIPS

Ballet and Opera

Coliseum, St Martin's Lane,
WC2. Tel: 7845 9300; www.eno.
org.
This elegant Edwardian theatre is easily distinguished on London's skyline by the illuminated golden globe on its roof. Home to the English National Opera (ENO), there English-language opera is performed. Production

Travel Tips provide all the practical knowledge you'll need before and during your trip: how to get there, getting around, where to stay and what to do. The A–Z section is a handy summary of practical information, arranged alphabetically.

THE BEST OF LONDON: TOP ATTRACTIONS

At a glance, everything you won't want to miss, from long-established icons like Tower Bridge and Big Ben to exciting newer landmarks such as Tate Modern and the London Eye.

▷ **Big Ben and the Houses of Parliament.** The clock tower of this flamboyant Gothic-style building is a symbol of London. Guided tours of the Houses of Parliament can be arranged during the summer recess in August and September. See page 70.

△ **Buckingham Palace.** The best time to see the palace is during Changing the Guard. If you would like to see inside, then you must time your visit to coincide with the Queen's annual trip to Balmoral (late July–Sept) when some of the State Rooms of the palace open for guided tours. See page 76.

◁ **The London Eye.** For the best views in London take a trip on the London Eye on the South Bank. The stately wheel takes 30 minutes to rotate, allowing plenty of time for picking out London's sights. On a fine day you will be able to see for 25 miles (40km). See page 182.

▽ **The British Museum.** This immense museum contains some of the world's most important treasures from antiquity. See page 142.

◁ **Trafalgar Square.** London's best-loved square has shooting fountains and Nelson's Column and is overlooked by the National Gallery. See page 95.

▷ **St Paul's Cathedral.** Built after the Great Fire of London of 1666, St Paul's is Christopher Wren's greatest work. See page 172.

▽ **Tower Bridge.** The famous bascule bridge is a triumph of Victorian engineering. See page 190.

◁ **Piccadilly Circus.** Presiding over this gateway to the West End and Theatreland is the famous statue of Eros. See page 85.

△ **Tate Modern.** For modern art in an inspired setting, visit this power station-turned-art-gallery on the South Bank. See page 194.

▽ **Tower of London.** Established by William the Conqueror, the Tower has a long and bloody history. See page 174.

THE BEST OF LONDON: EDITOR'S CHOICE

Here are our ideas on what to do once you've seen London's top sights, plus some tips and tricks even Londoners won't always know.

BEST FOR CHILDREN

The Natural History Museum. The Darwin Centre allows children to examine specimens and watch scientists at work. See page 215.

The Science Museum. The Who Am I? section is a great hands-on experience. See page 210.

Museum of Childhood. This outpost of the V&A appeals to adults and children alike. See page 247.

London Zoo. One of the world's top zoos. See page 125.

The London Aquarium. Sharks, seahorses, touch pools and much

Hamleys.

more. See page 181.

HMS Belfast. A World War II battleship moored on the Thames. See page 190.

Golden Hinde. The piratic-looking replica of Sir Francis Drake's ship. See page 187.

Madame Tussauds. Kids love spotting their favourite celebrities, even if they are made of wax. See page 130.

London Dungeon. Scary fun ideal for 10- to 14-year-olds. See page 181.

London Transport Museum. A huge hit with younger children. See page 100.

Ice-skating. In winter, ice rinks spring up outside the Natural History Museum and Somerset House. See pages 200 and 146.

Princess Diana Memorial Playground. With its pirate ship and teepees, this is the best playground in central London. See page 207.

Hamleys. Seven floors to explore in the 'world's finest toy shop'. See page 114.

Museum of Childhood.

BEST VIEWS

The Shard. London's iconic new skyscraper offers incredible views at a height of 800ft (244 metres). See page 189.

The London Eye. Unbeatable vistas whichever way you look. See page 182.

Monument. Climb the 311 steps for views over the City. See page 168.

Waterloo Bridge. Panoramas day and night. See page 183.

Westminster Cathedral. Take the lift to the top of the 330ft (100-metre) tower. See page 75.

One New Change. The sixth floor of this new shopping centre offers stunning views of St Paul's Cathedral. See page 168.

Richmond Hill. The pastoral view from here is protected by an act of Parliament. See page 234.

Parliament Hill. Far-reaching views across London. See page 240.

Restaurants and bars with views. Try the Tate Modern Restaurant (see page 192) or the Oxo Tower Restaurant (see page 192).

View from the Tate Modern.

Changing the Guard.

BEST WALKS

Old and new London.
An introductory walk,
starting from Westmin-
ster Abbey, crossing
Westminster Bridge,
strolling along the
South Bank past the
London Eye, Tate Mod-
ern and Shakespeare's
Globe, and then cross-
ing the Millennium
Bridge to St Paul's Ca-
thedral. See pages
73, 182 and 155.

Hampstead Heath.
Meadows, woods, lakes
and ponds, with great
views over London. See
page 240.

**Hyde Park and
Kensington Gardens.**
Sculptures, fountains,
gardens and
playgrounds in the
centre of the city. See
page 204.

Regent's Canal. Walk
all or part of the 8.5
miles (14km) from Pad-
dington to Limehouse,
taking in Camden Lock
and Little Venice. See
page 240.

Richmond. Offers fabulous views, a deer park,
interesting pubs and
17th-century Ham
House. See page 234.

ONLY IN LONDON

Harrods. The store that
has everything. See
page 199.

Shakespeare's Globe.
The play's the thing, as
in Elizabethan days.
See page 185.

Royal Pageantry. The
Changing the Guard cer-
emony at Buckingham
Palace takes place daily
at 11.30am May–July

(alternate days rest of
year). See page 78.

**Pearly Kings and
Queens.** You'll spot
these colourful charac-
ters at East End festi-
vals and markets. See
page 19.

The V&A. The world's
largest collection of
decorative arts. See
pages 200 and 212.

Deer grazing in Richmond Park.

HISTORIC PUBS

The George. This pub off Borough High Street, rebuilt in 1676, is London's only galleried coaching inn. See page 193.

Black Friar. Built in 1875 on the site of the Black Friars Monastery, this is London's only Arts and Crafts pub. The marble interior carries bronze friezes depicting the activities of monks. See page 152.

Lamb and Flag. Traditional pub tucked down a tiny alleyway in the heart of Covent Garden. See page 103.

The Grenadier. Hidden away in a quiet cobbled mews, this pub used to be the mess of the Duke of Wellington's officers. See page 225.

Jerusalem Tavern. Once an 18th-century coffee shop, this is now an intimate pub with cubicles, Georgian-style furniture and ales from Suffolk's St Peter's Brewery. See page 171.

The Mayflower. It was by this waterside pub in Rotherhithe that the Pilgrim Fathers moored their ship before setting off for Plymouth and thence the New World in 1620. See page 191.

Ye Old Cheshire Cheese. Famous olde-worlde pub off Fleet Street, rebuilt after the Great Fire but retaining a medieval crypt. Frequented by many well-known literary figures in the past, including Charles Dickens and Dr Samuel Johnson. See page 153.

Enjoying a drink in The George's cobbled courtyard.

The Savoy.

DISTINCTIVE HOTELS

The Savoy. Grand riverside hotel near Covent Garden, a favourite with Winston Churchill and Frank Sinatra. See page 280.

Brown's. Intimate luxury in the heart of Mayfair. See page 281.

The Goring. Where Kate Middleton spent the night before the royal wedding. See page 279.

Hazlitt's. A characterful 18th-century property in Soho. See page 280.

SUMMER IN THE CITY

River cruises. Cruise down to Greenwich or the Thames Barrier, or up to Hampton Court Palace. See page 296.

Open-air drama. Watch Shakespeare at the Globe Theatre on the South Bank or in Regent's Park. See pages 185 and 125.

The City in Bloom. See whole gardens recreated at the Chelsea Flower Show held in late May in Chelsea or visit the lovely Rose Garden (June through to late autumn) in Regent's Park. See pages 221 and 125.

Sporting greats. See tennis played at Wimbledon and cricket played at Lord's. See page 294.

Cool off. Swim in the bathing ponds on Hampstead Heath, in the Serpentine in Hyde Park, or in the Oasis, a heated outdoor pool, in Holborn. See page 295.

Picnic in the park. London's parks, such as Green Park or St James's Park, are great for lunching al fresco. See page 76.

Last Night of the Proms.

BEST FESTIVALS

Notting Hill Carnival.
This is Europe's biggest street festival, with Caribbean bands, extravagant costumes and floats. Held over the last weekend in August.
Chinese New Year.
Dancing dragons and exotic food in Soho's Chinatown. Late January/early February.

Trooping the Colour.
The Queen rides out on Horse Guards Parade, with the Household Cavalry in red tunics and bearskin hats. The Saturday closest to 10 June.
Lord Mayor's Show.
The Lord Mayor rides out in his gilded coach from the Guildhall to the Law Courts. Second

Saturday in November.
Last Night of the Proms. Exuberant finale to the annual BBC-sponsored Henry Wood Promenade Concerts in the Albert Hall and Hyde Park. Held on a Saturday night in mid-September.
For a full listing of festivals see page 292.

Dancer at Notting Hill Carnival, held on the last weekend in August.

MONEY SAVING TIPS

Half-price Theatre Tickets The tkts booth in Leicester Square sells same-day tickets for West End shows at up to 50% off, plus a £3 service fee (Mon–Sat 9am–7pm, Sun 11am–4.30pm; www.tkts.co.uk). Tickets for some plays at the National Theatre can be purchased for £12 through the Travelex scheme (www.nationaltheatre.org.uk).
Restaurant Vouchers A number of websites offer money off vouchers for some restaurants, especially chains like Pizza Express and Ask. Try www.

moneysavingexpert.com and www.vouchercodes.co.uk.
Museums and Attractions The national museums and galleries are free. The London Pass allows free entry to over 60 attractions. At press time, prices for an adult pass ranged from £56 for a one-day pass (including travel on Tube and bus) to £156 for a six-day pass including travel (children under 15 £34/£99). Details: tel: 0870 242 9988; www.londonpass.com.
Public Transport The Underground

(Tube) is expensive compared with most European metro systems, but money-saving Travelcards and Oyster cards are available. Children under the age of 11 can travel free on the network (as well as the Docklands Light Railway and buses), providing they are accompanied by an adult (see page 275). Buses are quite a bit cheaper than the Tube and offer a sightseeing tour along the way. Alternatively walk – many places, especially in the West End, are closer than you might think.

View over the Square Mile and Tower Bridge.

Walking in Green Park in autumn.

LONDON'S ALLURE

What attracts millions of visitors is a potent mixture of continuity and tradition plus the excitement of never knowing what they're going to find round the next corner.

Henry James described the capital as a 'giant animated encyclopaedia with people for pages'. With all its variety and history, it's hard to know where to start as a tourist, but James's emphasis is a good one. Even though the immensity of London makes it hard to embrace as a whole and you don't find long-time residents proclaiming their feelings through 'I Heart London' stickers, the people and the culture matter as much as the buildings. To most residents, the city is a collection of communities or villages, once independent but long since swallowed up, along with much of the surrounding countryside, by the expanding metropolis.

Getting a black cab.

At the centre of this patchwork city is a common area of shared London, a London of work and play. This book deals primarily with shared London, the essential London of the West End, the City and South Bank, but it also covers some of the interesting local 'villages' such as Hampstead, Islington, Greenwich and Brixton.

London, it is sometimes said, is as unrepresentative of the United Kingdom as New York is of the United States. There's some truth in this. Both cities have astonishingly cosmopolitan populations, their restaurants are almost as diverse as their immigrants, they are important centres of international finance, they pioneer the latest fashions, and their range of shops and theatres is absurdly disproportionate to their size.

Queen Anne architecture.

But London is umbilically linked to the rest of Britain in some crucial respects. Unlike New York, it is a capital city, spawning governmental institutions. It is also an ancient city, dating back to Roman times. Foreign forces have not occupied it since the Normans arrived in 1066 and, although it was bombed during World War II, most of its iconic buildings survived.

As a result, it exudes a palpable sense of the nation's history. You can walk in the footsteps of Shakespeare, or Dickens, or Churchill. You can journey along the Thames, as Henry VIII did. You can visit the room in the Tower of London where Sir Francis Drake lived out his last days. You can drink in the pubs where Dr Samuel Johnson drank. You can sit in the reading room where Karl Marx studied. This book will show you how to do all these things, and more.

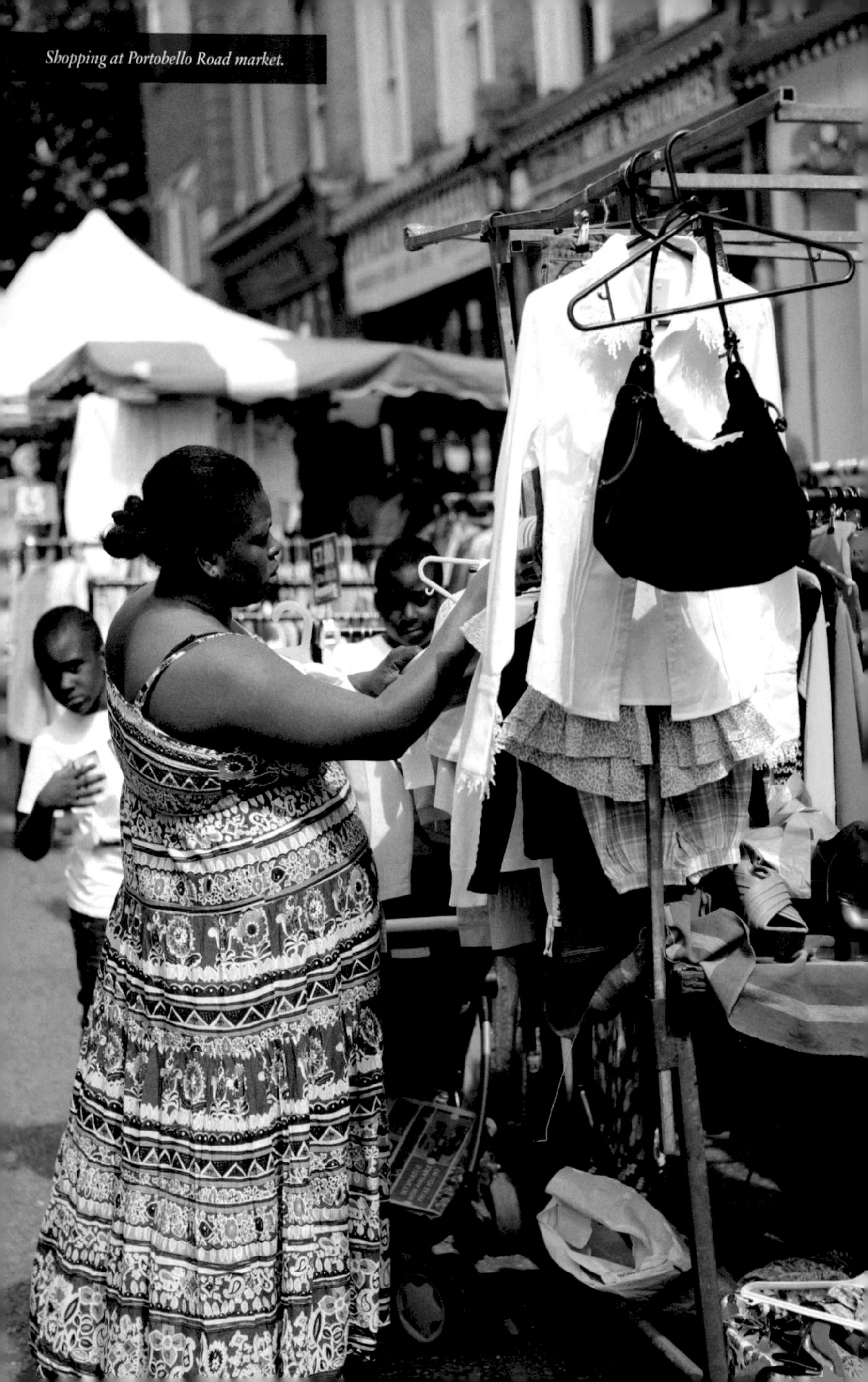

Shopping at Portobello Road market.

WHO LIVES IN LONDON?

The city has absorbed many waves of immigrants and, with more than a quarter of central London's population born outside the UK, is a truly international metropolis.

Celts, Romans, Saxons, Angles, Jutes, Danes and Normans were the first to tumble into London's melting pot. The first Far Eastern immigrants arrived in 1579, followed by Indians, Huguenots, Irish and the dispossessed of eastern Europe. And always there was the tide of new blood from the rest of Britain, drawn to London by hopes of fame, fortune, anonymity, or simply a new start. Today, nearly one in three of London's 8.3 million residents is from a minority ethnic group, and around 300 languages are spoken.

The Cockney

Is there, then, any such thing as a 'true' Londoner? Cockneys would seem to qualify, but being a cockney is as much a state of mind as it is a turn of phrase, and it is not exclusively genetic. Cockneys no longer need to be white and Anglo-Saxon; there are Italian, West Indian, Jewish and Pakistani cockneys. Nor do they necessarily have to be Londoners; the high cost of living has driven many out, and neighbouring towns such as Stevenage have large cockney populations. So what then makes a cockney? Certain traditions, being a member of an identifiable urban group, a distinctive language – and a quick sense of humour.

Cockney is a London accent with no use of the aspirant 'h', the 't' in the middle of words such as 'butter', or the final 'g' in words ending 'ing'. Cockneys traditionally spoke in a rhyming slang said to have originated among barrow boys who didn't want their customers to understand their conversations. A 'whistle' is a suit, short for whistle and flute, 'trouble and

Girls in Camden.

strife' means wife; new slang terms are continually being invented. News vendors and market traders are often cockneys – they are shrewd, street-wise people, who prefer to work for themselves and who value freedom more

The original definition of a cockney – someone born within the sound of Bow bells, the clarion of St Mary-le-Bow in Cheapside in the City – would today exclude most Londoners.

than wealth. The aristocracy of the cockneys are the pearly kings and queens, whose suits are embroidered with mother-of-pearl buttons – a marketing gimmick in the 19th century and now worn at festivals (see www.pearlysociety. co.uk for events).

Century of immigration

In the 19th century the port of London was the largest in the world, and clippers such as the *Cutty Sark* had races to bring the year's first tea crops home from China. The Chinese community was in Limehouse, where Sherlock Holmes went to mull over his latest conundrums in the relaxing atmosphere of the opium dens. Ming Street, Peking Street and Mandarin Street are the sole legacy of the community that was heavily bombed in World War II. Today, Chinatown is around Gerrard Street in Soho. Here resident Chinese opened restaurants after the end of World War II to cater for British and US forces. Although the streets and annual New Year's festivities mark this out as the centre of London's Chinese population of 80,000, they live in all parts of the capital.

Catching up on Paternoster Square.

Street performers on the South Bank.

The traumas of 19th-century Europe led to the mass exodus of Jews, and east London became England's Staten Island, with half a dozen refugee ships arriving every day. The Jews settled around the East End, giving it a dominant character. Since then the community, once around 250,000, has dispersed – to Stamford Hill, Golders Green and Finchley.

The Irish had been coming to Britain since the Anglo-Norman invasion of Ireland in the late 12th century. Mainly Catholic, they suffered for their faith in the Gordon riots of 1780, a dozen years before St Patrick's Catholic Church, which today holds services in Spanish, Portuguese and Cantonese, was built in Soho.

Irish immigration during the 19th century was brought about largely through the great famine of 1846–52. The Irish were a significant force in the 19th century's building boom,

Londoners frequently complain about overcrowding. But the population was just as high in 1931 when it reached over 8 million, almost the same as it is today.

Playing boules in Clerkenwell.

especially on the railways, and many settled in Camden and Kilburn. Today's population, around three percent of Londoners, is scattered across north and west London.

European settlers

Following the German invasion of Poland in 1939, the 33,000-strong Polish military in exile settled as a state-within-a-state in Mayfair and Kensington. Their pilots shot down one in seven German planes in the 1940 Battle of Britain. At the end of the war 150,000 were settled in London. While that number later dropped, a new wave of Polish immigrants from the EU in the 21st century meant 124,000 Poles were resident in London in 2013.

The Italians first settled around the church of St Peter's in Clerkenwell, in an area known

---

THE LONDON CABBIE

Perhaps the closest most visitors get to meeting a true Londoner is when they catch a cab. Taxi drivers, or cabbies, are experts on the city, and are essential to its life, coursing through its veins in their black cells (not that all the cabs are black any more: advertising has turned some of them into travelling billboards).

Cabbies take pride in their job, knowing that nowhere else in the world does a taxi driver need to know so much in order to qualify for a licence to work. Would-be drivers must spend up to four years learning London in minute detail (called 'doing the Knowledge') by travelling the streets of the metropolis on a moped and working out routes, before passing a special driving test.

About 25,000 drivers work in London, of whom half are owner-drivers. In all, there are more than 15,000 vehicles. The classic cab, known as the FX4, was launched in 1959 and some models are still going strong. The newer Metrocab, although more spacious, has taken a while to find the same place in customers' – and cabbies' – affections.

Only a small proportion of drivers are women, though the number is increasing. It is also very much a white, working-class occupation, and traditionally a large percentage of drivers are Jewish. Whatever their origins, most London taxi drivers, particularly the older ones, have a reputation for being garrulous.

Soaking up the sun in Grosvenor Square.

to the residents as The Hill and to Londoners as Little Italy. The population was at its height from 1900 to 1930 but, when Italians living in Britain were interned during World War II, their role as restaurateurs began to be eroded by Greek Cypriots, who had been filtering into Britain since the 1920s. Disruptions on Cyprus caused further immigration in the 1950s and 1960s, with Greek and Turkish Cypriots amicably settling side by side in north London. The densest Greek community is around Green Lanes in Haringey, north London, where traditions are maintained in male-only cafés.

WHERE TO SPOT THE ROYALS

On the second Saturday in June, the Queen's official birthday, she travels by carriage to Horse Guards Parade for the ceremony of Trooping the Colour. In November she is transported by state coach for the state opening of Parliament, escorted along the Mall by the Household Cavalry. Also in November, she attends the service of remembrance at the Cenotaph in Whitehall. The engagements of the Royal Family are listed daily in the *Court Circular* in the better national newspapers.

If you are more interested in spotting Prince Harry and Princesses Beatrice and Eugenie, you need to go to one of the more exclusive nightclubs, such as Boujis (members only) in Thurloe Street, South Kensington, or Mahiki in Dover Street, Mayfair.

Seasonal Arabs

In summer, when Middle East temperatures become too hot for comfort, London has traditionally attracted many Gulf Arabs, who spend much of their time enjoying the coolness of the parks and the shopping opportunities. First coming in the wake of the oil price hikes of the 1970s, they funded a mosque in Regent's Park, which can hold 1,800.

Seasonal Arabs are less common since the war in Iraq, but there are resident communities from Egypt, Iraq and Morocco. Most live in Kensington and Bayswater, and they congregate in Edgware Road, north of Marble Arch, where their restaurants, cafés and shops shine into the night. London is still one of the largest Arab media centres.

Commonwealth immigrants

The 20th century saw immigration mostly from the Commonwealth, and the resulting ethnic influence extends as far as Heathrow. The airport itself was largely built by construction workers from India's Punjab. After the Sikhs came the Caribbeans, who found work on London's buses, Underground railway network and in the health service.

But while London likes to think of itself as a multicultural society, it has few black or Asian top administrators or civil servants. You can pass through the City or the Inns of Court or Docklands without meeting many business tycoons, leading lawyers or top editors from the settlers' communities. Until the general election of 1987, there were no ethnic-minority members of Parliament; that situation has since changed and there are now around 26.

Why there's a welcome

Partly because London's vast number of hotels, bars and restaurants have a great need for cheap but hard-working labour, immigration has been a less contentious issue in the capital than elsewhere in the country. That said, in the current economic climate, there are worries about the pressures migrants place on public services, and the lifting of work restrictions on people

Happy shoppers at Camden Lock Market.

HOT PROPERTY

Over the past decade or so the dream of living in London has become unattainable for many young people unless they are prepared to rent with friends or strangers, or live with family.

London's long overheated property market has pushed the average price of a London home to over £500,000, with properties in the posher areas, such as Kensington and Chelsea, averaging £1.5 million. The economic downturn caused prices to drop in the rest of the country, but in London a return to City bonuses and very wealthy international buyers (Russian, Arab and American) have meant that prices continue to rise – in some boroughs by as much as 15 percent.

coming from Bulgaria and Romania from 2013 is causing concern to some.

Generally, though, London welcomes every type of visitor. Karl Marx, Mahatma Gandhi and Indira Gandhi all studied here. Charles de Gaulle lived in exile here. Writers Paul Theroux, Salman Rushdie and V.S. Naipaul chose to work here. Even Harrods, the quintessentially English store, was owned by an Egyptian, Mohamed Al-Fayed, from 1985 to 2010 and is currently owned by Quatar Holdings. It sells 40 percent of its merchandise to tourists.

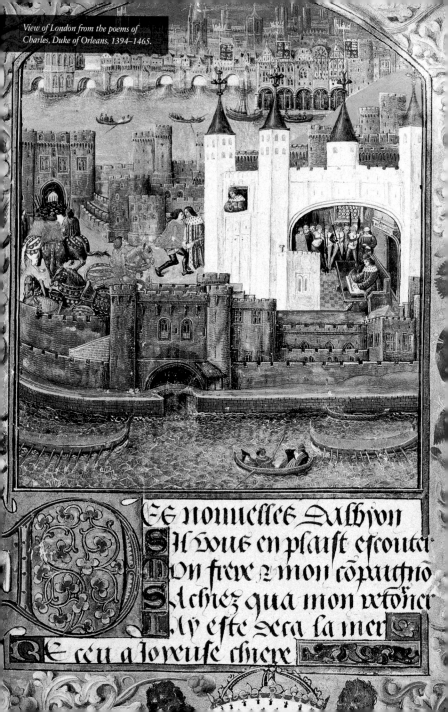

View of London from the poems of
Charles, Duke of Orleans, 1394–1465.

THE MAKING OF LONDON

Fire, plague, population explosions, aerial bombing, economic recessions, urban blight, terrorism... London has survived everything history could throw at it, yet it has remained one of the world's most seductive cities.

In AD 43 the invading Roman army chose gravel banks between what is now Southwark and the City as the site of a strategically important bridge. Roman London, the Celtic 'Llyn-din', the fort by the lake, quickly took shape, but suffered a setback 17 years later when British guerrillas led by Queen Boudicca attacked and burned areas around Lombard Street, Gracechurch Street and Walbrook so completely that archaeologists have identified a change in the colour of the earth.

A rebuilt Londinium, as the Romans called it, had by AD 100 supplanted Colchester as the capital as well as the trading centre of Britain. But in 410, Rome itself was threatened by the Germanic races from the north and recalled its garrison from England. Culture withered and Londinium crumbled as the Anglo-Saxons allowed the Roman buildings to become derelict.

Aerial view of Roman Londinium from the northwest, c. 2nd century AD.

Recovery and expansion

The city's position made it a natural trading centre and gradually it recovered its importance. In the 8th century the literary monk, the Venerable Bede, called it 'A market for many peoples coming by land and sea'. South of London Bridge, a residential area developed, later known as the Borough.

Two miles (3km) upriver on Thorney Island, the Monastery of St Peter was established, later the great West Minster. Following his accession in 1042, Edward the Confessor moved his court from the City to Westminster, creating the division of royal and mercantile power still in place today. In lieu of making

> Roman Londinium had a timber bridge, quays, warehouses, a governor's palace, baths and amphitheatre. Roads radiated to Colchester, York, Chester, Exeter, Bath and Canterbury.

the usual pilgrimage to Rome, he rebuilt the abbey, where most succeeding kings were crowned, married and, until George II (d.1760), buried.

City landmarks

In 1066 William the Conqueror brought the laws of Normandy to England, and gave London privileges that are still honoured today. Self-direction in local affairs was satisfied by the election of a first Mayor (later Lord Mayor) in 1189, with aldermen and a court. A new St Paul's Cathedral was started and the great keep of the White Tower completed in 1097. Westminster Hall was designed as a banqueting hall but, although the largest building of its kind in Europe, fell short of William's dreams – he said it was 'a mere bedchamber' compared to what he had expected. By 1176 work had begun on a stone London Bridge, and the suburb on the south bank was growing.

Union and plague

The city had grown to 50,000 by the time of Geoffrey Chaucer, the 'father of English poetry' – this in spite of the Black Death of 1348, when some 200 bodies a day were taken outside the city and buried in mass graves. This virulent bubonic plague, carried by rats and fleas, ravaged much of Europe but had a particularly

William the Conqueror accompanied by knights and soldiers, by an unknown artist (14th century).

Westminster Hall, c.1460.

devastating effect on London because of the city's narrow streets and insanitary housing.

London stopped growing in the 14th century. The City (now with a capital C) quite simply had no ambitions to get any bigger. Had it wanted to expand, it would have had to change its character, perhaps endangering in the process its hard-won privileges and sacrificing its unique position as a major European market and port. Whatever was happening outside the walls (not completely demolished until the 18th century), the City maintained a blinkered detachment that was not disturbed until Queen Victoria's reign.

The Golden Age

The much married and celebrated divorcé Henry VIII (1491–1547) almost qualifies as the 'father' of modern London, though the changes he brought about were the outcome of a bid for personal freedom from the Church. In 1534, after the Pope refused to annul his marriage to Catherine of Aragon so that he could marry Anne Boleyn, Henry cut all ties with Roman Catholicism. He had already pronounced himself head of the Church of England and

Detail, London from Southwark, c.1630 by an unknown artist.

persuaded Parliament to authorise the dissolution of the monasteries, their property and revenues being granted to the Crown. Cardinal Wolsey's house was added to an expanding palace in Whitehall. Hyde Park and St James's were enclosed as deer parks.

Convent (now Covent) Garden and Clerkenwell, Stepney and Shoreditch, Kennington and Lambeth all expanded during this time, taking London's population to 200,000. A lasting monument to the era is Henry VIII's Hampton Court Palace, southwest of London (see page 235).

Henry's daughter, Elizabeth I, whose mother, Anne Boleyn, had been beheaded for supposed adultery, came to the throne in 1558. She was truly London's queen and the 'Golden Age' began, in commerce, education and the arts. William Shakespeare, a Londoner by adoption, was far from adulated by the authorities. When the Lord Mayor banned theatrical performances from London, he and his fellow playwright Ben Jonson moved outside the Mayor's jurisdiction to new sites on the south bank of the Thames, an area notorious for bear pits, brothels and prisons.

Revolution and style

Being childless, the 'Virgin Queen' Elizabeth chose James VI of Scotland to succeed her as James I of England, thus launching the Stuart dynasty. Religious conflict continued, and a Catholic faction attempted to blow up Parliament in the infamous Gunpowder Plot. On 5 November 1605, Guy (Guido) Fawkes was caught about to ignite barrels of gunpowder in the cellars. Fawkes was executed, but 5 November, Guy Fawkes Day, is still marked with fireworks and the burning of an effigy.

Against a background of conflict between the king and Parliament, London responded to a new influence: the Italian architecture of Palladio as seen through the work of Inigo Jones. The purity of Jones's style is best seen

Little survives of Tudor London's wood-framed houses with their oversailing upper storeys, but a flavour can be found in the Old Curiosity Shop near Lincoln's Inn (see page 149).

The Great Fire of London 1666, by an anonymous artist, c.1675.

in the Queen's House at Greenwich, begun in 1616. Three years later came the Banqueting House in Whitehall.

Water, pestilence and fire

Great tragedies lay ahead for London. In 1665 the inadequate water supply and lack of sanitation brought the dreaded plague to the overcrowded city, and before it ran its course 100,000

BUNHILL FIELDS

Local parish burial grounds were unable to cope with the high mortality rate of the 1665 Great Plague and many victims were buried in plague pits such as the one in Bunhill Fields on City Road (see page 160), where these days city workers eat their lunches. The cemetery was specially built for plague victims, though the site had previously operated as a deposit for old bones from St Paul's churchyard, where space was at a premium. The burial ground was not consecrated and was later associated with Nonconformists, including many notable ones such as Daniel Defoe, John Bunyan, author of *Pilgrim's Progress*, and the poet and artist William Blake.

---

inhabitants died. The Great Fire, less than a year later, came as if to cleanse the stricken city. From a baker's shop on Pudding Lane, Eastcheap, the flames raged for five days, watched and recorded by the great 17th-century diarist Samuel Pepys. Miraculously, only half a dozen people were recorded as dead, although the number may well have been higher.

After the fire, 13,000 houses and 87 parish churches lay in ruins, but rebuilding was immediately planned.

Wren's dream

Christopher Wren, Surveyor General to the Crown, was inspired by Paris. London, too, he thought, should have *rond-points*, vistas and streets laid out in a grid pattern. But Wren's best ideas were never realised. Expediency dictated that the new should rise quickly on the sites of the old, with one prudent difference: new buildings were made of brick, not wood.

Wren turned his inventive powers to rebuilding 51 of the City's damaged churches. His achievements lie in the individuality of their soaring towers and steeples which rise above the rooftops. In 1675 work began on his masterpiece, a new St Paul's Cathedral.

House building spread through the green fields beyond Soho towards Hyde Park and across the Tyburn road. As the ripple of this 18th-century building ring moved outwards, the older centre was coming to the end of its useful life. The need for better communications brought demands for another river crossing. Westminster Bridge was completed in 1750, but nearly 20 years passed before the City had its own second bridge, at Blackfriars. Whitehall was beginning to take on its 20th-century character, the palace of kings being replaced by the palaces of government.

Splendour and sweatshops

By 1800 London was poised on the brink of a population explosion. In the next 35 years it was to double in size – and the railways were yet to come. While Britain was at war with Napoleonic France, work on public buildings withered, but housing swelled with the increasing numbers of civil servants. Paddington and Marylebone, Camberwell and Kensington, Knightsbridge and Chelsea forged their identities.

Queen Elizabeth I, attributed to George Gower.

Unlike the West End, the East End suffered ribbon building along the roads to Essex. Whitechapel High Street was "pestered with cottages", and Wapping with mean tenements. It was an area vulnerable to the impact of new developments in commerce following the Industrial Revolution. Canals had already linked the Thames with the industrial Midlands. Docks cruelly dismembered the riverside parishes. In 1825, 1,250 houses were swept away for St Katharine's Dock alone. The inhabitants were compressed, sardine-style, into accommodation nearby. The character of the modern East End was in the making. 'Sweatshops' and the labour to go with them multiplied in this fertile soil of ruthless competition, poverty and immigration.

By the 1830s the Industrial Revolution was making its impact on the Thames below Wapping. The marshy pools of the Isle of Dogs, long used for duck shooting and hunting, were deepened to make the West and East India Docks. Wharves and shipyards lined the banks of the river itself in Blackwall, Deptford and

Gin Lane, an engraving by William Hogarth, whose works vividly depict 18th-century London life.

Greenwich. With all this activity, London's air was dense with smog – smoke mixed with fog – although this word had not yet been coined.

Congestion and crime

By the early 19th century London was becoming impossibly congested, so bridges were built at Waterloo (1811–17) and Hammersmith (1824–27). London Bridge was rebuilt (1823–31) and foot passengers given a tunnel under the Thames at Wapping.

Courts of law and prisons responded to rising crime, while gentlemen's clubs met the Regency passion for gambling. In Bloomsbury's Gower Street, London University was born, and a fruit and vegetable market came to Covent Garden. Great collections were housed in the British Museum and National Gallery.

Londoners were on the move. In 1829 Mr Shillibeer introduced them to the omnibus, and the first steam train arrived with the London & Greenwich Railway of 1836. Terminal stations followed at Euston, King's Cross and Paddington by 1853, and at Blackfriars, Charing Cross and St Pancras by 1871.

Covent Garden, by Phoebus Leven, 1864.

> *London became increasingly affluent in the early 19th century. Visiting in 1814, the Emperor of Russia asked, 'Where are your poor?' Clearly he had not been east of the Tower of London.*

Cleaning up the Thames

At Westminster, the Houses of Parliament burnt down in 1834 when a furnace overheated, but soon Charles Barry and Augustus Pugin's Gothic extravaganza rose phoenix-like from the ashes: the House of Lords by 1847, the Commons and clock tower by 1858 and the Victoria Tower by 1860.

By this time, the 'sights' of London had dropped into place. The British Museum gave a home to the Elgin Marbles in 1816, and Trafalgar Square gave a hero's welcome to Nelson's column in 1843. The City Corporation, meanwhile, made efforts to unlock the congested streets, cutting swathes through Holborn's houses and cemeteries for the viaduct to bridge the Fleet valley. Fleet Street, the Strand and Whitehall were by-passed by the grand boulevard of the Victoria Embankment. Tower Bridge opened in 1894, steel dressed up in stone to make it look historic.

By 1859 another problem had arisen, serious enough to cause the adjournment of the House of Commons: the unbearable stench from the Thames. Londoners still depended largely on the river for drinking water, and at the same time disposed of their sewage in it. Cholera was common until the Board of Works' Chief Engineer, Joseph

THE GREAT EXHIBITION OF 1851

In 1851 Queen Victoria opened the Great Exhibition of the Works of all Nations in Hyde Park, its magnificent glass building – dubbed 'the Crystal Palace' – displaying Britain's skills and achievements to the world and attracting some 6 million visitors. With the profits of £186,000, Prince Albert, Queen Victoria's German-born husband, realised his great ambition: a centre of learning.

Temples to the arts and sciences blossomed in Kensington's gardens, nicknamed 'Albertopolis'. What was later named the Victoria and Albert Museum opened in 1852, moving to its present site in 1857, followed by the Royal Albert Hall in 1871, the Albert Memorial in 1872, and the Natural History Museum in 1881.

Bazalgette, devised a scheme to take the sewage well downstream to Barking in Essex and release it into the river after treatment. His scheme is still the basis of the modern drainage system.

Dickens and social reforms

But London had become polarised. In the east, there was poverty and overcrowding, and in the west affluence and spacious living. The novelist Charles Dickens described the refuge of down-and-outs and penny-a-nighters in novels such as *Bleak House* (1853). Public conscience was aroused by his writings and those of the social reformer Henry Mayhew. This encouraged both political action and private philanthrophy.

The railways and new roads did some of the reformers' work for them, sweeping away many insanitary dwellings. Soon London's city's edge opened up due to the first suburban railway, the Metropolitan, in 1863.

World War II and the Blitz

Britain's capital has evolved piecemeal over centuries, without any overall plans. Twice in its history, however, it has had to be rebuilt. On the first occasion, after the Great Fire of 1666, and on the second, after World War II and the Blitz, which killed 29,000 London civilians.

World War II left Britain impoverished and without the empire that had provided so much of its wealth. Utilitarian buildings, often of charmless concrete, replaced those destroyed in the Blitz and were condemned by Prince Charles, who said that modern town planners and architects did more damage than the Luftwaffe.

Swinging London

The 1950s were a time of post-war austerity with rationing still in place and efforts concentrated on regeneration in the face of a rapidly disintegrating empire. But there was also a massive

> By the end of the 19th century, London was throbbing with life and unloading the British Empire's fortunes across its wharves. Its docklands were called the warehouse of the world.

Detail from A Street Scene with Two Omnibuses, by James Pollard, 1845.

Firefighting during the Blitz, World War II.

London centred on Soho's Carnaby Street, the King's Road in Chelsea, where Mary Quant's shop Bazaar epitomised the new fashions, and Barbara Hulanicki's store Biba in Kensington.

Meanwhile, many of the East End's pre-war slums were replaced by new housing estates and tower blocks to meet the growing demand for decent public housing. The deep social problems created by the estates had yet to make an impact.

The roaring eighties

In the 1970s the pendulum swung the other way. Traditional industries collapsed all over Britain. Container ships made London's old wharves and warehouses redundant and the port that had once welcomed 14,000 vessels a year crumbled into dereliction.

By the time the economic boom of the 1980s created a demand for taller office buildings, there was somewhere convenient to put them: the former docklands. The area around Canary Wharf, with its 800ft (244-metre) -high One Canada Square tower, was dubbed Chicago-on-Thames. Meanwhile, for home buyers, the dream of living in London itself faded as the strong economy pushed London house prices and rents well beyond the pockets of the lower paid.

baby boom and by the mid-1960s, as the post-war babies became teenagers, times were a-changing. While Paris became the centre of serious political action, London was the place to have fun, where old notions of deference, responsibility and hierarchy were swept away, cultural and sexual attitudes were liberated, and fashion and pop music prevailed. Swinging

Male models pose in 1966. Second from left is clothes designer Ossie Clark, a leading figure in 1960s London.

LONDON'S MAYOR

In 1997 the UK elected a Labour government led by Tony Blair, ending 17 years of Conservative rule under which the Greater London Council, which had administered London, had been abolished. The new regime decided to restore a measure of self-government to the capital by creating a new post: an elected mayor (distinct from the ceremonial post of Lord Mayor, whose role is confined to the City). The first election was won by Ken Livingstone, who had controversially led the GLC. He was succeeded by the exuberant Tory MP Boris Johnson in 2008, distinguished by his unruly thatch of blond hair. He banned alcohol on public transport and introduced a cycle hire scheme (the Boris Bike); he was re-elected in 2012.

The South Bank soars

The next area to be revived was Bankside, the south bank of the Thames where Shakespeare first staged his greatest plays and Dickens mined the material for many of his novels. The London Eye, the giant observation wheel erected to mark the millennium (see page 182), indicates one end of this area, while at the other end towers the Shard, London's newest iconic landmark and Western Europe's tallest building.

In between are theatres, restaurants and river walks, recreating the lively hub of activity this area had been 400 years previously. Dominating the South Bank is the Tate Modern, a disused power station transformed into a fabulous modern art museum. A replica of Shakespeare's Globe Theatre is to the east, and in 2013 work started on a new indoor Jacobean theatre, the Sam Wanamaker Playhouse. The Millennium Bridge, the first new river crossing in central London for more than a century, allows you to walk from St Paul's Cathedral to Tate Modern in seven minutes.

London's Olympic legacy

London's 2012 Olympics were a huge success, with Danny Boyle's opening ceremony,

In 2012 London celebrated the Queen's Diamond Jubilee, marking 60 years since her accession to the throne. The high point was a river pageant, which saw thousands of people line the banks of the Thames to cheer on the royal barge.

described as 'a love letter to Britain', being particularly memorable. For two weeks in the summer, all eyes were on London as athletes from over 200 countries competed in 300 events.

'Legacy' was the key to London's successful bid, with a promise of large-scale redevelopment of some of the capital's most deprived areas, located in the east of the city. At the same time, the hitherto bleak area around King's Cross and St Pancras stations has been turned into a fitting setting for the new Eurostar terminal. The restoration and reopening of the 5-star St Pancras Hotel, designed in the 1860s by Sir George Gilbert Scott, seems to symbolise London's capacity for reinvention and renewal.

Eurostar platform at St Pancras International station.

Middle distance Olympic medallists Kelly Holmes and Steve Cram celebrate London's winning bid to host the 2012 Olympic Games.

DECISIVE DATES

Julius Caesar on an engraving from 1860.

Early times

55 BC
Julius Caesar discovers Britain. He launches an invasion and defeats Cassivellaunus, a British chieftain. However, Roman forces do not stay.

AD 43
Londinium settled during second Roman invasion; a bridge is built over the Thames.

AD 61
Boudicca, Queen of the Iceni tribe in East Anglia, sacks the city before being defeated.

c.200
Three-mile (5km) -long city wall built.

410
Troops are withdrawn to defend Rome.

449–527
Jutes, Angles and Saxons arrive in Britain, dividing it into separate kingdoms.

604
The first St Paul's Cathedral founded by King Ethelbert.

c.750
Monastery of St Peter is founded on Thorney Island, later to become Westminster Abbey.

8th century
Shipping and manufacturing flourish on the river bank near today's Strand.

884
London becomes the capital of Britain under Alfred the Great.

1042
Edward the Confessor moves his court from the city to Westminster and rebuilds the abbey.

After the Conquest

1066
William I, Duke of Normandy and descendant of the Vikings, conquers Britain. He introduces French and the feudal system.

1078
Tower of London's White Tower built.

1154
The Plantagenets, descendants of the French House of Anjou, take over throne.

1176
A new London Bridge is built of stone.

1189
City's first mayor is elected.

1240
First parliament sits in Westminster.

1290
Jews are expelled from the city – a ban not lifted until the 17th century.

Statue of Boudicca on a chariot on the north side of Westminster Bridge.

Richard I, a Plantagenet king.

1300
St Paul's Cathedral, now rebuilt in stone after a fire in 1087, is consecrated.

1381
Much of London is laid waste by the Peasants' Revolt led by Wat Tyler.

1485
The Tudor Age begins. Of Welsh descent, the Tudors preside over the English Renaissance, under Queen Elizabeth I (reigned 1558–1603).

1514
Building of Hampton Court Palace begins.

1532
Henry VIII builds Palace of Whitehall, the largest in Europe. It catches fire in 1698.

1534
Henry VIII declares himself head of the Church of England and dissolves the monasteries.

1536
St James's Palace is built.

1588
William Shakespeare (1568–1616) begins his dramatic career in London.

1605
Guy Fawkes tries to blow up Parliament.

1620
The Pilgrim Fathers set sail for America.

1642–9
Civil war between the Cavalier Royalists and the Republican Roundheads. Royalists are defeated. Charles I is executed.

1660
After 11 years, monarchy is restored under Charles II.

1660–9
Samuel Pepys writes his famous diary.

1664–6
The Great Plague kills one-fifth of the population.

The Gunpowder Plot conspirators.

Henry VIII.

1666
The Great Fire destroys 80 percent of London's buildings.

1675
Sir Christopher Wren (1632–1723) begins work on St Paul's Cathedral.

1694
The Bank of England is established.

1714
The House of Hanover is ushered in by George I. The architectural style prevalent

for the next 20 years is known as Georgian.

1735
George II makes 10 Downing Street available to Sir Robert Walpole, Britain's first prime minister.

1764
The Literary Club is founded by Samuel Johnson, compiler of the first English dictionary.

1783
Last public execution held at Tyburn (Marble Arch).

1811–20
The Prince Regent, later George IV, gives his name to the Regency style.

1820
Regent's Canal completed.

1824
The National Gallery is established.

1829
Prime Minister Robert Peel establishes a police force

Trafalgar Square, 19th century.

(nicknamed 'peelers' and later 'bobbies').

1834
Rebuilding of the current Houses of Parliament, after the old palace of Westminster is destroyed by fire.

The Age of Empire
1837
Queen Victoria comes to the throne at 18.

1840s
Trafalgar Square laid out on the site of royal stables to commemorate Nelson's victory.

1849
Tea merchant Henry Charles Harrod takes over a small grocer's shop in Knightsbridge.

1851
The Great Exhibition is held in Hyde Park.

1857
The Victoria and Albert Museum opens.

Queen Victoria and her family.

1859
A 13.5-tonne bell, nicknamed Big Ben, is hung in the clock tower of the Houses of Parliament.

1863
The first section of the Underground railway is built between Paddington and Farringdon Street.

1888
Jack the Ripper strikes in Whitechapel.

1890
First electric railway is built in deep-level tunnels, between the City and Stockwell.

1894
Tower Bridge is built.

1903
Westminster Cathedral is built. Marks & Spencer's first penny bazaar opens in Brixton.

1904
The first London motor taxi is licensed.

1914
World War I begins.

Canary Wharf.

1915
Zeppelins and, later, Gotha airplanes begin dropping incendiary and explosive bombs on the city.

1922
British Broadcasting Company transmits its first programmes from Savoy Hill.

1923
The first Football Association cup final is held at Wembley Stadium.

1939–45
World War II. Children are evacuated, and London is heavily bombed.

Modern London
1951
Festival of Britain; new concert halls built on South Bank near Waterloo.

1956
The Clean Air Act, introducing smokeless fuel, ends the asphyxiating smogs.

1976
National Theatre opens.

1982
Flood-preventing Thames Barrier is finished. Built after hundreds of people were killed when a storm caused a tidal surge in 1953.

1986
The Greater London Council is abolished.

1991
The first Canary Wharf tower is completed in Docklands.

1994
The first trains run through the Channel Tunnel to Paris and Brussels.

1997
Shakespeare's Globe opens on Bankside.

2000
Tate Modern opens on Bankside. The London Eye opens at County Hall.

2001
Greater London Authority is set up under mayor Ken Livingstone. Major museums drop entrance charge.

2002
The Millennium Bridge opens again after its unsettling wobble is cured.

2003
A £5 congestion charge is imposed on cars entering central areas.

2004
Planning permission is granted for 'The Shard', which becomes Western Europe's tallest building at

1,016ft (310 metres) when completed in 2012.

2005
On 6 July London is chosen to stage 2012 Olympic Games. The following day bombs explode on three Tube trains and a bus, killing 52 people.

2007
The new Wembley Stadium opens. Eurostar terminal opens at St Pancras.

2008
The 'credit crunch' – house prices crash and Northern Rock bank is nationalised.

2009
MPs' expenses scandal rocks Parliament.

2012
The nation celebrates Queen Elizabeth II's Diamond Jubilee – 60 years on the throne. London Olympics are held.

2013
The Duchess of Cambridge gives birth to Prince George on 22 July.

Sebastian Coe at London 2012.

Hackney Empire Theatre, which opened in 1901 as a music hall.

THEATRELAND

Shakespeare, Sondheim, ABBA and a host of stars – the best (and the worst) of plays and musicals turn up in the West End, and all kinds of innovative shows take place in fringe venues around the city.

On stage at the Globe.

The opening of Shakespeare's Globe on Bankside in 1997 was seen by some as a triumph of culture over commercialism. Here, for the price of a ticket, you can sit on rock-hard benches, squint through the sun streaming in through the large opening in the thatch roof, peer around pillars to try to catch lines from the acoustically challenged stage, and even, if the directors are to be taken at their word, cat-call and lob the occasional tomato if a performance is not to your liking.

This is theatre heritage to appeal to the tourist and even the purist, an Elizabethan playhouse risen from the rubble of time; many

make for its doors simply to savour the experience. The brainchild of American actor-director Sam Wanamaker, who didn't live to see it completed, the theatre is a replica of the 1599 auditorium in which William Shakespeare staged many of his plays. Like many theatres over the years, the original Globe was destroyed by fire. A new indoor theatre, the Sam Wanamaker Playhouse, was completed in 2014.

It is with good reason that London is famous for its amazing variety of theatre; here you can see everything from Shakespeare to sex farces, from cutting-edge fringe to long-running musicals.

That's show business

London's theatrical history goes back to a playhouse opened at Shoreditch in 1576 by James Burbage, the son of a carpenter and travelling player, and its development encompasses a strong tradition of taking sideswipes at social issues. In the *Roaring Girl* of 1611, for example, playwright Thomas Dekker dwelt at some length on London's traffic jams.

In modern times, live theatre was expected to succumb first to films, then to TV, yet it is still one of those essential attractions every visitor to London is supposed to experience, even if most opt for a blockbuster musical rather than anything more adventurous.

In the days when *South Pacific* and *Camelot* dominated musical theatre no one would have

Les Mis at the Queen's Theatre, Shaftesbury Avenue.

underwrite other work. Trevor Nunn master-minded the Royal Shakespeare Company's 1985 production of *Les Misérables*, which went on to conquer the world. More recently the National Theatre's production of *War Horse* is still going strong after opening in 2007.

Musicals dominate the modern West End and are its biggest money-spinners – Roald Dahl's much-loved story Matlida bursts into life as an award-winning musical, while Lloyd Webber has seen more success promoting the Bollywood-based *Bombay Dreams* and a revival of *The Sound of Music*, for which the starring role of Maria was cast via a reality TV show.

Broadway has reasserted its clout, whether in revivals of musical classics like *Guys and Dolls* and *Chicago* or recent successes such as *The Producers*, *Wicked* and *Monty Python's Spamalot*. The trend that gets critics tearing their hair out, though, is for the pop-music musical, reprising the song catalogue of favourite artists. Begun by ABBA-based *Mamma Mia!*, this has continued with *Dancing in the Streets* (Motown), *We Will Rock You* (Queen) and even *Daddy Cool* (Boney M). The

guessed the West End would hijack the genre from Broadway. Yet in the 1970s, Tim Rice and Andrew Lloyd Webber first demonstrated the possibilities of rock-musicals with *Jesus Christ Superstar* and *Evita*, before Lloyd Webber moved on to dominate the stage musical with Cats (a collaboration with the late T.S. Eliot) and *Phantom of the Opera*.

Critics might scoff, but shrewd theatre brains saw that income from musicals could

A Royal Shakespeare Company production of Hecuba.

WHERE TO SIT

It's useful to know the terminology of English theatre layout. What in America is called the 'Orchestra' (the seats at the lowest level) is in England called the 'Stalls'; then, in ascending order, come the 'Dress Circle' (or 'Royal Circle'), and the 'Upper Circle' (or 'Grand Circle' or 'Balcony'). The very top balconies, once known as 'The Gods', are not recommended to anyone with vertigo or a hearing impediment.

If in a party, consider asking for a box, which can sometimes work out cheaper than seats in the stalls. You can doze off more privately, too. As they tend to be at the sides of the theatre, however, boxes sometimes have a restricted view of the stage.

plots woven around the songs are wafer-thin, but the crowds keep coming in.

Some claim musical-mania has squeezed out new drama, but the theatre pages in *Time Out* don't really bear this out. New productions of classics still appear each year, new writing still gets aired in fringe and mainstream venues, and writers such as Tom Stoppard, Alan Bennett or Mark Ravenhill do not lack audiences.

Hollywood-on-Thames

As well as locally grown stars such as Michael Gambon, Ian McKellen, Maggie Smith, Diana Rigg and Judi Dench, American actors have never been strangers to the West End – Dustin Hoffman played Shylock in *The Merchant of Venice* here in 1989 – but lately this flow has become a flood, as nearly every Hollywood name has seemed to feel a need to add a London stage appearance to their resumé.

Nicole Kidman caused a great stir when she appeared naked in David Hare's *The Blue Room* in 1998, and Val Kilmer, Woody Harrelson, Glenn Close and Christian Slater are among

Kevin Spacey, artistic director of the Old Vic.

> With visitor numbers boosted by the Diamond Jubilee and the Olympics, London's theatreland enjoyed gross sales of £585 million in 2013, nearly 11 percent up on 2012, and 14.6 million people visited the theatre.

other famous faces seen on London stages, to varying reviews. Kathleen Turner won huge praise in a production of *Who's Afraid of Virginia Woolf*, but London's favourite American actor is Kevin Spacey. After scoring a massive hit in *The Iceman Cometh* in 1998, he accepted the job of artistic director of the venerable Old Vic theatre, where he has brought in a string of high-profile names and won critical acclaim. Spacey is now seeking to secure the future of the Old Vic by raising £20m before he steps down in 2015.

National companies

London has two major state-subsidised companies: the National Theatre and the Royal Shakespeare Company. The National has the advantage of its own huge building on the South Bank, with three auditoria. Not everyone was impressed with the stark concrete exterior when it opened in 1976, but today it is a firm favourite with the British public. By contrast, the RSC gave up its London home at the Barbican Centre in 2001 (its main base is in Shakespeare's home town, Stratford-upon-Avon) and now rotates between a number of theatres.

The director of the National Theatre, Nicholas Hytner, has introduced variety and innovation into the programme, and aided by business sponsorship has made many seats available for just £12. *War Horse*, with its stunning life-sized puppets, is just one example of the National's work, now very profitably transferred to the West End. Hytner's latest innovation is a massive project called NT Future, a £70 million scheme to open up the National's buildings and to contribute to the regeneration of the South Bank. Improved facilities for education and participation, and state-of-the-art new technologies, are the focus of the plans.

Off-West End to the fringe

There are many smaller or 'fringe' venues around London, from substantial theatres to

War Horse at the National Theatre.

tiny rooms above pubs. Their productions range from low-budget Shakespeare to political shows and international theatre. Much of new young British writing is dark, funny and well-observed.

The Royal Court, the Donmar Warehouse, the Young Vic, the Almeida in Islington and the Tricycle in Kilburn are the main outlets for new writing, which between them have pioneered many of London's most exciting recent productions. Lively pub theatres include the Bush (in Shepherd's Bush), the King's Head (Islington) and the Gate at Notting Hill Gate.

Every summer there is a very enjoyable open-air theatre season in Regent's Park, focusing on Shakespeare's comedies.

WAYS TO BUY YOUR TICKETS

Despite the popular notion that everything in London is so successful that it sells out fast, most shows have some seats, especially early in the week. It's the more expensive tickets – generally for the top musicals – that are usually hardest to obtain.

The best way to get tickets is from the theatre itself, either by calling at the box office or online. This cuts out the sometimes extortionate fees of ticket agencies. Agencies and hotels are most handy for obtaining hard-to-get tickets. A reputable agency should be a member of STAR (Society of Ticket Agents and Retailers), and follow a clear code of conduct.

Many theatres offer unsold tickets for performances the same day at reduced 'standby' prices, although some are only available to students. Tickets for same-day performances, or up to a week in advance, are also available at around half-price from the tkts ticket booths in Leicester Square (Mon–Sat 9am–7pm, Sun 11am–4.30pm). Matinees can be cheaper, but understudies may replace the stars. The National Theatre puts some same-day tickets on sale at 9.30am at its box office on the South Bank.

Tickets are offered outside theatres by touts for anything up to 10 times their face value. This isn't illegal, but check the ticket's face value and the position of the seat before purchasing.

EATING OUT

London's thousands of restaurants and cafés offer some of the world's best culinary experiences. New eateries open as frequently as new movies, so how do you find the good and avoid the bad?

Hipsters out to lunch.

London, once derided for mediocre cuisine, is today straining under a bombardment of Michelin stars. You can eat nachos and noodles, tapas and tempura, balti and bhajis; you can try pizza with Japanese toppings, choose from nearly 200 Thai restaurants or even eat English, a privilege reserved until a few years ago for diners at greasy-spoon cafés or, more tastefully, the traditional Rules or Simpson's in the Strand.

This revolution began in the 1980s, when the restructuring of London's financial world produced a legion of footloose brokers and traders looking for places to spend skyrocketing salaries. Innovative restaurants, like designer labels, were avidly sought out. At around the same time, the British discovered food. Cookery programmes proliferated on TV, book shops filled up with lavishly illustrated cookbooks and newspapers covered new restaurant openings with ever more

> The Conran empire marked a shift of emphasis away from chefs and towards restaurateurs. Famous chefs took to running their restaurant chains rather than doing much cooking.

excitement. The phenomenon of the 'celebrity chef' was born.

Until then it had been *de rigueur* for chefs to be French, and the country's best-known were Albert and Michel Roux of Le Gavroche. Now local stars emerged: the late Rose Gray, and Ruth Rogers, wife of the architect Sir Richard Rogers, opened their River Café alongside the architect's offices in Fulham, West London, presenting Tuscan cooking with a metropolitan twist. At the same time Terence Conran, the style-maker whose Habitat stores had brought the earthy kitchenware of Provence to Britain, opened Bibendum restaurant in the splendid Art Deco Michelin tyre company building in Fulham Road, the first of a string of Conran venues in striking locations with emphatically

Table at The Old Shoreditch Station café-bar.

FIRST, FIND YOUR TABLE

The downsides of London's top restaurants include terrifying prices, a growing air of exclusivity, and arrogance when it comes to dealing with anyone trying to make a reservation. Tables for dinner at Gordon Ramsay's main restaurant must be booked two months in advance, at The Ivy several weeks ahead; phone lines are often busy for hours, and when you do get through staff may be abrupt. One way to get around this is to go for lunch. Instead of booking, turn up early, just after noon. Tom Aikens, The Wolseley, Le Gavroche and The Ivy are among the prestigious venues that often have lunchtime tables free.

stylish decor. The epitome of the style is Quaglino's, near Green Park, with a look that deliberately recalls a 1930s ocean liner. This was food as entertainment, out-to-impress dining that symbolised the early 1990s, but – though some have maintained high standards – these are not restaurants where you can generally expect much individuality or charm.

Current movers and shakers

Nowadays, London's food scene has settled down a little: it's still devoted to fads – Moroccan one year, Argentinian the next – but alongside them there's also a more consistent idea of quality, as the city has got used to the idea of being one of the world's dining capitals. Some stalwarts have absorbed new trends while sticking to what they know their clients want: the River Café remains inviolate, The Ivy and Le Caprice are ever-popular with the rich and famous, the Savoy Grill with

Café in Camden Passage, Islington.

businessmen, and Le Gavroche with traditionalist gourmands. The fashion for 'mega-restaurants' has faded, as was indicated in 2007 when Terence Conran himself gave up control of his restaurant chain, passing it over to his former managers under a new name: the D&D Group.

Attention has shifted back from restaurant entrepreneurs to cooks, although London's best-known chef, Gordon Ramsay, manages to be both. A former footballer whose cooking skills won Michelin recognition and whose short temper made him a TV star, Ramsay still cooks himself (sometimes), installs talented young chefs in his restaurant stable and is an inescapable media face. London's grand hotels, traditional bastions of good cookery, have spruced up their restaurants to keep up with the dining boom, and Ramsay has taken astute advantage of this, taking over Claridge's restaurant. His protégée Angela Hartnett now has her own restaurant, Murano. There are many other inventive young British chefs around town, notably Heston Blumenthal. Like Ramsay,

Italian antipasti.

Vietnamese food in Hoxton.

most combine classical, French-based training with an eclectic, adventurous approach. Other stars of the moment include Chris Galvin, now in charge of the top-floor restaurant at the Hilton on Park Lane (as Galvin at Windows), and Tom Aikens, with his eponymous restaurant in Kensington.

AFTERNOON TEA

Throughout the world there are people still convinced that everyone in England sits down for 'afternoon tea' around 4pm every day, using best-quality porcelain. Sadly, this is a myth, and a full-scale, formal tea – with thin-cut sandwiches, cakes and a choice of fine teas – is nowadays a luxury. The venues that keep up the tradition are the grand hotels, most typically Brown's, The Ritz, the Langham and the Dorchester, which offer tea with all the trimmings in luxurious settings (reservations and smart dress are required).

Recently, too, there has been a bit of a tea revival, and several upscale restaurants now offer set afternoon teas, such as The Wolseley, as do smart stores like Fortnum & Mason.

The classic fish and chips.

Around the world, and back again

Many fans of eating out in London, however, say that what they enjoy most is the incredible variety of cuisines on offer. Its status as an international city attracts fine cooks from every part of the world to work here. French chefs are still prominent, such as Hélène Darroze (The Connaught) or Morgan Meunier (Morgan M), and even France's grandest current chef has a London operation, L'Atelier de Joël Robuchon. Far Eastern or South Asian restaurants are no longer just cheap options either: London has some of the finest Indian (Amaya, Café Spice Namaste), Japanese (Nobu) and Chinese (Bar Shu) restaurants in the world outside their countries of origin, and you can find regional variations, such as the superb south Indian vegetarian food of Rasa Samudra.

There has also been a re-evaluation of traditional British dishes, long dismissed as dreary. Pioneer of this new British style was Alastair Little in his Soho restaurant, but it was extended with still more zest by Fergus

WHERE TO EAT

The biggest concentration of restaurants is in the West End, with Soho providing the most interesting choice. Chinatown, north of Leicester Square, has a bewildering array of Asian eateries, and Covent Garden good-value pre-theatre suppers. Kensington and Chelsea, with their abundance of wealthy residents, contain many expensive restaurants but also a good sprinkling of reasonably priced bistros.

Islington and Notting Hill also offer a good choice, and Clerkenwell and Shoreditch house some of the most interesting new restaurants. The City, whose oyster bars and restaurants cater to business lunchers, tends to be a ghost town in the evenings and at weekends.

Henderson at St John. He has been hugely influential in showing that British favourites such as oxtail, smoked herrings and farm-reared pork, can be delicacies if prepared with care and flair.

Tom Aikens, holder of a Michelin star, in his restaurant Tom's Kitchen.

Since its appearance in the 1990s, the local gastropub has started to become London's equivalent of the Parisian street-corner bistro – essentially a restaurant serving good food in an informal setting.

The middle ground

The ever-rising standard of fine dining in London may grab the headlines, but it has to be said that for most people who do not have limitless wallets or full mastery of the strategems used to get a table in restaurants such as Gordon Ramsay's, these are places that are only visited for a special occasion. Among more regularly accessible eating places, London's fad-chasing can be a source of disappointment, as time and again restaurant promoters have placed 'concept' – decor, style, general trendiness – above quality of food, or value for money. This being so, it's pleasing to report that one of the best current trends has been for the new culinary flair at last to filter down into a wider range of restaurants at mid-range prices. Many 'new-British' restaurants, especially, are decently priced: even the prestigious St John is not expensive, particularly for lunch, and places such as Shoreditch's Canteen or Roast in Borough Market similarly offer flavour-rich, modern food in stylish settings. Eating out in London may still be more expensive than in many cities, but at least the difference is getting a little less.

City workers drinking in Leadenhall Market.

The trend for big institutions to re-examine their food has thrown up attractive novelties too: major museums such as the National Gallery, Tate Britain and Tate Modern all now have imaginative, good-value restaurants, and even the Royal Institute of British Architects has opened up its elegant Art Deco 'canteen' as a smart modern brasserie, the RIBA Café.

The great pub renaissance

Another vital element in making good food more accessible – as well as the unstoppable growth of 'ethnic' restaurants – has been the revolution in pub food. Realising there was

FISH AND CHIP SHOPS

A classic British dish, fish and chips originated in the 1850s. Today, fewer than 10,000 fish and chip shops remain in Britain, compared with over 30,000 in the 1930s. Many of the best were started by immigrants, especially Italians (Rock & Sole Plaice in Covent Garden, and the Fryer's Delight in Theobalds Road, Holborn) and Greek Cypriots (the Golden Hind, in Marylebone Lane since 1914, and Costas in Notting Hill). Nautilus in Fortune Green Road, West Hampstead, is Jewish and coats its fish in matzo flour.

Other notable fish and chip establishments are the long-standing favourites the Sea Shell in Lisson Grove,

and Geales in Notting Hill. Fish Central is a blessing to concert- and theatre-goers near the Barbican Centre, Seafresh in Wilton Road is handy for Victoria Station, and Masters Super Fish is convenient for Waterloo. These days you'll find more contemporary spins on the classic fish and chips, such as at the laid-back Fish Club in Clapham.

You generally get better value in a real fish and chip restaurant (attached to a takeaway shop) than in pubs or restaurants that offer fish and chips on their menus. One test, apart from truly fresh, sustainably sourced fish and crisp batter, is that they offer fresh lemon instead of just malt vinegar.

A Shepherd Market restaurant.

more money to be made from food and wine than just beer and crisps, pub after pub has become a 'gastropub', throwing out the limp sandwiches and plastic 'ploughman's lunches' of old-style pub fare in favour of chalkboard menus that mix traditional British favourites with French, Italian or Oriental influences.

Old standards like sausage and mash have been given new life by the use of Toulouse sausages and mustard sauces, and imaginative salads have become a hallmark. This combination of good food and a relaxed feel that preserves a fair bit of the atmosphere of a London pub, typified by The Eagle (159 Farringdon Road, EC1), the first of the breed, The Cow (89 Westbourne Park Road, W2) or trendier variants like the Lot's Road Pub & Dining Rooms (114 Lots Road, SW10), or the Princess Victoria (217 Uxbridge Road, W12), has been a real winner with both Londoners and visitors. The London gastropub can sometimes seem to have become a new cliché – every one has to have stripped floorboards and stressed furniture – but they're ideal for anyone looking for interesting food in relaxed surroundings.

The chain gang

As in every part of the world, in London plenty of restaurants, cafés, bars and pubs belong to chains.

They have their uses and some are worth looking out for. For Italian standbys (pasta, pizza) Carluccio's Caffè, ASK and Pizza Express are good bets, while Sofra branches provide enjoyable Turkish fare. If you want burgers, try Byron (upmarket but traditional) in several locations around town, or Honest Burger (quality British beef at good prices) in Brixton and Soho. The many Wagamama outlets are excellent Japanese-style noodle houses, or if you prefer sushi, try Itsu, a chain of Asian-inspired eat-in and takeaway restaurants. For tasty Mexican market food, head for Wahaca. Giraffes (South Bank and many more areas) are bright, modern brasseries with 'global fusion food' that are great for families.

RETAIL THERAPY

London's innovative department stores are redesigning the one-stop shopping experience.

The past decade has seen dramatic changes in that most traditional of London shops, the department store. The stuffy image has gone and stores are now imaginatively designed spaces stocking everything from freshly cut flowers and organic food to cutting-edge designer clothes and bespoke jewellery. Their hairdressers have become on-site spas, and they offer a host of bars and restaurants.

Oxford Street has the greatest concentration of department stores, headed by Selfridges. Marks & Spencer and John Lewis provide a more traditional shopping experience, while round the corner on Regent Street, Liberty is both eccentric and chic. Head to Knightsbridge for Harvey Nichols, the fashionista's choice, and Harrods.

Liberty's eye-catching 1920s mock-Tudor building was created using the timbers of two ships, HMS Impregnable and HMS Hindustan. The home interiors floor feels more like an exhibition of contemporary furniture. In the accessories department, the iconic William Morris Liberty print adorns everything from notebooks to bikinis.

Liberty was started by Arthur Liberty in 1875 and was originally known for its homewares and fabrics, both of which are still going strong today. Past collaborations with British designer Luella Bartley and Ronnie Wood of the Rolling Stones have made this Regent Street institution more fashionable.

Opened as a grocer's shop in 1849, today Harrods is a tourist destination in its own right. Harrods sells pretty much everything you can think of in surroundings that range from the sublime to the ridiculous. But whatever you think of Harrods, no trip to London would be complete without a visit to its wonderfully extravagant food halls.

BRITISH DESIGNERS

Carnaby Street storefront.

Creativity and eccentricity mark out British designers from the international fashion pack.

Many British designers have made their mark on the world stage. Stella McCartney's designs mix strong tailoring with feminine fabrics. Her popularity has sparked collaborations with Adidas and high street chain H&M. Punk diva Vivienne Westwood's theatrical clothes never fail to cause a stir. She has shops at 430 King's Road, SW10, and in Conduit Street, W1. For exquisite tailoring, silk ties and signature striped accessories, try Paul Smith.

British milliners have long been respected worldwide, and perhaps the most famous is Philip Treacy, whose sculptural headgear can be found in the top department stores, including Harrods. Mulberry is famous for its leather accessories – from personal organisers to weekend bags, all embossed with the classic tree logo. Another distinctive British designer is Cath Kidston; her floral and polka dot designs are used for everything from gifts, clothes and accessories to tents.

Selfridges has become the ultimate London department store. Combining luxury brands with high-street concessions, it manages to be both accessible and cool. The store has a changing programme of themed events to keep things interesting, as well as services ranging from leather repairs to ear piercing.

For a department store specialising in fine food and beverages visit Fortnum & Mason at 181 Piccadilly.

Designer necklaces at the Lesley Craze Gallery in Clerkenwell.

MARKETS

There are few better introductions to London's rich mix of cultures and tastes than a visit to one of its markets, where you can buy almost anything.

Many of the capital's markets have been in operation for centuries and a visit can conjure up images of an old London now largely lost to supermarket chains and developers. At the same time, London's markets have experienced a revival, and alongside the traditional stalls selling fruit and veg you'll find organic meat and fish and specialist produce from all over the world.

The resurgence of markets has encouraged the renovation of surrounding areas and all kinds of independent shops and restaurants are popping up. For some this has gone a step too far – for example, there is little doubt that the creation of a restaurant and boutique precinct at Spitalfields has damaged something of its original haphazard appeal – and the high prices charged for goods have taken the edge off bargain-hunting.

Despite this, a wander around places like Borough Market, Broadway Market and Spitalfields continues to be a treat for all the senses – you just have to be prepared to brave the crowds.

Handmade soaps, Spitalfields Market.

On Sunday mornings Londoners flood to Columbia Road Market in Hoxton (see page 246) for cut flowers, bulbs, shrubs, trees and garden ornaments. The old-fashioned streets around the market offer funky shops and cafés too.

Leadenhall Market (see page 167) is a fine example of one of London's great 19th-century covered markets. It was used as a setting for Diagon Alley in the film Harry Potter and the Philosopher's Stone.

The variety and quality of fresh produce at Borough Market is unrivalled in London, and some of the prices certainly reflect this. If you're happy to brave the lunchtime crowds, many of the stalls offer takeaway snacks – a firm market favourite are the hot chorizo and rocket rolls from Spanish supplier Brindisa's stand.

The Sunday UpMarket at Ely's Yard (Brick Lane) is a treasure-trove of second-hand clothing and one-off designs.

MARKET TREASURES

Directional vests at Camden Market.

A wide range of clothing, crafts and trinkets are available at Camden's various markets.

The covered market at Greenwich is the place for handmade jewellery and accessories. Quality varies and it's very crowded, but if it gets too much adjourn to the calmer antiques market a short walk away.

Portobello Road in Notting Hill is one of London's best-loved markets. For antiques explore the northern end of the street; for junk, offbeat fashions and arts and crafts (market Sat, shops Mon–Sat) head further north, towards the Westway flyover.

Trendy shoppers on Portobello Road.

THE ARCHITECTURAL LEGACY

London's haphazard development, together with the contribution of men of genius such as Christopher Wren, John Nash and Inigo Jones, has given the capital its principal allure: infinite variety.

Tudor building on Fleet Street.

Little remains of Roman Londinium, and even less of Saxon Lundenwic. Glimpses of the Roman city wall can be had at Tower Hill, and foundations of a Temple of Mithras have been exposed in Queen Victoria Street. The Saxons built mostly in timber, but were grateful for Roman stones. All Hallows-by-the-Tower has a Saxon arch, built with Roman tiles. Otherwise, they left little trace.

Norman to Gothic

The Norman Conquest of 1066 brought firmer resolution to the city, in the White Tower in the Tower of London, a sturdy box that showed the natives who was in control. Within it is St John's Chapel, with the squat pillars and round arches of Norman Romanesque architecture.

Medieval London grew out of the Gothic style, imported from France in the 13th century and in vogue until the 1550s. Far more delicate than Norman, it made outer walls thinner by supporting them with exterior buttresses, allowing larger windows. Southwark Cathedral is a fine example of simple, unadorned early English Gothic; Westminster Abbey, begun in 1245, was enhanced by royal mason Henry Yevele (1320–1400), London's first known architect. He also built the Jewel Tower and Westminster Hall in the Houses of Parliament, a vauntingly ambitious space with a timber roof by carpenter Hugh Herland.

> *The Tudor monarchs were great builders and brought the first real touches of grandeur and extravagance to London's buildings – fitting for what was by now the largest city in Western Europe.*

Tudor London

The finest work of Gothic architecture in London is the lavish Henry VII's Chapel in Westminster Abbey, completed by his son, Henry VIII. The Tudor monarchs oversaw constant expansion and building in London. Hallmarks of Tudor buildings – also called 'Elizabethan', after Queen Elizabeth I – are the use of half-timbering and red brick. Staple

St Paul's Cathedral.

London has only one example of the Jacobean style (from King James I): Prince Henry's Room (1610–11) above 17 Fleet Street. Its original ceiling, with geometric patterns, is still in place.

Inigo Jones and the Italian style

James I and his son Charles I brought a new elegance to London in the work of Inigo Jones (1573–1652). The court architect had studied in Italy, and was full of Italian Renaissance ideas. He introduced classical proportions in his Banqueting Hall in Whitehall and the Queen's House in Greenwich, and his original Palladian layout for Covent Garden, set out, with the neoclassical St Paul's church, London's first true square.

Wren and the Great Fire

Sir Christopher Wren (1632–1723) is undoubtedly London's greatest architect, but if there had been no Great Fire in 1666 his name would not be so well known. In three days 80 percent of London's buildings were destroyed: among the losses were the Guildhall and Old St Paul's, as well as 87 churches.

Inn in High Holborn is the sole survivor from this time, but the era also saw the building of London's first theatres such as Shakespeare's Globe, now reconstructed near its original Southwark site.

Brickwork was confined to the rich, used to produce octagonal towers, fancy chimneys and patterns of colours and shapes. Royal palaces were built like this at Greenwich, Hampton Court, St James's, Lambeth and Westminster.

Hampton Court.

OPEN HOUSE

During London Open House weekends more than 600 buildings of architectural and historical interest that are usually closed to the public open their doors, free of charge. The range of buildings participating is huge, from modern private residences to ancient sites – Billingsgate Roman House and Baths – to towering modern office blocks like Lloyd's of London and the Gherkin. The main weekend is usually in mid-September, but more limited Open House tours are run all year. See www.londonopenhouse.org for details. Queues can be long at the more popular attractions, such as the Bank of England or Horse Guards, and at some venues you will need to book.

Wren was a scientist and self-taught architect. His plans for the rebuilding of London were rejected, but he managed 53 churches in the City and Westminster (26 remain) as well as St Paul's. These very English classical-baroque monuments eschewed earlier styles, their windows bathing white and gold interiors with light. His mastery of design is also displayed in the superb Greenwich and Chelsea hospitals, and several royal palaces.

John Nash and Georgian London

John Nash (1752–1835) is the man who gave the West End style. He gained his reputation designing country houses, and in 1811 was commissioned by the Prince Regent, later George IV, to turn his 'Marylebone Farm' into Regent's Park, ringed by elegant neoclassical villas. Nash added theatrical terraces, colonnades and sculpted pediments, and his master plan included connecting the park with the Prince's residence – Carlton House Terrace, by The Mall – via Portland Place and Regent Street, London's first refined boulevards.

The Natural History Museum is another example of Gothic Revival.

St Pancras Station typifies Gothic Revival, a favourite of Victorian architects.

Nash's supremely elegant Regency style was the summit of Georgian architecture. The houses of Bedford Square are typically Georgian, with brick facades, sash windows and elaborate porticoes. As Italian influence waned, all things Greek became the vogue: Sir Robert Smirke (1780–1867) accordingly built the British Museum as a giant temple, to house Lord Elgin's plunder from the Parthenon.

Victorian revivals

Against this pagan Greek influence, Augustus Pugin (1812–52) contended it was time to return to 'true Christian architecture', the Gothic. His chance to lead the revival came on 16 October 1834, when the old Palace of Westminster burnt down. His design for the new Houses of Parliament, carried out with Charles Barry (1795–1860), took as inspiration the Henry VII chapel in Westminster Abbey.

Gothic Revival was the cornerstone of Victorian architecture. It produced a distinctive Tower Bridge, while Sir George Gilbert Scott (1811–78) built St Pancras Station as a romantic castle. Victorian eclecticism even allowed a Tudor Revival, as in New Hall at Lincoln's Inn.

View of The Shard from the Millennium Bridge.

Modern architecture

Britain was virtually bankrupted by World War II, which accounts for the number of utilitarian blocks that had to be built quickly and cheaply in the 1950s and 60s, which have not worn well. Buildings from the 1951 Festival of Britain such as the Royal Festival Hall, though, stand out beside more brutalist Modernist projects such as the all-concrete National Theatre (1967–77).

London's economic boom in the 1980s and the redevelopment of vast areas like Docklands have launched a whole new wave of construction, begun by Richard Rogers' futuristic Lloyd's

Building in 1986. A city that resisted tall buildings has acquired scene-stealing skyscrapers like the Shard at London Bridge, and the Gherkin, Cheesegrater and Walkie-Talkie in the City. London's nicknames for its new tall buildings reveal the affection in which they are held.

The latest focus for new building is the regeneration of the Olympic Park in east London. The site of the 2012 Games is being transformed into the Queen Elizabeth Olympic Park, incorporating the Olympic venues, thousands of new homes and acres of parkland and recreational space.

THE SKY'S THE LIMIT

Until the 1950s no new building in London was allowed to exceed the height of St Paul's Cathedral (355ft/108 metres). However, this has changed over the past few years with a wave of giant-scale building that is altering London's skyline dramatically.

The Leadenhall Building, a 740ft (225-metre) glass-and-steel wedge that soars up from the streets of the City, is the latest arrival in an ever-growing collection of novelty silhouettes. Due to be finished in 2014, the slanting, wedge-shaped design – hence its nickname, the Cheesegrater – means the view from Fleet Street to St Paul's will not be ruined as it would have been had the building not sloped off at the top. It has the characteristic

inside-out design of architect Richard Rogers, just like his Lloyd's Building which stands opposite, a symphony of pipes and ducts finished 30 years earlier.

Alongside the Cheesegrater stands Norman Foster's curvaceous Gherkin. To the south is the Walkie-Talkie (590ft/180 metres), also due for completion in 2014. The top-heavy design gives the building its nickname, and will allow for a 'sky garden' that will be open to the public. The Shard at London Bridge, completed in 2012 is, at 1,016ft (310 metres), the tallest building in Western Europe. This striking skyscraper, resembling a shard of glass, comprises exclusive apartments, offices, a hotel, restaurants and stunning 360° views from the 72nd floor.

Oxford Circus at Christmas.

The O2 arena and Canary Wharf skyline viewed from the Emirates Air Line cable car.

Wellington Arch, Hyde Park Corner.

ORIENTATION

The Places section details all the attractions worth seeing, arranged by area. Main sights are cross-referenced by number to the maps.

For a cosmopolitan city of 8.2 million people, London is quite parochial. Each neighbourhood, each street corner, is proud of its own identity. Central London is the shared London of all these groups and of nearly 20 million visitors a year as well. Symbols of London – the Beefeaters, the bobbies, the cabbies, the red buses, the pageantry, the Royal Family, the Houses of Parliament – all are here, along with the stock market, motorcycle messengers, dirty air and crawling traffic.

After an initial tour by boat or on an open-top bus to orientate yourself, the best way to see Central London is on foot. Although Greater London sprawls for 610 sq miles (1,580 sq km), the central area is surprisingly compact. Walkers have time to appreciate the infinite variety of architectural detail that traces the city's long development. What's more, they will be treading in the footsteps of some of history's most celebrated citizens – to aid the imagination, blue plaques (see page 138) show where the great, the good and the notorious once lived.

We begin the Places section by focusing on the royal and ruling heart of the city, Parliament and Buckingham Palace. The ensuing chapters cover the remainder of the central area, from Piccadilly to Chelsea, and cross the river to explore the vibrancy of Southwark and the South Bank. Village London (see page 229) tours some of the most interesting local communities outside the central area, usually reached by bus or Underground. Day Trips (see page 263) suggests a range of convenient excursions from London.

Tower Bridge.

All the sites of special interest are numbered on specially drawn maps to help you find your way around, and there is a street atlas towards the back of the guide.

As a visitor, you may be one of the 72 percent who visit the Tower of London, or the 92 percent who make their way to Piccadilly Circus. But you will probably also be one of the millions who find some small, distinctive corner of this remarkable city to be enthusiastic about.

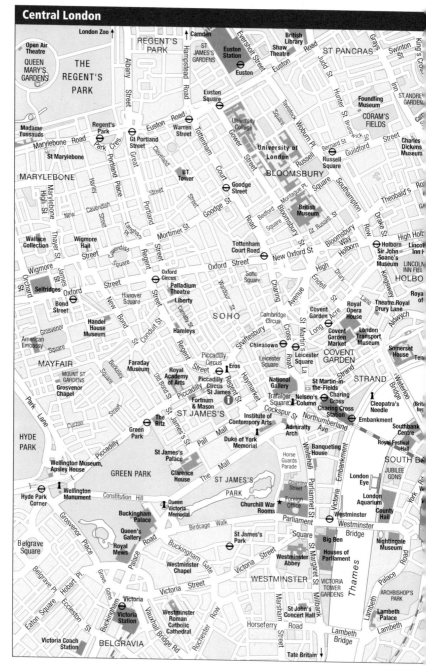

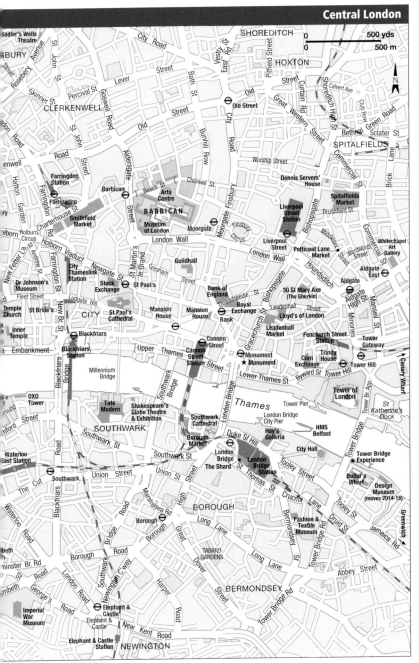

Soldier at Horse Guards.

WESTMINSTER AND BUCKINGHAM PALACE

Westminster is the centre of official London. Parliament meets here, the Queen and the prime minister have their London homes here, and state funerals are conducted in Westminster Abbey.

As the focus of government and the monarchy, Westminster contains within its ancient and easily walked boundaries the headquarters of the nation's policy-making civil servants, the prime minister and the Cabinet, and the Royal Family. Many kings and queens are buried in Westminster Abbey, founded by the last Saxon ruler, Edward the Confessor (1042–66).

WHITEHALL

Official London begins immediately south of **Trafalgar Square** (see page 95), where the broad and unmistakably official thoroughfare of **Whitehall ❶** stretches imperiously southwards towards the Houses of Parliament. Most buildings along here are government offices, built from Portland stone in an imposing classical style.

On the right, beyond the Trafalgar Studios, are the former offices of the Admiralty (for centuries the headquarters of the Royal Navy until the Ministry of Defence took over in 1964), and the offices of the Household Cavalry's headquarters, known as the **Horse Guards ❷**. Outside this colonnaded building are two mounted Life Guards in fancy uniforms, white gloves, plumes

and helmets, rigidly oblivious to the throng of camera-toting tourists. Changed every hour from 10am to 4pm, they guard the site of the main gateway to what was the Palace of Whitehall, used by King Henry VIII in the 16th century and burnt to the ground in 1698. Through the archway of Horse Guards and opening out on to St James's Park is the huge **Horse Guards Parade**. Here in June the Queen's birthday is honoured by a splendid pageant called **Trooping the Colour**; the name is derived

Buckingham Palace.

Downing Street gates.

from the regimental colours which are paraded.

Banqueting House ❸

Address: Whitehall, www.hrp.ork.uk
Tel: 0844 482 7777
Opening Hrs: Mon–Sat 10am–5pm
Transport: Embankment

Opposite Horse Guards, on the other side of Whitehall, is the Renaissance-style **Banqueting House**, built in 1620 by Inigo Jones, the man responsible for bringing this Italian style of architecture to England. It is the only surviving fragment of the palace destroyed by fire in 1698. Inside the huge hall upstairs, the ceiling is divided into nine large panels filled with rich baroque paintings by Rubens. They were commissioned by Charles I to glorify (or deify) the House of Stuart (Rubens was paid £3,000 and knighted for his work), but the Civil War followed and Charles I was beheaded on a scaffold outside the building. The hall is still used for official state banquets.

The prime minister's home

London's most famous address, **Downing Street ❹**, just off Whitehall,

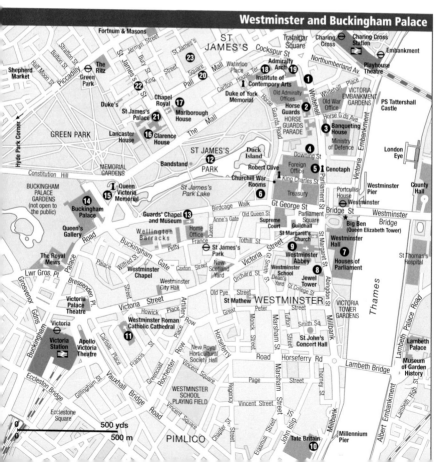

Westminster and Buckingham Palace

is little more than a terrace of four 18th-century houses, sealed off behind a heavy gate. The street is named after the diplomat Sir George Downing, who went to America with his parents in 1638 and became the second student to graduate from Harvard University. No. 10 is the official residence of the prime minister, and the venue for Cabinet meetings.

The plain black door and net-curtained windows suggest nothing of stylish rooms or of the state business conducted inside. Successive prime ministers have lived here since 1735. The chancellor of the exchequer has his official residence at No. 11.

Across Whitehall from Downing Street are the offices of the Ministry of Defence. Just south of here, the **Cenotaph** ❺, the national war memorial designed by Sir Edwin Lutyens, breaks Whitehall's monotony. On Remembrance Sunday in November it is the focal point of a service attended by the Queen and political leaders to remember the dead of two world wars as well as other conflicts.

Beyond the Cenotaph, Whitehall becomes **Parliament Street**. The stolid buildings on the same side as the Horse Guards house the Foreign and Commonwealth offices; its designer, Sir George Gilbert Scott, described it as 'a kind of national palace.'

Turn right into King Charles Street, which runs between the **Foreign Office** and the **Treasury** and **Cabinet offices** before reaching **Clive Steps** and a statue of Robert Clive (1725–74), a key figure in the establishment of British power in India. Beside the steps is a small wall of sandbags, the only above-ground sign of the Churchill War Rooms, one of London's best small museums.

The statue of Robert Clive, who rose from being a humble scribe in the East India Company to become governor of the Bengal Presidency, laying the foundations for British rule in India. His suicide at the age of 49 was linked to opium use and depression.

Churchill War Rooms ❻

Address: Clive Steps, King Charles Street, www.iwm.org.uk
Tel: 7930 6961
Opening Hrs: daily 9.30am–6pm
Transport: Westminster

This was the wartime bunker from which Sir Winston Churchill conducted World War II. Many of

Horse Guards.

David Lloyd George statue.

the 21 rooms were abandoned in 1945 and left untouched until the museum opened in 1984; others have been meticulously restored to their wartime condition, 'down to the last paper clip'. The Central Map Room and the rooms that served as a round-the-clock typing pool illustrate the problems of communications in the 1940s. A converted broom cupboard housed a pioneering hotline to the White House, enabling Churchill to have confidential talks with President Roosevelt, despite air raids.

The **Churchill Museum** within includes a selection of letters and other memorabilia, as well as an interactive table on which visitors can find information about Churchill's life.

PARLIAMENT SQUARE

Parliament Street empties out into **Parliament Square**, with its tall trees and lawns lined with statues of illustrious statesmen. This, the country's first official roundabout, is surrounded by national landmarks.

The Houses of Parliament ➐

Address: www.parliament.uk
Tel: 0844 847 1672 (for summer hours)
Opening Hrs: see page 73
Entrance Fee: charge for tours; free for UK residents if arranged through their MP
Transport: Westminster

The clock tower of the **Houses of Parliament** has become a symbol of London. Its elaborately fretted stone sides rise up nearly 330ft (100 metres) to a richly gilded spire and a 13.5-tonne hour bell supposedly nicknamed **Big Ben** after a rather fat government official called Sir Benjamin Hall who was commissioner of works when the bell was installed. Its chimes first rang out across Westminster in 1859, after an earlier bell was damaged while being tested three years previously.

Facing Big Ben is the odd-looking **Portcullis House**, a £250 million office block for members of Parliament; its prominent and much criticised 'chimneys' form part of the air-conditioning system.

The oldest part of the Houses of Parliament and one of the oldest buildings in London is **Westminster Hall**, begun in 1097. The thick buttressed walls are spanned with a magnificent hammer-beamed oak roof. This hall has witnessed many seminal events in British history: coronation celebrations, lyings-in-state and treason trials. Among those condemned to death were Sir Thomas More, who fell foul of King Henry VIII; King Charles I, accused of treason against Parliament; and the 17th-century revolutionary Guy Fawkes, who tried to blow up the buildings (see page 27).

Fire and reconstruction

In 1834 a fire achieved what Guy Fawkes had failed to do and most of the ancient Palace of Westminster was destroyed. Westminster Hall, a small crypt chapel and the Jewel Tower (see page 73) survived. Following this conflagration, the current purpose-built structure was created in exuberant Gothic style by Sir Charles Barry and Augustus Pugin.

The houses are embellished with gilded spires and towers, mullioned windows and intricate stone carving and statues. The complex, which took some 30 years to complete, covers 8 acres (3.2 hectares); there are 100 staircases and more than 1,100 rooms. Apart from the ceremonial state rooms and the two main debating chambers, the House of Lords and the House of Commons, there are libraries, dining rooms, offices and secretarial facilities for government ministers, opposition leaders and ordinary Members of Parliament.

Main points of interest

St Stephen's, on the western side of the building, is the main entrance to the House of Commons, and anyone can watch debates from the visitors' gallery, though there are almost always queues (see box). Beneath **St Stephen's Hall** is the ancient crypt chapel that survived the 1834 fire. Members can take their marriage vows and have their children baptised here. The **Commons chamber**

Churchill War Rooms.

The opulent House of Lords.

How Parliament Works

England is known as the mother of parliaments, and the Westminster Parliament has been a model for democracies all over the world.

The Houses of Parliament consist of the House of Commons and the House of Lords. The Commons, the House of locally elected Members of Parliament (MPs), known as the Lower House, wields virtually all the power but inhabits only half the building. Jutting out towards Parliament Square is Westminster Hall, with the offices, dining rooms and libraries of the Commons; in the centre is the Commons' debating chamber. To the right of Westminster Hall is the domain of the Lords, whose role is to examine and sometimes block bills proposed by the Lower House, although a bill can be reintroduced. Until recently, most lords governed by birthright, as descendants of the previous ruling classes, but the voting rights of many hereditary peers have been abolished and the make-up of the Lords has changed. Most members are now life peers, ennobled for services to the nation, and their titles cannot be passed to their children. Former MPs are often made peers in recognition of years of public service.

There are 650 elected MPs, yet the Commons seats only about 450. This is not usually a problem since MPs attend sessions when they wish. The governing party sits on one side, facing the opposition. Cabinet ministers sit on the front bench, opposite the 'Shadow Cabinet' (the leading members of the opposition). The Cabinet, consisting of up to two dozen ministers and chaired by the prime minister, meets at 10 Downing Street weekly to review major issues.

The General Election

Major parties represented are the Conservatives, Labour and the Liberal Democrats. General elections are run on the basis of local rather than proportional representation. Therefore, a party's presence in the house may not reflect its overall national standing. A party, however, needs an overall majority in the house to push through its bills, hence the need for the coalition after the 2010 election. The procedure of law making is so complex that a bill usually takes more than six months to be enacted. If it is still incomplete at the end of the parliamentary year, it is dropped. Various techniques are employed by the opposition to delay a bill.

The press can report on Parliament and the business of both houses is televised. A select group of journalists ('lobby correspondents') have daily informal 'background' briefings with ministers.

Parliament meets from October to July. In November, the government's plans for the year are announced in the Queen's Speech at the State Opening of Parliament. From the Visitors' Gallery, the public can watch the House of Commons at work, though seats are limited and security precautions tight. The weekly Prime Minister's Question Time – an unruly affair – usually attracts a full house.

The Queen's speech at the State Opening of Parliament.

was bombed in 1941; the current chamber only opened in 1950.

The immense **Victoria Tower** marks the grand entrance to the House of Lords. It is also the entrance used by the Queen when opening a new session of government.

Opposite Parliament is the moated **Jewel Tower** ❽, a relic of the Palace of Westminster dating from 1365. Its small museum of Parliament Past and Present (Apr–Oct 10am–5pm, Nov–Mar 10am–4pm) has more information panels than artefacts.

Opposite Parliament at the other end is the Supreme Court (Parliament Square, www.supremecourt.gov.uk; Mon–Fri 9.30am–4.30pm), the UK's highest court of appeal. Guided tours are available on Fridays (except public holidays) at 11.30am, 1.30pm and 3pm. Booking is advised.

Westminster Abbey ❾

Tel: 7222 5152, www.westminster-abbey.org
Opening Hrs: Mon–Tue, Thu–Fri 9.30am–4.30pm, last admission 3.30pm; Wed 9.30am–7pm, last admission 6pm; Sat 9am–2.30pm, last admission 1.30pm
Transport: Westminster

The most historic religious building in Britain is **Westminster Abbey**. It is also an outstanding piece of Gothic architecture, which is probably more striking from the detail on the inside than from its outward aspects. So many eminent figures are honoured in this national shrine that large areas of the interior have the cluttered appearance of an overcrowded sculpture museum. For full coverage of the abbey, see page 82.

St Margaret's Church

On the northeast side of Westminster Abbey facing the Houses of Parliament is **St Margaret's Church**, used by MPs for official services and for high-society weddings. Sir Walter Raleigh (1552–1618), the sea captain, poet and favourite of Queen Elizabeth I, who established the first British colony in Virginia and introduced tobacco and potatoes to Britain, was interred here after his execution. William Caxton (c.1421–92), who ran the first English printing presses nearby, is also buried here.

Beyond Westminster Abbey and Victoria Gardens a short street leads to one of London's most unobtrusive but notable concert halls, **St John's, Smith Square**. This former 18th-century church has fine acoustics and a reputation for a varied programme of classical music. In the crypt is a good wine bar-cum-restaurant (see page 81).

Tate Britain ❿

Address: Millbank, www.tate.org.uk/britain
Tel: 7887 8888
Opening Hrs: daily 10am–6pm
Entrance Fee: free except for feature exhibitions. Donation welcome.
Transport: Pimlico

The Jewel Tower has had several functions over the centuries. It was used to test official standards of weights and measures from 1869 until the 1930s, and its moat once supplied fish for the sovereign's table.

VISITING THE HOUSES OF PARLIAMENT

Guided tours of the Houses of Parliament are held most Saturdays throughout the year, and during Parliament's summer recess in August and September (Aug Mon 1.15–5.30pm, Tue–Fri 9.15am–5.30pm; mid-Sept–early Oct Tue–Fri 9.15am–4.30pm. Also most Sats all year 9.15am–4.30pm). If you are a permanent UK resident, you can contact your MP to arrange a free Member's tour up to six months in advance; otherwise there is a charge. To watch parliamentary debates at other times of the year from the public galleries overlooking the Commons or Lords chambers, queue outside the Cromwell Green visitor entrance. A wait of one to two hours is common, though usually less for the House of Lords. Note that Parliament is also in recess at Christmas and Easter.

Entry times vary depending on when Parliament is in session, but normal sitting times for the Commons are Mon 2.30–10.30pm; Tue–Wed 11.30am–7.30pm; Thur 9.30am–5.30pm. The Commons does not normally sit on Friday, but when it does the hours are 9.30am–3pm. Expect to queue for 1–1.5 hours, less in the evenings. The longest queues are for Prime Minister's Question Time (Wed noon–12.30); UK residents should contact their MP for an advance ticket, as ticket-holders have priority.

TIP

For art lovers in a hurry, a 220-seat catamaran runs every 40 minutes between Tate Britain on the Thames' north bank and Tate Modern on the south bank. It stops at the London Eye. Tel: 7887 8888.

A 10- to 15-minute walk along Millbank from the Houses of Parliament is **Tate Britain**, founded in 1897 by Henry Tate, of the Tate & Lyle sugar empire, and today the storehouse for the Tate's collection of British art from 1500 to the present. It is complemented by Tate Modern, further down the river on Bankside, which houses most of the Tate's modern and contemporary international collection (see page 194).

The galleries within Tate Britain are arranged by date and theme. The only criticism is that there isn't enough space: the majority of the collection has to be kept in storage out of the public view. A much-needed extension is being considered.

Among the British paintings are portraits by William Hogarth (1697–1764) and Thomas Gainsborough (1727–88), views of the English countryside by John Constable (1776–1837) and, in the Clore Gallery, seascapes and landscapes by J.M.W. Turner (1775–1851). Turner bequeathed the paintings to the nation on his death, with the stipulation that they should all be hung in one place, and should

The Cholmondeley Ladies, artist unknown, in Tate Britain.

The Union flag on top of Victoria Tower indicates that Parliament is in session. Night sessions are indicated by a light shining over the clock tower.

be available for the public to see without charge.

The most popular 19th-century painters represented are the Pre-Raphaelites, including Millais,

Holman Hunt, Rossetti and Burne-Jones. Modern British artists represented include Stanley Spencer, Francis Bacon and David Hockney. Sculptures include works by Jacob Epstein, Barbara Hepworth and Henry Moore. The Tate also stages free lectures and film shows, and has a reputation for the avant-garde, with the award of an annual Turner Prize. Its Rex Whistler-designed restaurant is a great place to have lunch (see page 81).

Across the river from Millbank, to the right, the modern green-and-cream building is **Vauxhall Cross**, headquarters of MI6's spymasters; this secret services building, designed by Terry Farrell, is built in a 'Faraday Cage' which stops electro-magnetic information passing in or out.

VICTORIA STREET

The west door of Westminster Abbey opens on to **Victoria Street**, important commercially but, since its rebuilding, a long grey canyon of undistinguished office blocks. Down this street, close to the Victoria Station end, is **Westminster Cathedral**.

Westminster Cathedral ⓫

Address: www.westminster cathedral.org.uk
Tel: 7798 9055
Opening Hrs: cathedral daily 7am – 7pm; tower Mon – Fri 9.30am – 5pm, weekends 9.30am – 6pm
Entrance Fee: free except for tower
Transport: Victoria

This is the most important Catholic church in London. Its bold red-and-white brickwork makes it look like a gigantic layer cake. Built at the end of the 19th century in an outlandish Italian-Byzantine style not seen elsewhere in London, it has a 273ft (83-metre) tower incorporating a lift. The views from the top are superb. The interior is sumptuous, with many chapels clad in coloured marble, but the decor was never finished; the numerous mosaics included in the original designs are absent, and the ceiling is largely bereft of decoration.

On the north side of Victoria Street behind St James's Park Underground station is **Queen Anne's Gate**, a small, quiet street which has retained much of its

The Italian-Byzantine-style facade of Westminster Cathedral.

Westminster Cathedral.

18th-century atmosphere. Lord Palmerston, who became prime minister in 1855, was born at No. 20.

ST JAMES'S PARK AND BUCKINGHAM PALACE

The formal arrangement of lakes and flora at **St James's Park** ⑫ is one of the most delightful in London. Formerly the grounds of St James's Palace acquired by Henry VIII in 1531, it was laid out in 1603, then re-landscaped in formal style by John Nash in 1827. It has always had a collection of ducks and water fowl, the highlight being the pelicans, fed every day between 2.30 and 3pm. In March 2013 another three pelicans were introduced to the park (a gift from the city of Prague), bringing the total to six.

Continuing the ornithological theme is **Birdcage Walk**, which takes its name from an 18th-century aviary, running along the south side of the park from Parliament Square to Buckingham Palace and dividing the park from the drilling ground of the **Wellington Barracks**, the home of the Royal Grenadier Guards and

Longcase equation clock next to a portrait of King George III.

the Coldstream Guards. Here the **Guards' Chapel and Museum** ⑬ (tel: 7414 3271; www.theguardsmuseum. com; daily 10am–4pm) are on the site of a former chapel which was hit by a bomb in 1944, killing 121 members of the congregation.

There are five of these aristocratic infantry regiments of Guards, first formed during the English Civil War (1642–9), and the museum provides a social history in uniform (including a uniform worn by the Duke of Wellington), as well as a large collection of toy soldiers.

Buckingham Palace ⑭

Address: Buckingham Palace Road, www.royalcollection.org.uk
Tel: 7766 7300
Opening Hrs: daily late July– late Aug 9.30am–7pm, last admission 4.45pm; Sep 9.30am–6.30pm, last admission 3.45pm; tickets are timed, and a visit lasts 2–2.5 hours
Transport: Green Park, Hyde Park Corner, Victoria

St James's Park.

Buckingham Palace has been the main London home of the royal family since Queen Victoria acceded to the throne in 1837. George IV had earlier employed John Nash (responsible for many of the grander parts of central London) to enlarge the building which had been built in the 17th century for the Duke of Buckingham (it originally became the property of the Crown when George III bought it for his wife in 1761). Nash added two wings that were later enclosed in a quadrangle, while the main facade came later still, being designed by Aston Webb in 1913.

Buckingham Palace.

A tour of the palace

The sumptuous **State Rooms** are open to the public for a few weeks in late summer when the Queen is not in residence. These include the Dining Room, Music Room, White Drawing Room and Throne Room, where there are paintings by Vermeer, Rubens and Rembrandt. The tour includes a stroll through part of the 40-acre (16-hectare) Palace Gardens where the cream of society mingles with the good and the worthy from all walks of life at the celebrated garden parties. The guests are invited because of some commendable contribution made to the nation, but few of the 8,000 people a year get to shake the Queen's hand.

Only the invited get further into the 775-room palace, although one enterprising intruder penetrated as far as the Queen's bedroom one night in 1982. She talked to him quietly while managing to summon

State Banquet table.

The bronze statue of Frederick, the Duke of York, at the top of the Duke of York Steps.

Admiralty Arch.

palace security. The Queen and the Duke of Edinburgh occupy about 12 of the rooms, on the first floor of the north wing, overlooking Green Park. If the Queen is in residence, the royal standard flies from the flagpole.

Next to the Royal Mews on Buckingham Palace Road, the **Queen's Gallery** (tel: 7766 7300; daily 10am–5.30pm; combined tickets with admission to Buckingham Palace and the Royal Mews are available late July–late Sept) holds one of the top private art collections in the world, including an exceptional collection of Leonardo da Vinci drawings, portraits by Holbein and Rubens, and watercolour views of Windsor by Paul Sandby. A significant new addition to the gallery is a gift of 97 works by the Royal Academy of Arts to celebrate the Queen's Diamond Jubilee in 2012. The portfolio includes prints, drawings, photographs and works in oil, watercolour and mixed media by 93 Academicians, among them Tracey Emin, David Hockney, Anish Kapoor, Grayson Perry and Tom Phillips.

The adjoining **Royal Mews** (tel: 7766 7300; Mar–Oct daily 10am–5pm, Nov–Feb Mon–Sat 10am–4pm) contain royal vehicles, ranging from coaches to Rolls-Royces. The Gold State Coach, built for George III in 1762, is still used by the Queen on major state occasions.

Most of the everyday crowds come to see the **Changing the Guard** ceremony which takes place outside the palace on alternate mornings at 11.30am, and daily in May, June and July. The New Guard, which marches up from Wellington Barracks, meets the Old Guard in the forecourt of the palace and they exchange symbolic keys to the accompaniment of regimental music. The Foot Guards are distinctive for their bearskin hats.

The **Queen Victoria Memorial** ⓑ in front of the palace was built in 1901. It encompasses symbolic figures glorifying the achievements of the British Empire and its builders.

The Mall

The Mall, the wide thoroughfare leading from Buckingham Palace

CLUB LAND

Each of London's members' clubs has its own character and attracts a certain type of person; most are the near-exclusive preserve of men. It is said that bishops and Fellows of the Royal Society join the Athenaeum, the foremost literary club, while actors and publishers opt for the Garrick or Saville Club. Diplomats, politicians and spies prefer Brooks', the Traveller's, Boodles or White's, while journalists gather at the Groucho Club in Soho. Jules Verne used the Reform Club (Pall Mall), the leading liberal club, as the setting for Phileas Fogg's wager that he could travel around the world in 80 days.

Dukes join the Turf Club, while top Tories like to dine at The Carlton on St James's Street.

to Trafalgar Square, was laid out by Charles II as a second course for the game of *paille maille* (a kind of croquet which spread from Italy to France, and then to Britain), when the one in Pall Mall (see page 78) became too rowdy. The Mall is the venue for the autumn **State Opening of Parliament**, when the Queen rides in a gold stagecoach surrounded by more than 100 troopers of the Household Cavalry wearing armorial breastplates. A further eccentricity are two farriers who accompany the procession, bearing spiked axes that would once have been used to kill any horse lamed in the parade and chop off its hooves to prevent the horse flesh being sold to a butcher.

The Mall is lined with a succession of grand buildings and historic houses reflecting different styles and periods. The ducal palaces have been used as royal residences: **Clarence House** 16 is home to Prince Charles; at **Lancaster House** Chopin gave a recital for Queen Victoria; **Marlborough House** 17, designed by Sir Christopher Wren, was the home of Queen Mary, consort of George V (1865–1936) until her death in 1953. Now it is a Commonwealth conference and research centre. The brick Tudor **St James's Palace** faces onto Pall Mall (see page 80).

Near the end of the Mall is **Carlton House Terrace**, built by John Nash, part of which houses the headquarters of **The Royal Society**, a learned body for the promotion of natural sciences. The oldest society of its kind, it was founded in 1660.

At the Trafalgar Square end, the terrace incorporates the **Mall Gallery** and the **Institute of Contemporary Arts** 18, a venue for avant-garde exhibitions, cinema and theatre, held in the restored Nash House.

The reinforced concrete structure across the Mall on the corner of the park is a bomb-proof shelter built for the Admiralty and nicknamed the Citadel, or Lenin's Tomb.

Admiralty Arch 19, leading from The Mall to Trafalgar Square, is a five-arched gateway commissioned by King Edward VII in memory of his mother, Queen Victoria, and completed in 1911. Traffic passes

ICA gallery.

Lobb's, the bootmaker.

through the two outer arches: the central arch is opened only for state occasions, letting royalty in and out of the city. In 2013 plans were announced to turn Admiralty Arch into a luxury hotel.

PALL MALL AND ST JAMES'S

Along elegant **Pall Mall** ⓴ exclusive gentlemen's clubs mingle with the grand homes of royalty. Their lofty book-lined rooms, picture-lined dining rooms and chandeliered lounges can be seen from the street. The area has been the haunt of men of influence since the 17th century, and it is reassuring to learn that the clubs generally enjoy a reputation for dull food and snobbish company.

In **Waterloo Place**, at the east end of Pall Mall and the bottom end of Regent Street, the statue of Frederick, the 'grand old' Duke of York (whose 10,000 men are fruitlessly marched up and down hill in a popular nursery rhyme), overlooks the Mall and St James's Park from its 124ft (37-metre) column. His monument's cost was met by extracting a day's wages from every man in the armed services.

One building that is unmistakable in Pall Mall is the red-brick **St James's Palace** ㉑ at the western end, built by Henry VIII in 1540 in a style that echoes his palace at Hampton Court. The state apartments are not open to the public and the chief relic of the original Tudor palace, the Gatehouse or **Clock Tower**, one of the finest examples of Tudor architecture in the city, is best viewed from the street. Clarence House is part of the complex.

North of St James's Palace **St James's Street** ㉒ leads into an area traditionally associated with gentlemen's tailors and shoemakers. The characterful shop frontages include **Berry Bros and Rudd**, at

St James's Palace.

No. 3, which could be straight out of a Dickens novel. **James Lock and Co**, at No. 6, is the birthplace of the bowler hat. A few doors up is **Lobb's**, shoemakers to Queen Victoria, and now to the Duke of Edinburgh.

St James's Square

Also off the north side of Pall Mall is **St James's Square** ㉓ laid out by Henry Jermyn, 1st Earl of St Albans, in about 1660. The Dukes of Norfolk had a town house in the square from 1723 until 1938. The building was used by General Eisenhower when he was preparing to launch the invasions of North Africa and northwest Europe in World War II. Also here is the London Library, an independent subscription library whose past members have included Dickens and George Eliot.

BEST RESTAURANTS, PUBS AND BARS

Restaurants

British

Boisdale
15 Eccleston St, SW1. Tel: 7730 6922. www.boisdale.co.uk Open: Mon–Fri, D Mon–Sat. **££££** [❶ p320, A1]
Classic Scottish restaurant serving dishes such as lobster bisque, haggis and Aberdeen Angus steaks. Live jazz every night and a full malt whisky line-up.

Goring Dining Room
Goring Hotel, Beeston Place, SW1. Tel: 7396 9000; www.thegoring.com Open: Sun–Fri, D daily. **££££** [❷ p320, A1]
Traditional fare such as potted shrimps, filet of venison, and proper puddings. Sunday roast lunch is a speciality.

Rex Whistler Restaurant
Millbank, SW1. Tel: 7887 8825. Open: daily. **£££** (set menu **££**) [❸ p320, C2]
Tate Britain's main restaurant reopened in 2013 after complete refurbishment, and now serves an excellent contemporary British menu to suit a broad range of tastes. The Tate wine list is exceptionally good.

Smith Square Café and Restaurant
St John's, Smith Square, SW1. Tel: 7222 2779. Open: Mon–Fri, D on weekday concert evenings and weekends. **££–£££** [❹ p320, C1]
Beneath one of London's top concert venues, this brick-vaulted restaurant offers good food and excellent service. Sandwiches and snacks are also on offer, and there is a long wine list.

French

Le Caprice
Arlington House, Arlington St, SW1. Tel: 7629 2239. www.le-caprice.co.uk Open: L & D daily. **££££** [❺ p306, A4]
Chic, buzzy bistro with Art Deco decor. The food – sophisticated salads, seafood and wonderful desserts – is more for picking over than wolfing down. Vegetarian dishes are also available.

Quaglino's
16 Bury St, SW1. Tel: 7930 6767. www.quaglinos-restaurant.co.uk Open: L & D Mon–Sat. **£££** [❻ p306, B4]
Glamorous brasserie that also does a set lunch menu. Live music most Friday and Saturday nights adds to the atmosphere.

Indian

The Cinnamon Club
Old Westminster Library, Great Smith St, SW1. Tel: 7222 2555. www.cinnamonclub.com Open: L & D Mon–Sat. **££££** (set lunch **££**) [❼ p320, C1]
Set in a beautifully refurbished Victorian library. The menu has a fine selection of specialities, ranging from Wagyu beef to tandoori lamb.

Pubs and Bars

Pubs

The Red Lion
48 Parliament S, www.redlionwestminster.co.uk [❶ p314, C4]
A stone's throw from No. 10 Downing Street and favoured watering hole of the political elite.

St Stephen's Tavern
10 Bridge St; www.ststephenstavern.co.uk [❷ p314, C4]
Traditional pub popular with politicians, unsurprisingly given its location opposite the Houses of Parliament.

Bars

Balls Brothers
50 Buckingham Palace Road; www.ballsbrothers.co.uk [❸ p320, A1]
Part of a small chain of London wine bars with an excellent selection of wines, this one is convenient for Victoria Station and Buckingham Palace.

Cinnamon Club Bar
30–32 Great Smith St; www.cinnamonclub.com [❹ p320, C1]
This is the high-tech downstairs bar of the trendy restaurant (see Restaurants).

Millbank Lounge
30 John Islip St [❺ p320, C2]
This modern bar decked out in red and chrome is great for speciality whiskies as well as cocktails.

Tapster
3 Brewers Green, Buckingham Gate; www.davy.co.uk/tapster [❻ p320, B1]
Traditional wine bar with a good menu.

Zander
45 Buckingham Gate [❼ p320, B1]
Sleek bar in the trendy Bank Restaurant serving classic and seasonal cocktails.

The Goring Hotel.

WESTMINSTER ABBEY

More than 3,000 notable people are buried here. The clutter of monuments make it seem like an ecclesiastical Madame Tussauds, with stone replacing wax.

The Tomb of the Unknown Warrior.

Monarchs were interred here until George II in 1760, and they are still crowned here. Among the royal tombs, look out for those of Elizabeth I and her half-sister Queen Mary, both in the Lady Chapel. Poets lie close by, beginning with Geoffrey Chaucer in 1400, who had been Clerk of the King's Works to the Palace of Westminster.

Other tombs include those of the naturalist Charles Darwin, the explorer David Livingstone and the scientist Sir Isaac Newton.

The Tomb of the Unknown Warrior houses a body brought back from France at the end of World War I. As the national shrine, Westminster Abbey was the natural resting place for this anonymous representative of the war dead.

Royal weddings also take place in the Abbey.

Much of the present abbey, the third on the site, was built in the 13th century in early English Gothic style by Henry III. In the 16th century, Henry VII added the chapel in the late Gothic Perpendicular style. During the 18th century, Nicholas Hawksmoor designed the towers at the main west entrance.

The Essentials

Tel: 7222 5152;
www.westminster-abbey.org
Opening Hrs: Mon–Fri 9.30am–4.30pm, Wed until 7pm (last admission 6pm), Sat 9.30am–2.30pm
Transport: Westminster

The Lady Chapel where King Henry VII is buried.

SOME HIGHLIGHTS

The south rose window and lancets.

Poets' Corner. The remains of Chaucer, Edmund Spenser, Samuel Johnson, Dryden, Sheridan, Browning, Tennyson, Dickens and Kipling lie here. Ben Jonson is buried standing up because he didn't wish to occupy too much space.
Coronation Chair. This has been used for every coronation in the Abbey since 1308.

Henry VII's Chapel. Contains exquisite fan-vaulting and the statues of nearly 100 saints.
Chapter House. Parliament met here in the 14th century. It has a fine tiled floor from 1259 and some lurid wall paintings based on the Apocalypse.
Undercroft Museum. This 11th-century room contains many of the Abbey's treasures as well as waxworks and death masks of various monarchs.
Sculptures. There are superbly carved angels in the south transept, and the chapels of Henry V and Henry VII are packed with saints and philosophers.
Brass band concerts are often held in a garden off the Cloisters in July and August.

Poets' Corner consists of a mixture of burials and commemorations of playwrights, poets and writers. Shakespeare's memorial comprises the central feature of this group memorial.

The choir is the part of the abbey where the monks worshipped. This area includes the abbey organ; famous organists who played here include Henry Purcell, who is also buried in the abbey.

The marble effigy of Queen Elizabeth I sits over her tomb and that of her half-sister, Queen Mary Tudor, in the Lady Chapel. Originally buried in the vault of King Henry VII, Elizabeth's tomb was moved here in 1606. Her crown, collar, orb and sceptre are replacements, the originals having been stolen.

Gateway to Chinatown.

SOHO AND CHINATOWN

Soho, Chinatown and Leicester Square form London's main entertainment centre, where you'll find abundant clubs, pubs, cinemas and theatres, and cuisines from all over the globe.

Main Attractions
Piccadilly Circus
Old Compton Street
Soho Square
Berwick Street Market
Carnaby Street
Chinatown

Maps and Listings
Map, page 86
Shopping, page 90
Restaurants, page 91
Accommodation, page 280

The West End has long been seen as the place to head for a night out in London. Piccadilly Circus is a springboard for London's theatreland while Leicester Square is the gateway to Chinatown and the location of the Empire cinema, the venue for UK film premieres. Over the past few decades, however, as tacky shops and chain restaurants have muscled in on these famous squares, their glamour has begun to look a little tarnished. Neighbouring Soho, on the other hand, has largely shed its once-dubious image as London's dark underbelly to become one of the capital's foremost destinations for drinking and dining.

PICCADILLY CIRCUS

At the heart of the West End is **Piccadilly Circus ❶**, star of millions of postcards. The first illuminated advertising signs appeared here in 1890, offering lucrative rental income to shopkeepers but contrasting harshly with the elegant architecture of neighbouring Regent Street. The statue of Eros, Greek god of love, was erected in 1893 as the Angel of Charity in honour of the philanthropic seventh Earl of Shaftesbury (1801–85), who drove the broad thoroughfare

bearing his name through the squalid slums that had grown up to the northeast.

Adding to Piccadilly's bright lights are the refurbished Criterion theatre on the south side, a huge branch of fashion retailer The Sting on the west and the 19th-century facade of the London Pavilion, a former music hall, on the east, which is now part of the **Trocadero Centre**, a complex of shops and restaurants on Holland Street. It includes Ripley's Believe It or Not! (daily 10am–midnight),

Sitting under Eros, Piccadilly Circus.

Bar Italia in Soho's Frith Street.

a collection of hundreds of weird objects from fossilized dinosaur eggs to a replica of Tower Bridge made from matchsticks.

In 2012 plans were approved to transform the Trocadero Centre into a 583-bedroom hotel across seven floors, incorporating Tokyo-style 'pod' rooms, apartments, shops and a rooftop bar.

BUSTLING SOHO

On the north side of Shaftesbury Avenue lies Soho, a bustling area of narrow streets long popular with immigrants. Flemish weavers, French Huguenots, Greeks, Italians, Belgians, Maltese, Swiss, Chinese and Russian Jews have sought refuge here at various times. Their influence is still felt in the patisseries, delicatessens, restaurants and shops.

Four hundred years ago Soho was an area of open fields, and its name is said to come from a hunting cry: 'So-ho, so-ho!'.

Bars and clip joints

Once infamous as the centre of London's sex industry, Soho occupies a middle-ground between the edgy, seedier Soho of its past and the tourist-friendly hotspot of smart bars and restaurants that populate the area today. 'Anything you like, sir' is still a phrase murmured to passers-by, but most of the strip joints and sex shops have been pushed towards the side streets. There are also venues for drag artists and transvestites that have been going long enough to have become almost respectable, and several of the attractive late-night bars and restaurants designed for the discerning gay crowd draw visitors of all persuasions.

Old Compton Street ➋

This is Soho's main artery, where a few of the celebrated continental food stores, cafés and specialist shops that once dominated the street, live on. Most have been replaced by

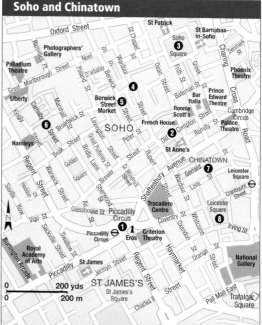

modern coffee shops, bars and more outlandish establishments, such as the body-piercing shop.

Situated at the Charing Cross Road end of Old Compton Street, the **Prince Edward Theatre** dates back to 1930. It was here that cabaret artiste Josephine Baker made her London debut in 1933.

Just off Old Compton Street is the French House in Dean Street, the centre of the Free French in World War II, an artists' haunt and still fiercely French. Artists such as Francis Bacon and Lucian Freud used to take advantage of the liberal licensing arrangements at the Colony Club in Dean Street. At 22 Frith Street, opposite Ronnie Scott's jazz club, is Bar Italia, a narrow café-bar with pavement seating and a retro Italian feel, which serves the best cappuccino in town and is open 24 hours a day. It is also a great place to watch international football matches; the large screen at the back of the bar is visible from the street.

Soho Square ❸

At the top of Frith Street, **Soho Square** was one of London's best

addresses when it was built in the 17th century. Today various film, new media and design companies are based here, their minimalist receptions lit up by plasma screens or statement art. During the summer the garden at the heart of the square is crowded with office workers grabbing a bit of sun with their sandwich. In the centre of the square are a 17th-century statue of Charles II and a 19th-century mock-Tudor gardeners' tool shed from which steps lead down to an underground cavern, used as a workshop during World War II and now waiting to be put to good use.

The red-brick tower of St Patrick's Catholic Church lends a bit of variety to the architectural proceedings. Established in 1893 on the site of an earlier church, a £3.5 million restoration has returned St Patrick's to its former glory.

A hint of Soho Square's former glory can be seen in the 18th-century house of charitable works, caring for the destitute, **St-Barnabas-in-Soho**, on the corner of Greek Street. Once a residential hostel, it is now a 'life skills' centre

The raunchier side of Soho.

Old Compton Street.

HISTORIC STREETS

Many famous people are associated with Soho, from the painters Thomas Gainsborough (1727–88) to Francis Bacon (1909–92), from Casanova (1725–98) to Oscar Wilde (1854–1900). A blue plaque reminds you that 41 Beak Street was the home of Canaletto, the Venetian painter, from 1749 to 1751. In 1926 John Logie Baird transmitted the first television images from an attic at 22 Frith Street (now Bar Italia), next door to where Mozart stayed as a boy. The house at 26 Dean Street, now Quo Vadis restaurant, is where Karl Marx wrote *Das Kapital*. Further down, at No. 49, Dylan Thomas once left the manuscript of *Under Milk Wood* under his chair at the French House pub.

Royal Events

'The events that I have attended to mark my Diamond Jubilee have been a humbling experience.' Her Majesty Queen Elizabeth II.

For millions of visitors, London is the Royal Family. Buckingham Palace, St James's Palace, the Tower of London and Kensington Gardens all symbolise the enduring presence of a dynasty that has played a significant role in British life for more than a thousand years. The wedding of Prince William and Kate Middleton in 2011 boosted the royals' popularity, which reached its apogee in 2012 in the euphoria of the Olympics and Diamond Jubilee.

In 2012, the Queen celebrated a landmark 60 years on the throne: only Queen Victoria has reigned for longer. The anniversary was celebrated (as her coronation had been) by street parties across the UK over an unprecedented four-day public holiday in June. Official celebrations included a Diamond Jubilee concert in front of Buckingham Palace, a rather cold and damp Thames Jubilee Pageant, a service of thanksgiving at St Paul's Cathedral and a carriage procession through London watched by a crowd estimated at a million people. The following year a special service was held in Westminster Abbey to celebrate the 60th anniversary of the Queen's coronation.

Royal Wedding

The wedding of Prince William to Kate Middleton in 2011 attracted a global television audience of around two billion people. Thousands of onlookers descended on London to share in the party atmosphere, with many spending the night sleeping in the streets to ensure a good view of the procession and get a glimpse of the bride's much-awaited dress – an elegant ivory satin creation, designed by Sarah Burton of Alexander McQueen, decorated with lace hand-made by the Royal School of Needlework at Hampton Court.

The wedding was an intriguing mix of the ancient and modern: while the couple were making their vows, for instance, the internet practically melted as people tweeted their admiration for Pippa Middleton's bottom. The couple emerged from the cathedral with new titles, the Duke and Duchess of Cambridge, and later delighted the crowds in the Mall with two balcony kisses. After a buffet reception at Buckingham Palace for around 650 guests, hosted by the Queen, William drove away his new bride in his father's borrowed Aston Martin.

Royal Baby

As soon as William and Kate tied the knot, speculation was rife as to how long it would be before Britain would be celebrating the birth of a new heir to the throne, so the official announcement on 3 December 2012 that the Duchess was expecting her first child was met with great excitement. Young Prince George Alexander Louis was duly born on 22 July 2013, weighing 8lb 6oz. Described by his proud father soon after his birth as 'a little bit of a rascal', he is third in line to the throne, after Prince Charles and Prince William.

All these royal events have been good for Britain's economy, boosting visitor numbers to London and retail spending nationwide, if only temporarily. So when is the next one?

Prince William and Kate Middleton process down the aisle in Westminster Abbey.

for homeless people. Its elegant interior of fine woodcarvings, fireplaces and plasterwork is not open to the public but a monthly series of events are held here.

Wardour Street ❹

Continuing west from Soho Square past Dean Street, the next main road is **Wardour Street**, once sarcastically known as the only street in the world which was shady on both sides. It is still the heart of London's film and recording industries, and during weekday lunch times the surrounding bars and restaurants are full of 30-something media bods discussing the next big thing.

Wardour Street has become a restaurant hotspot, and venues such as Busaba Eathai and Floridita (Cuban) ensure the street is busy long after office hours.

At the Shaftesbury Avenue end of Wardour Street, a tower is all that remains of Sir Christopher Wren's church of **St Anne's**, bombed in the war, though its beautifully kept gardens provide some shade and benches for a rest on a hot day.

Berwick Street Market ❺

The fruit and vegetable market in parallel **Berwick Street** is well laid out and inexpensive, and its stalls also sell cheese and flowers. The traders represent the most dense concentration of cockneys in central London apart from the taxi cafés, and their language is colourful.

Carnaby Street ❻

A detour away from Soho via Broadwick Street will take you towards **Carnaby Street**. The street now hosts up-market branches of some of the hipper high-street chains (Vans, Jack Wills, Lee Jeans and American Apparel, for example). You will still find examples of the sort of fashion creativity that first put the area on the map, but for this you'll need to leave Carnaby Street itself and explore the pedestrianised streets to the east.

CHINATOWN ❼

Returning to Soho and continuing down Wardour Street, walk along the south side of Shaftesbury Avenue to **Gerrard Street** and

Leicester Square.

Berwick Street Market.

Chinatown building.

parallel **Lisle Street**, home of Chinese grocers, restaurants and stores. Kitsch Chinese street furniture, lamps and archways in Gerrard Street make this the heart of Chinatown. Established in the 1950s after the first Chinatown in Limehouse was damaged by World War II bombing, it has some of the best Oriental cuisine in town, although quality varies.

There are also herbal and medicine shops. On Sundays, a family outing day for the city's Chinese, there is a Chinese food market. Chinese New Year in late January or early February is celebrated in style, with massive papier-mâché lions dancing through the streets.

LEICESTER SQUARE ❽

Just south of Chinatown, Leicester Square is home of the big cinemas and host to the capital's film premieres. Until the 17th century, this was the garden of Leicester House, and at the four corners of the garden are busts of famous people associated with the square. At the centre is the **Shakespeare monument** (1874), surrounded by brass plates in the ground giving distances to

Carnaby Street.

cities all over the world. Facing the bard is a **statue of Charlie Chaplin**, born in Southwark, south London, in 1889. Around the square is a regular contingent of caricature artists, buskers, Bible-thumpers and, on special occasions, a funfair carousel and amusement rides.

SHOPPING

Art

Frith Street Gallery
17–18 Golden Square, W1
Tel: 7287 3733; www.frithstreetgallery.com
The gallery was established in 1989. It began life as a gallery for contemporary drawing but quickly expanded into artists working in film, photography, painting and sculpture.

Clothes

Agent Provocateur
6 Broadwick St, W1
Tel: 7439 0229; www.agent provocateur.com

The place to go for decadently sexy lingerie.
Michiko Koshino Japan Co Ltd
59 Broadwick St, W1
Tel: 7434 3686; www.michikokoshino.co.uk
Koshino made her name with a line of menswear called Motorking. She derives her inspiration from urban streets and dance clubs and now has outlets in London and Japan.
Size?
33–34 Carnaby St, W1
Tel: 7287 4016; www.size.co.uk
Trainers specialist, stocking a good range of technical sports shoes as well as classic and old-school trainers.

Gifts and Souvenirs

Pylones (formerly Octopus)
28 Carnaby St, W1
Tel: 7287 9164; www.pylones.com
Bright, often witty designs in bags, watches, jewellery, umbrellas, ties and much more.

Specialist Shops

Vintage Magazine Shop
39–43 Brewer St, Soho, W1
Tel: 7439 8525; www.vinmag.com
A cardboard cut-out of Harrison Ford or Marilyn Monroe? They've got it, as well as a huge collection of vintage mags.

BEST RESTAURANTS, PUBS, BARS AND CAFÉS

PRICE CATEGORIES

Prices for a three-course dinner per person with a half-bottle of house wine:

£ = under £25
££ = £25–35
£££ = £35–55
££££ = over £55

Restaurants

American

Ed's Easy Diner
Old Compton St, W1. Tel: 7434 4439.
www.edseasydiner.com. Open: daily, all day from noon. **£** [8 p306, C2]
Beefburgers, veggie burgers, chicken burgers dished up in 1950s American-style surroundings. There is another Ed's diner at the Trocadero on Rupert Street.

British

Dean Street Townhouse
69–71 Dean St, W1. Tel: 7434 1775; www.deanstreettownhouse.com. Open: L & D daily. **££££** [9 p306, C2]
The restaurant of this stylish Soho hotel manages to combine the style of a French brasserie with the delights of simple English food – the fish and chips are particularly good. The ambience is cool and sexy and the service is attentive.

Chinese

Harbour City
46 Gerrard St, W1. Tel: 7439 7859. Open: daily, all day. **££** (set menu **£–££**) [10 p306, C3]
A recommended choice with a window table overlooking Gerrard Street. Dim sum served from noon–5pm.

Joy King Lau
3 Leicester St, WC2. Tel: 7437 1133.
www.joykinglau.com
Open: daily, all day. **£££** (set menu **££–£££**) [11 p306, C3]
This is a popular choice for those who know Chinese food well. Set

menus from around £28 feature sizzling veal with black pepper sauce, plus a range of noodle dishes. Dim sum is available until 5pm.

Mr Kong
21 Lisle St, WC2H. Tel: 7437 7341.
www.mrkongrestaurant.com Open: daily, all day till 2.45am, Sun until 1.45am. **££** (set menu **£–££**) [12 p306, C3]
This is one of the more authentic (and claustrophobic) Chinese restaurants in the area. It offers many unusual dishes such as baked lobster with black beans and chilli, and deep fried oysters. Has a lively vegetarian selection too.

Royal Dragon
30 Gerrard St, W1. Tel: 7734 1388.
www.rdklondon.co.uk Open: daily, until 3am. **££** (set menu **£**) [13 p306, C3]
A noisy place where karaoke is as much a feature as the food, and sizzling, quick-fire dishes descend from on high. Set menus

are reliable. Dim sum served noon–5pm.

Yauatcha
15 Broadwick St, W1. Tel: 7494 8888.
www.yauatcha.com Open: daily, all day.
£££ [14 p306, B2]
This stylish, Michelin-starred tea-room and dim sum emporium offers delicious, if expensive, dim sum from noon until midnight (until 10.30pm on Sun). Created by the founder of Wagamama, the popular chain of noodle restaurants.

Fish

Randall & Aubin
16 Brewer St, W1. Tel: 7287 4447.
www.randallandaubin.com Open: L & D daily.
£££ [15 p306, B2]
Piles of lobster, crab and oysters greet you as you enter this bustling place, which serves seafood of the highest quality, but also classic French and British dishes.

Chinatown cuisine.

Welcome

French

L'Escargot Marco Pierre White
48 Greek St, W1. Tel: 7439 7474.
www.lescargotrestaurant.co.uk Open: Mon–Fri, D Mon–Sat. **£££** (set menu **££**) [16] p306, C2]
The grand-père of London's French restaurants, with its lovely 1920s decor, is now run by Marco Pierre White. It offers a choice between the exciting hubbub of the ground floor or the more intimate Picasso room upstairs, with à la carte and set menus.

Hungarian

Gay Hussar
2 Greek St, W1. Tel: 7437 0973. www.gay hussar.co.uk Open: L & D Mon–Sat. **£££** [17] p306, C2]
In polished, gentleman's club surroundings, a mix of hearty British and Hungarian dishes are served. Pork and potatoes are prominent.

Indian

Masala Zone
9 Marshall St, W1. Tel: 7287 9966.
www.masalazone.com Open: L & D daily.

Drinking outside the French House pub on Dean Street.

£–££ [18] p306, B2]
Bright and always busy, this offers reasonably priced, if slightly sanitised, Indian food in fast-paced surroundings.

International

Balans
60 Old Compton St, W1. Tel: 7439 2183.
www.balans.co.uk Open: daily (Mon–Thu, Sun 8am–5am, Fri–Sat 8am–6am). **££** [19] p306, C2]
Sets out to bring a buzz and glamour to gay eating in Compton Street with its range of New York brunch-style dishes – including melt-in-your-mouth eggs benedict – and an extensive all day menu.

Floridita
100 Wardour St, W1. Tel: 7314 4000.
www.floriditalondon.com Open: Tue–Wed 5.30pm–2am, Thur–Sat 5.30pm–3am. **£££**. Admission £10 after 8pm on Fri and Sat. [20] p306, B2]
Eat to a Latin beat in this buzzy, Cuban-themed restaurant. Live jazz, funk, soul and Latin music every night of the week.

Italian

Amalfi
29–31 Old Compton St, W1. Tel: 7437 7284.
www.amalfi-restaurant.co.uk Open: L & D daily. **££** [21] p306, C2]
The cooking is of the 1970s bistro variety, but pizzas, vegetable pastas and other Italian fare are filling and you can be sure of quick service and a table without reservation.

Bocca di Lupo
12 Archer St, W1.Tel: 7734 2223.
www.boccadilupo.com Open: L daily, D Mon–Sat. **££–£££** [22] p306, B3]
Vibrant trattoria serving regional dishes such as courgette flower risotto and Florentine steaks.

Kettners
29 Romilly St, W1. Tel: 7734 6112. www.kettners.com Open: daily, all day. **££** [23] p306, C2]
This sprawling, always busy grande dame fuses an extensive champagne list with a menu of dishes such as pearl barley risotto or seared turbot. Pudding bar, too.

Quo Vadis
26–29 Dean St, W1. Tel: 7437 9585.
www.quovadissoho.co.uk Open: L Mon–Fri, D Mon–Sat. **£££–££££** [24] p306, C2]
A venerable institution in the one-time home of Karl Marx serving high-end modern Italian food. Brit art on the walls, and an expensive but excellent wine list.

Japanese

Satsuma
56 Wardour St, W1. Tel: 7437 8338.
www.osatsuma.com Open: daily, all day. **££** [25] p306, C2]
Fast food but well presented, with some good udon and ramen noodle dishes, plus sushi.

Ten Ten Tei
56 Brewer St, W1. Tel: 7287 1738. Open: L and D Mon–Sat. **££** [26] p306, B3]
A small place with an excellent reputation for delicious Japanese dishes at affordable prices. The restaurant has a casual, thrown-together appearance, but that doesn't stop people coming back for more.

Mediterranean

Hummus Bros
88 Wardour St, W1. Tel: 7734 1311.
www.hbros.co.uk Open: L & D daily. **£** [27] p306, B2]
Very popular budget café serving, as its name suggests, hummous with various toppings such as salad or Mexican beef. Ideal mopped up with fresh pitta bread.

Modern European

Bar du Marché
19 Berwick St, W1. Tel: 7734 4606.
www.bardumarche.co.uk Open: all day, Mon–Sat. **££** [28] p306, B2]
Tucked behind Berwick Street Market, this is a surprisingly unpretentious Soho hangout. Serves a mix of French brasserie-style food, salads and seafood.

Mildred's
45 Lexington St, W1. Tel: 7494 1634.
www.mildreds.co.uk Open: Mon–Sat noon–11pm. **££** [29] p306, B2]
This is a friendly, laid-back place. The vegetarian food ranges from veggie burgers to tofu stir fries and ale pie, accom-

panied by organic beer and soft drinks.

Spanish

Barrafina
54 Frith St, W1. Tel: 7813 8016; www.barrafina.co.uk Open: L & D daily. **££** [30] p306, C2]
Delicious Spanish tapas served as you sit at the counter in stylish surroundings. All dishes are for sharing, and the produce is of the highest quality. Extensive list of Spanish wines; no reservations.

Pubs, Bars and Cafés

Pubs

For those who like their ale from a barrel and not a bottle, Soho has plenty of classic Victorian pubs.

The Argyll Arms
18 Argyll St; www.nicholsonspubs.co.uk [8] p306, A1]
Close to Oxford Circus, this is a traditional pub in a lovely 18th century building. Food is served all day.

The Coach & Horses
29 Greek St; www.coachandhorsessoho. co.uk [9] p306, C2]
Best known for its association with the columnist Jeffrey Bernard, and as a haunt of other Soho personalities, this was also the home of 'London's rudest landlord', Norman Balon. A Soho institution.

The Dog & Duck
18 Bateman St [10] p306, C2]
In the heart of Soho, this traditional pub is famous for having served John Constable and George Orwell.

Bars

Alphabet
61–3 Beak St [11] p306, B2]
If you're in search of a hip hang-out, head for West Soho and this place. Arranged over two floors, it caters for a media in-crowd.

Café Boheme
13–17 Old Compton St; www.cafeboheme. co.uk [12] p306, C2].
A French bistro offering quality Martinis and an excellent selection

of wines.

La Casa del Habano
100 Wardour St; www.floridita.co.uk [13] p306, B2]
Luxurious cocktail lounge and a vast selection of Havana's finest available from the Cigar Boutique.

Experimental Cocktail Club
13A Gerrard St; www.chinatownecc.com [14] p306, C3]
A popular plush bar appealing to a hip crowd offering top cocktails and absinthe. Vintage gins add a classy flavour.

The French House
49 Dean St; www.frenchhousesoho.com [15] p306, C2]
This iconic Soho spot offers a decadent and beautiful old bar that was the centre of the French Resistance in London during World War II, and the regular haunt of painter Francis Bacon and writer Samuel Beckett. The upstairs restaurant serves good French fare.

Cafés

The best in Soho are found in and around Compton Street.

Patisserie Valerie.

Bar Italia
22 Frith St; www.baritaliasoho.co.uk [16] p306, C2]
This is a Soho legend, serving great Italian coffee and snacks around the clock.

Maison Bertaux
28 Greek St; www.maisonbertaux.com [17] p306, C2]
The most wonderful, boho French café this side of the Channel, where the surroundings appear as if they'll crumble to the touch, just like their exquisite cakes.

Patisserie Valerie
44 Old Compton St; www.patisserie-valerie. co.uk [18] p306, C2].
Come here for a gentle continental experience and delicious cakes and pastries amid the bustle of Old Compton Street.

PRICE CATEGORIES

Prices for a three-course dinner per person with a half-bottle of house wine:
£ = under £25
££ = £25–35
£££ = £35–55
££££ = over £55

TRAFALGAR SQUARE AND COVENT GARDEN

With its shooting fountains and soaring column, Trafalgar Square is one of London's most popular open spaces. It is also a short hop from vibrant Covent Garden.

South of Leicester Square is Trafalgar Square, from where the Strand heads east, flanked on one side by Covent Garden and on the other by the riverside Victoria Embankment leading down to Waterloo Bridge.

TRAFALGAR SQUARE ❶

The closest that London has to the kind of large public square common in other European capitals was designed in 1838 by Sir Charles Barry. In 1841 it was named **Trafalgar Square** to commemorate Admiral Lord Nelson's 1805 victory against Napoleon's navy at Trafalgar, off the Atlantic coast of Spain.

At the centre of the square is **Nelson's Column**, a 169ft (51.5-metre) monument, made up of a Corinthian column topped by a statue of Horatio Nelson, battle-scarred with only one arm but without a patch on his blind eye. He is gazing towards the Mall, inspecting the fleet of model ships attached to pillars on the avenue. The four iconic lions (1847) are by Edwin Landseer.

Around the square, Canada House, South Africa House and Uganda House are memories of distant Empire days. Also celebrating the old Empire are statues of General

Charles Napier and Major General Sir Henry Havelock, on the plinths in the two southern corners of the square. The statue in the northeast corner depicts George IV.

Controversy over who should occupy the northwest corner's fourth plinth – left empty after plans in 1841 to erect an equestrian statue collapsed through lack of funds – caught Londoners' imaginations, and a committee was formed to commission works of art that could take their turn on the plinth. Anthony

Main Attractions
Trafalgar Square
National Gallery
National Portrait Gallery
St Martin-in-the-Fields
Covent Garden Market
Royal Opera House
St Paul's Church
London Transport Museum
London Coliseum
Charing Cross Bookshops

Maps and Listings

Covent Garden street performer.

Gormley's One and Other was perhaps the most popular, as members of the public were able to adopt the plinth for an hour at a time and do whatever they wished. The unveiling in 2013 of a giant blue cockerel by German artist Katharina Fritsch met with controversy, with some not happy about having the national symbol of France in a square that celebrates a historical victory over the French.

The square has long been the site of public gatherings, political demonstrations and New Year celebrations. A mayoral campaign to rid it of its traditional plague of pigeons was largely successful, and in 2003 the north side of the square was pedestrianised to give people a sporting chance of reaching the fountains without being mown down by traffic.

In the southwest corner of the square, Admiralty Arch marks the start of The Mall, leading to Buckingham Palace (see page 76). Whitehall, the other exit, will lead you to the Houses of Parliament (see page 70).

National Portrait Gallery.

The National Gallery ❷

Address: Trafalgar Square, www.nationalgallery.org.uk
Tel: 7747 2885
Opening Hrs: Sat–Thu 10am–6pm, Fri 10am–9pm
Entrance Fee: free except some special exhibitions
Transport: Charing Cross

Dominating the north side of Trafalgar Square is the neoclassical **National Gallery**, designed by William Wilkins in 1838 with a modern wing by Robert Venturi completed in 1991. This is the country's most important art gallery, home to around 2,000 west European masterpieces, including works by Rembrandt, Rubens, El Greco, Vermeer and Van Gogh. For full details, see page 104.

The National Portrait Gallery ❸

Address: St Martin's Place, www.npg.org.uk
Tel: 7306 0055 or 7312 2463
Opening Hrs: Mon–Wed, Sat–Sun 10am–6pm, Thu–Fri 10am–9pm
Entrance Fee: free except for some special exhibitions
Transport: Charing Cross

Behind the National Gallery is the **National Portrait Gallery**, housed

in a Florentine Renaissance building originally designed by architect Ewan Christian and opened in 1896. Only a fraction of the collection's 10,000 artworks, plus half a million photographs of the nation's illustrious men and women, is on display at any one time. For full details, see page 106.

St Martin-in-the-Fields ❹

Address: Trafalgar Square, www.st martin-in-the-fields.org
Tel: box office (evening concerts) 7766 1100
Opening Hrs: Mon–Tue, Thu–Fri 8.30am–6pm, Wed 8.30am–5pm, Sat 9.30am–6pm, Sun 3.30pm–5pm)
Entrance Fee: free except evening concerts
Transport: Charing Cross

Across the road is the church of **St Martin-in-the-Fields**, the oldest building in Trafalgar Square, built in 1726 by a Scottish architect, James Gibbs, when this venue was in fields outside the city. Nell Gwynne, the mistress of Charles II, is one of several famous people buried in this parish church of the royal family, which was so chic in the 18th century that pews were rented out on an annual basis. The royal box is on the left of the altar. The crypt, which houses a soup kitchen for the homeless, a café and the London Brass Rubbing Centre, was used as an air-raid shelter during the bombing blitz of World War II.

Regular classical music concerts are held in the church on Wednesday, Thursday, Friday and Saturday, at either 7.30pm or 8pm. There are also free lunchtime concerts.

AROUND THE STRAND

The mundane modern architecture in the Strand, the main thoroughfare connecting the West End with the City, camouflages the fact that it was once a very fashionable street, home in the 18th and 19th centuries to the poet Samuel Taylor Coleridge and

Nelson's Column.

The entrance to the National Gallery, seen from the side.

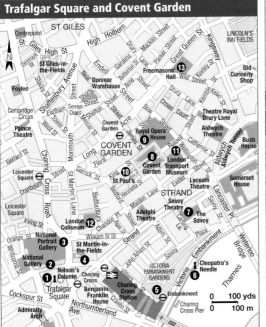

Trafalgar Square and Covent Garden

0   100 yds
0   100 m

the novelist George Eliot. Although the street is well past its glory days, a sense of history is not altogether lost: you can still dine in traditional style at Simpson's, opened in 1848, or take tea in the Thames Room of the Savoy.

At the Strand's western end, near Trafalgar Square, is **Charing Cross** railway station. In front of it is a replica of the last of 12 crosses set up by Edward I in 1291 to mark the funeral procession of his queen, Eleanor of Castile, from Nottinghamshire to Westminster Abbey. "Charing" is thought by some to come from "*chère reine*" (dear queen) Eleanor, although it is more likely to have come from the Old English word "*cierran*", meaning to turn.

Victoria Embankment

At this point, cut down Villiers Street, which for a while was home to Rudyard Kipling, author of *The Jungle Book* (a blue plaque marks the spot). Nearby is Craven Street, where the Founding Father of the USA, Benjamin Franklin, lived from 1757 to 1775. His Georgian

Browsing at the Apple Market in Covent Garden piazza.

Soaking up the sunshine on the entrance steps to St Martin-in-the-Fields.

mansion is now a fascinating and lively museum, the Benjamin Franklin House (36 Craven Street; tel: 7839 2006; www.benjaminfranklin house.org; historical experience shows Wed–Sun noon–4.15pm; architectural guided tours Mon noon, 1pm,

2pm, 3.15pm and 4.15pm; book in advance).

Back on Villiers Street, at its southern end, is **Victoria Embankment**, built in 1870 to ease traffic congestion and carry sewage pipes needed to improve London's crude sanitation system. In the Victoria **Embankment Gardens ⑤** a restored **Water Gate** once marked the river entrance to York House, London home of the archbishops of York, birthplace of philosopher and statesman Francis Bacon (1561–1626) and home of the dukes of Buckingham.

On the river front is **Charing Cross Pier**, a starting point for boats heading east to Greenwich. This is also the site of the 60ft (18-metre) **Cleopatra's Needle ⑥**, carved in Aswan, Egypt, c.1475BC and presented to Britain in 1819 (see box). The needle is flanked by two bronze sphinxes.

The Savoy

Back on the Strand are several theatres, including the **Adelphi**, opened in 1806. Richard D'Oyly Carte (1844–1901), sponsor of Gilbert and Sullivan operas at the splendid Art Deco **Savoy Theatre**, also financed the building of the **Savoy Hotel ⑦**, which opened in 1889 as one of the first in London with private bathrooms, electric lights and lifts (elevators). From the Strand, the Savoy is unimposing, but it is grand enough to have its own private forecourt and the only road in Britain where traffic drives on the right.

D'Oyly Carte is commemorated in a stained-glass window in the **Queen's Chapel of the Savoy** (www. duchyoflancaster.co.uk; Oct–July Mon–Thur 9am–4pm, Sun 10am–4pm services permitting), behind the hotel. It was founded in the 16th century when the former Savoy Palace became a hospital. Built by Peter, 9th Count of Savoy, in 1246, the palace had its heyday under John of Gaunt (1340–99), when it was 'the fayrest manor in Europe, big enough for a large part of an army'.

Covent Garden ⑧

Named after a convent whose fields occupied the site, **Covent Garden** was for centuries the principal market in London for vegetables, fruit and flowers, and the workplace of Eliza Doolittle, the flower girl in George Bernard Shaw's *Pygmalion*, who later burst into song in the film and musical *My Fair Lady*. The main piazza was originally laid out with colonnaded town houses designed by Inigo Jones c.1630, and inspired by the 16th-century Italian architect Andrea Palladio. A small market was founded here as early as 1656.

After the market moved out in 1974, the area became a blueprint for turning old commercial buildings into a mall of stores and stalls. Restaurants, cafés and shops occupy the old warehouses in the streets around the market square. There is a good line in street entertainers, who undergo auditions before they are granted a licence to perform here.

FACT

Since the 18th century, Charing Cross has been the spot from which distances to and from London are measured.

One of the sphinxes flanking Cleopatra's Needle.

Cleopatra's Needle, on the Victoria Embankment.

London Transport Museum.

Royal Opera House ❾

Address: Bow Street, www.roh.org.uk
Tel: 7304 4000
Opening Hrs: Daily 10am–3.30pm
Entrance Fee: free except for tours
Transport: Covent Garden

In 1733, a theatre was established in the northeast corner of Covent Garden, on the site now occupied by the **Royal Opera House**. A fire ravaged the first building in 1808, consuming Handel's organ and many of his works. The Opera House has had to contend with unimpressed audiences: price riots were common in the 19th century, and in 1809 lasted 61 nights. The Floral Hall, which acts as a reception space prior to performances and during intervals, is spectacular.

St Paul's Church ❿

Address: Bedford Street, www.actors church.org
Tel: 7836 5221
Opening Hrs: Mon–Fri 8.30am–5pm, Sun 9am–1pm and for services
Entrance Fee: free
Transport: Covent Garden

The portico of **St Paul's**, the actors' church, built in 1633 by Inigo Jones, and used as a backdrop in *My Fair Lady*, dominates the western end of the square. The vaults and grounds of this Tuscan-style church are said to contain the remains of more famous people than any other church except Westminster Abbey. The headstones have long been removed, but residents include master wood carver Grinling Gibbons (died 1720), the composer of **Rule Britannia**, Thomas Arne (1778) and the actress Ellen Terry (1928).

London Transport Museum ⓫

Address: Covent Garden Piazza, www.ltmuseum.co.uk
Tel: 7379 6344 or 7565 7299
Opening Hrs: Sat–Thu 10am–6pm, Fri 11am–6pm
Entrance Fee: free to accompanied children under 16
Transport: Covent Garden

The old flower market, in the southeastern corner of the square, is now occupied by **London Transport Museum**, which brings alive the development of London's transport network, from trams and trolleybuses to the Routemaster bus. There is plenty of hands-on fun, so it's great for children. You can take the wheel of an old double-decker bus, try your hand as a Tube conductor or bump around with other passengers in the back of a train.

Around Drury Lane

Neighbouring **Drury Lane** is closely linked with the theatre. Its principal venue is the Theatre Royal, which, when it opened in 1663, was only the second legitimate playhouse in the city. The mistress of Charles II, Nell Gwynne, depicted by cartoonists as a voluptuous orange seller, trod the boards here. Being one of the largest in the West End, its stage can mount blockbuster musicals.

Opposite its white Corinthian portico is the former **Bow Street police**

Music shop on Charing Cross Road.

station, home in the 18th century of the scarlet-waistcoated Bow Street Runners, the prototype policemen.

Long Acre and St Martin's Lane

Long Acre cuts through Covent Garden, from Neal Street to Leicester Square tube station. At 12–14 Long Acre is Britain's best travel bookshop, **Stanford's**. South of Long Acre is St Martin's Lane, home of the English National Opera's **London Coliseum** ⑫ (see page 289), where productions are sung in English, with subtitles.

Great Queen Street is the site of the **Freemasons' Hall** ⑬ (tel: 7831 9811; www.ugle.org.uk; Mon–Fri 11am–4pm), an imposing white behemoth that houses a museum on the history of freemasonry, a library and tavern.

CHARING CROSS ROAD

Long Acre leads to **Charing Cross Road**, a centre for rare and second-hand books. **Foyles** is a maze of more than 4 million volumes but has become better organised, if duller, since the death of its eccentric former owner, Christina Foyle. **Zwemmer's** is known for fine art and photography books, while Denmark Street is known as **Tin Pan Alley**, a home of early British rock 'n' roll.

KIDS

On the second Sunday in May, the Covent Garden May Fayre and Puppet Festival is held in the garden of St Paul's church. The day commemorates the Punch and Judy puppet tradition, first noted here in May 1662 by diarist Samuel Pepys. There's a brass band procession around the area at 10.30am and puppetry performances in the afternoon. The Punch & Judy pub inside the market marks the spot where the puppet show was first mounted.

SHOPPING

Books

Bertram Rota
31 Long Acre, WC2
Tel: 7836 0723; www.bertramrota.co.uk/
Bertram Rota specialises in modern first editions, books on architecture and the applied arts.

Blackwell's
100 Charing Cross Rd, WC2
Tel: 7292 5100;
www.blackwell.co.uk
As with its namesake in Oxford, Blackwell's concentrates on academic books (particularly business and law) but also sells more popular titles.

Foyles
107–109 Charing Cross Rd, WC2
Tel: 7434 1574; www.foyles.co.uk
In 2014, Foyles moved from its famous premises spread over five buildings to a new site on the same road. It also houses Grant & Cutler, the UK's largest foreign language bookseller.

Stanfords
12–14 Long Acre, WC2
Tel: 7836 1321; www.stanfords.co.uk
Stanfords was established in 1853 and is the UK's leading specialist retailer of maps, travel books and other travel accessories. It claims to have the world's largest stock of maps and travel books under one roof.

Clothes

Paul Smith
40–44 Floral St, WC2
Tel: 7379 7133; www.paulsmith.co.uk
Designer famous for his original take on classic tailoring and use of colourful patterns. Men's and women's clothing is found here, which was his first store, opened in 1979.

Ted Baker
9–10 Floral St, WC2
Tel: 7836 7808; www.tedbaker.com
A UK brand of stylish clothing that

started in Glasgow in 1988 and now has shops across the world.

Whistles
24 Long Acre, WC2
Tel: 7240 8195; www.whistles.co.uk
One of the best places to shop for good clothing with an individualistic take on trends.

Specialist Shops

Ellis Brigham
10–12 Southampton St, WC2
Tel: 7395 1010; www.ellis-brigham.com
The ideal store for stocking up on outdoor equipment, for camping, climbing and sports. They also sell a good range of rucksacks and their staff are very knowledgable.

Neal's Yard Remedies
15 Neal's Yard, WC2
Tel: 7379 7222; www.nealsyard remedies.com
Alternative health shop which also sells aromatherapy blends, shampoos, skin protection and gift boxes.

BEST RESTAURANTS, PUBS AND BARS

PRICE CATEGORIES

Prices for a three-course dinner per person with a half-bottle of house wine:

£ = under £25
££ = £25–35
£££ = £35–55
££££ = over £55

Restaurants

American

Christopher's
18 Wellington St, WC2. Tel: 7240 4222.
www.christophersgrill.com Open: B Sat–Sun, L & D daily. **£££** (set menus **£–££**) [❸❶] p306, E3]
The dishes on the contemporary American menu are imaginative and usually well prepared, but the elegant dining rooms, refurbished in 2013, are the main attraction. The Martini Bar is a theatrical spot for a drink and a light snack. Has good-value pre- and post-theatre menus.
Joe Allen
13 Exeter St, WC2. Tel: 7836 0651.

Rules restaurant.

www.joeallen.co.uk Open: daily noon–midnight. **£££** (brunch, pre-theatre and late supper menus **£–££**) [❸❷] p306, E3]
Tucked away below street level, this relaxed diner has a predictable enough menu – salads, steaks, spareribs, pecan pie – and average-quality food, but it's ever popular with customers, who sip cocktails until 12.45am.

British

Rules
35 Maiden Lane, WC2. Tel: 7836 5314.
www.rules.co.uk Open: L & D daily. **£££–££££** [❸❸] p306, E3]
Rules (est. 1798) is London's oldest restaurant, and the decor, notably the wonderful Art Nouveau stained-glass ceiling and the wood panelling, reflects its heritage. The robust food is very English, with beef, lamb and a variety of game from Rules' own estate in the Pennines. Upstairs, the cocktail bar serves a very fine Bloody Mary.
Simpson's-in-the-Strand, Grand Divan
100 The Strand, WC2. Tel: 7836 9112.

www.simpsonsinthestrand.co.uk Open: B Mon–Fri, L & D daily. **££££** (breakfast **£**, set menu **££**) [❸❹] p306, E3]
This bastion of Britishness retains all the grandeur of bygone days – chandeliers, oak panelling and tail-coated waiters – while managing a surprisingly relaxed atmosphere. The menu is traditional (beef fillet, duck and Dover sole); for many the famed roast beef, wheeled in on a silver-domed carving trolley, is the only choice. A good place to breakfast like a king.

Fish

J. Sheekey
28–32 St Martin's Court, WC2. Tel: 7240 2565; www.j-sheekey.co.uk Open: L & D daily. **££££** (weekend lunch menu **££**) [❸❺] p306, D3]
Think chargrilled squid with gorgonzola polenta, Cornish fish stew and New England baby lobster, followed by rhubarb pie or the famed Scandinavian iced berries with white chocolate sauce. Impressive wine list. Chic. Booking essential.

French

L'Atelier de Joel Robuchon
13–15 West St, WC2. Tel: 7010 8600.
www.joelrobuchon.co.uk Open: L & D daily. **£££–££££** (pre-theatre menu available) [❸❻] p306, C2]
French food with Spanish influences at this two Michelin-starred restaurant. Foie gras ravioli, free range quail, Scottish scallops, lobster and steak are just some of the offerings. Diners sit at a counter surrounding the kitchen so you can see the chefs at work.

International

Asia de Cuba
St Martin's Lane Hotel, 45 St Martin's Lane, WC2. Tel: 7300 5588. Open: B, L & D daily. **££££** [❸❼] p306, D3]
Attached to one of London's hippest hotels is this buzzing restaurant, with eccentric decor and fusion menu comprising a mix of

Cuban and Asian cuisine. Lobster parcels, pot-roast pork and melt-in-your-mouth tuna are a few of the treats on offer.

Bali Bali

150 Shaftesbury Ave, WC2. Tel: 7836 2644. www.balibalirestaurant.com. Open: L Mon–Sat, D daily. **££** [38 p306, D2]

This authentic Indonesian restaurant serves up good value curries and spicy meat and vegetarian dishes. The service can be slow but the flavoursome food is worth the wait.

Modern European

Belgo Centraal

50 Earlham St, WC2. Tel: 7813 2233. www.belgo-restaurants.co.uk Open: L & D daily. **££** [39 p306, D2]

Belgian fare of mussels and chips and excellent beers. Long benches, shared tables and waiters dressed as monks add to the atmosphere. The 'Beat the Clock' option offers great value from 5 to 6.30pm.

The Ivy

1 West St, WC2. Tel: 7836 4751. www.the-ivy.co.uk Open: L & D daily. **££££** (set menu **££**) [40 p306, D2]

Begun in 1917, The Ivy is one of London's best-known celebrity haunts. The menu is British but includes international favourites. The wine list is strong and the surreptitious star-spotting irresistible. Open late so useful for post-theatre meals. The only problem is getting a table – reserve months, not just days, ahead, although you might be lucky if you want lunch rather than dinner.

The Portrait Restaurant

National Portrait Gallery, St Martin's Place, W1. Tel: 7312 2490. www.npg.org.uk Open: L daily, D Thur–Sat. **£££** [41 p306, D4]

When it comes to location, few can beat the top floor of the National Portrait Gallery. It offers views of Trafalgar Square, Big Ben and the London Eye. The food is above average by gallery restaurant standards. The menu includes game, pork belly and fish, with a delicious array of desserts.

Sarastro

126 Drury Lane, WC2. Tel: 7836 0101. www.sarastro-restaurant.com Open: L & D daily. **££**–**£££** [42 p306, E2]

'The show after the show' is this restaurant's slogan. The flamboyant decor, with velvet drapes, golden chairs, opera boxes, chandeliers and props, is a stage set in itself. The Turkish-influenced menu is more straightforward, and there is live music most evenings.

Vegetarian

Food for Thought

31 Neal St, WC2. Tel: 7836 0239. www.food forthought-london.co.uk Open: B Mon–Sat, L daily, D Mon–Sat until 8.30pm (last orders 8pm). **£** [43 p306, D2]

This pleasant eatery does an imaginative selection of dishes, with a daily changing menu. Tom-yam soup might be followed by gnocchi with gorgonzola and oyster mushrooms. A BYOB (no corkage) policy keeps the cost down. No credit cards.

Pubs and Bars

Cafés, wine bars and pubs are ten a penny in the Covent Garden area – ideal for a relaxed lunch or a night on the town, with happy hours/late closing hours commonplace.

Pubs

Lamb and Flag

33 Rose St; https://lambandflagcovent garden.co.uk [19 p306, D3]

Tucked away down the tiniest of alleyways, this is one of several historic pubs in the area.

The Punch & Judy

40 The Market, Covent Garden Piazza; www.taylor-walker.co.uk [20 p306, E3]

This pub, dating from 1787, is on the upper level of the Market itself, which means you have a great view of the street performers on the piazza below.

Bars

American Bar

Savoy Hotel, Strand; www.fairmont.com/savoy-london [21 p306, D3]

Classic hotel bar with a history going back to the 1920s, the golden age of cocktails.

Brasserie Blanc at the Opera Terrace

Royal Opera House; www.roh.org.uk [22 p306, E2/3]

Raymond Blanc opened Brasserie Blanc at the Opera Terrace in 2012. With its arched glass ceiling and fabulous views across the piazza, this is a wonderful spot for a drink at the cocktail bar, or something more substantial at the brasserie.

Brasserie Max

10 Monmouth St; www.firmdalehotels.com [23 p306, D2]

Set in the Covent Garden Hotel, this is popular with trendy urbanites.

Christopher's Martini Bar

18 Wellington St; www.christophersgrill.com [24 p306, E3]

A theatrical American Deco interior and creative cocktails appeal to a discerning crowd.

Cork & Bottle

44–46 Cranbourn St; www.thecorkandbottle. co.uk [25 p306, C3]

This is an old favourite with Londoners, pulling in the crowds for its comfort factor and excellent wine lists.

Gordon's Wine Bar

47 Villiers St; www.gordonswinebar.com [26 p306, E4]

On the way to Embankment Tube is this favourite London watering hole, where drinkers sit under the arches on chilly nights (though keep an eye on your bag) and out on the terrace in summer. Sherry and port are specialities here.

Lobby Bar at One Aldwych

1 Aldwych; www.onealdwych.com [27 p306, E3]

Regularly voted top hotel lobby bar in the world, this is one of London's most glamorous drinking spots.

Lowlander

36 Drury Lane; www.lowlander.com [28 p306, E2]

A Belgian bar and brasserie boasting an impressive lager and ale list.

The Portrait Bar

National Portrait Gallery; www.npg.org.uk [29 p306, D4]

For location, it's hard to top the bar and restaurant of the National Portrait Gallery, which has wonderful views over Trafalgar Square and beyond.

THE NATIONAL GALLERY

Dominating Trafalgar Square is one of the world's finest art collections, bringing together masterpieces from over seven centuries – and entry is free.

Rembrandt's Self Portrait at the Age of 63, 1669.

The National Gallery was founded in 1824, when a private collection of 38 paintings was acquired by the British Government for the sum of £57,000 and exhibited in the house of the owner, banker John Julius Angsterstein, at 100 Pall Mall. Included in the collection were *Bacchanal* by Poussin, *St Ursula* and *The Queen of Sheba* by landscape master Claude, paintings by Van Dyck, two admirable Rembrandts, a superb Aelbert Cuyp, and William Hogarth's narrative, six pictures called *Marriage à la Mode*. As the collection grew, a new building was needed. William Wilkins' long, low construction, with its neoclassical facade and dome, opened in 1834 in the then-recently created Trafalgar Square. The building has been remodelled in various ways. The most prominent addition is the Sainsbury Wing, added in 1991.

J.M.W. Turner's The Fighting Téméraire, voted the nation's favourite picture in a poll in 2005.

Among the gallery's Post-Impressionist works is Georges Seurat's Bathers at Asnières.

The West Wing contains paintings from 1500–1600, including Raphael's *Saint Catherine of Alexandria* (c.1507), pictured, Michelangelo's *The Entombment* (c.1500–1) and Leonardo's *The Virgin of the Rocks* (1491–1508).

Botticelli's *Venus and Mars* (c.1485) in the Sainsbury Wing.

GALLERY LAYOUT

Constable's *The Hay Wain*.

The National Gallery's collection is arranged chronologically, from the 13th century to the end of the 19th century, through four wings, starting in the Sainsbury wing containing works from the 13th–15th centuries.

Many people enter the gallery through its grand main entrance, from where a magnificent flight of stairs offers you a choice of three directions. Take the left flight to the West Wing and the Renaissance galleries. Go straight ahead, through the Central Hall, for the North Wing, where you will find several portraits by Rembrandt as well as Velázquez's *Rokeby Venus*, the Spanish painter's only surviving nude, or turn right for the East Wing. Here you will find portraits and landscapes, including work by Gainsborough, Constable, J.M.W. Turner and Stubbs.

For special exhibitions held in the main wing, it is best to take the Getty Entrance, which also offers level access and wheelchairs.

NATIONAL PORTRAIT GALLERY

Five centuries of portraits of Britain's most famous and important figures are showcased here.

Portrait of Elizabeth I by an anonymous artist.

A British Historical Portrait gallery was founded in 1856, the initiative of the 5th Earl of Stanhope. With no collection as such, it relied on gifts and bequests, the first of which was the 'Chandos' picture of William Shakespeare, attributed to John Taylor, c.1610, and arguably the only portrait of Britain's most famous playwright done from life. From the start, additions to the collection (initially comprising traditional paintings, drawings and sculpture, with photography a later addition) were determined by the status of the sitter and historical importance of the portrait, not by their quality as works of art; these criteria still pertain today. Portraits of living people were not admitted until 1968, when the policy was changed to encourage younger artists and a fresh exploration of the genre.

Room 12 is devoted to portraits of those closely involved with the arts in the late 18th century, such as Samuel Johnson, Handel and the prolific landscape architect Capability Brown. A self-portrait of the artist Gainsborough, and a bust of poet Alexander Pope, can also be found here.

Among the 17th- and 18th-century portraits on the second floor is this one of Lady Emma Hamilton, the wife of the British Ambassador to Naples and the mistress of Lord Nelson (see page 96), painted by George Romney in 1785. Emma Hamilton was known for her great beauty and vitality; there are 28 portraits of her in the gallery's collection.

The Essentials

Address: St Martin's Place; www.npg.org.uk
Tel: 7312 2463 or 7306 0055
Opening Hrs: daily 10am–6pm, Thu–Fri until 9pm
Entrance Fee: free except some exhibitions
Transport: Charing Cross

SPECIAL EXHIBITIONS

Changing exhibitions are held on the ground floor, and it is worth checking the website to see if anything interesting is on. Recent examples include George Catlin's American Indian Portraits, and the annual Taylor Wessing Photographic Portrait Prize, showcasing the work of professional and amateur portrait photographers. Other

A visitor looks at Andy Warhol's Marilyn.

recent displays include Hidden: Unseen Paintings Beneath Tudor Portraits (2013).

Gallery Layout

The displays are broadly chronological, starting on the second floor (reached by the vast escalator from the main hall) and ending on the ground floor. There are thematic subdivisions within each period: the Tudors, 17th-century and 18th-century portraits on the second floor; the Victorians and 20th-century portraits until 1990 (including special displays on the Balcony Gallery and landing) on the first floor, and, on the ground floor, the ever-popular British portraits since 1990 and temporary shows.

Other themes range from science and technology in Room 27, featuring this portrait of evolutionist Charles Darwin, to politics, expansion and empire.

The official portraits of the Victorian and Edwardian periods, which fill the bulk of the first floor, are some of the last examples of stylish formality. Works are organised by theme, including the arts in Room 24, home to this Romantic portrait of poet Alfred Tennyson by Samuel Laurence.

Getting shoes shined inside Burlington Arcade, a classy place to shop.

MAYFAIR TO OXFORD STREET

Mayfair has consistently retained its social prestige since the building of its great estates began in the 1660s. With its Georgian residences, gentlemen's clubs and exclusive shops, it is synonymous with wealth.

West of Trafalgar Square and Piccadilly Circus is Mayfair, the smartest part of town. This is where a broom cupboard costs as much as a house in the country, where shoes are handmade and where life is bespoke.

The area is divided in two by Piccadilly. To the south of this famous thoroughfare lies St James's (see page 80), which grew up around the life of the royal court; to the north Mayfair, the most expensive place to land on the English Monopoly board. The second most expensive, Park Lane, forms the western boundary of the area, while Oxford Street, the capital's most famous shopping street, is on its northern side.

PICCADILLY

Court fops and dandies were a source of moneymaking for London's traders. In the 18th century Robert Baker grew rich by selling them 'pickadils', fashionable stiff collars, and built a mansion on what was then Portugal Street. It became known as **Piccadilly**, and it remains a fashionable street and a favourite location for airline and national tourist offices.

Royal Academy of Arts ❶

Address: Burlington House, Piccadilly,

www.royalacademy.org.uk
Tel: 7300 8000
Opening Hrs: daily 10am–6pm, Fri until 10pm; John Madejski Fine Rooms (guided tours) Tue 1pm, Wed–Fri 1pm and 3pm, Sat 11.30am
Entrance Fee: permanent collection free
Transport: Green Park

Behind the imposing Renaissance-style facade of **Burlington House** on the north side, fronted by a handsome courtyard, the Academy stages big, thematic exhibitions and is famous

Fortnum & Mason.

for its Summer Exhibition to which any artist may present work for selection. The fun of this massive assemblage of paintings is that it ranges from the sublime to the risible.

In the **John Madejski Fine Rooms**, tucked to the rear of the main staircase, much of the RA's little-known permanent collection is rotated on a yearly basis. In contrast to the Academy's top-lit galleries, these smaller rooms have been restored to reveal heavy gilding and panelled doors crowned by plaster putti – the *gusto italiano* as interpreted by William Kent in the 1720s. The Academy's most famous bequests include Michelangelo's marble *Taddei Tondo* (in the high-tech Sackler wing), Constable's *The Leaping Horse* and Gainsborough's *A Romantic Landscape*.

Fine living

At No. 181 Piccadilly is **Fortnum & Mason** ❷, grocers to the Queen and famous for its food hampers, food hall and shop assistants in tails. A tercentenary refurbishment has seen the food hall expand into the basement, with a new wine bar and an ice-cream parlour. The hourly changing of the guard on the mechanical clock above the shop front is a free attraction.

A little further along Piccadilly is **The Ritz** ❸, where afternoon tea in the Palm Court is a tradition. The hotel, built in 1906, was fashionable in the 1930s and 1940s, when Winston Churchill was among the guests. In 1995 the hotel was bought for £75 million by the Barclay brothers, David and Frederick, who have restored it to its former glory. The elegant Louis XVI dining room overlooks Green Park.

Piccadilly Arcade, known for its glass and chinaware shops, has graceful, bow-fronted Regency windows which belie the fact that it was built in 1910. Almost opposite and beside

The Royal Academy is famous for its Summer Exhibition, the largest open contemporary art exhibition in the world.

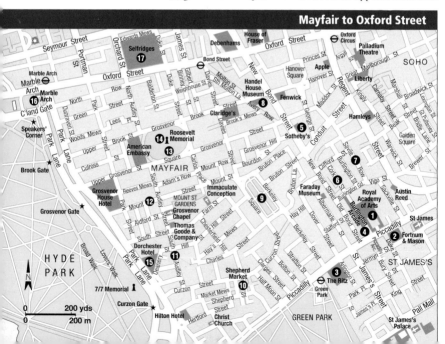

Mayfair to Oxford Street

Entrance to The Ritz hotel.

the Academy, **Burlington Arcade** ❹, built in 1819, is a beautiful covered shopping street lined with traditional purveyors of luxury goods. This is one of Britain's first shopping arcades (the gates are closed at night and on Sundays).

MAYFAIR

The region bounded by Piccadilly and Park Lane, Oxford and Regent streets has been a place of wealth and power since the early 18th century, when it was first laid out by the Grosvenor family, dukes of Westminster. **Mayfair** takes its name from the fair which was held annually on the site of what is now Shepherd Market. In the best British tradition, it clings to its exclusivity, although many of the magnificent Georgian homes of business barons and princes of property are now overrun with hotels, luxury offices, embassies and clubs.

The high street of Mayfair is **Bond Street**, divided into Old Bond Street at its southern end leading north to New Bond Street. Here are London's most exclusive couturiers and designer boutiques, jewellery shops, antiques emporia and art galleries.

The headquarters of **Sotheby's** ❺, the auctioneers founded in 1744 and now American-owned, is at No. 34. World-record prices for art works are notched up here, but not every sale is for millionaires. Admission is free, as long as you look reasonably presentable, and there is a small café.

Asprey the jeweller and Fenwick's the department store are also part of

The place to come for gentlemen's bespoke tailoring.

The Burlington Arcade was built in 1819. This Regency promenade of Lilliputian shops is patrolled by Beadles. In their top hats and livery, they ensure good behaviour, with "no undue whistling, humming or hurrying". Only a Beadle knows what constitutes undue humming.

Italian restaurant Da Corradi, Shepherd Market.

Bond Street's fabric and are worth checking out. Art galleries proliferate in Bond Street and adjacent Bruton Street, but the best place for art is **Cork Street ⑥**, parallel to Bond Street to the east, with such prestigious premises as Waddington's and The Gallery in Cork Street, where Britain's top artists are represented. In 2013 Westminster Council approved plans to demolish part of the street to make way for a £90 million development, meaning the closure of several art galleries. A 'Save Cork Street' campaign was set up to ensure the street retains its significance as the headquarters of the art trade.

Just beyond is **Savile Row ⑦**, the home of several gentlemen's outfitters, where even off-the-peg items are highly priced. The offices of Apple, the Beatles company, were at No.3 Savile Row, and in 1969 the group staged what was to be their last ever live concert from its roof, included in the film *Let It Be*.

Handel House Museum ⑧

Address: 25 Brook Street, www.handel house.org

Tel: 7495 1685
Opening Hrs: Mon–Sat 10am–6pm, Sun noon–6pm
Transport: Bond Street, Oxford Circus

On **Brook Street**, which runs from the west side of New Bond Street, stands the house in which Handel wrote his *Messiah*. His home for 35 years until his death in 1759, it has been refurbished in early 18th-century style. While the composer's life and work is well documented with information sheets, CD listening posts, and paintings, prints and old musical scores, the sparsely furnished rooms come into their own as evocative settings for intimate chamber music concerts – often with the Handel House harpsichord as their focus – and other special events.

Another musical resident here was Jimi Hendrix, who occupied a flat at No. 23 from 1968 to 1969 (tours available once a year). A small corner of the museum is given over to a series of photographic portraits showing the guitar legend at home, and the flat is set to become a proper museum dedicated to Hendrix.

Smart addresses

Brook Street is also home to **Claridge's Hotel**, one of London's premier luxury hotels, built in the 1890s, though mostly in Art Deco style. Here also is the Savile Club, haven of the literary establishment; past members include Thomas Hardy and the poet Yeats.

BERKELEY SQUARE ⑨

Nightingales rarely sing in **Berkeley Square**, though they may have done when the song was written in 1915, and this once highly aristocratic square has been much spoilt by dull office buildings. In 1774 Lord Clive of India committed suicide at No. 45. The Earl of Shelburne, the prime minister who conceded the independence of the United States in 1783, lived in Lansdowne House,

now the site of the private members' Lansdowne Club. Berkeley Square House is built on the site of the house where Queen Elizabeth II was born in 1926.

SHEPHERD MARKET ⓾

From Berkeley Square, Curzon Street leads to Shepherd Market, Mayfair's 'village centre', by way of a side passage. This small pedestrian enclave is incongruous amid the grand town houses and exclusive hotels. Built around 1735 by the architect Edward Shepherd, it was established to supply the daily needs of local residents and obliterated the open space which had accommodated the May Fair – commemorated by a blue plaque at 7 Trebeck Street – whose riotousness offended the well-off residents.

Even today Shepherd Market maintains a quaint air. There are specialist shops, pubs and restaurants, all on a village scale. At night, the area is a haunt of up-market prostitutes.

SOUTH AUDLEY AND MOUNT STREETS

Along **South Audley Street** ⓫ is the former residence of Charles X, the last Bourbon king of France, who lived here 1805–14. At No. 19, **Thomas Goode & Co**, the china, silverware and crystal shop once almost exclusively the preserve of international royalty, has occupied its own block since the 1840s.

Behind neat miniature hedges, a marble colonnade frames the window displays. Stealing the show are the pair of howdah-bearing ceramic elephants, 7ft (2 metres) tall in their regalia, which are the establishment's trademark. Produced by Minton for Thomas Goode, they took the Paris Exhibition of 1889 by storm. The shop incorporates a design archive and museum section.

The original wood pannelling and chandeliers of the Audley pub set the tone for the unbridled Victoriana of

Mount Street ⓬, whose eastern portion especially, lined with fine shops, is strikingly homogeneous: wholly rebuilt from 1880 to 1900 in the pink terracotta Queen Anne style, its red-brick facades are enthusiastically decked out with terracotta features.

GROSVENOR SQUARE ⓭

A pleasing, friendly statue of General Eisenhower and Winston Churchill having a chat on a bench in Bond Street is a sign of the interest Americans have always had in Mayfair. In 1785 John Adams, the first United States Minister to Britain and later the nation's president, took up residence at **9 Grosvenor Square**. No fewer than 31 of the 47 households in the square then belonged to titled families. Plans were made in 2007 to move the United States embassy to a larger and more secure suburban location south of the Thames; the move is hoped to be complete by 2017.

The cost of the statue of **Franklin D. Roosevelt** ⓮ in the gardens was met by grateful British citizens after World War II.

The window of Thomas Goode & Co.

SHOP

Oxford Street is known for its department stores and chain stores, but Regent Street is also worth exploring. Shops include **Hamleys**, the world's biggest toy store, at Nos. 188–96 and the gigantic **Apple Store** at No. 235. **Austin Reed**, at No. 103–13, has an Art Deco barber's in its basement (now a beauty salon). Just off Regent Street on the fringes of Soho is **Liberty** (see pages 50 and 117).

The entrance to Claridge's.

PARK LANE

Park Lane, running from Hyde Park Corner to Marble Arch, forms the western boundary of Mayfair. Its once magnificent homes overlooking Hyde Park (see page 207) have largely been replaced by modern hotels and apartments. These include the **Hilton Hotel** and the **Dorchester Hotel** , General Dwight D. Eisenhower's HQ in World War II, and popular with visiting film stars. To the north, the residence of the Grosvenor family (owners of a 300-acre/120-hectare estate covering Mayfair and Park Lane) was knocked down in 1928 to make way for the **Grosvenor House Hotel**, whose Great Room is London's largest banqueting hall.

MARBLE ARCH AND OXFORD STREET

At the top of Park Lane, the **Marble Arch** ⓰, designed by John Nash and based on the Arch of Constantine in Rome, was placed here, then known as Tyburn, in 1851 after being removed from the front of Buckingham Palace where it was originally erected in 1827. It now sits in the middle of a busy traffic island.

Statue of Franklin Roosevelt in Grosvenor Square.

Crowds first came to **Oxford Street** to see the condemned being taken to Tyburn (see box): this produced a ready clientele for shopkeepers, and stores first appeared along 'Ladies' Mile' between Tottenham Court Road and Marylebone Lane, just short of Bond Street Underground station. This was where the first department

---

HANGMAN'S HAUNT

A stone slab on a traffic island opposite Marble Arch at the west end of Oxford Street, London's principal shopping thoroughfare, marks the spot where public hangings took place. The first recorded one was in 1196, of populist leader William Fitz Osbern, and the last was in 1783, of highwayman John Austin. Up to 50,000 convicted felons died here. The site of London's main place of execution took its name from Tyburn Brook, which flowed into the Westbourne River at what is now the Serpentine in Hyde Park. The condemned were transported here along what is now Oxford Street (formerly Tyburn Street) from Newgate Prison or the Tower of London. The gallows stood right in the middle of the major western route into London, and so was a prominent symbol of law and order to passing travellers.

Hanging days were public holidays, attracting huge crowds, and London apprentices were given a day off to attend them. The victims dressed in their best, carried nosegays of flowers and took a last mug of ale; they were allowed to speak to the crowd before being hanged. The site of the now demolished Newgate Prison contains the Central Criminal Court.

stores were built. One of the finest to this day, **Selfridges** , was built further west by Gordon Selfridge, a Chicago retail millionaire. The food halls are hard to resist, and the shop window displays at Christmas are spectacular. Marks & Spencer, the drapers, opened their largest shop next door in 1930, still the site of their flagship store.

Only buses and taxis are allowed to drive down most of Oxford Street and its widened pavements are usually packed with tourists. New developments indicate that, despite the congestion, Oxford Street is still the retail heart of central London. Near Bond Street Underground station, designer boutiques in St Christopher's Place – with its pavement cafés and hanging baskets – offer an escape from the masses, as do Bond Street and South Molton Street on the south side.

At Oxford Circus, Oxford Street crosses over **Regent Street** which continues north, part of Nash's scheme to connect the Prince Regent's home at Carlton House with his newly acquired property at Regent's Park.

Shoppers on Oxford Street.

Among Regent Street's restaurants are **Veeraswamy's** (entrance on Swallow Street), London's first Indian restaurant.

The Café Royal, also a haunt of Winston Churchill, and the high-living Edward VIII (when he was Prince of Wales) and George VI, has now reopened as a luxury hotel.

Fun at Hamleys.

SHOPPING

Antiques

London has an enormous selection of antiques shops and markets. Many of the most elite dealers are in Mayfair, centring around Old Bond Street, many at **Grays Antique Market** at 58 Davies Street, W1, with valuable collections of silver, fine art, jewellery, porcelain, carpets, furniture and antiquities.

Art

Agnews Gallery
35 Albemarle St, W1⬚
Tel: 7290 9250; www.agnewsgallery.com
Founded in 1817, the gallery deals in Old Master paintings, British paintings and watercolours, prints of original masters and contemporary artists. To view you will need to book an appointment.

Annely Juda Fine Art
23 Dering St, London W1
Tel: 7629 7578; www.annelyjudafineart.co.uk
Annely Juda represents contemporary British, European and International artists. The gallery also exhibits masters of the 20th century avant-garde.

Bernard Jacobson Gallery
6 Cork St, W1
Tel: 7734 3431; www.jacobsongallery.com
Bernard Jacobsen was founded in 1969 and specialises in modern and contemporary British and international art, both sales and exhibitions.

Browse and Darby
19 Cork St, W1
Tel: 7734 7984; www.browseanddarby.co.uk
Browse and Darby specializes in British and French paintings, drawings and sculpture. It is particularly associated with figurative English painting and late 19th and early 20th century European Art.

Colnaghi & Co Ltd
15 Old Bond St, W1
Tel: 7491 7408; www.colnaghi.co.uk
Colnaghi is one of London's oldest art dealers (1760) and holds regular exhibitions. It specializes in Old Master paintings and drawings from the 15th to the 19th centuries.

The Fine Art Society
148 New Bond St, W1
Tel: 7629 5116; www.faslondon.com
The Fine Art Society was established in 187 and specialises in 19th- and 20th-century British art and design. The gallery is closed in August.

Flowers Gallery
21 Cork St, London W1
Tel: 7439 7766; www.flowersgallery.com
The Flowers Gallery specializes in prints and contemporary international photography.

The Mayor Gallery
22A Cork St, W1
Tel: 7734 3558; www.mayorgallery.com
The gallery was founded in 1925 and specializes in the work of non-British artists, particularly from the United States. Surrealism and the avant-garde are its specialities.

Waddington Custot Galleries
11–12 Cork St, W1
Tel: 7851 2200; www.waddingtoncustot.com
Waddington Custot Galleries deals in modern and contemporary works of art. As well as sales, there are also regular exhibitions of works by the gallery's artists.

Books

Hatchard's
187 Piccadilly, W1
Tel: 020 7439 9921; www.hatchards.co.uk
Hatchards is the oldest bookshop in the UK, and still occupies the site where it was first opened in 1797. Every Christmas up to 20 well-known authors hold special book signing events.

Quaritch
40 South Audley St, W1
Tel: 020 7297 4888; www.quaritch.com
Quaritch was founded in 1847 and specialises in buying and selling rare books and manuscripts. It also sells photographs, books on photography and propaganda poster material.

Waterstones
203–206 Piccadilly, W1
Tel: 0843 290 8549; www.waterstones.com
The Piccadilly branch of this chain now claims to be Europe's largest bookstore. Occupying eight floors, there are around 150,000 titles spread over more than 8 miles (13km) of shelving!

Clothing and Shoes

Alexander McQueen
4–5 Old Bond St, W1
Tel: 7355 0088
McQueen was one of Britain's most famous designers, known for his imaginative, cutting-edge fashions. His label has continued after his premature death, led by Sarah Burton, who designed Kate Middleton's wedding dress.

Anderson and Sheppard
32 Old Burlington St, W1
Tel: 7734 1420; www.anderson-sheppard.co.uk
Anderson and Sheppard has been making bespoke suits since 1906. Near the main shop is an outlet selling items of haberdashery.

Anya Hindmarch
118 New Bond Street, W1
Tel: 7493 1628; www.anyahindmarch.com
London's bag queen sells lines ranging from the classic and bespoke leather to totes with pictures or environmental slogans printed on.

Browns
25 South Molton St, W1
Tel: 7514 0016; www.brownsfashion.com
With over 100 leading labels stocked in Browns' five interconnecting shops, this is a very popular one-stop fashion boutique. Browns Labels for Less and the directional Browns Focus are alternatives on the same street.

Burberry
21–23 New Bond St, W1
Tel: 7980 8425; www.uk.burberry.com
Traditional trenchcoats and accessories in the famous plaid are sold

alongside the stylish Prorsum range, which offers a fresh, contemporary take on a classic British aesthetic.

Dover Street Market
17–18 Dover St, W1
Tel: 7518 0680; www.doverstreetmarket.com
At the height of cutting-edge cool is this fashion bazaar, with lines by directional designers displayed in conceptual spaces.

Gieves and Hawkes
1 Savile Row, W1
Tel: 7432 6403; www.gievesandhawkes
Gieves and Hawkes is one of the oldest bespoke tailors in the world and has one of the smartest addresses to go with it. It now provides ready-to-wear tailoring as well as hand-made articles.

Jaeger
200 Regent St, W1
Tel: 7979 1100; www.jaeger.co.uk
Tailored classic English clothes for men and women with formal, business and casual ranges.

James Lock
6 St James's St, SW1
Tel: 7930 8874; www.lockhatters.co.uk
The company was founded in 1676, making it the oldest hat shop in the world! Once a postcard was sent to the shop addressed simply 'the best hatters in the world, London'.

Jimmy Choo
27 New Bond St, W1
Tel: 7493 5858; www.jimmychoo.com
Footwear of choice for many celebrities and girls-about-town. Glamorous, vertiginous stilettos abound.

John Lobb Bootmaker
9 St James's St, SW1
Tel: 7930 3664; www.johnlobbltd.co.uk
John Lobb has been making bespoke boots and shoes for a century and a half. The company now sells ready-to-wear lines as well as its luxury hand-made items.

Joseph
23 Old Bond St, W1
Tel: 7629 3713; www.joseph.co.uk
Sexy trousers and sleek classics make up the basis of this label's success; stores also stock a smattering of other designers such as Gucci and Diane von Furstenberg. Another branch in Brook Street.

Matthew Williamson
28 Bruton St, W1

Tel: 7629 6200; www.matthewwilliamson.com
Brightly coloured and patterned womenswear, often intricately embellished and ethnic-inspired.

Mulberry
50 New Bond St, W1
Tel: 7491 3900; www.mulberry.com
Modern clothes along classic British lines, but most renowned for the leather pieces. Their range of handbags is enormously popular and the men's accessories are interesting too.

Nicole Farhi
25 Conduit St, W1
Tel: 7499 8368; www.nicolefarhi.com
Smart, yet comfortably casual, classic separates in soft fabrics.

Ozwald Boateng
30 Savile Row, W1
Tel: 7437 2030; www.ozwaldboateng.co.uk
Boateng opened his first Savile Row tailors at the age of 28. His name is now synonymous with bespoke tailoring, classical but with a modern twist.

Stella McCartney
30 Bruton St, W1
Tel: 7518 3100; www.stellamccartney.com
Femininity with an edge and 'vegetarian' (non-leather) shoes is the house style of this high-profile British designer.

Topshop
216 Oxford St, W1
Tel: 08448 487487; www.topshop.com
No shopping trip in London would be complete without scouring for a bang-on-trend bargain. The largest fashion store in the world, this flagship branch is fast becoming iconic.

Vivienne Westwood
44 Conduit St, W1
Tel: 7439 1109; www.viviennewestwood.co.uk
This is formal compared to Westwood's eccentric World's End boutique on the King's Road, and is the outlet for her more tailored collections. Her menswear collection is available at 18 Conduit Street, W1.

Department Stores

Fortnum & Mason
181 Piccadilly, W1
Tel: 0845 300 1707; www.fortnumand mason.com
Fortnum & Mason opened their

store in the 18th century with the grocery needs of the Palace in mind. They began importing exotic and unusual foodstuffs, which have long been the basis of the shop's success. The Queen's grocer also stocks fine clothes and household goods. At Christmas the window displays are a joy to behold and many hanker after one of their famous hampers. A fashionable place to have tea.

Liberty
Regent St, W1
Tel: 7734 1234; www.liberty.co.uk
The goods on sale in this distinctive store are still largely based along the same lines as the Oriental, Art Nouveau and Arts and Crafts furniture, wallpaper, silver, jewellery and fabrics Liberty began selling in the late 19th century. There is a particularly fine fashion-accessory department and an exotic bazaar in the basement.

Selfridges
400 Oxford St, W1
Tel: 0800 123 400; www.selfridges.com
For sheer variety of quality goods, this 100-year-old institution has cornered the market, in a massive one-stop shop. Home furnishings, china, stationery, beauty products, food and a vast selection of fashions are just some of what's on offer. Selfridges is also the most fashionable of the department stores, managing to combine a sense of its history with contemporary style.

Food and Drink

Berry Bros & Rudd
3 St James's St, SW1
Tel: 0800 280 2440; www.bbr.com
Dating back to the 17th century, Berry Bros has a superb range of wines and spirits, with prices ranging from £5 to £5,000.

Paxton & Whitfield
93 Jermyn St, SW1
Tel: 7930 0259; www.paxtonandwhitfield.co.uk
As Winston Churchill once observed, 'a gentleman only buys his cheese and Paxton & Whitfield'. The cheesemonger has been selling quality British and European cheeses since 1797.

BEST RESTAURANTS, PUBS AND BARS

PRICE CATEGORIES

Prices for a three-course dinner
per person with a half-bottle of
house wine:
£ = under £25
££ = £25–35
£££ = £35–55
££££ = over £55

Restaurants

American

Burger and Lobster
29 Clarges St, W1. Tel: 7409 1699;
www.burgerandlobster.com Open: L & D
Mon–Sat, Sun noon–5.30pm **££** [44
p314, A3]
A good choice if you don't like
being faced with an exhaustive
menu as there are only three
options – burgers, lobster and
lobster roll. The atmosphere is laid
back and there is a good range of
cocktails.

Hard Rock Café
150 Old Park Lane, W1. Tel: 7514 1700.
www.hardrock.com Open: L & D daily. **££**

Ye Grapes, Shepherd Market.

[45 p312, E4]
Long established member of the
global chain. Expect long queues,
huge portions of nachos, chicken
wings, sundaes and hamburgers,
and homage to rock 'n' roll memorabilia. The 'vaults museum' next
door exhibits guitars belonging to
Hendrix, Presley et al.

Chinese

Kai
65 South Audley St, W1. Tel: 7493 8988.
www.kaimayfair.co.uk Open: L & D daily.
££££ (set lunch **£££**) [46 p312, E3]
Opulence pitched at a wealthy
clientele. Specialities include
abalone in a white truffle jus
reduction and tiger prawns with
crisp curry leaves. Holder of one
Michelin star.

Princess Garden
8–10 North Audley St, W1. Tel: 7493 3223.
www.princessgardenofmayfair.com Open: L
& D daily. **£££** [47 p312, E2]
An upmarket Chinese (specifically
northern Chinese) in the heart of
Mayfair, popular for business
lunches. The dim sum are

excellent, especially the steamed
buns – hot little clouds of
perfection.

Fish

Scotts
20 Mount St, W1. Tel: 7495 7309.
www.scotts-restaurant.com Open: L & D
daily; Oyster Bar daily all day. **££££** [48
p312, E2]
This restaurant is more than 150
years old. Seafood (good fish pie,
scallops, and Dover sole) in grand
surroundings. Popular celebrity
hangout, so book if you can.

French

Alain Ducasse
The Dorchester, Park Lane, W1. Tel: 7629
8866. Open: L Tue–Fri, D Tue–Sat. **££££**
[49 p312, E3]
Three Michelin stars at this elegant
hotel restaurant. Menus are seasonal, but dishes might include
Anjou pigeon, fillet of halibut or
wild sea bass. A tasting menu
allows you to sample seven
courses for £120.

Le Gavroche
43 Upper Brook St, W1. Tel: 7408 0881.
www.le-gavroche.co.uk Open: L Mon–Fri, D
Mon–Sat. **££££** [50 p312, E2]
French haute cuisine is given a
lighter touch with hints of Asian
influence. A chic, civilised operation with polished service. Male
diners are expected to wear a
jacket.

Hélène Darroze
The Connaught, Carlos Place, W1. Tel: 7107
8880. Open: Brunch Sat, L Tue–Fri, D Tue–
Sat. **£££–££££** [51 p312, E2]
Hélène Darroze has earned two
Michelin stars for her modern
French cuisine. Service is formal
and prices are high in the evening,
but the lunch time set menu repre-
sents good value.

Truc Vert
42 North Audley St, W1. Tel: 7491 9988.
www.trucvert.co.uk Open: Mon–Fri 7am–
10pm, Sat 9am–10pm, Sun 9am–6pm.
£££ [52 p312, E2]

Informal, buzzy restaurant in a wonderful deli, offering salads, pâtés, quiches and pastries plus charcuterie/cheese plates made to order.

Indian
Benares
12a Berkeley Square House, Berkeley Square, W1. Tel: 7629 8886. www.benares restaurant.com Open: L & D Mon–Sat. **£££** [53] p314, A2]
Hits on the menu include butter poached lobster tail with mussel kedgeree. Recipient of a Michelin star. All lamb and chicken is halal.

Italian
Cecconi's
5A Burlington Gardens, W1. Tel: 7434 1500; www.cecconis.co.uk Open: B, L & D daily, also brunch Sat–Sun. **£££** [54] p306, A3]
Specialises in classic Italian gems. Menu features tartares, carpaccios and Italian tapas.
Mayfair Pizza Company
4 Lancashire Court, W1. Tel: 7629 2889; www.mayfairpizzaco.com Open: L & D daily. **££** [55] p314, A2]
Modern Italian serving wood-fired pizzas and pasta in a pretty, traffic-free enclave off New Bond Street.

Japanese
Nobu
Metropolitan Hotel, 19 Old Park Lane, W1. Tel: 7447 4747. Open: L & D daily. **££££** [56] p312, E3]
Haunt of A-list celebrities, this stylish restaurant is on the first floor of the Metropolitan hotel overlooking Hyde Park. Great Japanese food with a Peruvian twist is on offer in what was the first European venture for eponymous chef Nobu Matsuhisa. On the downside, the tables are close and there are two-hour time limits.
Umu
14–16 Bruton Place, W1. Tell: 7499 8881. www.umurestaurant.com Open: L Mon–Fri, D Mon–Sat. **£££–££££** [57] p314, A2]
The food here has been awarded a Michelin star, and consists of sushi, sashimi and a Kaiseki tasting menu.

Modern European
Criterion Grill
224 Piccadilly, W1. Tel: 7930 0488. www.criterionrestaurant.com Open: L & D daily. **£££** (set menu **££**) [58] p306, C3]
The Criterion has a please-all menu, featuring British produce such as Scottish beef and Cornish crab. The real draw is the neo-Byzantine interior.
Dover Street Restaurant & Jazz Bar
8–10 Dover St, W1. Tel: 7629 9813. www.doverst.co.uk Open: D Mon–Sat until 2am. **£££** [59] p306, A4]
Attracts an affluent post-work crowd who come here to unwind over drinks and the live jazz, soul and Latin sounds. The brasserie-style menu is unadventurous but reliable. Charge after 10pm; no jeans or trainers.
Maze
10–13 Grosvenor Sq, W1. Tel: 7107 0000. www.gordonramsay.com Open: L & D daily. **££££** (set lunch **£££**) [60] p312, E2]
This Rockwell-designed, Gordon Ramsay-owned restaurant is a runaway success. The French-Asian dishes are intensely flavoured, for example boiled beef cheeks with cardamom and star anise. Sushi at Maze offers authentic sushi and sashimi dishes prepared in front of you at the counter.

Others
Momo
25 Heddon St, W1. Tel: 7434 4040. www.momoresto.com Open: L Mon–Sat, D daily; tearoom daily noon–1am. **£££** (set lunch **££**) [61] p306, A3]
Theatrical decor, authentic Moroccan cuisine and a party atmosphere. Share excellent pastilla (sweet and sour pigeon pie), couscous or tagines.
The Wolseley
160 Piccadilly, W1. Tel: 7499 6996. www.thewolseley.com Open: B, L & D daily. **£££–££££** [62] p306, A4]
Always busy, always glamorous, The Wolseley is the place to come for afternoon tea and pre-theatre light meals as well as lunch or dinner.

Pubs and Bars
Pubs
Audley
41–43 Mount St; www.taylor-walker.co.uk/pub/audley-mayfair [30] p312, E2]
Old-fashioned boozers are thin on the ground in Mayfair, but there are a few gems and this is one of them. This posh, high Victoriana pub attracts a local well-heeled crowd.
Coach & Horses
5 Bruton St; www.shepherdneame.co.uk/pubs/london/coach-horses [31] p314, A2]
Pleasant cosy pub, the oldest in Mayfair (1744). It used to be a coaching inn and still retains some historic features like the cellars and a cold room.
Ye Grapes
16 Shepherd Market [32] p314, A3]
Lively pub is this pretty enclave of Mayfair.

Bars
Mayfair drinkers frequent some of London's grandest hotel bars, where the scale of the free nibbles can offset the steep drinks prices.
Claridge's Bar
55 Brook St; www.claridges.co.uk [33] p312, E2]
Very fashionable bar in an elegant setting.
Coburg Bar at the Connaught
Carlos Place; www.the-connaught.co.uk [34] p312, E2]
Stately grande dame of hotel bars.
Dorchester Bar
53 Park Lane; www.thedorchester.com [35] p312, E3]
Mirrored piano bar with an opulent interior perfectly suited to enjoying fabulous cocktails.
Met Bar
Metropolitan Hotel, 19 Old Park Lane; www.comohotels.com [36] p312, E3]
Enjoy creative cocktails at this celeb hang-out.
Rivoli Bar at The Ritz
150 Piccadilly; www.theritzlondon.com [37] p306, A4]
Glorious Art Deco bar in this historic hotel. During World War II, Churchill, De Gaulle and Eisenhower held summit meetings here in one of the dining rooms.

LONDON'S PARKS

The city has more green spaces than any comparable conurbation – and they're used for everything from sunbathing to speechmaking.

Parliament Hill, Hampstead Heath.

St James's Park.

London's eight royal parks – Hyde Park, Kensington Gardens, Regent's Park, St James's Park, Green Park, Greenwich Park, Richmond Park and Bushy Park – are all owned and run by the Crown. Many were once royal hunting grounds, and they retain an elegant air.

The largest is Hyde Park (350 acres/140 hectares), a vast open space only a few paces away from bustling Oxford Street. The corner of the park near Marble Arch is known as Speakers' Corner, where freedom of speech is given full rein on Sunday afternoons.

Hyde Park adjoins Kensington Gardens, a lovely green space on the west side of which stands Kensington Palace, home to the Duke and Duchess of Cambridge. The oldest park is St James's, beautifully landscaped with fountains and views of Buckingham Palace and Whitehall. Regent's Park, in Marylebone, houses London Zoo and has a very fine rose garden.

In addition there are several good suburban parks, some of them established in the 19th century to alleviate the unhealthy living conditions of the poor. The other great open space is Hampstead Heath in north London.

Boats on the Serpentine, Hyde Park.

Lavender beds at Kew Gardens. Main attractions include the Palm House (the Victorian glasshouse containing a tropical rainforest), a rose garden next to the Palm House, the Temperate House and the Princess of Wales conservatory.

MUSIC, WILDLIFE AND THEATRE IN THE PARKS

Enjoying live music in Regent's Park.

The sight of people sitting in striped deckchairs in a park on a warm summer's day listening to a brass band is reassuringly English. In Greenwich Park you can listen to a band or jazz orchestra playing free concerts at weekends.

Throughout the summer, all sorts of events are held in the parks; bat walks are held in Hyde Park, when you can see and hear different bat species in the park at night.

In Kensington Gardens you can follow in Peter Pan's footsteps and experience the magic that inspired J.M. Barrie's tales. A statue of Peter Pan stands on the east side of the gardens, near the lake. Or you can get a close-up view of the herons and other wildlife in Regent's Park.

Great houses provide other venues for music and theatre, with picnic concerts at Kenwood House featuring artists such as Tom Jones. Concerts and opera are also held in the grounds of Holland House in Holland Park, west London, and make a delightful evening, as do the open-air Shakespeare productions in Regent's Park in the summer. Bring cushions and blankets.

For more information, see www.royalparks.org.uk/whats-on.

The fountain at Regent's Park's Inner Circle.

Skating in Greenwich Park.

MARYLEBONE AND FITZROVIA

North of Oxford Street lies Marylebone, a characterful area of elegant squares and terraces bordered by Regent's Park. Among its attractions are Madame Tussauds, London Zoo and the Sherlock Holmes Museum.

The residential area of Marylebone (pronounced *marry-le-bun*) lies between Oxford Street and Regent's Park. It is largely Georgian in character, its streets and squares named after the Cavendish, Harley and Portland families, who progressively developed the district from the beginning of the 18th century. The need to relieve congestion in Oxford Street inspired the creation of a new road running from Paddington to Islington through the parish of St Mary-by-the-bourne.

Today, Marylebone still retains an air of genteel village dwelling, an oasis framed by multicultural Edgware Road to the west, Oxford Street to the south and Tottenham Court Road to the east. The section known as Fitzrovia, traditionally an artists' enclave and retaining a bohemian atmosphere, nestles around the BT Tower.

NORTH OF OXFORD STREET

St Christopher's Place, a pedestrian enclave lined with boutiques and cafés, is accessible through a narrow passageway on Oxford Street (see page 115) and leads via cobbled James Street to Wigmore Street. The latter contains several good restaurants as well as various medical specialists spilling over from Harley

Street, the preferred haunt of private physicians since the 1840s.

On the north side of the road stands **Wigmore Hall ❶** (see page 289), a delightful concert venue, particularly at lunchtimes. BBC Radio 3 broadcasts live from here on Mondays. The Art Nouveau building, which has notable acoustics, was erected in 1901 by a German piano company.

Wallace Collection ❷

Address: Hertford House, Manchester Square, W1,

Main Attractions
Wallace Collection
Madame Tussauds
Sherlock Holmes Museum
Regent's Park
London Zoo

Maps and Listings
Map, page 124
Shopping, page 127
Restaurants, page 128
Accommodation, page 282

Fitzrovia townhouses.

www.wallacecollection.org
Tel: 7563 9500
Opening Hrs: daily 10am–5pm
Entrance Fee: free
Transport: Bond Street

This remarkable display of art ranges from 17th- and 18thcentury English and European paintings to Sèvres porcelain. In addition to pictures by Velázquez, Boucher and Fragonard, it contains Rembrandt's *Self-Portrait in a Black Cap*, Rubens' *Rainbow Landscape*, Poussin's *Dance to the Music of Time*, and Frans Hals's *The Laughing Cavalier*. The Great Gallery is currently undergoing refurbishment and

The Great Gallery in the Wallace Collection contains Old Master paintings and French and Italian furniture.

is due to reopen in autumn 2014; all other galleries remain open.

MARYLEBONE VILLAGE

Tucked amongst quiet residential terraces, **Marylebone High Street ❸** is a hub of homeware shops, boutiques and restaurants, its urban village atmosphere providing an oasis from the surrounding bustle. It also has several specialist food shops, from charcuteries to fishmongers. On Sundays there is a good *farmers' market* (10am–2pm) at Cramer Street car park.

More pubs and small shops are dotted along narrow Marylebone Lane,

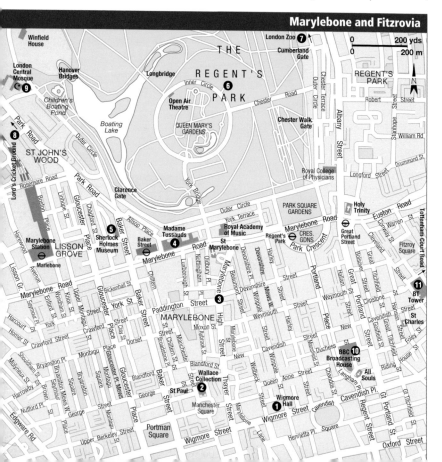

Marylebone and Fitzrovia

which winds along the course of the subterranean River Tyburn.

MARYLEBONE ROAD AND BAKER STREET

Marylebone Road is one of London's busiest east–west thoroughfares. Its intersection with north–south Baker Street is marked by two attractions, Madame Tussauds and the Sherlock Holmes Museum.

Madame Tussauds ❹

Address: Marylebone Road,
www.madametussauds.com
Tel: 0871 894 3000
Opening Hrs: Mon – Fri 9.30am – 5.30pm, Sat – Sun and during peak times 9am – 6pm
Transport: Baker Street

With its high-tech special effects and increasing emphasis on contemporary celebrities, Madame Tussauds waxwork museum is one of London's top attractions, especially for teenagers. For more information, see page 130.

Not far past the scrum outside Madame Tussauds is the **Royal Academy of Music**, which hosts daily recitals, workshops, seminars and concerts, most of which are free (tel: 7873 7300). Opposite the Academy stands St Marylebone Parish Church, which was depicted by Hogarth in the wedding scene of *A Rake's Progress*. Lord Byron (1788) was baptised here, and Lord Nelson worshipped here.

Sherlock Holmes Museum ❺

Address: 221b Baker Street,
www.sherlock-holmes.co.uk
Tel: 7224 3688
Opening Hrs: daily 9.30am – 6pm
Transport: Baker Street

On Baker Street, north of the intersection with Marylebone Road, this museum re-creates the Victorian home of Arthur Conan Doyle's fictional detective. Some rooms are detailed representations of his living quarters, others contain waxwork tableaux of characters and scenes described in the stories. A Victorian 'maid' is on hand to answer questions.

REGENT'S PARK

Baker Street, Marylebone High Street and Portland Place all lead to **Regent's Park ❻**, an elegant 470-acre (190-hectare) space surrounded by John Nash's Regency terraces. Shakespeare plays are performed at the Open Air Theatre in summer. The boating lake is a tranquil spot, the rose gardens are stunning in summer, and Regent's Canal runs through the north of the park.

London Zoo ❼

Address: Outer Circle, Regent's Park,
www.zsl.org/london-zoo
Tel: 0844 225 1826
Entrance Fee: daily Mar – Oct 10am – 5.30pm, mid-July – early Sept 10am – 6pm, Nov – Feb 10am – 4pm
Transport: Camden Town

Increasingly placing an onus on conservation breeding, London Zoo includes a tropical birdwalk in the Blackburn Pavilion, the Gorilla Kingdom, and the Clore Rainforest

Regent's Park's rose garden in the heart of the Inner Circle contains some 20,000 roses. They bloom from June through to Christmas.

The Sherlock Holmes Museum.

TIP

An alternative and more romantic route to London Zoo is to take a canal boat from Camden Lock or Little Venice along Regent's Canal. The London Waterbus Company runs regular services in summer (tel: 7482 2550; www.london waterbus.com) with a reduced service during winter.

Lookout displaying South American mammals, birds and reptiles.

In March 2013 a flagship exhibit called Tiger Territory opened, home to Jae Jae and Melati, a pair of Sumatran tigers. You can see them hanging out in their custom-built pool, or relaxing on heated rocks in their indoor dens. The Penguin Beach has a pool with windows set below water level, allowing you to watch the penguins swimming underwater. On a more tactile level, the revamped children's enclosure allows visitors to handle animals such as goats and llamas.

Around the park

On the northwest side of the park is **Lord's Cricket Ground** ❽ (nearest Tube: St John's Wood), belonging to the Marylebone Cricket Club, which runs the English game. To access the ground and the portrait-packed Long Room through which players walk on their way to the field, see the honours boards in the players' dressing rooms and visit the museum, you must take the 100-minute tour (tel: 7616 8595;

Penguins at London Zoo.

All Souls' Church, Langham Place.

www.lords.org; daily noon and 2pm, except on major match or preparation days, also 10am and 11am on weekends and Apr–Sept).

Just around the corner from Lord's is Abbey Road and the zebra crossing immortalised by the eponymous Beatles album recorded in the studios nearby. It's hard to miss as there are usually tourists stopping to pose on the crossing.

Nearby is the **London Central Mosque** ❾ and Islamic Cultural Centre. The site for the mosque was a gift from the government to the Muslim community during World War II, in recognition of the substantial Islamic population of the British Empire. Visitors are welcome but note that clothing to below the knee is required; women can borrow headscarves from the bookshop.

Portland Place

The eastern stretch of Marylebone leads to Park Crescent and **Portland Place**, conceived by the Adam brothers as a home for the rich. John Nash included it in his grand design to connect Regent's Park with St James's but the plan was never realised. The Adam houses in Portland Place are home to several embassies, institutes and learned societies, such as the Royal Institute of British Architects (RIBA).

Langham Place, which curves round to connect Portland Place with Regent Street, has a trio of dramatic buildings: the circular All Souls' Church built by Nash in 1822–24,

the Langham hotel and the rebuilt **Broadcasting House** ❿, headquarters of the BBC, where the first public television transmission was made in 1932. In June 2013 the Queen opened the new Broadcasting House, home to the BBC's television, radio, news and online services.

FITZROVIA

Dominating the skyline of this former bohemian enclave is the 620ft (189-metre) -high **BT Tower** ⓫, one of the tallest structures in London. Fitzroy Square is central to the area's literary heritage (see page 127); George Bernard Shaw, Virginia Woolf and Ian McEwan have all lived here.

Cosmopolitan **Charlotte Street** used to be known mainly for Greek eateries but now has a variety of chic restaurants. Running parallel is Tottenham Court Road, home to electrical goods and home furnishing stores such as Heal's, and the eastern boundary of Fitzrovia.

FITZROVIA'S LEGACY

Fitzrovia is famous for attracting a bawdy bohemian set between the 1920s and 1950s. Welsh poet Dylan Thomas and the painter Augustus John frequented the Fitzroy Tavern, while writer Julian Maclaren-Ross drank away his publishing advance at The Wheatsheaf, ultimately becoming better known for his 'King of Fitzrovia' persona, complete with silver-topped cane, than for his short stories.

George Orwell was another regular and the Newman Arms on Rathbone Street features in his novels *Nineteen Eighty-Four* and *Keep the Aspidistra Flying*. Other inhabitants included Anthony Powell, Wyndham Lewis and Francis Bacon. The scene dissolved in the 1950s. Today creativity comes in other forms: many media companies are based here.

SHOPPING

Books

Daunt Books
83 Marylebone High St, W1
Tel: 7224 2295; www.dauntbooks.co.uk
Daunt books is a specialist in travel writing and is famous for its long oak galleries and William Morris prints. It claims to be the first custom built book shop in the world.

French's Theatre Bookshop
52 Fitzroy St, W1
Tel: 73879373; www.samuelfrench-london.co.uk
French's is a specialist theatre shop, stocking play manuscripts as well as works on the world of theatre, speech CDs and DVDs.

Food

Natural Kitchen
77 Marylebone High St, W1

Tel: 3012 2123; www.thenatural kitchen.com
Well stocked deli/café that uses as much local, seasonal and free-range produce as possible.

Gifts and Souvenirs

Cath Kidston
51 Marylebone High St, W1
Tel: 7935 6555; www.cathkidston.com
Homeware, bags and gifts all in Kidston's unmistakeable patterns: flowers, strawberries and stars.

Specialist Shops

The Button Queen
76 Marylebone Lane, W1
Tel: 7935 1505; www.thebuttonqueen.co.uk
Lots of antique and modern buttons.

BEST RESTAURANTS, PUBS, BARS AND CAFÉS

PRICE CATEGORIES

Prices for a three-course dinner per person with a half-bottle of house wine:
£ = under £25
££ = £25–35
£££ = £35–55
££££ = over £55

Restaurants

British

Riding House Café
43 Great Titchfield St, W1. Tel: 7927 0840. www.ridinghousecafe.co.uk Open B, L & D daily. **££** [63] p308, E4]
A shabby chic look reigns here in this all-day brasserie, with British/Mediterranean dishes and good puddings providing plenty of choice. Lively atmosphere.

Fish

Fishworks
89 Marylebone High St, W1. Tel: 7935 9796. Open: L Mon–Fri, D Mon–Fri and Sun. **££**

St Christopher's Place is full of good spots to eat.

[64] p308, C4]
Member of a well-regarded chain selling fresh fish and seafood in the front, with an excellent restaurant behind.

Golden Hind
73 Marylebone Lane, W1. Tel: 7486 3644. Open: L Mon–Fri, D Mon–Sat. **£** [65] p312, E1]
Vintage chippie (1914), with a magnificent 1930s fryer now purely decorative. Fabulous, glisteningly fresh fish in crispy golden batter. There are a few tables outside, great for people-watching. BYOB. No corkage.

French

Galvin Bistrot de Luxe
66 Baker St, W1. Tel: 7935 4007. www.galvinrestaurants.com Open: L & D daily. **£££** [66] p312, D1]
Critically adored brasserie serving traditional Gallic dishes; simple recipes crafted with quality produce makes a winning formula. Affordable set menus available at lunch and 6–7pm.

Pied à Terre
34 Charlotte St, W1. Tel: 7636 1178. www.pied-a-terre.co.uk Open: L & D Mon–Sat. **££££** (set lunch £££) [67] p308, E4]
Michelin-starred cuisine from Marcus Eaves. A sample dish is slow-cooked rabbit leg with courgettes, smoked garlic, soft polenta and tarragon jus. There's a ten-course tasting menu (£99; vegetarian tasting menu £89).

Italian

Caffe Caldesi
118 Marylebone Lane, W1. Tel: 7487 0754. www.caldesi.com Open: L & D Mon–Sat. **£££** [68] p312, E1]
This is a gem, with a ground floor café/wine bar and a first floor restaurant. A sample dish is sea bass with saffron sauce. Set lunch available.

Da Paolo
3 Charlotte Place, W1. Tel: 7580 0021. www.dapaolo.co.uk Open: L Mon–Fri, D

daily. **£££** [69] p308, E4]
Pleasant village atmosphere, serving authentic Italian dishes that include linguine with langoustines and beef fillet with blue cheese, and desserts such as Sicilian lemon cheesecake.

Locanda Locatelli
Churchill Intercontinental, 8 Seymour St, W1. Tel: 7935 9088. Open: L & D daily. **££££** [70] p312, D1]
Tucked away off Regent Street is this Michelin-starred restaurant, where Giorgio Locatelli conjures up magical Italian dishes.

Japanese

Roka
37 Charlotte St, W1. Tel: 7580 6464; www.rokarestaurant.com Open: L and D daily. **££££** [71] p308, E4]
See and be seen at this rustic-style, uber-stylish place, where the food is based on robatayaki cuisine (cooked on an open charcoal grill).

Modern European

Orrery
55 Marylebone High St, W1. Tel: 7616 8000; www.orrery-restaurant.co.uk Open: L & D daily. All menus are set. **££–££££** [72] p308, C4]
Located on the first floor of a converted stable block, dinner here is a romantic gastro experience. Sample dishes include Kentish fillet of lamb, beetroot purée, gratin dauphinois and olive lamb jus; and pannacotta, orange and champagne terrine with fennel essence. There's a rooftop terrace too.

Oscar Bar and Restaurant
Charlotte Street Hotel, 15–17 Charlotte St, W1. Tel: 7980 1007; www.firmdalehotels.com Open: L & D daily. **££–££££** [73] p308, C4]
Behind an elegant façade of Georgian townhouses is the Charlotte Street Hotel, whose restaurant takes up the ground floor. It's a busy, vibrant place, with walls brightly painted with scenes of

21st-century London. This is a great place to come for breakfast, but it's also popular for lunch with the media crowd who work round here.

Salt Yard
54 Goodge St, W1. Tel: 7637 0657. www.saltyard.co.uk Open: L and D Mon – Sat. **£–££** [74] p308, E4]
Bar and restaurant serving tapas inspired by the flavours of Spain and Italy, with inventive options such as courgette flowers stuffed with goats' cheese. Charcuterie and bar snacks available too.

North African
Original Tagines
7a Dorset St, W1. Tel: 7935 1545. www.original-tagines.com Open: L and D daily. **££** [75] p308, C4]
A buzzy little restaurant which specialises in deliciously spiced Moroccan tagines and couscous. Laid-back atmosphere.

Spanish
Navarro's
67 Charlotte St, W1. Tel: 7637 7713. www.navarros-tapas-london.co.uk Open: L Tue–Sat, D Mon–Sat. **££** [76] p308, E4]
A choice of some 50 tapas in a cheerful, popular restaurant. Seafood dishes generally excel and there are plenty of vegetarian options.

The Providores and Tapa Room
109 Marylebone High St, W1. Tel: 7935 6175. www.theprovidores.co.uk. Open: L & D daily. Tapa Room **££**, Providores **££££** [77] p308, C4]
Interesting ingredients are used to create exciting fusion dishes. The downstairs Tapa Room is more informal, where you can sit elbow to elbow along the counter – the food more than makes up for the squish. Upstairs is the more formal restaurant. Great weekend brunches and Sunday roasts.

Other
Reuben's
79 Baker St, W1. Tel: 7486 0035; www.reubensrestaurant.co.uk Open: L & D Mon–Fri and Sun. **££** [78] p308, C4]
Kosher middle European food

served in no-frills surroundings. Famed for its traditional favourites such as salt beef and chicken soup. There's a deli and café, plus a takeaway menu.

Pubs, Bars and Cafés

Pubs
Fitzroy Tavern
16 Charlotte St [38] p308, E4]
Popular with media types, given the proximity of the BBC's Broadcasting House in Langham Place. George Orwell's journalists' union card is on display.

Golden Eagle
59 Marylebone Lane [39] p312, E1]
For a down to earth, old-fashioned pub try the Golden Eagle, with its traditional ales and regular piano sing-alongs.

The Marquis of Granby
2 Rathbone St; www.nicholsonspubs.co.uk [40] p314, B1]
Popular amongst the 1930s literary set – T.S. Elliot used to drink here. Offers a choice of real ales.

Newman Arms
23 Rathbone St; www.newmanarms.co.uk [41] p314, B1]
Built in 1730, this lovely old pub is famed for its pies.

Bars
Artesian at Langham Hotel
1 Portland Place; www.artesian-bar.co.uk [42] p314, A1]
For sheer indulgence, this is the place to come. Voted 'World's Best Bar' by Drinks International, you can choose from the extensive cocktail menu, which includes the Langham Cobbler, made with sake.

Bradley's Spanish Bar
42–44 Hanway St [43] p306, C1]
Scruffy bar just off Oxford Street with a nice vibe.

Coco Momo
79 Marylebone High St; www.foodandfuel.co.uk [44] p308, C4]
Hip Marylebone hang-out, with good food.

Jerusalem
33–34 Rathbone Place; www.jerusalembarandkitchen.com [45] p314, B1]
Cultish basement bar with reasonable prices.

Long Bar in the Sanderson Hotel
50 Berners St; www.sandersonlondon.com [46] p314, B1]
Modish bar in a luxury hotel.

Cafés
La Fromagerie
2–6 Moxon St; www.lafromagerie.co.uk [47] p308, C4]
A fabulous cheese shop with a tasting café.

Lantana
13–14 Charlotte Place; www.lantanacafe.co.uk [48] p308, E4]
Popular café offering Aussie-style brunches tucked away off Goodge Street.

Pâtisserie Valerie
105 Marylebone High St; www.patisserie-valerie.co.uk/café-marylebone [49] p308, C4]
All the best in breads, cakes and pâtisserie, perfect for a day-time treat.

The Wallace
The Wallace Collection, Manchester Square [50] p308, C4]
For a civilised lunch or tea break, in an airy glass-roofed courtyard, this restaurant in the delightful art gallery of the Wallace Collection is hard to beat.

Coco Momo, Marylebone High Street.

SEEING STARS AT MADAME TUSSAUDS

When computer animation creates miraculous images on screen, what is the appeal of mute effigies with fibreglass bodies and wax heads?

Madame Tussauds logo.

A key ingredient in the success of Madame Tussauds is that the models are no longer roped off or protected by glass cases. You can stroll right up to them – an impertinence their bodyguards would never permit in real life. You can be photographed with your arm around the Queen or Tom Cruise. Whatever impulse draws crowds to see a minor television personality declare a supermarket open is at work here in overdrive, and the reactions are similar. Is Lady Gaga really wearing a telephone hat? Is Beyoncé's skin really that perfect? An additional talking point is provided by the fact that, while the best models are astonishingly lifelike, a surprising proportion just aren't all that good. To ring the changes, Tussauds mounts temporary groupings based on films, or TV shows such as *The X Factor*.

The Beatles – age cannot wither them, nor will they be melted down while fans want to pose with them.

The Essentials

Address: Marylebone Road; www.madame tussauds.com
Tel: 0871 894 3000
Opening Hrs: Mon–Fri 9.30am–5.30pm, Sat–Sun and during peak times 9am–6pm
Transport: Baker Street

A waxwork of Rihanna was unveiled in 2011, in the museum's Pop Stars section where she joins Justin Bieber and the late Amy Winehouse, amongst others.

It can take 800 hours of specialist sculpting to create figures such as Princes William and Harry. Some donate clothing for their waxwork – Nicolas Cage provided a pair of jeans, Kylie Minogue a mini-dress and Tony Blair a suit.

Humphrey Bogart's likeness is passable, though Marlon Brando and Alfred Hitchcock fare less well. You can hug Marilyn Monroe as her skirt billows up as it did in The Seven Year Itch.

THE WOMAN BEHIND THE WAXWORKS

Marie Grosholtz.

The story began during the French Revolution in 1789 when Marie Grosholtz, trained by a doctor in modeling anatomical subjects in wax, was asked to prepare death masks of famous victims of the guillotine. She married a French engineer, François Tussaud, in 1795, but left him in 1802 to spend the next 33 years touring Britain with a growing collection of wax figures. The London waxworks began in Baker Street and moved to Marylebone Road in 1884.

Today those gory beginnings are echoed in the waxworks' Chamber of Horrors, which contains the blade that sliced off Marie Antoinette's head and recreates various none-too-scary tableaux of torture.

You can enter a dark section of the chamber where actors portraying deranged serial killers lunge at you and yell in your face. Since you are forewarned that this will happen and assured that they won't touch you, it's hard to be seriously terrified.

A better bet is the audio-animatronic Spirit of London ride, which carries you past well-made historical tableaux.

Football star Wayne Rooney.

BLOOMSBURY AND KING'S CROSS

Home to the British Museum and the traditional base of publishing in London, Bloomsbury has an intellectual reputation, while King's Cross is reinventing itself as a new cultural zone.

The eastern side of Tottenham Court Road marks the beginning of Bloomsbury, London's literary heart, and home to the British Museum and the University of London. The area was laid out in the late 17th and early 18th centuries, initially by Thomas Wriothesley, Earl of Southampton, and later by the Russell family, the Dukes of Bedford. Both are commemorated in the place names of the area.

Publishing houses occupy many of the fine Georgian properties lining the streets and squares. Bloomsbury is blue plaque territory *par excellence* (see page 138). Charles Dickens lived in Doughty Street between 1837 and 1839 (see page 136) and in the early part of the 20th century it nurtured the Bloomsbury set, a group of writers who laid the foundations for modernism in Britain. Virginia Woolf, Vanessa Bell, Duncan Grant, Dora Carrington, E.M. Forster, Roger Fry, Maynard Keynes and Queen Victoria's biographer, Lytton Strachey, all lived at addresses in the area. They probably had more influence as a body than as individuals, and were bookish men and women in a bookish world.

The ever popular Egyptian mummies.

The British Museum ❶

Address: Great Russell Street, www.britishmuseum.org
Tel: 7323 8299
Opening Hrs: daily 10am–5.30pm, Fri until 8.30pm
Entrance Fee: free except some special exhibitions
Transport: Russell Square

The British Museum on Great Russell Street is the nation's greatest treasure house. It opened in 1759, in smaller premises in South Kensington, and now owns more than 6.5 million

Main Attractions
The British Museum
Coram's Fields
King's Cross
St Pancras Station
London Canal Museum
The British Library

Maps and Listings
Map, page 134
Restaurants, page 140
Accommodation, page 282

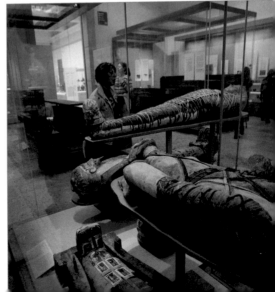

items, ranging from the oldest neo-lithic antiquities to 20th-century manuscripts (see pages 142).

Access to the collections is via the **Great Court**, roofed with a steel and glass canopy in 2000 and one of the most spectacular spaces in London. The museum's famous circular Reading Room, where Karl Marx did much of his research for *Das Kapital*, is open to all as an information centre and a home to temporary exhibitions, its library having moved to Euston Road (see page 139).

Probably the most famous arte-fact in the British Museum is the Rosetta Stone, a stele from 196 BC that provided the key to deciphering Egyptian hieroglyphics.

Near the museum

From the museum three short streets (**Museum Street**, **Coptic Street** and **Bury Place**) lead to Bloomsbury Way. Among their antiquarian bookshops and cafés look out for the **London Review Bookshop** (14 Bury Place), which regularly hosts author readings and interviews; **Blade Rubber Stamps** (12 Bury Place), selling a huge range of rubber stamps as well as

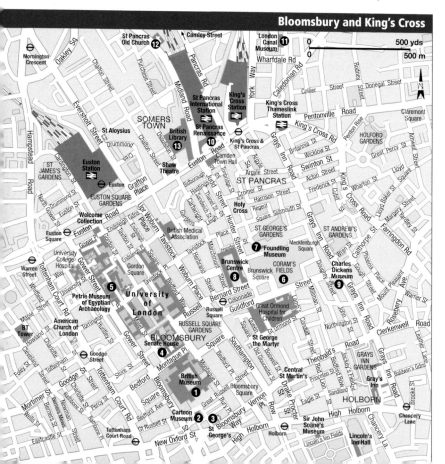

Bloomsbury and King's Cross

everything needed to make home-made greetings cards; and, next door to one another at the northern end of Bury Place, **It's All Greek** and **Parthenon**. These both sell quality replicas of ancient artefacts (though the British Museum's own shop is also very good for these).

In Little Russell Street, running between Museum Street and Coptic Street, the **Cartoon Museum ❷** (35 Little Russell St; tel: 7580 8155; www.cartoonmuseum. org; Mon–Sat 10.30am–5.30pm, Sun noon–5.30pm) charts the history of British cartooning from Hogarth and Bateman to Steve Bell and Gerald Scarfe, taking in comic book characters such as Dennis the Menace and comic postcards by Donald McGill.

The British Museum's collection had an effect on the architecture of the area. Nicholas Hawksmoor's **Church of St George ❸** (1731) in Bloomsbury Way was inspired by the Mausoleum of Halikarnassos, one of the Seven Wonders of the Ancient world, remnants of which can be seen in the museum (see page 144). This is best appreciated by looking at its unusual stepped tower with lions and unicorns at its base and a statue of George I wearing a toga on top. The church often holds free choral performances on Sunday afternoons (www.stgeorges bloomsbury.org.uk).

THE UNIVERSITY OF LONDON

Just north of the British Museum is the University of London, identified by the grey turret of **Senate House ❹**, built in 1936, on the western side of Russell Square.

Close by, at 46 Gordon Square, is the house to which Virginia Woolf and her siblings moved after their father's death in 1904, thus becoming a magnet for other 'Bloomsberries'.

The **Petrie Museum of Egyptian Archaeology ❺** (University College London, Malet Place; Tue–Sat 1–5pm; free) is a two-room collection of treasures, of interest mainly to students and academics.

CORAM'S FIELDS ❻

East of the British Museum, across **Russell Square**, the area is dissected

TIP

The Tavistock Hotel on Tavistock Square sits above a wonderful retro-look bowling alley (entrance Bedford Way, not part of the hotel). This is a great option for children on a wet day, but be aware that they are not admitted after 4pm. In the evenings and at weekends it is essential to book (tel: 7183 1979; www.blooms burybowling.com).

Cartoon Museum.

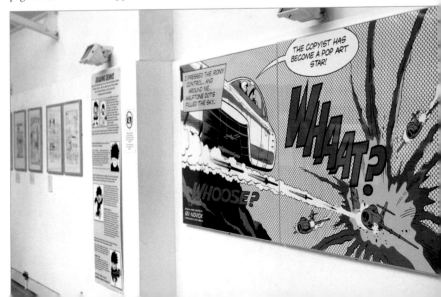

Charles Dickens Museum.

by Southampton Row. On the east side of the square, just beyond the children's hospital in Great Ormond Street, are Coram's Fields, where children rule the roost (adults may only enter the park if accompanied by children). As well as playgrounds, sports facilities, and a nursery, it has rabbits, chickens and sheep.

Thomas Coram was a sea captain who started a hospital and school for foundling children and persuaded artists of the day, including William Hogarth, to donate works of art to raise funds. The collection, which includes paintings by the great 19th-century portraitists Thomas Gainsborough and Joshua Reynolds, is displayed in **The Foundling Museum** ❼, adjacent to the site of the old Foundling Hospital on the north side of Coram's Fields (40 Brunswick Square; tel: 7841 3600; www.foundlingmuseum.org.uk; Tue–Sat 10am–5pm, Sun 11am–5pm; children free).

The ground floor traces the history of the hospital and of the philanthropic movement set against the background of 19th-century

Nicholas Hawksmoor's tower on the Church of St George.

social conditions. Upstairs, in a fine rococo drawing room, are items belonging to or related to George Frideric Handel, one of the hospital's benefactors.

Shopping and eating

The **Brunswick Centre** ❽, a 1960s shopping-cum-housing development on the west side of Coram's Fields, has been given a makeover. It includes several good eating options as well as the Renoir, an art-house cinema. Alternatively, south of Coram's Fields is **Lamb's Conduit Street**, a characterful street with interesting shops and The Lamb pub.

CHARLES DICKENS MUSEUM ❾

Address: 48 Doughty St, www.dickens museum.com
Tel: 7405 2127
Opening Hrs: daily 10am–5pm
Transport: Russell Square

A five-minute walk southeast of Coram's Fields is the house-museum where Dickens lived with his family between 1837 and 1839 and wrote *Oliver Twist* and *Nicholas Nickleby*. In a reverential atmosphere, visitors

can inspect a huge collection of furniture, memorabilia, paintings, books and documents. The displays on the upper floors illustrate his one great passion besides literature – the plays that he produced, directed and acted in at various times.

South of Dickens Museum, **John Street**, lined with handsome Georgian properties, some with a full complement of 18th-century ironwork, leads to Theobald's Road and Holborn (see page 146). North of Coram's Fields, and best reached along Hunter Street, lies the newly booming area of King's Cross and St Pancras.

King's Cross and St Pancras

The area around St Pancras and King's Cross stations, for many years run down and sleazy, is undergoing massive regeneration in the 21st century. Triggered by the construction of the Eurostar rail terminal, which opened in 2007, the area is fast becoming a new cultural zone, called King's Cross Central, attracting creative industries and contemporary art galleries, as well as bars, restaurants and luxury apartments.

Housing the new terminal, **St Pancras Station ❿**, an immense redbrick edifice by Sir George Gilbert Scott, the master of Victorian Gothic, has been superbly restored, with a 5-star hotel and a spa.

Regent Quarter

The area behind the two stations, for long an industrial backwater crossed by roads and railway lines, is also being regenerated, especially the so-called Regent Quarter, near the Regent's Canal. Occupying an old icehouse on the wharf of Battlebridge Basin is the **London Canal Museum ⓫** (12–13 New Wharf Road, accessed from Wharfdale Road; tel: 7713 0836; www.canalmuseum.org.uk; Tue–Sun

Playing in Coram's Fields.

10am–4.30pm). As well as portraying canal life, the museum tells the hard story of London's 19th-century ice trade, when ice was imported from Norway. One of two ice pits is open to view.

Camley Street

Behind St Pancras Station, Camley Street leads north towards Camden.

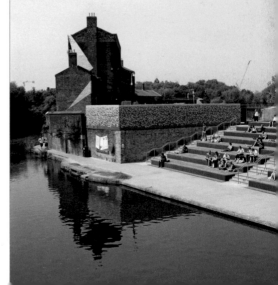

The King's Cross Central development.

Blue Plaques

Numerous famous writers, artists and intellectuals have made Bloomsbury their home. Commemorating their presence are scores of blue plaques.

One of many pointers to London's varied past are the blue plaques on sundry sites to commemorate famous people, events and buildings. There are plenty in Bloomsbury, but they are strewn all across London. Almost 900 have appeared on the former homes of the famous and the long dead. The first plaque was erected by the Royal Society of Arts in memory of the poet Lord Byron in 1867. In those days the round plaques were often brown rather than blue, and were pithily known as 'indications of houses of historical interest in London'. Today the service is administered by English Heritage, although it was temporarily suspended in 2013 due to budget cuts.

A blue plaque marking one of John Lennon's former London residences.

Bona fide plaques are ceramic with white lettering on a circular blue base. To ensure legibility, the design allows for only 19 words of inscription, including dates; they are bald statements of fact, giving little biographical information – simply the name, dates, profession and usually the period he or she lived in the building.

Who gets a plaque?

The awarding of a plaque is almost haphazard: there is no overall register of famous people who have lived in London. Many plaques are put up because descendants or adherents of the deceased put forward the suggestion to English Heritage. Thus plaques function as a barometer of public taste, as notions change about what constitutes fame. The range has been dominated by 19th-century politicians and artists, but in 1997 the first plaque to commemorate a rock star – Jimi Hendrix – went up in Brook Street. In 2013 Harry Beck, the man who designed London Underground's iconic tube map, received a blue plaque on the house where he was born in Leyton.

A plaque-spotting tour would not lack variety. Captain William Bligh of Bounty fame lived at 100 Lambeth Road, SE1; Charlie Chaplin lived at 287 Kennington Road, SE1; Sir Winston Churchill lived at 34 Eccleston Square, SW1; Benjamin Franklin lived at 36 Craven Street, WC2; Charles Dickens lived at 48 Doughty Street, WC1; Henry James lived at 34 De Vere Gardens, W8; Karl Marx lived at 28 Dean Street, W1; George Bernard Shaw lived at 29 Fitzroy Square, W1; and Mark Twain lived at 23 Tedworth Square, SW3.

Most candidates for traditional plaques are submitted to lengthy scrutiny. They must have been dead for at least 20 years; they must be regarded as eminent by luminaries in their profession; they should have made an important contribution to human welfare; the well-informed passer-by should recognise their name; and they should, by the kind of infuriatingly nebulous 'general agreement' that has characterised British decision-making, deserve recognition.

Opposite Euston Station, on Euston Road, look out for St Pancras New Church. Its eight caryatids (four on each side) were inspired by the Erechtheum on the Acropolis in Athens.

On the left is **St Pancras Old Church** ⑫, one of the oldest Christian sites in London. Its cemetery contains the graves of several notable figures, including the

celebrated architect and art collector Sir John Soane (see page 148).

Also on Camley Street, opposite the cemetery and flanking the canal is a slim **nature park** (free) with a trail, wildlife pond and child-friendly activities at weekends.

The British Library ⑬

Address: 96 Euston Road, www.bl.uk
Tel: 0843 208 1144
Opening Hrs: Mon, Wed–Fri 9.30am–6pm, Tue 9.30am–8pm, Sat 9.30am–5pm, Sun 11am–5pm; tours available
Entrance Fee: free
Transport: King's Cross

Back on Euston Road, next door to St Pancras, is the British Library, which moved here from the British Museum in 1998. It houses over 14 million books and periodicals, including a Gutenberg Bible, the Magna Carta and original texts by Shakespeare, Dickens and Leonardo da Vinci. In addition to guided tours of the highlights, the library holds temporary exhibitions. The spacious courtyard (with café) is a peaceful refuge from busy Euston Road.

One of the 11 reading rooms in the British Library.

THE BRITISH LIBRARY

Researchers can use the reading rooms by applying in person or through the website (www.bl.uk) for a reader's pass. Two forms of identification, including proof of home address and proof of signature, must be produced. Your need to use the library will be ascertained, so documentation or a business card supporting your application is useful. Free 45-minute induction sessions help users find their way around the vast resources.

Members of any local library in the UK can also access the collection, if the book required cannot be obtained from any other library. This is done through the local library service.

BEST RESTAURANTS, PUBS, BARS AND CAFÉS

PRICE CATEGORIES

Prices for a three-course dinner per person with a half-bottle of house wine:
£ = under £25
££ = £25–35
£££ = £35–55
££££ = over £55

Restaurants

African

Addis Restaurant
40–42 Caledonian Rd, N1. Tel: 7278 0679. www.addisrestaurant.co.uk Open: L and D daily. **££** [79 p310, B2]
With brightly coloured walls and Ethiopian pop music playing, this is the place to come for something a bit different. If you're unfamiliar with Ethiopian food, try the Addis Special, which includes a number of different vegetable and meat options. Many of the dishes are served on injera, the local bread, which is like a big sour crumpet and definitely an acquired taste.

The Lamb pub.

British

The Gilbert Scott
St Pancras Hotel, Euston Rd, NW1. Tel: 7278 3888; www.thegilbertscott.co.uk aB, L & D daily. **££–£££** [80 p310, A2]
An elegant bar and brasserie run by Marcus Wareing in a spectacular gothic setting. Named in honour of the original architect, the building is magnificent, and the classic British food more than matches the location. The menu celebrates traditional dishes such as Dorset jugged steak, lemon sole, Cornish hake and Yorkshire fishcakes.

Fish

North Sea Fish Restaurant
7–8 Leigh St, WC1. Tel: 7387 5892. www.northseafishrestaurant.co.uk Open: L & D Mon–Sat. **£–££** [81 p308, B3]
Veteran chippie serving straightforward fish and chips, but also a good range of fish, including Dover sole, plaice, halibut, trout and scampi, plus British puddings. You may see lots of black cabs parked outside as London cabbies get a discount here.

Indian

Malabar Junction
107 Great Russell St, WC1. Tel: 7580 5230. www.malabarjunction.co.uk Open: L & D daily. **££** [82 p314, C1]
Much classier than its frontage suggests, this elegant, long-established Indian restaurant specialises in spicy and nutty Keralan cuisine. Lovely atrium for light-filled dining.

Salaam Namaste
68 Millman St, WC1. Tel: 7405 3697. www.salaam-namaste.co.uk Open: L & D daily. **££** [83 p310, B3]
A light and modern restaurant which won the award for best chef of the year in the 2012 Asian Curry Awards. Excellent pan-Indian cuisine with a special emphasis on seafood. Lots of familiar Indian dishes, but many inventive options too.

Italian

Cosmoba

9 Cosmo Place, off Southampton Row, WC1.
Tel: 7837 0904; www.cosmoba.co.uk Open:
L & D Mon–Sat. **££** [94 p310, B4]

A hidden gem in an alley connecting Southampton Row and Queen Square. Unpretentious and run by the same family for 65 years,Cosmoba specialises in homely Italian food, such as gnocchi with gorgonzola, or grilled sea bream.

Pizza Express

30 Coptic St, WC1. Tel: 7636 3232.
www.pizzaexpress.com Open: L & D daily. **£**
[85 p314, C1]

This branch of the quality pizza-pasta chain occupies a fabulous old dairy decorated in Art Nouveau tiles. A stone's throw from the British Museum.

Japanese

Abeno

47 Museum St, WC1. Tel: 7405 3211.
www.abeno.co.uk Open: L & D daily. **££**
[86 p314, C1]

Oriental pancake house specialising in okonomi-yaki, which are tasty, if messy, omelettes and pancakes crammed with meat, vegetables or fish, cooked on a hotplate at the table.

Spanish

Camino

3 Varnishers Yard, N1. Tel: 7841 7331.
www.camino.uk.com Open: L & D daily.
£££ [87 p310, B2]

Spanish hotspot, with an informal atmosphere and friendly staff. The wide selection of tapas is served either in the large bar area on one side or in the restaurant (noisy) on the other. Across the courtyard is Pepita, an Andalusian 'bodega' specialising in a wide variety of sherries.

Cigala

54 Lamb's Conduit St, WC1. Tel: 7405 1717.
www.cigala.co.uk Open: L & D daily. **£££**
(set lunch **£**) [88 p310, B4]

Set up by Jake Hodges, founder of Moro, Cigala serves real Spanish food in an attractive modern dining room. Excellent

Spanish wine list, including many sherries. Tapas served in the basement.

Others

Konaki

5 Coptic St, WC1. Tel: 7580 9730.
www.konaki.co.uk Open: L Mon–Fri, D Mon–Sat. **£–££** [69 p314, C1]

Long-established and popular Greek restaurant near the British Museum. Serves Greek staples and has a small terrace for summer dining.

The Brunswick Centre

This shopping mall [90 p310, B3] in the heart of Bloomsbury has several of the better chain restaurants, offering good-value dining. They include **Strada** (Nos 15–17; tel: 7278 2777; **£**) for good wood-oven pizzas, **Carluccio's** (No. 1, tel: 7833 4100; **£–££**), for pastas, which also has a small Italian deli-cum-bakery attached; and **Giraffe** (Nos 19–21; tel: 7812 1336; **£–££**), a café-bar with a global menu including great breakfasts and healthy options for children. Also popular with families is **Nando's** (No. 3, tel: 7713 0351; **£**) serving spicy Portuguese-style chicken with salads, rice or chips, followed by frozen yoghurts and cheesecake for pudding.

Pubs, Bars and Cafés

Bloomsbury has several traditional pubs tucked into its quiet corners.

Pubs

The Lamb

94 Lamb's Conduit St; www.youngs.co.uk
[51 p310, B4]

A classy old-timer, serving Young's beer and pub food and with a small pavement terrace.

Perseverance

63 Lamb's Conduit St; www.the-perseverance.moonfruit.com
[52 p310, B4]

Popular pub with a friendly atmosphere, and a few outdoor seats. Tasty and well-presented dishes are served in the bar or

the more secluded first-floor dining room.

Bars

Truckles

off Bury Place; www.davy.co.uk/truckles
[53 p310, B4]

Near the British Museum, this wine bar has a light and airy ground floor, a sawdust-sprinkled basement, and a large courtyard.

Vats Wine Bar

51 Lamb's Conduit St; www.vatswine bar.com
[54 p310, B4]

Long-time neighbourhood favourite, offering a convivial atmosphere, quality food (fish, hearty casseroles, home-made pies, etc) and a lengthy wine list.

Café

Court Restaurant

British Museum; www.britishmuseum.org/visiting/eating
[55 p310, A4]

For traditional English or Viennese afternoon tea, try the British Museum's restaurant, high up under the spectacular glass roof; some tables have views into the circular Reading Room. Also pleasant for lunch.

The Lamb sign.

THE BRITISH MUSEUM

Opened in 1759, this world-class institution on Great Russell Street contains some 6.5 million objects.

Devote just 60 seconds to each object owned by the British Museum and you'd be there, without sleep or meal breaks, for more than 12 years. Even though only 50,000 objects are on display at any given time, this is not a place to 'do' in a couple of hours. It is a treasure house that caters for scholars as well as tourists and, as the scholars do, it is best to concentrate initially on what interests you most. A tour of the highlights is a good start (see page 143 or join one of the organised tours).

The best time to visit is soon after opening. This is also an ideal time to appreciate the Great Court, a dramatic glassed-over space in the heart of the complex, added for the millennium, and the round Reading Room, where Marx and Lenin once studied, which now functions as an information and research centre.

A new wing, the World Conservation and Exhibition Centre, is due to open in 2014 with a special exhibition on the Vikings.

The Portland Vase, a superbly crafted cameo glass vessel from the early 1st century.

The Essentials

Address: Great Russell Street, WC2; www.thebritishmuseum.org
Tel: 7323 8299
Opening Hrs: daily 10am–5.30pm, Fri 10am–8.30pm
Entrance Fee: free except some exhibitions
Transport: Russell Square

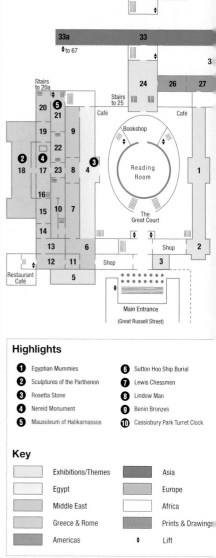

Ground Floor

Highlights

1. Egyptian Mummies
2. Sculptures of the Parthenon
3. Rosetta Stone
4. Nereid Monument
5. Mausoleum of Halikarnassos
6. Sutton Hoo Ship Burial
7. Lewis Chessmen
8. Lindow Man
9. Benin Bronzes
10. Cassiobury Park Turret Clock

Key

Exhibitions/Themes	Asia
Egypt	Europe
Middle East	Africa
Greece & Rome	Prints & Drawings
Americas	↕ Lift

THE MAIN COLLECTIONS
Greece and Rome

The museum's vast holdings from the Classical world are divided between Rooms 11–23 and Rooms 69–73 on the first floor.

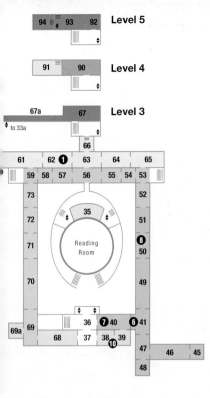

The museum exterior.

TOP 10 HIGHLIGHTS

The Egyptian mummies
This is the richest collection of Egyptian funerary art outside Egypt.

The Sculptures of the Parthenon
Commonly known as the Elgin Marbles, these 5th century BC sculptures have a wondrous muscular detail.

The Rosetta Stone
This granite tablet from the 2nd century BC provided the elusive key to deciphering ancient Egypt's hieroglyphic script.

The Nereid Monument
The imposing facade of this 4th-century monument from Xanthos in Turkey was reconstructed after an earthquake.

The gilded wooden inner coffin of Henutmehyt, a Theban priestess, dating from c.1250 BC.

The Mausoleum of Halikarnassos
This giant tomb, finished around 350 BC in southwest Turkey, was one of the Seven Wonders of the Ancient World.

The Sutton Hoo Ship Burial
The richest treasure ever dug from British soil, an early 7th-century longboat likely to have been the burial chamber of an East Anglian king.

The Lewis Chessmen
82 elaborately carved 12th-century chess pieces, found in the Outer Hebrides, off the Scottish coast.

Lindow Man
A well-preserved 2,000-year-old body found in a peat bog in England and dubbed Pete Marsh.

The Benin Bronzes
Brass plaques found in Benin City, Nigeria, in 1897. They depict court life and ritual in extraordinary detail.

The Cassiobury Park Turret Clock
This intricate 1610 weight-driven clock is part of a remarkable collection of timepieces.

The 12th-century Lewis Chessmen, found in the Outer Hebrides.

Room 18, the **Parthenon Gallery**, is lined with an exquisitely detailed frieze from the colonnade of the Parthenon, removed from the Acropolis by Lord Elgin, British Ambassador in Constantinople, at the end of the 18th century.

Nearby, in Room 17, is the **Nereid Monument**, a magnificent Lycian tomb (c.390–380 BC) from Xanthos, and, in Room 21, fragments and sculptures from the **Mausoleum of Halikarnassos** (modern day Bodrum; mid-4th century BC), the tomb of Maussollos and considered to have been one of the Seven Wonders of the Ancient World. A large-scale model of the mausoleum shows how it would have looked in its splendid entirety.

Early Europe

As well as highly crafted Celtic artefacts and Roman treasures, look out for Lindow Man, a 1st-century man discovered in a peat bog in Cheshire.

Medieval and Modern Europe

Apart from the Sutton Hoo treasure, objects include richly decorated ecclesiastical artefacts such as an intricately decorated 12th-century gilt cross from Germany.

Africa

The Sainsbury African Galleries in the basement combine ancient and modern, showing how cultural traditions are still alive today. This is one of the most colourful and vibrant collections in the museum.

Of special interest are the Benin Bronzes, from the Kingdom of Benin (now in Nigeria), a powerful state in West Africa between the 13th and 19th centuries.

The Americas

The museum has superb collections from Central and North America in Rooms 26–27 on the ground floor (far-right corner off the Great Court). There are a number of impressive Olmec statues and other works from around 1000 BC, plus magnificent carved Mayan slabs from the 8th century AD. Relics

A 16th-century European mechanical galleon.

from the Aztec civilisation include turquoise mosaic work that may have been given to Hernán Cortés by Moctezuma II and a very rare pre-Conquest manuscript painted on deer skin.

Asia

The museum's collections of Chinese, Japanese and Korean artefacts are astonishingly large, with a series of vast galleries given over to them (33–33b on the ground floor, 67 and 92–95 on the upper floors).

Human-headed winged bull, one of a pair of marble bulls that guarded either side of a gateway at Khorsabad, Assyria (710 BC), in modern day Iraq.

Nebamum hunting birds in the marshes (1450 BC).

Lindow Man, the 1st-century bog man.

The ceremonial helmet from the Sutton Hoo treasure.

TREASURES OF ANCIENT EGYPT

The Egyptian Galleries are a must-see.

The Egyptian Galleries filled with funerary artefacts (Rooms 61–66, on the upper floor), are the rooms to see first, simply because they can get wildly overcrowded as the day goes on – 98 percent of visitors want to see the Egyptian mummies in rooms 62–63. They're worth seeing, too: thanks to the enthusiastic plundering by 19th-century explorers, this is the richest collection of Egyptian funerary art outside Egypt.

The size and ornamentation of the coffins and sarcophagi are immediately striking. The richly gilded inner coffin of the priestess Henutmehyt (see page 143), for example, dating from 1250 BC, is a work of considerable art. Scans displayed beside the coffin of Cleopatra (not the Cleopatra) show how well the body inside is preserved, and the process of embalming is explained in detail.

Apart from the noble humans who were destined to spend their afterlife in London's Bloomsbury, there are various mummified cats, dogs, fish and crocodiles, plus amulets and assorted jewellery.

Look out for the paintings from the Tomb of Nebamun, a Theban official, dating from the 18th Dynasty (c.1350 BC), in Room 61.

Assistant to a Judge of Hell, a 16th-century stone figure from Ming-Dynasty China. The figure is holding a bundle of scrolls recording the sins of the deceased.

HOLBORN AND THE INNS OF COURT

Once the haunt of Samuel Johnson, Dickens and Thackeray, this area on the cusp of the City has long been the centre of the legal profession and was for centuries the irrepressible hub of Britain's newspaper industry.

Holborn encompasses what can be termed legal London, with landmarks such as the Royal Courts of Justice, the Old Bailey and the historic Inns of Court clustered around Fleet Street, the former centre of the national newspaper industry. The area is wedged in between London's financial and political centres, and is markedly different from both: away from the busy thoroughfares, quiet courtyards, leafy parks and some of the city's oldest buildings lend a sense of a bygone London.

KINGSWAY AND THE EASTERN STRAND

Somerset House ❶

Address: The Strand, www.somerset house. org.uk; www.courtauld.ac.uk
Tel: 7848 2526
Opening Hrs: Courtauld Institute of Art daily 10am–6pm
Entrance Fee: reduced entry Mon
Transport: Temple

Somerset House became the city's first office block in 1775 when the original 16th-century palace was rebuilt. For many years it housed the official registry of births, marriages and deaths; the inland revenue offices remain, but the northern and southern wings now accommodate a series of galleries and museums. The complex is divided into two main sections by its large courtyard, which contains a fanciful statue of George III wearing a toga. From mid-November to early January the courtyard is turned into a **skating rink**, the classical facade providing a magical setting.

Entering from the Strand, you'll come to the **Courtauld Institute**, home to a fine collection of 20th-century European art, notably some major Impressionist and post-Impressionist paintings: works

Middle Temple Lane.

include Van Gogh's *Self-Portrait with Bandaged Ear* and Manet's *A Bar at the Folies-Bergère*. Temporary exhibitions are held in the Embankment galleries.

The Seamen's Hall gives access to the splendid River Terrace, which in summer has a café with great views.

Across the Strand from Somerset House is **Bush House** ❷, the former headquarters of the BBC's World Service, which is due to be transformed into offices in a £52 million refurbishment deal. The World Service has moved to the BBC's expanded Broadcasting House near Oxford Circus. To the north, Kingsway marks the western boundary of Holborn and legal London. It was named after George V, and its tunnel, opened in 1906 for trams to dive beneath the buildings of Aldwych before emerging at Waterloo Bridge, was a miracle of urban engineering in its day.

Two baroque churches sit on traffic islands in the Strand: by Bush House is **St Mary le Strand**, built by James Gibbs from 1715; a short distance further east by a statue of Gladstone is **St Clement Danes** ❸, completed by Wren in 1682. The name is a reference to the first structure on the site, built by the Vikings in the 9th century. The church has an association with the Royal Air Force, who rebuilt it after bomb damage in WWII.

At the end of the Strand on the left are the **Royal Courts of Justice** ❹, which deal with libels, divorces and all civil cases. The courts moved here from Westminster Hall in 1884. The neo-Gothic confection of towers and spires has around 1,000 rooms, and newspaper and television journalists often hang around its entrance awaiting verdicts. Visitors are free to sit in the public galleries of the 58 courts when trials are in session. There are public tours of the building on the first and third Tuesday of each month, running at 11am and 2pm. It is necessary to book in advance (tel: 7947 7684).

THE INNS OF COURT

All around this area are the **Inns of Court**, home of London's legal profession. The 'Inns' were once, much

The Royal Courts of Justice.

Courtauld Institute gallery.

TIP

There are free guided tours of the buildings of Somerset House every Thursday at 1.15 and 2.45pm, and Saturday at 12.15, 1.15, 2.15 and 3.15pm. Tickets are available on the day from 10.30am from the Information Desk.

as they sound, places of rest and comfort for trainee lawyers. From the 19th century onward, law was taught at King's College, next to Somerset House in the Strand, and at University College in Gower Street. Before then, the only way to obtain legal training was to serve an apprenticeship in one of the Inns.

Four still remain, and still function as accommodation and offices for the legal profession: **Middle Temple** ❺ and **Inner Temple** ❻ between Fleet Street and the Embankment, and Gray's Inn (see page 149) and Lincoln's Inn further north. With their cobbled lanes and brass plaques bearing Dickensian names, they are atmospheric places to stroll around. Note that the entrances to Middle Temple Lane and Inner Temple Lane are easily missed – the gates are usually closed and access is via a small side passageway.

These Inns take their name from the crusading Knights Templar, who bought land here in the 12th century and built the **Temple Church** (charge), inspired by the Church of the Holy Sepulchre in Jerusalem.

Temple Church.

There are a number of the knights' tombs inside, and a tiny punishment cell by the altar. The church contained one of the clues featured in Dan Brown's The Da Vinci Code. Sloping down to the Embankment, the grassy swards of the Temple Gardens are a pleasant place to take a break from sightseeing.

North of the Royal Courts of Justice, between Kingsway and Chancery Lane, is **Lincoln's Inn** ❼, alma mater of Oliver Cromwell, and the two great 19th-century prime ministers, William Gladstone and Benjamin Disraeli.

Lincoln's Inn Fields were created for the students' recreation, but the best sport was watching the early city planners try to outmanoeuvre each other: Inigo Jones sat on a 17th-century Royal Commission to decide the area's fate.

Sir John Soane's Museum ❽

Address: 13 Lincoln's Inn Fields, www.soane.org
Tel: 7405 2107
Opening Hrs: Tue–Sat 10am–5pm;

also 6–9pm (candlelit opening) first Tue of each month
Entrance Fee: free except Tue evenings
Transport: Holborn

This marvellous museum is a self-endowed monument to John Soane (1753–1837), one of London's most important architects and collectors, who left his house and collection much as they had been during his lifetime. He built his private home on three sites along the edge of Lincoln's Inn Fields (No. 13) and it is a delight to visit, like being in a miniature British Museum.

Among the highlights are an Egyptian sarcophagus, Hogarth's *Rake's Progress* and some fine Canalettos, but much of the pleasure of visiting is derived from the building itself.

As the museum is undergoing phased restoration until 2015, in a project called "Opening up the Soane", some rooms may be closed during your visit.

Dickens's world

The ghost of the great Victorian writer Charles Dickens (1812–70) haunts the streets of Holborn. Just south of Lincoln's Inn Fields is the **Old Curiosity Shop**, a tiny 16th-century structure – now a shoe shop – likely to have been the inspiration for Little Nell's antiques shop.

On the other side of Lincoln's Inn, Dickens's first marital home was on the site of the neo-Gothic Prudential Assurance building in Holborn, opposite a half-timbered row of shops at the bottom of Gray's Inn Road. This is **Staple Inn** ❾, one of the former Inns of Chancery that dealt with commercial law. Dating from 1586 and a survivor of the Great Fire of London, it shows how much of the city must have looked before 1666.

Dickens underwent his legal apprenticeship at **Gray's Inn** ❿ (Mon–Fri 10am–4pm), one of Holborn's four Inns of Court. Dating

Barrister's wig in a Middle Temple Lane shop window.

Lincoln's Inn Fields.

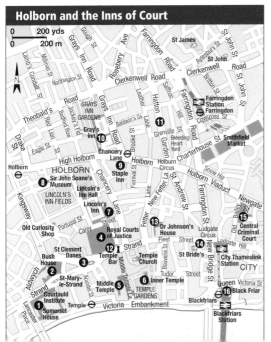

Holborn and the Inns of Court

0   200 yds
0   200 m

Diamond merchant in Hatton Garden. This part of London has retained a core of shops selling a particular item: opticians and other optical-related goods (such as camera lenses) as well as watch repair shops along Fleet Street, and diamonds in Hatton Garden.

Lincoln's Inn.

from the 14th century, its grounds lie just to the west of Gray's Inn Road. The magnificent garden (Mon–Fri noon–2.30pm) was laid out by Francis Bacon, the Elizabethan philosopher and statesman. With an irony that must have tickled Dickens's sense of the law's ridiculousness, Gray's Inn Hall saw the first production of Shakespeare's *Comedy of Errors*.

Further east is **Bleeding Heart Yard**, scene of much of the domestic action in *Little Dorrit*. Only a step or two away is **Hatton Garden** ⓫, the centre of London's diamond trade, and Leather Lane, where market stalls sell fresh food and household goods.

FLEET STREET

Just beyond the Temple Inn and the Royal Courts of Justice is **Temple Bar** ⓬, where a mean-looking heraldic dragon marks the boundary between Westminster and the City of London, beyond which, theoretically, the monarch cannot pass without the Lord Mayor's permission.

Stretching eastwards is **Fleet Street**, the former home of Britain's national newspapers from 1702, when the first daily newspaper, the *Daily Courant*, was published here. In the 1980s, new technology enabled the press barons to move to cheaper sites in Docklands and elsewhere.

There is still evidence of the street's illustrious past. Dr Samuel Johnson (who quipped, 'A man who is tired of London is tired of life') lived in the back courts at 17 Gough Square from 1748 to 1759 where, with the help of six assistants, he compiled the first comprehensive English dictionary. **Dr Johnson's House** ⓭ is an evocative museum of this great man of letters (tel: 7353 3745; www.drjohnsonshouse.org; Mon–Sat 11am–5.30pm, Oct–Apr until 5pm; cash only). The creaky old building dates from 1700; Johnson paid rent to the tune of £30 per year, equivalent to around £3,000 today. (The alleyway leading to Gough Square is immediately east of No. 167 Fleet Street.)

The crime writer Edgar Wallace (1875–1932) is immortalised on a plaque on the northwest corner of **Ludgate Circus**, at the far end of

The Old Curiosity Shop.

Fleet Street. As an 11-year-old he sold newspapers at this junction.

Wedged in behind the Reuters Building designed by Sir Edwin Lutyens in 1935 is 'the journalists' and printers' church', **St Bride's** (tel: 7427 0133; www.stbrides.com). It was near here that the aptly named Wynkyn de Worde, an associate of William Caxton, set up the street's first press. There is a small museum of Fleet Street in the crypt, where a magpie collection of Roman mosaics from a villa on this site, Saxon church walls, and human remains are stored – much was revealed when the building was bombed in World War II. The ossuary is visible if you join a guided tour (Tue 3pm; charge; check website for dates). Samuel Pepys was baptised at St Bride's (he was born in 1633 in Salisbury Court, off Fleet Street) and he records in his diary how

Ye Olde Cheshire Cheese pub is just off Fleet Street.

DR JOHNSON'S DICTIONARY

Samuel Johnson (1709–84) was one of the great figures of the Enlightenment, rising from a humble background to become a member of London's intellectual elite. Having arrived in the city in 1737 after his attempt at a teaching career failed, he started writing for The Gentleman's Magazine, as well as penning various plays and poems. In 1746 he was commissioned by a group of publishers to produce a dictionary for a fee of £1,575 – a large sum at the time, but the work ended up taking 10 years instead of the three originally estimated, and Johnson had to pay for his staff and materials out of it. In 1762, however, his financial stability was assured with the award of a £300 annual pension by the king in recognition of his efforts (and thanks to his influential friends, actor and educator Thomas Sheridan and the Earl of Bute).

While some words in the dictionary have changed in meaning over the years (for example, 'nice' was defined as 'superfluously accurate'), many of his pithy definitions still fit the bill. One of the more oblique entries is for 'lexicographer', which Johnson ruefully defined as 'a harmless drudge'.

On top of the Old Bailey's dome, a golden figure of justice stands with a sword in her right hand and, in her left, scales to weigh the evidence.

The dragon at Temple Bar.

he had to bribe the sexton to find room for his brother's corpse here. The church's elegant spire is Sir Christopher Wren's tallest and is said to have inspired the first tiered wedding cake. Lunchtime concerts are held here on Tuesday and Friday at 1.15pm except for Lent, August and December.

LUDGATE HILL

The River Fleet, which once marked the division between Westminster and The City, used to be a 'disembouging stream' according to the 18th-century poet Alexander Pope. Acting as a sluice for Smithfield Market, and notorious since the 14th century for its foetid stench, it was bricked over in the 18th century, although the subterranean waters still have the propensity to make their presence felt by periodically flooding basements in the area.

The Fleet Prison for debtors was on the Fleet's right bank, Newgate Prison on the left. Public executions took place here until 1868, when a law brought an end to the rowdy spectacles they had become.

Johnson portrayed in a window of his former home.

On the site of the former prison, just beyond Ludgate Circus, is the **Central Criminal Court** ⓯, universally known by the name of the street in which it is located, Old Bailey. Some of the country's most unpleasant criminals have been brought to account here, and in the forbidding No. 1 Court, until the abolition of the death penalty in 1965, convicted murderers were sentenced to be hanged, the judges placing black caps on their heads as they passed sentence. You can still watch cases from the visitors' gallery (Mon–Fri 10am–1pm and 2–5pm approx, closed Aug).

BLACKFRIARS

The underground river enters the Thames at Blackfriars Bridge, named after a friary that was here from 1278 to 1538. A fine monument to this Dominican order is the 1905 **Black Friar** ⓰, on the corner of Queen Victoria Street: a most spectacular Arts and Crafts pub.

Heading west along Victoria Embankment from Blackfriars takes you back to Somerset House, past the permanently moored ships HMS *President* and HQS *Wellington*, opposite the gardens of the Inns of Court.

BEST RESTAURANTS, PUBS AND BARS

PRICE CATEGORIES

Prices for a three-course dinner per person with a half-bottle of house wine:

£ = under £25
££ = £25–35
£££ = £35–55
££££ = over £55

Restaurants

Asian

Asadal
227 High Holborn, WC1.
Tel: 7430 9006. www.asadal.co.uk
Open: L Mon–Sat, D daily. **££–£££** [**91**] p314, E1]
Basement restaurant by Holborn tube station, offering a wide choice of Korean dishes. Try *kalbi* (beef and sauce), *kimchi* (seasoned vegetables) or hae mool jeon gol (a spicy seafood and tofu stew).

Chi Noodle and Wine Bar
5 New Bridge St, Bride Court EC4.
Tel: 7353 2409. www.chinoodle.com
Open: L & D Mon–Fri. **££** [**92**] p314, E2]
Airy restaurant and takeaway offering pan-Asian noodle and rice dishes.

Pu's Thai Brasserie
10 Gate St, WC2. Tel: 7404 2126.
www.pus-brasserie.com Open: L & D Mon–Sat. **£–££** [**93**] p306, E1]
Reasonable Thai restaurant located around the corner from Sir John Soane's Museum.

French

Bleeding Heart Restaurant and Bistro
Bleeding Heart Yard, Greville St, EC1.
Tel: 7242 2056 for restaurant. www.bleeding heart.co.uk Open: L Mon–Sat, D daily. **£££** [**94**] p310, D4]
Comprises three establishments: the tavern, the bistro (No. 7) and the restaurant, each in separate premises. The latter is the place to go for superb French cuisine and alfresco dining in the cobbled courtyard.

Modern European

The Delauney
55 Aldwych, WC2. Tel: 7499 8558.
www.thedelauney.com Open: L and D daily.
£££ [**95**] p314, D2]
Large busy restaurant in the grand tradition of European cafés, with dark wood panelling and very smart waiters. The varied menu includes such classics as choucroûte à l'Alsacienne, moules frites and steaks. Good afternoon teas.

Other

Gaucho
125–126 Chancery Lane, WC2. Tel: 7242 7727. www.gauchorestaurants.co.uk
Open: L Mon–Fri, D Mon–Sat. **£££** [**96**] p312, E2]
An Argentinian-style chain specialising in steaks, but the odd pasta, fish and chicken dish are also available.

Pubs and Bars

This area has several historic pubs.

Pubs

Black Friar
174 Queen Victoria St; www.nicholsonspubs.co.uk [**56**] p316, A2]
The Arts and Crafts interior (stained glass, wood panelling, marble and mosaics) of this 1905 pub is worth a visit in itself, but it is also known for its good choice of ales.

Old Bank of England
194 Fleet St; http://oldbankofengland.co.uk [**57**] p314, E2]
Situated in the former law courts of the Bank of England, this is a beautifully opulent pub. It serves good food and has a decent outside space – rare in this part of the city.

Punch Tavern
99 Fleet St; www.punchtavern.com [**58**] p314, E2]
Another striking interior, this time Victorian, is offered by this historic city pub, which has a tiled

entrance, dark panelling and serves decent food.

Ye Olde Cheshire Cheese
145 Fleet St [**59**] p314, E1]
This is easily dismissed as a tourist trap, but its age and history are impressive: it was frequented by many famous Londoners, including Dickens and Samuel Johnson. A warren of nooks and crannies, its cosy chop room serves good steak and kidney pies.

Bars

El Vino
47 Fleet St; www.elvino.co.uk [**60**] p314, E2]
This was once the favourite wine bar of hard-drinking journalists and is now popular with lawyers. Its cellar restaurant serves traditional British food and tapas.

Pearl Bar
Chancery Court Hotel, 252 High Holborn; www.pearl-restaurant.com [**61**] p314, D1]
Part restaurant, part high-end cocktail bar, with over 50 wines available by the glass.

Black Friar pub.

ST PAUL'S AND THE CITY

The City, covering just one square mile, is Britain's main financial centre. This was the original London, once contained by Roman walls, and it retains its own government and police force.

The City, London's financial quarter, is a world apart from the rest of the capital. It runs its own affairs, has its own police force and a distinct set of hierarchies. Even the Queen treads carefully here: on her coronation drive in 1953, she was obliged – if only by tradition – to stop at Temple Bar and declare that she came in peace. The name 'Square Mile' is given to this financial district that was at one time regarded as 'the clearinghouse of the world', but it signifies far more than a limited geographical area. For most of its 2,000-year history, the City *was* London.

Today, more than 300,000 workers stream into the City every weekday. Known for their work-hard-play-hard attitude, they are driven by competition and substantial annual bonuses. On weekends, under 9,000 City residents are left to savour the stillness that settles across the Square Mile, an area where a strong sense of tradition has helped a potentially faceless financial world retain a certain degree of character.

The City has been devastated twice. In 1666 the Great Fire devoured fourfifths of the area, and during the winter of 1940–1 Germany's Luftwaffe left one-third of it in ruins.

St Paul's Cathedral ❶

Address: www.stpauls.co.uk
Tel: 7246 8357
Opening Hrs: Mon–Sat 8.30am–4pm, tours at 10am, 11am, 1pm, 2pm
Transport: St Paul's

At the top of Ludgate Hill, the western approach to the City, stands St Paul's, the first cathedral built after the English Reformation and Sir Christopher Wren's greatest work. A tablet above his plain marble tomb reads: *'Lector, si monumentum*

Main Attractions
St Paul's Cathedral
St Bartholomew the Great
Smithfield Meat Market
Charterhouse Square
Museum of London
Bank of England
Leadenhall
Monument
Tower of London

Maps and Listings
Map, page 156
Restaurants, page 170
Accommodation, page 283

The Gherkin.

TIP

Like any closed world, the City doesn't open up easily to outsiders. Peering out of a tourist bus at acres of glass and concrete is far too superficial an examination; time and legwork in the network of alleys and backstreets which thread through the office blocks will reveal much more.

requiris, circumspice' ('Reader, if you wish to see his memorial, look around you'). For full coverage of St Paul's, see page 172.

Paternoster Square

St Paul's needs room to breathe, but the area around it – in particular the ancient market site known as **Paternoster Square** – has been intensively developed. In spite of recent remodelling, it forms a disappointing setting for Wren's masterpiece.

In 2004 the **London Stock Exchange** abandoned its long-held base near the Bank of England in Threadneedle Street for new premises in Paternoster Square that were better suited to electronic trading.

With origins going back to merchants trying to raise money for a Far Eastern trip in 1553, the Stock Exchange has changed enormously since the Big Bang reforms of 1986, when it agreed to radically change its practices. Fixed commission systems were abolished, and jobber and broker functions were merged and transferred to a computerised quotation system. The trading floor, once crowded with frantic pin-striped figures engaged in open

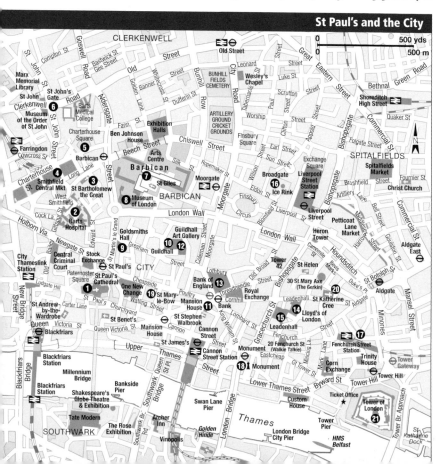

St Paul's and the City

outcry, fell silent. As a result, the Stock Market is a fairer but duller place. It is no longer open to the general public.

Historic churches

In the warren of roads that lead from St Paul's to the river, there are several Wren churches. **St Andrew-by-the-Wardrobe** in St Andrew's Hill was so named because it stood near a royal storage area. **St Nicholas Cole Abbey** is followed by **St Benet's**, which serves as the Metropolitan Welsh Church.

On the other side of Queen Victoria Street is the **College of Arms** (www.college-of-arms.gov.uk; entrance hall open when receptionist is present Mon–Fri 10am–4pm; free; Record Room tours by arrangement, tel: 7248 2762; charge), which has a handsome, refurbished 17th-century interior by William Emmett and a library of heraldry and genealogy, which, for a fee, deals with genealogy enquiries.

Other Wren churches in the vicinity include **St James Garlickhythe** on busy Upper Thames Street,

Sign on the College of Arms.

which was disastrously struck by a crane that demolished its rose window in 1991, and **St Michael Paternoster Royal**, the burial place of Dick Whittington (1423), a Lord Mayor of London, who, with his cat, has entered British mythology as a pantomime figure. This rags-to-riches story sets out to prove that even country bumpkins could be elected Lord Mayor of the City,

St Paul's Cathedral.

though the real Whittington came from a wealthy county family and amassed a fortune as a merchant.

WEST SMITHFIELD

Northwest of St Paul's is the great block of St Bartholomew's Hospital.

Barts Hospital ❷

Address: Museum, North Wing
Tel: 7837 0546
Opening Hrs: Tue–Fri 10am–4pm, tours by arrangement Fri 2pm
Entrance Fee: free; charge for tour
Transport: Barbican, St Paul's

Founded in1123, St Bartholomew's Hospital is the oldest in London. Like many early hospitals, it was founded as a monastery offering 'hospitality' to pilgrims and the needy. The care provided was initially a combination of shelter, comfort, food and prayer, and only in later centuries evolved into medical treatment. Patients were tended by monks and nuns (hence the term 'sister' still in use today).

The hospital includes an interesting little **museum** on changes in medicine over the centuries. A door at the rear of the museum opens to reveal two William Hogarth murals dressing the staircase of the entrance hall of the North Wing. Some of the figures are believed to have been modelled on patients. For a closer look, book one of the guided Friday tours.

Opposite the hospital, on the wall at the corner of **Giltspur Street** and **Cock Lane**, is a golden figure of a urinating boy, symbolising the extinguishing of the 1666 Great Fire at this point. Just beyond, in **West Smithfield**, are memorials to the Scottish hero William Wallace, victim of a spot of judicial butchery here in 1305, and to the 270 'Marian martyrs', Protestants burned at the stake for religious heresy by Queen Mary in the 1550s.

St Bartholomew the Great ❸

Address: West Smithfield, www.great stbarts.com
Tel: 7248 2294
Opening Hrs: Mon–Fri 8.30am–5pm (mid-Nov–mid-Feb until 4pm), Sat 10.30am–4pm, Sun 8.30am–8pm

Barts Hospital.

Transport: Barbican

One of the oldest and finest churches in the City stands in a corner of the square, perhaps a trifle shocked by what has passed before, for this was also the site of the Bartholomew Fair, immortalised in Ben Jonson's play of the same name. Film-makers, too, have been drawn to this corner of London: scenes in *Four Weddings and a Funeral* and *Shakespeare in Love* were filmed inside the church. The monk Rahere, who founded St Bartholomew's Hospital, is buried here.

SMITHFIELD TO CLERKENWELL

The unlikely confection of iron and plaster adjacent to St Bartholomew's is **Smithfield Central Markets** ❹, at its busiest early in the morning. Here the porters and workers known as 'bummarees' thunder about with barrow loads of carcasses and the knife grinders shower sparks out of the backs of their vans. Through all the commotion, it's still possible to hear 'backchat', Smithfield's equivalent of Billingsgate profanity, designed to fool unwanted listeners.

The last of the great markets still on its original site, Smithfield is now one of the most modern meat markets in the world, thanks to a £70 million overhaul. The renovation was accomplished without sacrificing the Victorian shell of the Central Markets. Although Smithfield has resisted becoming a shopping piazza like Covent Garden, the area has gone up-market, with a number of good-quality restaurants in St John Street.

Tombstones in Bunhill Fields, where many famous people are buried, including John Bunyan, author of The Pilgrim's Progress.

Barts Hospital museum.

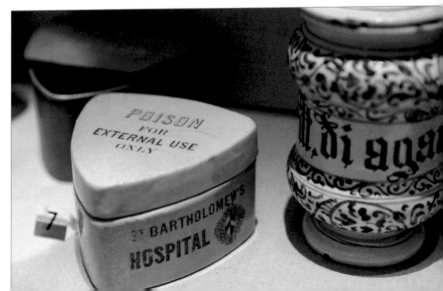

Smithfield butcher.

Inside St Bartholomew the Great.

Just north of Smithfield is Georgian **Charterhouse Square** ❺. With its gas lamps and cobbles, it is a favourite location for period film-makers. The Carthusian order **London Charterhouse** still has around 40 residents, some of whom conduct guided tours between April and September (tel: 7253 9503; www.thecharterhouse.org; book in advance).

St John's Gate ❻

Address: St John's Lane, www.museum stjohn.org.uk
Tel: 7324 4005
Opening Hrs: Mon–Fri 10am–5pm (Sat until 4pm), tours Tue, Fri–Sat 11am, 2.30pm
Entrance Fee: free
Transport: Farringdon

To the left of London Charterhouse, approached through the medieval St John's Gate off Clerkenwell Road, is **St John's** Priory, founded by the crusading Order of the Knights of St John. Little remains of the buildings dissolved by Henry VIII, but there is a small **museum** in the Gate House, and guided tours of the Grand Hall and remains of the Priory Chapel, which, like the Temple Church off Fleet Street, was round.

Clerkenwell

Further north, beyond Old Street is **Clerkenwell**, historically a district of immigrants (notably Italian) and revolutionary traditions, as well as the traditional centre of the city's watchmaking industry. In the 19th century, Chartists and campaigners for Home Rule collected around Clerkenwell Green.

Guiseppe Mazzini, the Italian revolutionary, lived at No. 10 Laystall Street and Lenin edited a newspaper in what is now the Marx Memorial Library at 37a Clerkenwell Green (tel: 7253 1485; www.marx-memorial-library.org; open to the public for guided tours Mon–Thu 1–2pm or by appointment).

To the east, just south of Old Street Underground station on City Road, is **Bunhill Fields** (Apr–Sept closes 7pm, Oct–Mar at 4pm), the burial ground for many notable nonconformists including Daniel Defoe, William Blake and John Bunyan. Across the road is **Wesley's House and Chapel** (tel: 7253 2262;

THE ROMANS

The Romans established the City in AD 43, but there are few remains of the original Roman settlement. The Roman Wall, which was 2 miles (3km) long, 20ft high and 9ft wide (6 by 3 metres) and had six magnificent gates (Ludgate, Aldersgate, Cripplegate, Newgate, Bishopsgate and Aldgate) is now found only in fragments. Good sections can still be seen at London Wall, Noble Street, Cooper's Row and the Museum of London. There are also remains on the approach to the Tower of London from Tower Hill Underground station. The wall's course can be traced with the help of maps which have been set up on the City's pavements.

The Barbican.

www.wesleyschapel.org.uk; Mon–Sat 10am–4pm, Sun 12.30–1.45pm, closed Thu lunch time;), built by the founder of Methodism, John Wesley, in 1778. There is a museum in the crypt and Wesley's house, next to the chapel, is also open to the public. In the men's public toilets are Victorian fixtures manufactured by Thomas Crapper.

THE BARBICAN

Based around three 42-storey towers, the **Barbican Centre** ❼ (www.barbican.org.uk; architecture tours Wed 4pm, Thur 7pm, Sat 11am and 2pm, Sun 2pm; hidden Barbican tours, check website for times) is the main residential block in the City and contains Europe's largest arts centre. It was devised as council housing by the Corporation of London in the 1950s to attract residents and boost a falling City population. It took more than 20 years to build and is renowned for its inaccessibility and maze-like design. Later the flats were sold at exorbitant prices. The complex contains two art galleries, a cinema, two theatres and the London Symphony Orchestra, and is now listed as being of architectural and historical importance.

Beside the Barbican Centre, on the site of a Roman fort, is the Museum of London.

TIP

During the day there are often foyer performances and live music on the terrace of the Barbican's Waterside Café overlooking the fountains.

Get your bearings and find key attractions.

CITY OF LONDON

Museum of London ❽

Address: London Wall, www.museum oflondon.org.uk
Tel: 7001 9844
Opening Hrs: daily 10am–6pm, last entry 5.30pm
Entrance Fee: free
Transport: Barbican

With more than a million objects in its stores, this is the world's largest urban history museum and an essential stop for understanding how the City developed.

Aside from important prehistoric and Roman collections, it has a vast archaeological archive, a costume and decorative arts collection, a photographic archive of 280,000 images and more than 5,000 hours of oral life-story recordings.

London's history is presented chronologically from prehistory to the early Stuarts. The same thematic threads run through each period: architecture, trade and industry, transport, health, religion, fashions, leisure pursuits. There are many detailed information panels; you may find that, an hour into your visit, you're still with the Romans.

Here are some highlights:

London Before London
This surveys life in the Thames Valley from 450,000 BC to AD 50. The centrepiece of the exhibition is the 'River Wall' displaying 300 artefacts found in the Thames.

Roman London
This gallery has a hoard of gold coins (1st–2nd century AD), a Roman leather bikini, and the gilded arms of what must have been a life-size statue of a god or emperor.

Medieval London
Telling the story of London from the end of Roman rule to the accession of Elizabeth I, this gallery displays items such as a gold and garnet brooch found in a Covent Garden grave, and some extremely pointy medieval shoes.

War, Plague and Fire
This tells the story of London in the turbulent 17th century, when Civil War, plague and then the Great Fire of 1666 ravaged the city. Objects include a death mask of Oliver

Museum of London exhibit.

Cromwell, primitive fire-fighting equipment and fire-damaged floor tiles from Pudding Lane (where the fire began in a baker's shop).

Galleries of Modern London

These galleries bring the story of London up to the present day, and display the stunning Lord Mayor's Coach. There is also a reconstructed 18th-century pleasure garden and pavilion, a cell from a debtors' prison, an Art Deco lift from Selfridges, and exhibits such as the elaborate Fanshawe dress made from Spitalfields' woven silk.

THE GUILDS

Craftsmen with the same trade tended to congregate in small areas, and clubbed together to form medieval guilds. Like trade unions, the guilds operated to ward off foreign competition and established an apprenticeship system. They set standards for their goods and working practices, and ran mutual-aid schemes which helped members in difficulty. The more prosperous guilds built halls to meet and dine in and wore lavish uniforms or 'liveries', in due course becoming livery companies.

Down the centuries the livery companies joined the establishment, promoting charities and founding some of England's better educational institutes, including Haberdashers' College and Goldsmiths' College.

The Livery Halls

Today some of the most impressive portals in the City belong to livery halls. Behind their elaborate carvings members dine as lavishly as ever.

Most spectacular is **Goldsmiths Hall** ❾ in Foster Lane (tel: 7606 7010; www.thegoldsmiths.co.uk/hall), between the Museum of London and St Paul's, where the integrity of coins made by the Royal Mint are checked in an annual ceremony. The use of the word 'hallmark' as a seal of value originated here and the company is still responsible for assaying gold. Unfortunately, visitors are not usually allowed inside the livery halls, except on open days held a few times a year (tel: 7606 3030 to book). While the 108 livery companies today have little connection

The Lord Mayor's Coach in the Museum of London.

FACT

Behind Mansion House is St Stephen Walbrook, the Lord Mayor's church, rebuilt after the Great Fire and considered by many to be Christopher Wren's best. Its dome is believed to be a dry run for St Paul's and its controversial 'cheeseboard' altar is by Henry Moore.

with their original crafts, they still exert influence in their home territory. The City is governed by the City Corporation, chaired by the **Lord Mayor** (whereas the rest of the capital comes under the wing of the Mayor of London, who presides over the Greater London Authority). The office of Lord Mayor dates from 1189. The new Mayor is elected each year on Michaelmas Day, 29 September, when the reigning Lord Mayor and his aldermen parade through the streets carrying posies of flowers to ward off the stench which filled the City in medieval times.

Guildhall ⑩

Address: Gresham Street, www.cityof london.gov.uk
Tel: 7606 3030
Opening Hrs: Mon–Sat 10am–4.30pm
Entrance Fee: free
Transport: St Paul's

In November the Mayor is sworn in here, taking up his symbols of office in a ceremony known as the Silent Change, so called because no words are spoken. The Guildhall is the best place to glimpse the guilds' past. Dating from the 15th century, and several times restored, the Great Hall is decorated with the liveries' banners and shields, and contains statues of Gog and Magog, the legendary founders of London. A small museum (tel: 7332 1868; Mon–Sat 9.30am–4.45pm; free) in a room adjacent to the Library displays the timepieces owned by the Clockmakers' Company. This splendid collection is the oldest and largest of its kind. There are 15 marine timekeepers, including one by John Harrison.

The Lord Mayor's Show is held a day after his swearing in. This colourful parade starts at the Guildhall and passes through the City, culminating at **Mansion House** ⑪, opposite the Bank of England. This is the Lord Mayor's official residence, designed by George Dance the Elder in 1758, but its magnificent rooms are not open to the public. However, there are guided tours every Tuesday at 2pm (charge) – meet at the A-board near the porch entrance to Mansion House, in Walbrook.

An ornate memorial to Admiral Horatio Nelson (1758–1805), the Guildhall.

BANK AND BEYOND

The triangular intersection known as **Bank** can intimidate. Imposing civic architecture abounds, with Sir Edwin Lutyens' **HSBC** building on the north west side, Mansion House on the western corner, the **Royal Exchange** building to the east and Sir John Soane's implacable facade of the Bank of England to the north.

All the City's great institutions grew from the fulfilment of the most basic needs and only later acquired their grandiose headquarters. Banking first came to the City in the 12th century when Italian refugees set up lending benches (*banca* in Italian) in **Lombard Street**, running eastwards from the Bank of England.

The Bank of England ⑬

Address: Museum entrance in Bartholomew Lane, www.bankof england.co.uk
Tel: 7601 5545;
Opening Hrs: Mon–Fri 10am–5pm
Entrance Fee: free
Transport: Bank

The **Bank of England** dominates the Bank square as it does the British

The Guildhall.

Guildhall Art Gallery ⑫

Address: Guildhall Yard, www.cityof london.gov.uk
Tel: 7332 3700
Opening Hrs: Mon–Sat 10am–5pm, Sun noon–4pm
Transport: Mansion House or St Paul's

Established in 1886, the Guildhall's gallery was destroyed in the Blitz but reopened in 1999. John Singleton Copley's immense *The Defeat of the Floating Batteries at Gibraltar*, around which the new gallery was designed, commands attention, but allow time to linger over the smaller-scale works depicting London life. You can take a free tour of the collection's highlights on Fridays (hourly between 12.15 and 3.15pm).

Shortly before work began on the present building, the remains of a **Roman amphitheatre** were discovered under the yard. The arena, including well-preserved timber drains bearing original carpentry tool marks, may now be viewed in a lower-level gallery.

Mansion House.

Leadenhall Market sits on the site of the Roman Forum.

Leadenhall Market.

financial scene. Popularly known as the Old Lady of Threadneedle Street, a nickname which probably originates from a late 18th-century cartoon depicting an old lady (the bank) trying to prevent the then prime minister, Pitt the Younger, from securing her gold. The name stuck because it aptly describes the conservative, maternalistic role the bank played in stabilising the country's economy – a role strengthened in 1997 when the new Labour government freed it from direct government control.

The Bank of England was set up in 1694 to finance a war against the Dutch. In return for a £1.2 million loan, it was granted a charter and became a bank of issue (with the right to print notes and take deposits). Today it prints 5 million notes daily, destroys another 5 million and stores the nation's gold reserves. Its present home was largely rebuilt between 1925 and 1939.

It covers 3 acres (1.2 hectares) and contains the **Bank of England Museum**. The presentations narrate how the bank helped to finance Britain's war effort against France in 1688, how it became one of the first institutions in the City to employ women and how it controlled government borrowing during World War II. There is a display of gold, including Roman and modern bars.

Lloyd's of London

The financial boom of the 1980s brought immediate demands for new office buildings which would be purpose-built for modern communications and, by 1991, 1.7 sq miles (4.4 sq km) of office space had been built in the City. One of the first, and the most dramatic, was the 1986 **Lloyd's of London** ⓮ building in Lime Street, designed by Sir Richard Rogers (now Lord Rogers).

For so long the biggest insurance group in the world, Lloyd's started in the 17th-century coffee house of Edward Lloyd, where underwriters, shippers and bankers gathered and began to strike deals. Its practices remained largely unchanged for 300 years, but in the late 1980s sundry international disasters led to some huge payouts and millions

of pounds were lost. Many of the 'names' – investors who shouldered the insurance risks, often through syndicates – lost life savings and owed more than they could ever possibly pay; tragically a few committed suicide.

The building is no longer open to visitors, but the exterior is a highlight of the City. Hidden from sight on a magnificent marble floor is a rostrum housing the **Lutine Bell**, which was rung once for bad news and twice for good. It was rung following the 9/11 terrorist attacks in 2001.

Beside this modern building is the more accessible **Leadenhall ⓯**, once the wholesale market for poultry and game, and now a handsome commercial centre. The magnificent airy Victorian cream and maroon structure has a collection of up-market chain shops, book shops, sandwich bars and stylish restaurants, attracting City workers at breakfast and lunch time.

Grand stations

London's other steel-and-glass Victorian constructions – the

The 30 St Mary Axe building, aka the Gherkin.

railway stations – were also given facelifts during the 1980s building boom. **Liverpool Street** was overhauled along with neighbouring **Broadgate ⓰**, one of the most ambitious developments in the City, with 16 office-block buildings around three squares including, at

Liverpool Street station.

Visits to the Tower of London are exhausting, but refreshment is within easy walking distance. The Ship pub in Talbot Court off Eastcheap, and The Samuel Pepys pub down Stew Lane, off Upper Thames Street on the river, have real character and real ale.

Broadgate Square, an ice rink with sushi, coffee and sandwich stalls dotted around the perimeter. There are now plans afoot to redevelop the site.

Fenchurch Street with its arched roof and graceful windows was the City's first railway station. Originally situated in the Minories, it moved in 1854 to its present location and has the 1930s Manhattan-style office building, **1 America Square**, over its railway lines.

To stand out in such an architectural playground, new buildings have to be innovative. A much-loved new feature of the London skyline is the **30 St Mary Axe building**, a 40-storey tapering glass tower designed by Lord Foster and better known as the Gherkin. Richard Rogers' latest addition to the novelty silhouettes in the City is the 'Cheesegrater', a 740ft (225-metre) -tall skeletal glass-and-steel wedge that soars skywards. And at 20 Fenchurch Street is the latest skyscraper to be built, also with an affectionate nickname, the Walkie-Talkie, because of its distinctive top-heavy shape.

Less obvious is **One New Change** on Cheapside, the City's newest shopping centre designed by Jean Nouvel. Its 6th floor roof terrace offers stunning views of the City and St Paul's.

Monument ⓲

Address: Monument Yard, www.the monument.info
Tel: 7626 2717
Opening Hrs: viewing gallery daily 9.30am–5.30pm
Transport: Monument

Erected according to Wren's designs to commemorate the 1666 fire, this Roman Doric column stands 202ft (61 metres) high. The height happens to be the same as the distance between the monument's base and the king's baker's house in Pudding Lane where the fire began.

The Great Fire lasted four days and spread through 460 streets, destroying 87 churches and more than 13,000 houses. Inside the column, 311 steps wind up to a small platform, from which the view is spectacular. Appropriately enough, the gallery affords a chance to appreciate the remarkable vision Wren imposed on the City through his spires. There are so many Wren spires that you risk severe Wren-fatigue if you attempt to see them all.

St Mary-le-Bow ⓳ is the home of the famous Bow bells, which define a true cockney – you have to be born within earshot. There have been many sets of bells over the centuries; the current ones were cast after World War II. The church interior after restoration is rather plain, but the Norman crypt, now a restaurant called The Café Below, is worth a visit. Wren was able to leave his significant mark on London because so much of it had been destroyed in the Great Fire, but some churches survived the conflagration, including **St Katherine Cree** ⓴, a mix of

Exterior of the Lloyd's of London building.

Classical and Gothic, in Leadenhall Street. Henry Purcell played its fine 17th-century organ, and the painter Hans Holbein, a plague victim, was buried here in 1543.

Tower of London ㉑

Address: Tower Hill,
www.hrp.org.uk
Tel: 0844 482 7777
Opening Hrs: Mar–Oct Tue–Sat 9am–5.30pm, Sun–Mon 10am–5.30pm; Nov–Feb Tue–Sat 9am–4.30pm, Sun–Mon 10am–4.30pm
Transport: Tower Hill

East of the Monument, across the river from the oval-shaped City Hall, from which the Greater London Authority's power is exercised, is the City's oldest structure. At first sight the **Tower of London** can look like a cardboard model rather than a former seat of power, but closer inspection reveals an awesome solidity which encompasses much of Britain's history. The Tower has contained at various times a treasury, public record office, observatory, royal mint and zoo, and was so frequently remodelled for these

Monument, commemorating the Great Fire of London. Climb its 311 steps for superb views.

purposes that its interiors look less ancient than one expects.

For full coverage of the Tower of London, see page 174.

The Tower of London.

BEST RESTAURANTS, PUBS AND BARS

PRICE CATEGORIES

Prices for a three-course dinner per person with a half-bottle of house wine:

£ = under £25
££ = £25–35
£££ = £35–55
££££ = over £55

Restaurants

British

The Café Below
St Mary-le-Bow, Cheapside, EC2. Tel: 7329 0789. www.cafebelow.co.uk Open: B and L Mon–Fri. **£–££** [97] p316, B2]
An excellent café in the church crypt of St Mary-le-Bow, with seats in the churchyard in summer. The menu changes daily, is seasonal, includes plenty of vegetarian options, and all food is home-made.

Hix Oyster and Chop House
36–37 Greenhill Rents, off Cowcross St, EC1. Tel: 7017 1930. www.hixoysterand chophouse.co.uk Open: L and D daily **£££**

Outdoor dining in Clerkenwell.

[98] p310, D4]
Chef Mark Hix showcases his modern British cooking. Dishes, which vary with the seasons, might include beef and oyster pie, Porterhouse steaks and grilled fish.

One New Change
Cheapside. www.onenewchange.com [99] p316, B2]
The City's new shopping centre has several bars and restaurants. These include a Searcy's Champagne Bar (tel: 7871 1213), Madison Restaurant (tel: 8305 3088) on the roof terrace, and the chic café Bea's of Bloomsbury (tel: 7242 8330).

St John
26 St John St, EC1. Tel: 7251 0848. www.stjohnrestaurant.com Open: L Mon–Fri and Sun, D Mon–Sat. **££££** [100] p310, D4]
This little restaurant, a stone's throw from Smithfield's meat market, is a Clerkenwell favourite. It offers simple but curious dishes such as Middle White belly and dandelion. One Michelin star.

Fish

Sweetings
39 Queen Victoria St, EC4. Tel: 7248 3062. www.sweetingsrestaurant.com Open: L only Mon–Fri. **££** [101] p316, B2]
First-rate restaurant with bags of traditional City atmosphere, and well-prepared dishes such as grilled skate or turbot in mustard sauce, and old-fashioned puddings such as treacle tart.

French

Café du Marché
22 Charterhouse Square, Charterhouse Mews, EC1. Tel: 7608 1609. www.cafedu marche.co.uk Open: L Mon–Fri, D Mon–Sat. **£££** [102] p310, D4]
Rustic ambience, including a countrified courtyard, and traditional French menu. The food can seem a little on the rich side. Ideal for a romantic meal or lunchtime treat. There are three restaurants, each with a different atmosphere, under the same roof.

Club Gascon
57 West Smithfield, EC1. Tel: 7600 6144. www.clubgascon.com Open: L Mon–Fri, D Mon–Sat. **£££** [103] p316, A1]
Though tradition is not totally dispensed with, there's more to this Michelin-starred restaurant than the foie gras and magret de canard standards. Dishes and ingredients of southwestern France are prepared with an inventive touch and served tapas style, with a fine selection of regional wines to match. Booking essential.

Italian

Caravaggio
107 Leadenhall St, EC3. Tel: 7626 6206. www.etruscarestaurants.com Open: L & D Mon–Fri. **££££** [104] p316, C2]
Grand and rather showy Italian restaurant in a converted bank. Fish is a good option and the grilled rib-eye of beef with thick-cut chips is a carnivore's dream.

Modern European

Bonds

5 Threadneedle St, EC2. Tel: 7657 8088. www.bondsrestaurant.co.uk Open: B daily, L & D Mon–Fri. **££££** (set lunch **££**) [⑩⑤ p316, C2]

Set in the classy Threadneedles boutique hotel, overlooking the Bank of England, this top-class restaurant draws clients of the silk-lined wallet variety. Dishes include plenty of British fish and meat. There is a tapas menu too.

The Don

20, St Swithin's Lane, EC4. Tel: 7626 2606. www.thedonrestaurant.com Open: L & D Mon–Fri. **£££–££££** [⑩⑥ p316, C2]

Hidden in a courtyard off St Swithin's Lane, this is a cosy and welcoming brick-walled bistro. The food is a flavour-packed mélange of influences, with a French bias. There is also a more formal restaurant.

Eagle

159 Farringdon Rd, EC1. Tel: 7837 1353. Open: L daily, D Mon–Sat. **££** [⑩⑦ p310, C3]

This was the pub that launched a thousand gastropubs with its pioneering menu of inventive dishes. The food has a Mediterranean bias and there's a good choice of European beers.

Little Bay

171 Farringdon Rd, EC1. Tel: 7278 1234. www.littlebayfarringdon.co.uk Open: daily, all day. **£** [⑩⑧ p310, C3]

For honest food, keenly priced, this bizarre little bistro, lit by hand-crafted copper sculptures, is hard to beat.

Searcy's

Level 2, Barbican, Silk St, EC2. Tel: 7588 3008. www.barbican.org.uk L Mon–Fri, D Mon–Sat. **£££** [⑩⑨ p310, E4]

A classy place that serves up well-executed dishes for an arts-centre restaurant. Ring first as it doesn't open at night if there's no performance at the Barbican.

Pan-Asian

Cicada

132–136 St John St, EC1. Tel: 7608 1550. www.rickerrestaurants.com Open: L Mon–Fri, D Mon–Sat. **££** [⑪⑩ p310, D3]

Offers a range of well-executed pan-Asian dishes such as black cod with sweet miso, and duck, watermelon and cashew salad.

Spanish

Moro

34–36 Exmouth Market, EC1. Tel: 7833 8336. www.moro.co.uk Open: L & D Mon–Sat. **£££** [⑪⑪ p310, C3]

Laid-back restaurant serving Moorish cuisine, where lamb is charcoal grilled, tuna is wind-dried, monkfish wood-roasted, and manzanilla sherry partners prawns and garlic. Tapas available all day.

Pubs and Bars

Given that some of London's oldest streets as well as its newest buildings are here, the mix of watering holes is diverse, ranging from hip bars and contemporary cafés to quaint pubs full of character and history. Fewer and farther between are the no-nonsense Victorian pubs, but with a bit of effort, traditionalists or anyone craving a quiet pint and a packet of peanuts can root them out.

Pubs

The Counting House

50 Cornhill; www.the-counting-house.com [⑫ p316, C2]

This is a bank-turned-pub, with high ceilings and chandeliers, which make for a very impressive interior. The food is good here, especially the pies.

Jerusalem Tavern

55 Britton St; www.stpetersbrewery.co.uk/london-pub/ [⑬ p310, D4]

A lovely intimate little pub dating from 1720, with cubicles, Georgian-style furniture and a selection of real ales and fruit beers from St Peter's Brewery in Suffolk.

Ye Olde Watling

Watling St; www.nicholsonspubs.co.uk [⑭ p316, B2]

Standing on the main Roman road out of the City, Ye Olde Watling has a fascinating history. One of its upstairs rooms was used by Sir Christopher Wren when he was building St Paul's Cathedral. It serves real ales and good pub food in generous portions.

Bars

1 Lombard Street

www.1lombardstreet.com [⑮ p316, B2]

This popular and very swanky restaurant in the City is also a good place to come for a drink. Sit at the circular bar, under a dramatic domed skylight, and enjoy one of their fine cocktails or something from the extensive wine list.

The Folly Bar

41 Gracechurch Street; www.thefollybar.co.uk [⑯ p316, C2]

Enjoy cocktails and bar snacks surrounded by off-duty city workers in this beautifully decorated venue.

Prism

147 Leadenhall St; www.harveynichols.com/prism-london [⑰ p316, C2]

In the vaults of the former Bank of New York building, this Harvey Nichols-run bar is a fashionable watering hole in the City. On the ground floor is a brasserie.

Royal Exchange Grand Café and Bar

The Courtyard, Royal Exchange, Bank [⑱ p316, B2]

Offering breakfast, lunch, dinner and drinks in opulent surroundings with prices to match.

Smiths of Smithfield

67–77 Charterhouse Street; www.smithsofsmithfield.co.uk [⑲ p310, D4]

Vast restaurant and bar spread over four floors in the heart of Smithfield Market (London's only meat market). The lounge and cocktail bar is on the first floor, and serves great snacks as well as a wide range of cocktails.

Vertigo 42

Tower 42, Old Broad St; www.vertigo42.co.uk [⑳ p316, C2]

This bar lives up to its name, serving Champagne and Champagne-based cocktails to accompany great views from on high in the 42-storey skyscraper.

Vinoteca

7 St John St; www.vinoteca.co.uk [㉑ p310, D4]

Popular wine bar with an excellent wine list, good, unpretentious food and reasonable prices.

ST PAUL'S CATHEDRAL

Sir Christopher Wren built more than 50 churches in London after the Great Fire of 1666, but this is the one that remains his masterpiece.

Sir Christopher Wren.

Historians believe that the first church on the St Paul's site was built in the 7th century, although it only really came into its own as Old St Paul's in the 14th century, and by the 16th century it was the tallest cathedral in England. Much of the building was destroyed in the Great Fire of 1666. Construction on the new St Paul's Cathedral began in 1675, when its architect, Sir Christopher Wren, was 43 years old.

The architect was an old man of 76 when his son Christopher finally laid the highest stone of the lantern on the central cupola in 1710. In total, the cathedral cost £747,954 to build, and most of the money was raised through taxing coal imports. Prior to the 300th anniversary of the 'topping out' of the cathedral in 2008, centuries of soot and grime were scrubbed away as part of a £40 million restoration project.

Just below the 24 windows in the dome is the Whispering Gallery, nearly 100ft (30 metres) of perfect acoustic. A whisper can be heard across the gallery, 107ft (33 metres) away.

The Essentials

Tel: 7246 8350; www.stpauls.co.uk
Opening Hrs: Mon–Sat 8.30am–4pm, tours begin at 10am, 11am, 1pm and 2pm
Transport: St Paul's

Admiral Lord Nelson (1758–1805) is entombed in the crypt.

THE HIGHLIGHTS

Features: marble steps (A); oak pulpit (Q); High Altar ®; Dean's pulpit and stairs to crypt (U); stairs to dome (V). **Chapels:** St Dunstan's (B); All Souls' (C); St Michael & St George's (D); American Chapel of Remembrance (S). **Tombs & Monuments:** Lord Leighton (E); General Gordon (F); Viscount Melbourne (G); Duke of Wellington (H); Joshua Reynolds (I); Dr Samuel Johnson (J); Admiral Earl Howe (K); Admiral Collingwood (L); J.M.W. Turner (M); Sir John Moore (N); General Abercromby (O); Lord Nelson (P); John Donne (T).

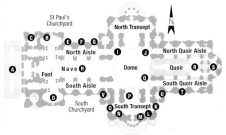

The superb craftsmanship was supervised during the 35-year construction by one master builder, Thomas Strong, and by Wren himself.

The cathedral's appearance is deceptive. The famous dome viewed from afar would look over large if seen from inside the building. The dome you look up at from within is in fact a much smaller dome, on top of which is built a brick cone. The cone's purpose is to support the massive weight of the external Portland stone dome, which weighs more than 64,000 tonnes.

A chapel behind the High Altar, damaged during the Blitz, was restored as the American Chapel, with a book of remembrance paying tribute to the 28,000 American citizens based in the UK who died in World War II.

THE TOWER OF LONDON

Queens were beheaded here, princes murdered and traitors tortured. Once a place to be avoided, it is now one of London's top visitor attractions.

Encircled by a moat (now dry), with 22 towers, the Tower, begun by William the Conqueror around 1078, is Britain's top military monument and a reminder of how power was once exercised in the nation.

Two of Henry VIII's wives, Anne Boleyn and Catherine Howard, were beheaded here, in 1536 and 1542. So were Sir Thomas More, Henry's principled Lord Chancellor (1535), and Sir Walter Raleigh, the last of the great Elizabethan adventurers (1618). The uncrowned Edward V, aged 12, and his 10-year-old brother Richard were murdered in 1483, allegedly on the orders of Richard III. William Penn, the future founder of Pennsylvania, was imprisoned here in 1669, and the diarist Samuel Pepys in 1679. As recently as 1941, Rudolph Hess, Germany's deputy führer, was locked in the Tower.

The Imperial State Crown.

At the centre of the fortress is the imposing White Tower with its four weathervane-topped turrets, each of a different style. The name followed Henry III's order to whitewash the exterior.

Tower of London armoury.

Given that the Tower's 18 acres (7.3 hectares) contain enough buildings and collections to occupy three hours, you may prefer to skip the one-hour Beefeater-led tour and strike out on your own. A multimedia guide can be hired.

In summer, it's best to arrive early to beat the queues, giving priority to the Crown Jewels and

The Essentials

Address: Tower Hill; www.hrp.org.uk
Tel: 0844 482 7777
Opening Hrs: Mar–Oct Tue–Sat 9am–5.30pm, Sun–Mon 10am–5.30pm; Nov–Feb Tue–Sat 9am–4.30pm, Sun–Mon 10am–4.30pm
Transport: Tower Hill

Traitors' Gate.

THE SIGHTS WORTH SEEING

Historic view of the Tower.

The Medieval Palace

Just before Traitor's Gate is the entrance to the residential part of the Tower, used by monarchs when they lived here. St Thomas's Tower, built in 1275–79 but much altered, displays archaeological evidence of its many uses. Parts of the Wakefield Tower (1220–40), such as the King's Bed Chamber, are furnished in 13th-century style and a torture exhibition has been added. A spiral staircase leads to a walkway on top of the south wall, which provides a good view of the riverside defences. The wall runs to the Lanthorn Tower (1883) containing 13th-century artefacts.

The White Tower

The oldest part of the fortress, the White Tower, was probably designed in 1078 by a Norman monk, Gandulf, a prolific builder of castles and churches. It has walls 15ft (5 metres) thick. Its original form remains, but nearly every part has been refurbished or rebuilt: the door surrounds and most windows were replaced in the 17th and 18th centuries, and much of the Normandy stone was replaced with more durable Portland stone from Dorset. The first floor gives access to the austere Chapel of St John the Evangelist, a fine example of early Norman architecture. Much of the remaining space is devoted to displays of armour, swords and muskets, taken from the Royal Armouries. Legend has it that London will fall if the ravens who nest here ever leave the Tower – so their wings are clipped to ensure they stay.

A Tower raven.

the Bloody Tower. Note that the spiral staircases in some of the towers require a degree of agility. Within the Tower walls, picnics are permitted on any of the seats. There are also snack kiosks and a restaurant in the New Armouries. In winter you can go ice-skating just outside the Tower's walls, with lovely views of the river.

MORE MODERN THAN MEDIEVAL

Given that so much of the country's turbulent history was played out within these walls, the Tower conspicuously lacks the romantic aura that many visitors expect. The reason is that, until comparatively recently, its buildings were functional – as well as serving as a fort, arsenal, palace and prison, it also contained at various times a treasury, public record office, observatory, royal mint and zoo. As a result, it was frequently remodelled and renovated, especially in the 19th century, so that many floors and staircases, for example, look more modern than medieval. But then, how could the boards that Henry VIII trod hope to survive the footfalls of 2.5 million tourists a year?

Any sense of awe is also undermined by the brightly uniformed 'Beefeaters'. Although all have served in the armed forces for at least 22 years, some have enthusiastically embraced showbiz, apparently auditioning for the role of pantomime villain by alternating jocular banter with visitors and melodramatically delivered descriptions of torture and beheadings. In contrast, pike and musket drills by the English Civil War Society are conducted with the masterful lethargy of confirmed pacifists.

The upper chamber of Wakefield Tower was used as a throne room by Henry III and later converted into an anteroom of the King's private chambers by his son, Edward I. Wakefield Tower also housed the state archives from 1360 to 1856 and, for a time, served as the Jewel House.

Attired in Tudor uniforms, Yeoman warders first took up their posts under Edward VI and have been guarding the Tower for more than 500 years. Their nickname

"Beefeaters" may derive from the French word buffetier, meaning servant, although an "eater" was also used in English to describe a servant. In 2007 the first female Beefeater, Moira Cameron, was appointed. Like her fellow male Beefeaters she has a military background. Among the perks of the job of a Beefeater is the use of a subsidised apartment within the Tower of London.

Sir Walter Raleigh's room in the Bloody Tower (1603–16).

In character as Isaac Newton, former Master of the Royal Mint at the Tower of London.

THE HIGHLIGHTS

The Wall Walk
The walk along this defensive outer wall takes in the eastern towers. Access is through the Salt Tower, often used as a prison. Next are the Broad Arrow Tower, also once a lock-up, the Constable Tower, which contains a model depicting the Tower in the 14th century, and the Martin Tower, which houses an exhibition on the Crown Jewels.

The Royal Fusiliers' Museum
In the centre of the Tower is the modest but elegantly housed Royal Fusiliers' Museum. Opened in 1962, it follows the regiment's campaigns from its first battle for William of Orange against the French in Walcourt up to its more recent peace-keeping involvement in the Balkans and Northern Ireland. The regiment was almost destroyed in the American War of Independence.

The Crown Jewels
These are displayed in the neo-Gothic Waterloo Barracks, built in 1845. The queues here can be long, with airport-style barriers. At the centre of the display are a dozen crowns and a glittering array of swords, sceptres and orbs used on royal occasions. A moving walkway ensures that visitors cannot linger over the principal exhibits, but many other glass cases contain gold dishes, chalices and altar dishes that can be viewed at leisure. The collection includes the notorious Koh-i-Noor diamond.

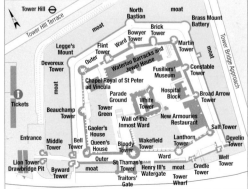

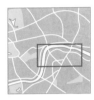

SOUTHWARK AND THE SOUTH BANK

The historic area south of the Thames has been transformed into a vibrant entertainment centre. Its multiple attractions, ranging from the London Eye and Tate Modern to Tower Bridge, are linked by an attractive riverside walk.

Southwark is one of the oldest parts of the capital. The first bridge across the Thames was built by the Romans near London Bridge, and the community around it developed separately from the City, as it lay beyond the City's jurisdiction. In Shakespeare's day it was the place for putting on unlicensed plays and for setting up brothels, and it retained its reputation as an area of vice well into the 19th century. The regeneration around Tate Modern, Borough Market and Butler's Wharf – coupled with Renzo Piano's new giant tower, The Shard – has transformed the area.

AROUND LAMBETH BRIDGE

Opposite the Houses of Parliament, beside Lambeth Bridge, is the red-brick **Lambeth Palace** ❶, which has been the London residence of the Archbishops of Canterbury since the 12th century. The fine Tudor brickwork of the entrance tower dates from 1485, but much of the rest is Victorian. The rare occasions on which the palace is open to the public include the annual Open House weekend (see page 55).

Adjacent, by Lambeth Bridge on Lambeth Palace Road, the garden and deconsecrated church of St

Second-hand book market outside the BFI.

Mary contains the **Garden Museum** (tel: 7401 8865; www.gardenmuseum. org.uk; Sun–Fri 10.30am–5pm, Sat 10.30am–4pm, closed first Mon of every month). It is based on the work of two 17th-century royal gardeners, the elder and younger John Tradescant, father and son, who introduced exotic fruits such as pineapples to Britain. The old-fashioned roses and herbaceous perennials are delightful, and the church's rich history is evident in its memorials, including one remembering HMS

EAT

The Garden Café, within the Garden Museum, is a great option for a bite to eat in the Lambeth Bridge area. The café serves home-cooked, vegetarian food, from aubergine and black bean chilli to delicately spiced soups and good cakes.

Lambeth Palace.

Bounty's Captain William Bligh, who lived locally in his later years.

Imperial War Museum ❷

Address: Lambeth Road, www.iwm. org.uk
Tel: 7416 5000
Opening Hrs: daily 10am–6pm
Entrance Fee: free except some special exhibitions
Transport: Elephant & Castle, Lambeth North

A 15-minute walk south from Lambeth Bridge, along Lambeth Road, leads to the **Imperial War Museum** (IWM London). The museum is currently undergoing extensive remodelling, creating new gallery spaces and improved facilities to do justice to this incredible collection and to mark the centenary of the outbreak of World War I in 2014.

The museum, of what Churchill termed 'the Age of Violence', was founded in 1917; at the opening ceremony it was stated that the museum 'was not a monument of military glory, but a record of toil and sacrifice'. In 1936 the museum was moved to the present building, which stands on the site of a 19th-century psychiatric hospital known as Bedlam, an inspired choice for a museum chronicling the horrors of modern warfare.

After World War II the museum began to gather material from this and later conflicts, and three smaller sites, including the warship HMS *Belfast* (see page 190), were acquired.

As part of the refit, the atrium space at the heart of the museum will be reworked to display iconic objects, including aircrafts, tanks and artillery, and there will be new shops and a park-side café. Other exhibits include one of Britain's leading collections of 20th-century art.

St Thomas's Hospital

Back by the river, close to Westminster Bridge, **St Thomas's Hospital** includes a reminder of warfare's

Southwark and the South Bank

nobler side: the **Florence Nightingale Museum** ❸ (2 Lambeth Palace Road; tel: 7620 0374; www.florence-nightingale.co.uk; daily 10am–5pm). Don't be deterred by the walk down Lambeth Palace Road, which is unattractive at this point; this small museum is worth the detour. It has a rich collection of memorabilia, and there are audio hotspots around the museum on the life and achievements of the woman whose work in the Crimean War of 1853–6 helped transform nursing.

COUNTY HALL ❹

Just downstream from Westminster Bridge and facing the Houses of Parliament is the majestic **County Hall**, designed in 1908 by architect Ralph Knott and for years the seat of the Greater London Council, which ran London until the government of Margaret Thatcher abolished it in 1986. It now incorporates the London Aquarium, the London Dungeon, an up-market hotel (the five-star Marriott), a budget hotel (a Premier Inn), a games arcade and several restaurants.

The first attraction as you walk eastwards along the river is **Namco Funscape** (www.namcofunscape-londonevents.co.uk; 10am–midnight), home to bumper cars, video games and a bowling alley. Better for children is the **London Sea Life Aquarium** (tel: 0871 663 1678; www.visitsealife.com/london; Mon–Thu 10am–6pm, last entry 5pm, Fri–Sun 10am–7pm, last entry 6pm). Thousands of specimens represent some 500 species of fish, and atmospheric sounds, smells and lighting are all employed to great effect. Highlights include the sharks and the touch pool.

County Hall is also the new home of the **London Dungeon** (tel: 0871 423 2240; www.thedungeons.com; Fri–Wed 10am–5pm, Thu 11am–5pm, weekends until 6pm; longer opening hours in school holidays).

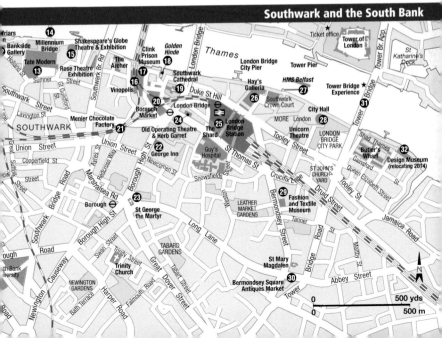

Southwark and the South Bank

The tour of the **London Dungeon** begins with an obligatory photo opportunity – head in the stocks, a blackened chopper at your neck. It's lots of fun for kids who are keen on the macabre, but it is pretty scary and the entire visit is spent in darkened corridors (often made more atmospheric by bloodcurdling shrieks), so it's not recommended for children under eight. Even under-12s must be accompanied by an adult. Queues tend to be long, so book in advance.

The London Eye.

Lasting about 1.5 hours, the actor-led tour features ghoulish exhibits of the Black Death, the Great Fire of 1666, Jack the Ripper's exploits, Sweeney Todd the barber's gruesome deeds, and a boat ride to hell. Guaranteed to make you jump at some point.

London Eye ❺

Address: County Hall, www.london eye.com
Tel: 0871 781 3000
Opening Hrs: daily Sept–Mar 10am–8.30pm, Apr–June 10am–9pm, Jul–Aug 10am–9.30pm. Closed 25 Dec and 1 week in Jan
Transport: Waterloo

Towering over County Hall is the **London Eye**, one of the world's largest observation wheels (the largest being the newer Singapore Flyer), designed by architects David Marks and Julia Barfield for the turn of the millennium.

The 32 enclosed capsules take 30 minutes to make a full rotation – a speed slow enough to allow passengers to step in and out of the capsules while the wheel keeps moving. On a clear day, you can see for 25 miles (40km). Book ahead (by phone or online) if you hope to ride the Eye at busy periods, although check the weather forecast first.

The area around the London Eye has been redeveloped into a pleasant park, called the Jubilee Gardens.

SOUTHBANK CENTRE ❻

The Southbank Centre (bookings tel: 0844 875 0073; www.southbankcentre. co.uk) is Britain's most vibrant arts centre. Its cafés, bars, book and record shops are open throughout the day, and there's usually something going on in one of the foyers.

Concert halls

The 2,900-seat **Royal Festival Hall** (RFH), the oldest and largest of the three concert halls on the South Bank, was constructed on the site of the Lion Brewery, destroyed by bombing during World War II. The building was opened in 1951 as part of the Festival of Britain, intended to improve the country's

morale after years of post-war austerity. Reopened in 2007 after extensive renovation, the hall now has improved acoustics, better facilities in the foyer and a renovated restaurant, Skylon.

There are two other concert halls within the complex, the 917-seater **Queen Elizabeth Hall**, opened in 1967 for music theatre and opera, and the 372-seater Purcell Room, intended for solo recitals and chamber music.

Hayward Gallery

Set on the upper level of the Southbank Centre complex is the **Hayward Gallery** (tel: 0844 875 0073; Mon noon–6pm, Tue–Wed, Sat–Sun 10am–6pm, Thu–Fri 10am–8pm), an outstanding example of 1960s brutalist architecture. Its cutting-edge programme focuses on the world's most adventurous and innovative artists. Recent exhibitions include William Eggleston, Dan Flavin, Antony Gormley, Ray Lichtenstein, Tracey Emin and Sam Taylor Wood.

The Hayward's mirrored **Waterloo Sunset Pavilion**, designed by Dan Graham as part of the regeneration of the Southbank, remains open in between main exhibitions. The gallery roof is often used as exhibition space.

BFI Southbank

Next door is BFI Southbank (the former National Film Theatre; www.bfi.org.uk), Britain's leading art house cinema since 1952. With four cinemas, it holds over 2,400 screenings and events each year, from restored silent movies (with live piano accompaniment) to world cinema productions.

In the Mediathèque, visitors can browse the British Film Institute's archive free. The Riverfront Bar in front of the building, with trestle tables sheltering under Waterloo Bridge, is complemented by the chic Benugo Bar & Kitchen.

The BFI also runs the **BFI London IMAX Cinema ⑦**, which rises from the roundabout at the south end of Waterloo Bridge. Large format film is projected onto a screen 66ft high by 85ft wide (20 by 26 metres), the biggest in the UK. It also specialises in screening films in 3-D.

The National Theatre ⑧

On the other side of Waterloo Road, still by the river, is the concrete **National Theatre** (www.nationaltheatre.org.uk; see page 289). The theatre company first opened its doors in 1963 as the Old Vic under Laurence Olivier, but in 1976 the company moved to its new premises on the river, which incorporates three theatres: the large 1,200-seater Olivier; the 900-seater Lyttelton, a two-tier proscenium theatre; and the Cottesloe, a more intimate space, accessed at the side of the building.

For a peek behind the scenes, book a backstage tour (tel: 7452 3000; tours run six times a day Mon–Fri, twice on

see page 289

FACT

At 450ft (135 metres), the London Eye is one of the highest structures in London. The hub and spindle weigh 330 tonnes – more than 40 double-decker buses. On average, a whopping 10,000 people take a 'flight' on it every day – that's around 3.5 million people per year.

Fountain outside Queen Elizabeth Hall.

TIP

The area around the Southbank Centre is great for free entertainment, from lunch time concerts and 'Commuter Jazz' (Friday 5.15–6.45pm) at the concert halls to talks at the National Theatre. Further along the river, there are often free concerts and talks at Tate Modern.

The BFI London IMAX Cinema.

Sat and once on Sun, and last 1 hour 15 mins).

At this point, a detour down Waterloo Road, past the IMAX cinema (see page 183), leads to The Cut and the elegant **Old Vic Theatre** ❾ (www.oldvictheatre.com), erected in 1811. A music hall in its early days, it is now a repertory theatre with Hollywood star Kevin Spacey as artistic director. Backstage tours are available (tel: 7928 2651 for dates).

Located a little further along The Cut is the **Young Vic** ❿, a theatre especially known for nurturing the talent of young theatre directors.

GABRIEL'S WHARF TO BANKSIDE

Back on the riverfront, to the east of the National Theatre, is Gabriel's Wharf, a cluster of shops and restaurants. East again is the **Art Deco Oxo Tower** ⓫. Architect Albert Moore had grand ideas for this project: as well as erecting what was to become London's second highest commercial building, he wanted to use electric lights to spell out the name of the gravy powder. When planning permission was refused due to an advertising ban, Moore came up with the idea of using three letters – O, X and O – as 10ft (3-metre) -high windows looking out north, south, east and west. Inside the tower are several smart restaurants.

Beyond Blackfriars Bridge, the riverside walk leads past the **Bankside Gallery** ⓬ (tel: 7928 7521; www.bankidegallery.com; daily 11am–6pm), home of the Royal Watercolour Society and the Royal Society of Painter-Printmakers, which holds exhibitions.

Tate Modern ⓭

Address: Bankside, www.tate.org.uk
Tel: 7887 8888
Opening Hrs: Sun–Thu 10am–6pm, Fri–Sat 10am–10pm
Entrance Fee: free except for special exhibitions
Transport: Southwark or London Bridge

Easily identifiable by its tall brick chimney, Tate Modern occupies the former Bankside Power Station and houses the Tate's international modern art collection and part

of its contemporary collection. A new building is being added to the south of the Tate which will create new galleries and more public space. Work is expected to be completed by 2016, but the main gallery remains open.

In addition to the art, a highlight of the Tate Modern is the view across the Thames to St Paul's Cathedral from the upper floors. (For full coverage, see page 194.)

Millennium Bridge ⑭

Giving easy access to Tate Modern from St Paul's Cathedral, the Millennium Bridge was the first new river crossing in central London since Tower Bridge opened in 1894.

Designing the footbridge was tricky: it had to be slender enough not to spoil the view of St Paul's from Bankside, yet it also had to make an impact as a significant millennial sculpture. The solution, a sort of stainless-steel scalpel, was provided by architect Norman Foster, sculptor Anthony Caro and engineers Ove Arup and Partners. However, opening-day crowds caused the bridge to sway excessively, and it had to be closed for two years for adjustments.

Shakespeare's Globe ⑮

Address: New Globe Walk, www.shakespearesglobe.com
Tel: box office 7401 9919
Opening Hrs: tours regularly
Entrance Fee: charge for tours
Transport: London Bridge or Southwark

Bankside and Southwark are the most historic areas of the South Bank. They grew up in competition with the City opposite, but by the 16th century had become vice dens. Bankside was famous for brothels, bear- and bull-baiting, prize fights and the first playhouses, including the Globe.

The replica of the 1599 building opened in 1996 and is worth a visit even if you're not seeing a play. It has been painstakingly re-created using the original methods of construction and has an open roof (the season runs from May to early October). It can accommodate around 1,500 people – 600 standing (called 'groundlings'

Skateboarders on the South Bank.

Street performer.

THE NATIONAL THEATRE

The idea of a National Theatre was suggested in 1848, but it wasn't until 1912, when Lilian Baylis became manager of the Old Vic Theatre, that the basis for a National Theatre was established. Baylis turned the old Victorian music hall into 'the home of Shakespeare and opera in English', but finding a site for a permanent theatre proved difficult. During World War II, the government introduced funding for the arts as part of the war effort, the London County Council made land available on the South Bank, and in 1949 the National Theatre Bill was passed through Parliament. In 1962 Laurence Olivier was named artistic director, and his first play opened the following year.

The Old Vic remained the company's home while the new theatre was being built, by architect Denys Lasdun. In 1976, after more than a century of controversy, the National Theatre was opened by the Queen, by which time Peter Hall was the director. He was succeeded by Richard Eyre in 1988 and Trevor Nunn in 1997. The current director, Nicholas Hytner, has had some success in broadening the theatre's appeal by offering some cheaper seats. In 2013 the National Theatre celebrated its 50th anniversary with a series of special events drawing on its history.

TIP

A novel way to travel
between Tate Modern
and Tate Britain (see
page 73) is to take the
Tate Boat. It runs every
40 minutes during
gallery hours and also
stops at the London Eye.

and liable to get wet if it rains) and
the rest seated. The wooden benches
feel rather hard by Act III, but you
can bring or rent cushions.

A new indoor theatre will open
in 2014, named after the Globe's
founder Sam Wanamaker. This
will be a candlelit venue in keeping with theatre performances in
Shakespeare's time.

The Rose Theatre

Shakespeare also acted at the Rose
Theatre, whose foundations were discovered close to the Globe in 1989.
Turn down New Globe Walk (by
the Globe's box office) and then left
into Park Street. This was Bankside's
first theatre, built in 1587. Events
are staged here and tours take place
when guided tours of the Globe are
not possible (tel: 7261 9565; charge).

BANKEND

Back on the riverside walk, past
Southwark Bridge on the stretch
known as Bankend, is the Anchor
Inn. The present building (1770–5)
is the sole survivor of the 22 busy
inns that once lined Bankside. Dr

The Oxo Tower.

Samuel Johnson, of dictionary fame,
drank here.

Vinopolis, City of Wine ⓰

Address: 1 Bank End, www.vinopolis.
co.uk
Tel: 7940 8300
Opening Hrs: Wed 6–9.30pm, Thu–
Fri 2–10pm, Sat noon–9.30pm, Sun

*The Millennium Bridge,
looking towards St
Paul's Cathedral.*

1–5pm; last tour 2 hours before closing
Transport: London Bridge

Opposite the eastern side of the pub, occupying 2.5 acres (1 hectare) of cathedral-like space under railway arches, the sprawling Vinopolis, City of Wine offers a visual wine tour through exhibits of the world's wine regions. Individual audio units give access to four hours of recorded commentary in six languages, and the admission charge includes tickets for wine tastings. Guided tours are held on Sundays at 1pm.

Clink Street

Like most country bishops, the bishops of the powerful see of Winchester had a London base. A single gable wall remains of Winchester Palace, their former London residence. They had their own laws, regulated the many local brothels and were the first authority in England to lock up miscreants. The prison they founded, in what is now Clink Street, remained a lock-up until the 18th century. The **Clink Prison Museum** ⓱ (tel: 7403 0900; www.clink.co.uk; Jul–Sep daily 10am–9pm, Oct–June Mon–Fri 10am–6pm, Sat–Sun until 7.30pm) recalls the area's seedy past.

Clink Street leads on to Pickfords Wharf, built in 1864 for storing hops, flour and seeds, and now converted into an apartment block. At the end of the street, in **St Mary Overie Dock**, is a replica of Sir Francis Drake's splendid galleon, the **Golden Hinde** ⓲ (tel: 7403 0123; www.golden hinde.com; daily 10am–5.30pm).

Launched in 1973, the ship is the only replica to have completed a circumnavigation of the globe, and has now clocked up more nautical miles than the original, in which Drake set sail on his voyage of discovery in 1577.

Southwark Cathedral ⓳

Address: London Bridge,
https://cathedral.southwark.anglican.org
Tel: 7367 6700
Opening Hrs: daily 8am–6pm
Entrance Fee: free
Transport: London Bridge

Southwest of London Bridge and hemmed in by the railway, Southwark

Note that there are no tours of Shakespeare's Globe theatre during performances. If you are visiting when a matinée is on, you will be given a tour of the Rose, Bankside's first playhouse, instead.

Shakespeare's Globe.

The Golden Hinde.

Cathedral is a rich fund of local history. A memorial to Shakespeare in the south aisle, paid for by public subscription in 1912, shows the bard reclining in front of a frieze of 16th-century Bankside. Above it is a modern (1954) stained-glass window depicting characters from his plays. Shakespeare was a parishioner for several years. John Harvard, who gave his name to the American university, was baptised here, and is commemorated in the Harvard Chapel.

The cathedral holds free organ recitals every Monday (1pm) and classical concerts on Tuesday (3.15–4pm).

BOROUGH

The area around London Bridge is in the throes of a regeneration programme. Much of its Dickensian character lingers, adding greatly to its appeal. In addition to Borough Market, there are several quirky museums and many restaurants, cafés and specialist shops.

Borough Market ❷⓿

Address: Southwark Street, www.boroughmarket.org.uk
Tel: 7407 1002

The George.

Opening Hrs: Thu 11am–5pm, Fri noon–6pm, Sat 8am–5pm
Transport: London Bridge

The highlight of the area is Borough Market, a wholesale food market dating from the 13th century. On Thursday, Friday and Saturday (the last two are the busiest days) a popular retail market offers gourmet and organic products. Apart from basics such as fruit and vegetables, you will find stalls specialising in seafood, game, oils and vinegars, cakes, preserves, fresh pasta, juices, wines and beers.

Southwark Street

A brief diversion down Southwark Street is the splendid Victorian Hop Exchange (now offices), with The Wheatsheaf in its cellar. A cross between bar and pub, it serves hearty pub grub, shows Sky sports, has black and white photographs decorating its walls and is often lively.

Further along Southwark Street, the **Menier Chocolate Factory ❷❶** (51–3 Southwark Street; box office: 7378 1713; www.menierchocolatefactory. com) sits on the corner of O'Meara Street. Housed within this 1870s

Tate Modern.

chocolate factory is a 150-seat theatre, plus bar and restaurant.

Borough High Street

Situated on Borough High Street, the main road south from London Bridge, is the 17th-century **George Inn** ㉒ (No. 77), the only remaining galleried coaching inn in London and mentioned in Dickens' Little Dorrit. Further down the street is the renovated **Church of St George the Martyr** ㉓ (www.stgeorge-the martyr.co.uk), also known as 'Little Dorrit's Church', because Dickens' heroine was baptised and married there. She is represented in stained glass in the east window. There are free recitals at 1pm on the third Thursday of each month.

London Bridge area

Back towards London Bridge, at 9a St Thomas Street, is the **Old Operating Theatre Museum & Herb Garret** ㉔ (tel: 7188 2679; www.thegarret.org. uk; daily 10.30am–5pm), the only surviving 19th-century operating theatre in Britain. It offers insights into the fearsome medical techniques of the day. The Herb Garret displays herbs and equipment used in the preparation of medicines.

Next to London Bridge station is **The Shard** ㉕. The tallest building in Western Europe, at 1,106ft (310 metres) high, it is a mix of residential and office space, and includes a restaurant and 5-star hotel. You can take a lift to the 72nd floor for unobstructed views of the city and beyond

EAT

There are lots of opportunities to sample the produce free at Borough Market. Many stalls also do takeaway food, from venison burgers to scallops that are pan-fried while you wait. For a posh sit-down meal, try Roast (see page 192), on the first floor; breakfast (Mon–Fri till 11am, later on Saturday) is a great way to enjoy the up-market dining experience at a fraction of the cost of lunch or dinner.

Southwark Cathedral.

LONDON BRIDGE

The present London Bridge, dating from 1967–72, is the latest of many on this site. Until Westminster Bridge opened in 1750, the crossing here was the only bridge across the Thames in London. A wooden bridge had existed here since the Romans, but the first stone bridge, later lined with houses, was erected in 1176 and completed 33 years later. In 1823–31 a new bridge of five stone arches was built, but in 1972, having been sold to American businessman Robert P. McCulloch for US$2.46 million, it was dismantled and re-erected in Arizona. Some claimed that McCulloch bought London Bridge in error, thinking that it was the much grander Tower Bridge. He denied this.

The Old Operating Theatre Museum.

(www.theviewfromtheshard.com; check website for opening times; book in advance).

Down Tooley Street is **Hay's Galleria** , a setting for shops, craft stalls and restaurants. The 60ft (18-metre) kinetic sculpture in the centre is David Kemp's The Navigators.

HMS *Belfast* ㉗

Downstream from Hay's Galleria is HMS *Belfast*, the last of the warships to have seen action in World War II (tel: 7940 6300; www.iwm.org.uk/visits; daily Mar–Oct 10am–6pm, Nov–Feb 10am–5pm; last entry one hour before closing). You can explore the whole ship, from the bridge to the engine rooms; there's an interactive Operations Room, and a taste of battle in the Gun Turret Experience.

To its east, the oval-shaped building is **City Hall** ㉘, seat of the Greater London Authority, the body that governs London. In front is The Scoop, a sunken amphitheatre staging free theatre, music and films in summer.

City Hall.

Bermondsey Street

A 10-minute detour southeast leads to hip Bermondsey Street, lined with stylish restaurants, bars, boutiques and galleries. At No. 83, you can't miss the pink-and-orange **Fashion and Textile Museum** ㉙ (tel: 7407 8664; www.ftmlondon.org; Tue–Sat 11am–6pm), the creation of British designer Zandra Rhodes. It celebrates fashion via exhibitions and its own academy.

At the other end of the street, on Friday morning only, is **Bermondsey Square Antiques Market** ㉚, which has successfully shed its bad reputation. Arrive early if you are after a bargain as the hundreds of traders start gathering at 4am.

Tower Bridge ㉛

Dating from 1894 the Victorian Gothic Tower Bridge is one of London's most iconic structures. Despite its mock-medieval cladding, it contains 11,000 tons of steel, and sophisticated engineering raises its middle portion to allow tall ships

SHOPPING

Antiques

Bermondsey's early-morning Friday antiques market at Bermondsey Square, SE1, is a major trading event. The best items change hands by 10am.

Food and Drink

Konditor & Cook
10 Stoney St, SE1
Tel: 0844 854 9363; www.konditorandcook.com
Delicious cakes plus hot and cold lunches.

Vinopolis
1 Bank End, SE1
Tel: 7940 8300; www.vinopolis.co.uk
A large branch of Majestic Wines and the well-stocked Whiskey Exchange, attached to the wine-tasting and dining complex.

Historical characters at the Clink Prison Museum.

opens around 500 times a year, with its bascules taking 90 seconds to lift.

The structure contains **Tower Bridge Experience** (tel: 7403 3761; www.towerbridge. org.uk; Apr–Sept 10am–6pm, Oct–Mar 9.30am–5.30pm), an exhibition detailing the history of the bridge and explaining how the mechanism works. The view from Tower Bridge's high walkways is magnificent.

Around Butlers Wharf

The old warehouses east of Tower Bridge contain a gourmet's delight. The gourmet in question is Habitat founder Sir Terence Conran, who opened several restaurants, such as Le Pont de la Tour (see page 192) in the biscuit-coloured **Butlers Wharf**.

The adjacent **Design Museum** ㉜ (tel: 7403 6933; www.designmuseum. org; daily 10am–5.45pm), inspired by Conran, showcases influential (mainly 20th-century) design through its permanent collection and excellent changing exhibitions. In late 2014 the museum will move to its new home in the former Commonwealth Institute building in Kensington.

through. When the capital was a flourishing port, it opened several times a day. In 1954 a bus driver was awarded a medal for putting his foot on the accelerator when, to his horror, he saw the bridge yawn open before him. The bus leapt over a 3ft (1-metre) gap. These days the bridge

DRINK

Further east along the south bank from Tower Bridge and the Design Museum is Rotherhithe, which has several good traditional pubs, including the Mayflower, where the Pilgrim Fathers moored their ship before sailing to Plymouth and America in 1620. It is close to the Brunel Museum (Railway Avenue; www.brunel-museum.org.uk; daily 10am–5pm) on the site of the Thames Tunnel: built by Isambard Kingdom Brunel it was the world's first under-river tunnel.

Tower Bridge.

BEST RESTAURANTS, PUBS, BARS AND CAFÉS

Restaurants

British

Butlers Wharf Chop House
Butlers Wharf Building, 36e Shad Thames, SE1. Tel: 7403 3403. www.chophouse-restaurant.co.uk Open: L & D daily. **££££** (set menu ££) [112 p316, D4]
Carnivores should go straight for the steak and kidney pudding, served with oysters, or pork loin and crackling. There are fish dishes for non-meat eaters. Other attractions include great river views and a terrace.

Roast
Floral Hall, Stoney St, SE1. Tel: 0845 034 7300. www.roast-restaurant.com Open: B

Paella at Borough Market.

Mon–Sat, bar brunch Mon–Thur, L daily, D Mon–Sat. **£££** [113 p316, B3]
Spectacularly set on the upper floor of Borough Market, with gorgeous views. Sourced from the market, the excellent food is resolutely British.

Fish

fish!
Cathedral St, SE1 Tel: 7407 3803. www.fishkitchen.com Open: L & D daily. **£££** [114 p316, B3]
Specialises in tasty GM-free fish in the shadow of Southwark Cathedral. Bar seats are fun but noisy.

Masters Super Fish
191 Waterloo Rd, SE1. Tel: 7928 6924. Open L Tue–Sat, D Mon–Sat. **£** [115 p314, E4]
Need a taxi? You'll find cabbies galore tucking into huge portions of fish and chips in this old-fashioned eatery.

French

RSJ
33a Coin St, SE1 Tel: 7928 4554. www.rsj.uk.com Open: L Mon–Fri, D Mon–Sat. **££–£££** [116 p314, E3]
This pretty restaurant offers pleasant dishes such as Gressingham duck with beetroot salad, but the real attraction is the excellent selection of wines from the Loire.

Italian

Zucca
184 Bermondsey St, SE1. Tel: 7378 6809. www.zuccalondon.com Open: L Tue–Sun, D Tue–Sat. **££–£££** [117 p316, C4]
Stylish restaurant serving deliciously authentic Italian food in a great location on hip Bermondsey Street. The signature dish is the deep fried pumpkin (zucca in Italian).

Modern European

The Anchor and Hope
36 The Cut, SE1. Tel: 7928 9898 Open: L Tue–Sun, D Mon–Sat. **££** [118 p314, E4]
Meat and offal feature strongly on the gastropub menu. Reasonable prices, hefty portions and friendly staff. The no-booking policy can mean long queues.

Cantina Vinopolis
1 Bank End, SE1. Tel: 7940 8333. www.cantinavinopolis.com Open: L Thur–Sat, D Mon–Sat. **£££** [119 p316, B3]
Full marks to the wine list (over 150 choices) at the restaurant in London's only wine museum. Then comes the decor – soaring cathedral-style arches. Appealing menu, too, with some dishes suitable for vegetarians.

Oxo Tower
Oxo Tower Wharf, Barge House St, SE1. Tel: 7803 3888. www.harveynichols.com Open: L & D daily. **££££** (set lunch £££) [120 p314, E3]
Some find it overpriced, but this iconic spot is still hugely popular. The biggest draw is the fabulous view of the Thames through huge windows.

Le Pont de la Tour
Butlers Wharf Building, 36d Shad Thames, SE1. Tel: 7403 8403; www.lepontdelatour.co.uk. Open: L & D daily. **££££** (set lunch £££) [121 p316, D4]
Prime ministers and presidents have enjoyed the splendid view of Tower Bridge from here, where the stress is on seafood. Impeccable but very expensive.

Southwark Cathedral Refectory
Southwark Cathedral, London Bridge, SE1. Tel: 7407 5740 Open: B & L daily. **£** [122 p316, B3]
This restaurant does hearty, well-priced soups and main dishes. The terrace is a bonus in summer. Open for morning coffee, lunch and afternoon tea (until 6pm).

Tate Modern Restaurant
Bankside, SE1. Tel: 7887 8888. Open: L daily, D Fri–Sat (last order 9.30pm). **££££** [123 p316, A3]
Great views, a buzz and an arty crowd are the attractions here. Level 2 Café is good for lunch, too, but lacks the views.

Union Street Café
47 Great Suffolk Street, SE1. Tel: 020 7592

7977. www.gordonramsay.com/uk-restaurants/union-street-café Open: L & D daily £££ [124] p316, A4]
Hidden a few streets behind the Tate Modern, this Gordon Ramsay project focuses on southern European dishes in an open industrial setting.

Spanish

Mesón Don Felipe
53 The Cut, SE1. Tel: 7928 3237. www.mesondonfelipe.com Open: L & D Mon–Sat. ££ [125] p314, E4]
Londoners in the know flock to this excellent tapas bar. Tables fill up fast, but there's often room at the bar.

Tapas Brindisa
18–20 Southwark St, SE1. Tel: 7357 8880. www.brindisa.com B Fri–Sat, L daily, D Mon–Sat. £££ [126] p316, B3]
Connected to one of the most popular stalls in Borough market, this restaurant is usually packed. Authentic tapas and a buzzing ambience. Some outside tables. No reservations taken.

Others

Baltic
74 Blackfriars Rd, SE1. Tel: 7928 1111. www.balticrestaurant.co.uk Open: L & D daily. ££ [127] p314, E4]
A cool bar filled with media types leads to the skylit dining room. Eastern European dishes feature, such as roast pork and spiced meatballs. Alternatively, try vodka and blinis at the bar.

The Cut Bar
Young Vic Theatre, 66 The Cut, SE1. Tel: 7928 4400. www.thecutbar.com Open: B, L & D Mon–Sat. ££ [128] p314, E4]
Set over two floors, this stylish bar/restaurant serves burgers alongside an eclectic mix of dishes, such as Alpine salad or watermelon curry.

Pubs, Bars and Cafés

Pubs

In Chaucer's *Canterbury Tales*, the Miller declares, 'And if the words get muddled in my tale, just put it down to too much Southwark ale.' Sobriety has never been a characteristic of this area, which still has many pubs.

The George Inn
77 Borough High St; http://gkpubs.co.uk/pubs-in-london/the-george-inn-pub [72] p316, B4]
Owned by the National Trust, this is London's only galleried coaching inn, and was a favourite haunt of Charles Dickens (it is mentioned in *Little Dorrit*).There are several wood-panelled rooms and a big courtyard where you can sit outside.

The Market Porter
9 Stoney St; www.markettaverns.co.uk/the_market_porter.html [73] p316, B4]
Real-ale pub in a great setting opposite Borough Market. Monday to Friday it opens its doors 6–8.30am for market workers.

The Wheatsheaf
6 Stoney St; www.wheatsheafborough.co.uk [74] p316, B4]
This popular pub moved back to its premises opposite Borough Market in December 2012 and is now even better. Nice cosy atmosphere in the main bar area, and there's a new heated garden with its own campervan bar. Great food too.

Bars

Boot and Flogger
10–20 Redcross Way; www.davy.co.uk/bootandflogger [75] p316, B4]
For a traditional wine bar, try the Boot and Flogger, named after a corking device. Reminiscent of a gentleman's club, it has lots of dark panelled cubby holes and an excellent wine list.

Brew Wharf
Brew Wharf Yard, Stoney St; www.brew wharf.com [76] p316, B3]
Set under the railways arches near Borough Market, Brew Wharf has a micro-brewery and does gastropub-style food. There's a pleasant outdoor space for alfresco dining and drinking.

Pit Bar
The Old Vic, The Cut; www.oldvictheatre.com/fooddrink/ [77] p314, E4]
The bar in the basement of the Old Vic is open till late (closed Sundays).

The Wine Wharf
Stoney St [78] p316, B3]
Part of Vinopolis and one down from Brew Wharf, this wine bar offers great wines and light meals in a cool under-the-railway-arches setting (closed Sunday).

Cafés

Café 171
171 Union St [79] p316, A4]
In the Jerwood Space, a new gallery and rehearsal rooms, this café serves good food (salads, omelettes, soups) at reasonable prices.

Konditor & Cook
Stoney St and Cornwall Rd [80] p314 and p316, B3]
There are a couple of tables outside the Stoney Street branch, but this is more the place to come for takeaway food – it's lost favour now that so many eating places have opened up in the market nearby, but the food is still excellent. Hot and cold dishes, quiches, pizzas and great sandwiches.

Monmouth Coffee Co.
2 Park St; www.monmouthcoffee.co.uk/shops/the-borough [81] p316, B3]
Lovely place for fresh coffee and incredibly helpful knowledgeable staff to help you choose the best beans for your brew. Pastries and scrumptious chocolates.

Catching up at Borough Market.

TATE MODERN

Once it generated electricity. Now it is a powerhouse of modern and contemporary art.

Exploring the exhibits.

Tate Modern has caught the public's imagination in a quite unprecedented way, both for its displays and its building, a magnificent presence on the South Bank. The redundant Bankside Power Station, a massive horizontal block with a huge central tower, has been transformed into a gallery showcasing the Tate's collection of modern and contemporary art. Machinery from within the power station was removed to create an entrance the height of the building; three gallery floors, shops and cafés, a restaurant and an auditorium were piled into a compact bank on one side. From the windows are fabulous views of St Paul's Cathedral across the river. On the other side is the vast Turbine Hall, a stunning exhibition space. A new gallery is being built to the south of the Tate Modern (due for completion in 2016), and a bridge across the Turbine Hall will provide the link between the two galleries.

Whaam! by Roy Lichtenstein (1923–97), on show at Tate Modern. Lichtenstein's interest in Americana dated from the early 1950s, but his involvement in pop art received a crucial boost from one of his young sons, who showed him a Mickey Mouse comic book and said: "I bet you can't paint as good as that."

Kandinsky's Swinging (1925). Kandinsky began his artistic career as a figurative landscape painter in Russia, but moved towards abstraction through the influence of German Expressionism. He used colour for emotional effect. Also in Tate Modern's permanent collection is Kandinsky's Cossacks (1910–11).

The Essentials

Address: Bankside; www.tate.org.uk
Tel: 7887 8888
Opening Hrs: Sun–Thu 10am–6pm, Fri–Sat 10am–10pm
Entrance Fee: free except for special exhibitions
Transport: Southwark or London Bridge

Chinese artist Ai Weiwei's Sunflower Seeds, one of the many installations that have graced the Turbine Hall. This installation was made up of around 100 million individually crafted ceramic 'seeds' that covered 1000 sq m (10,764 sq ft).

THE COLLECTION

An exhibit from the permanent collection.

In order to make the permanent collection more accessible to, and more popular with, the general public, the works are ordered by theme. Note that the displays change from time to time, so the examples picked out here may not all be on show when you visit.

The permanent collection is hung in four suites, over three floors. On level 2 is 'Poetry and Dream', where the focus is on Surrealist artists and their associates. A large central room (Room 2) includes works by Joan Miró, Picasso, Giacometti, Max Ernst, Salvador Dalí, Francis Bacon, Joseph Beuys and Giorgio de Chirico. Transformed Visions is on level 3, exploring abstract art and its influences. This is where you'll find Mark Rothko's Seagram Murals, paintings which were originally commissioned for the Four Seasons Restaurant in Manhattan but which Rothko eventually decided to give to the Tate.

On level 4 are Energy and Process and Structure and Clarity, with the former showcasing artists, such as the Italian Arte Povera movement of the 1960s and 70s, who are interested in transformation and natural forces. Structure and Clarity explores the development of abstract art since the early 20th century, includingi Cubism, Futurism and Vorticism, with work by Georges Braque, Paul Cézanne, Fernand Léger, Roy Lichtenstein, Auguste Rodin, Henri Matisse and Bridget Riley.

Tate Modern posters.

Natural History Museum entrance.

KNIGHTSBRIDGE, KENSINGTON AND NOTTING HILL

Knightsbridge and Kensington have long been the home of the British upper classes, and the areas' cultural attractions reflect their dilettantish interests. Neighbouring Notting Hill Gate is more diverse, younger and edgier.

These three areas of London encompass many of its best features: Knightsbridge has grand architecture, designer shops and two of London's top department stores; Kensington is home to three world-class museums and Queen Victoria's monuments to her husband Prince Albert; Notting Hill Gate, the stamping ground of the young, hip and famous, has Portobello Road, one of London's funkiest street markets.

In the heart of all this is a huge area of parkland, where you can skate, jog, hire a boat or just stroll around and forget you're in the city, and throughout the area are pretty cobbled mews and squares lined with elegant town houses that make venturing off the main streets rewarding.

This chapter begins at Hyde Park Corner, proceeds via Knightsbridge to Kensington and Notting Hill Gate, and then dips into Kensington Gardens and Hyde Park.

HYDE PARK CORNER

At the junction of Piccadilly, Park Lane and Knightsbridge, **Hyde Park Corner** is a major hub of traffic now, but it used to stand on the outskirts of London.

Apsley House ❶

Address: 149 Piccadilly, Hyde Park Corner, www.english-heritage.org.uk
Tel: 7499 5676
Opening Hrs: Apr–Oct Wed–Sun 11am–5pm, Nov–Mar weekends only 10am–4pm
Transport: Hyde Park Corner

The mansion on the northern side of Hyde Park Corner is known colloquially as No. 1, London, as it was the first house you came to after passing through the tollgates at the top of Knightsbridge. Built in

Outdoor drinks on Beauchamp Place.

1770 by Robert Adam, and owned by Arthur Wellesley, the first Duke of Wellington, in 1816, just after he had defeated Napoleon at Waterloo, it is still lived in by the Wellesley family. Inside are collections of furniture, silver and porcelain, and paintings by Velázquez, Rubens, Van Dyck and Goya. Among its sculptures is a huge nude of Napoleon by Canova.

Wellington Arch ❷ (tel: 7930 2726; Apr–Oct Wed–Sun 10am–5pm, Nov–early Dec until 4pm; may close for functions so ring ahead), in the middle of Hyde Park Corner, was designed in 1828 as part of a grand approach to London. The huge bronze statue of a charioteer and four horses (the *Quadriga*) depicts the angel of peace descending on the chariot of war.

KNIGHTSBRIDGE

Running west of Hyde Park Corner is Knightsbridge, where you'll find

A cabmen's shelter in front of the V&A Museum, one of 13 still dotted around London. Now Grade II-listed, they provide shelter and refreshment for cab drivers.

two of London's most famous stores: Harrods and Harvey Nichols.

Harvey Nichols ❸, well known for its innovative window displays, opened on the corner of Knightsbridge and Sloane Street in the 1880s; with eight floors of fashion, beauty and home collections, it caters to a

Knightsbridge, Kensington and Notting Hill

discerning – and affluent – clientele. The Fifth Floor is a very smart place to eat (see page 209).

Harrods ❹

Address: 87–135 Brompton Road, www.harrods.com
Tel: 7730 1234
Opening Hrs: Mon–Sat 10am–8pm, Sun noon–6pm
Transport: Knightsbridge

Nearby in Brompton Road, **Harrods** is hard to miss, especially at night when it is brightly illuminated. The food hall is ornately decorated and sells a wide range of gourmet items; it's worth looking, even if you only come out with a tin of speciality tea. The store's famous January sales see the British lose their dignity in the scramble to save hundreds of pounds.

The store was started by Henry Charles Harrod when his grocery business opened in 1849, although the present building was opened in 1905. The Egyptian Al-Fayed brothers bought the store and other House of Fraser outlets for £615 million in 1983, and the flamboyant Mohamed Al-Fayed (whose son Dodi died with Princess Diana in the 1997 Paris car crash) owned the store until 2010, when he sold it to Qatar Holdings.

Beauchamp Place ❺ (pronounced *Beecham*), a stylish street west of Harrods lined with designer stores and expensive restaurants, is the stamping ground of the well-heeled, including sundry royals.

Beyond Harrods, at the point where Brompton Road branches left, is the Roman Catholic **Brompton Oratory ❻** (www.bromptonoratory.com; daily 7am–6pm), a flamboyant Italian baroque building designed by a 29-year-old architect, Herbert Gribble. Opened in 1884, its huge dome, extravagant decor and gilded mosaics are seldom seen in British churches.

SOUTH KENSINGTON

South Kensington exudes affluence; Christie's has an auction house here, in Old Brompton Road, and there are plenty of designer shops and up-market restaurants.

It's also very cosmopolitan: the Lycée Français is at 35 Cromwell Road, teaching the children of the many French people who live in the area, and the German Goethe Institute is in Princes Gate.

You can take a lift inside Wellington Arch up to the galleried balconies, from where there are good views all around, including into the gardens of Buckingham Palace.

Harrods lights up at night.

Exhibition Road is pedestrianised.

Three Victorian museums

At the heart of South Kensington are three world-class museums: The Victoria and Albert Museum, the Natural History Museum and the Science Museum, which owe their existence to the spirit and enterprise of the Victorian age. In 1851, the Great Exhibition, held in Hyde Park, was an astonishing success. For the first time elements of the far-flung Victorian Empire were brought under the curious gaze of the public. The idea for the exhibition had come from Henry Cole (1808–82), chairman of the Society of Arts, and it had been taken up enthusiastically by Prince Albert.

More than 6 million visitors came to the park to see the Crystal Palace, and after it moved to Sydenham, south London, the following year, the profits were used to purchase 87 acres (35 hectares) of land in adjoining South Kensington to build a more permanent home for the arts and sciences.

Dinosaur in the central hall.

Greatest of them all is undoubtedly the **Victoria and Albert Museum** ❼, popularly known as the V&A, which Henry Cole began assembling the year after the Great Exhibition, though Queen Victoria did not lay the foundation stone of the current building until 1899, 38 years after Albert died. It was the first museum to be gas-lit, allowing working people to visit in the evening after finishing their jobs. For a detailed guide to its collections, see page 212.

On the other side of Exhibition Road is the neo-Gothic pile of the **Natural History Museum** ❽, built between 1873 and 1880. With its collection of 75 million plants, animals, fossils, rocks and minerals and, of course, its dinosaurs, it is justly celebrated and a big hit with children. For details, see page 214.

The **Science Museum** ❾, round the corner in Exhibition Road, traces the history of inventions from the first steam train – Stephenson's Rocket – to the battered command module from the Apollo 10 space mission, and is a particular favourite of children. The Wellcome Wing focuses on contemporary science and technology. See page 210 for more details.

Music and geography

Further up Exhibition Road, on Prince Consort Road, is the **Royal College of Music**, containing the **Museum of Music** ⑩ (tel: 7591 4842; www.rcm.ac.uk; Tue–Fri 11.30am–4.30pm in term time and summer holidays only; free), a collection of over 1,000 instruments from 1480 to the present.

On the corner of Exhibition Road and Kensington Gore is the **Royal Geographical Society** (tel: 7591 3000; www.rgs.org; Mon–Fri 10am–5pm). Only exhibitions in the Pavilion, and the Foyle Reading Room are open to the public.

Royal Albert Hall ⑪

Address: Kensington Gore, www.royal alberthall.com
Tel: 020 7838 3105(tours); 020 7589 8212 (tickets)
Transport: South Kensington

The **Royal Albert Hall**, an ornate building with a capacity of 5,500, was opened in 1871 in honour of Prince Albert. The frieze around the outside illustrates 'The Triumph of Arts and Sciences'. Events here range from

Facade of the Natural History Museum.

On the corner of Queen's Gate Terrace, opposite the Natural History Museum, is **Baden-Powell House**, with a statue of the Boy Scouts' founder standing on watch outside. It is now a budget hostel, but there is a small exhibition area dedicated to Lord Baden-Powell (1857–1941).

PRINCE ALBERT

Albert of Saxe-Coburg-Gotha, born in Germany in 1819, was Queen Victoria's first cousin. When they married in 1839, both aged 20, his English was limited, but he worked to improve it. Initially unpopular with the British public and with no official role, his position was not easy at first, although over time he gained considerable influence in both royal and state affairs. He enjoyed hunting and winter sports, and sired nine children. His great interest in the sciences and the natural world made him a typical Victorian and he was largely responsible for establishing the museums in South Kensington. Victoria was shattered when he died in 1861, spending the next 40 years mourning.

The Royal Albert Hall.

The Albert Memorial has been restored to its former gilded – some say gaudy – glory.

Edward Burne-Jones's house in Kensington Square.

clutching in his right hand the catalogue of the Great Exhibition which he masterminded. Marking the corners of the monument are symbols for the spread of the British Empire: a camel for Africa, a bull bison for America, an elephant for Asia and a cow for Europe (Australia, then the Empire's dumping ground for convicts, failed to merit a mention).

In a 1960s building next door to the Albert Hall is the **Royal College of Art**, where annual graduation exhibitions allow the public to buy the works of future greats. David Hockney and Henry Moore studied here.

KENSINGTON HIGH STREET

Kensington Gore runs into Kensington High Street, a useful shopping area, more compact and stylish than Oxford Street but with most of the big-name stores and fewer people. **Kensington Church Street**, branching off to the right towards Notting Hill Gate, is the place for antiques. On the corner behind the flower stall stands **St Mary Abbots Church** **⑬**, designed by Victorian architect Sir George Gilbert Scott, and a fine example of Victorian Gothic Revival. Walk through the cloisters to reach St Mary Abbots Gardens, a quiet spot away from the crowds. To the right, Kensington Church Walk is lined with exclusive boutiques. At the top, Holland Street, running off Kensington Church Street, has designer shops and a pretty pub, the Elephant and Castle.

Back on Kensington High Street, walk down Derry Street to the entrance to the **Roof Gardens** (tel: 7937 7994; call to check opening hours), a members' club and restaurant (Babylon, see page 208), six storeys above street level. With 1.5 acres (0.6 hectares) of ornamental gardens and views over west London, this is one of the most original places to eat in the city. The

boxing to rock concerts, but the hall is best known for the Proms, a series of BBC-sponsored classical concerts running for eight weeks in the summer. Named after the promenading audience, they provide a rich diet of affordable music.

Queen Victoria's most expressive tribute to her **husband is the Albert Memorial ⑫** in Kensington Gardens, opposite the Albert Hall. Designed by Sir George Gilbert Scott, it depicts the prince as a god or philosopher, gardens are themed with Spanish and English woodland areas and have resident flamingos.

Further down Derry Street is **Kensington Square** ⑭, one of the oldest in London, and an elegant mix of architectural styles dating from the late 17th century. The Pre-Raphaelite painter Edward Burne-Jones lived at No. 41, and the philosopher John Stuart Mill, another eminent Victorian, at No. 18.

West down Kensington High Street is the former Commonwealth Institute, which from late 2014 will be home to the **Design Museum** (see page 191). At the end of the street is **Leighton House Museum** ⑮ (12 Holland Park Road; tel: 7602 3316; Wed–Mon 10am–5.30pm; free guided tour Wed 3pm). The red-brick exterior conceals an extraordinary interior. The home of the Victorian artist Lord Leighton (1830–96), president of the Royal Academy, it is a mix of lavish Orientalism and conventional Victorian comforts. It contains his highly romanticised works, as well as many by fellow Pre-Raphaelites, but the centrepiece

Holland Park.

KIDS

Holland Park is great for kids. As well as the wildlife – rabbits, peacocks and squirrels – there is an adventure playground (for ages 6–15 approximately), and a smaller sand pit play area for children under 8. After they've let off steam, take them to the Japanese garden, which has a waterfall and stepping stones.

of the house is the grand Arab Hall, displaying Leighton's collection of Islamic tiles.

South of here is cosmopolitan **Earl's Court**, named after the earls of Oxford who owned the land in the 12th century. It is famous for its massive exhibition centre, built in 1937, which hosted the volleyball events in the 2012 Olympics.

Vintage shops line Portobello Road.

Dating from 1912, Peter Pan's statue in Kensington Gardens was erected secretly one night so it might seem as if it had appeared by magic.

Italian Garden, Kensington Palace.

To the west is **Olympia**, another exhibition centre. To the north is **Holland Park** , the grounds of the Jacobean Holland House, mostly destroyed in World War II. Peacocks preen among the formal gardens, and the ruins provide an appealing set for open-air concerts. For refreshments, try the restaurant in the Orangery, or the more informal café nearby.

NOTTING HILL

The northeastern exit of Holland Park leads to Holland Park Avenue, at the top of which is Notting Hill Gate, one of the hip areas of London.

Portobello Road Market

Address: Portobello Road, www.portobelloroad.co.uk
Opening Hrs: Mon–Wed, Fri–Sat 8am–6pm, Thu 8am–1pm; antiques market Sat 8am–6pm
Transport: Ladbroke Grove, Notting Hill Gate

On Saturdays, Notting Hill's Portobello Road is home to a vast antiques market. The antiques are concentrated in the more genteel southern end of the street, while further north, under the Westway flyover, a flea market mixes junk, cutting-edge fashion and arts and crafts (Fri–Sun). Between these two, the traditional fruit, veg and flower stalls blend with traders selling global foodstuffs.

As a backdrop to the stalls, the refurbished Electric Cinema is London's oldest surviving cinema (1905).

Off Portobello Road, on Blenheim Crescent, is the former **Travel Bookshop** (now a Book Warehouse), the setting for the 1999 romantic comedy *Notting Hill*, in which Hugh Grant improbably wooed Julia Roberts. What the film didn't convey is that Notting Hill is a melting pot in which many races and just about every social class rub shoulders.

Ladbroke Grove

Notting Hill's main north–south artery, **Ladbroke Grove**, is the parade route for the **Notting Hill Carnival**, a three-day Caribbean festival which takes over the area on the last weekend of August. West of Notting Hill (Shepherd's Bush or White City tube stations) is **Westfield**, a huge urban shopping centre where high street names rub shoulders with Armani, Louis Vuitton, Ted Baker and Ugg. There is a second branch by the Olympic Stadium in Stratford.

QUEENSWAY AND KENSINGTON GARDENS

Westbourne Grove heads eastwards to **Queensway** , home to Whiteleys Shopping Centre, which has cafés, restaurants and a cinema. At the top of Queensway, past the ice rink, is Kensington Gardens.

London's great green lung is **Hyde Park** and **Kensington Gardens**, which cover 1 sq mile

(2.5 sq km) – the same area as the City of London. Although they are a single open space, they are two distinct parks, divided by West Carriage Drive.

Kensington Palace ⑲

Address: Kensington Gardens, www.hrp.org.uk
Tel: 0844 482 7777
Opening Hrs: Mon–Sat 10am–5pm (last admission 4pm)
Transport: Notting Hill Gate, Queensway

On the west side of Kensington Gardens, overlooking the Round Pond, is **Kensington Palace**, the former home of Diana, Princess of Wales.

The palace was given its present appearance by Sir Christopher Wren and Nicholas Hawksmoor, and was the centre of the Court after William III bought the mansion in 1689. Several monarchs were born here, the last of them Victoria in 1819, who 18 years later was called from her bed to be told she had become Queen.

Portobello Market stallholder.

The state apartments have undergone major redevelopment, making previously unseen areas open to the public. A new display focuses on Princess Diana's clothes and

Hyde Park.

SHOPPING

Antiques

Westbourne Grove in W11 has many interesting dealers. The whole area comes to life on Friday and Saturday mornings when hordes of tourists descend on the antique arcades and stalls of Portobello Road market. **Kensington Church Street** in W8 is filled with a great variety of expensive antiques shops dealing in everything from fine art to porcelain. **Alfie's Antique Market** in Church Street, NW8, is London's largest indoor antiques bazaar and has a lively atmosphere. Many former dealers have now set up shops along the same road.

Clothing

Anya Hindmarch
15–17 Pont St, SW1
Tel: 7838 9177; www.anyahindmarch.com
London's bag queen sells lines ranging from the classic and bespoke leather to totes with pictures or environmental slogans printed on.

Rellik.

The Cross
141 Portland Rd, W11
Tel: 7727 6760; www.thecrossshop.co.uk
An eclectic mix of designers, both home-grown and imported, alongside own-brand cashmere at this trendy shop.

Lulu Guinness
3 Ellis St, SW1
Tel: 7823 4828; www.luluguinness.com
Fun, retro bags and other pieces, stylistically positioned between ladylike and kitsch.

Myla
77 Lonsdale Rd, W11
Tel: 7221 9222; www.myla.com
Sensual, gorgeous lingerie boutique. Also sells swimwear.

Rellik
8 Golbourne Rd, W10
Tel: 8962 0089; www.relliklondon.co.uk
Probably the most fashionable of London's many vintage emporiums, specialising in retro pieces from the 1920s to 1980s, many by iconic designers.

Temperley
6–7 Colville Mews, W11
Tel: 7229 7957; www.temperleylondon.com

Romantic, slightly bohemian dresses and daywear, popular with fashionistas.

Urban Outfitters
36–38 Kensington High St, W8
Tel: 7761 1001; www.urbanoutfitters.co.uk
Since the late 1990s this branch, the first Urban Outfitters in the UK, has been championing local young designers and quirky homewares.

Department Stores

Conran Shop
Michelin Building, 81 Fulham Rd, SW3
Tel: 7589 7401; www.conranshop.co.uk
Sir Terence Conran's unique and stylish shop sells designer furniture and household accessories, and in many ways resembles a design museum. Set within the beautiful Art Nouveau-tiled Michelin Building, it is worth a visit just to browse.

Harrods
87–135 Brompton Rd, SW1
Tel: 7730 1234; www.harrods.com
One of the world's largest and most famous department stores. Since the 19th century Harrods has maintained a reputation for quality and service, priding itself on stocking the best of everything. No one should miss the fabulous displays in the Edwardian tiled food halls, but some may find the rest of the store a little dark and claustrophobic. Harrods sales are major events but be prepared to queue.

Harvey Nichols
109–125 Knightsbridge SW1
Tel: 7235 5000; www.harveynichols.com
London's leading fashion department store, with an excellent range of women's designer fashions and footwear. Men and children are also well catered for.

Food and Drink

Justerini & Brooks
61 St James's St, SW1
Tel: 7484 6400; www.justerinis.com
Top range of wines and whiskies.

style, while another new exhibition explores Queen Victoria's story, with visitors being able to see the room in which she was born and the spot where she met Prince Albert.

Around the palace grounds are an attractive sunken garden and an Orangery, designed by Nicholas Hawksmoor in 1704 and modified by Sir John Vanbrugh. It has wood carvings by Grinling Gibbons and is now a café (see page 208).

A path east of the gilded main gates of Kensington Palace leads to **Kensington Gardens**. The lake on the eastern side (called The Long Water here, and the Serpentine in Hyde Park) has, at its northern edge, the delightful **Italian Garden**, commissioned by Prince Albert, with fountains and a statue of Edward Jenner, who developed the vaccination against smallpox. The loggia in Italian Renaissance style was originally the fountains' pumphouse.

Along the path by the water is a statue, by George Frampton, of J.M. Barrie's **Peter Pan** – the full title of this classic children's story is *Peter Pan in Kensington Gardens*.

The **Serpentine Gallery** ⑳ (tel: 7402 6075; www.serpentinegallery.org; daily 10am–6pm; free) by the road bridge is a dynamic exhibition space for contemporary art. In 2013 a new gallery by prize-winning architect Zaha Hadid opened nearby. The Magazine, a Grade II listed building near the Serpentine, is a dynamic new space called the Serpentine Sackler Gallery. The modern extension, used as a café/restaurant and social space, presents the best in emerging talent across all art forms.

HYDE PARK

Across the road is Hyde Park which, as the *Domesday Book* of 1086 records, was inhabited by wild bulls and boars. First owned by the monks of Westminster Abbey, it was turned into a royal hunting ground

by Henry VIII and then opened to the public in the 17th century. The **Serpentine** ㉑ was created in the 1730s as a royal boating lake, and boats can still be hired from the north bank. **Rotten Row**, William III's Route du Roi, running along the southern edge, is where the Household Cavalry, based in the barracks on Knightsbridge, exercise their horses.

The **Princess Diana Memorial Fountain** ㉒, a ring of flowing water surrounding a landscaped area, was designed by Seattle-based landscape architect Kathryn Gustafson.

At the northeast corner, near Marble Arch, is **Speakers' Corner** ㉓, where anyone can pull up a soap box and sound off, especially on Sunday afternoons. This tradition goes back to when the Tyburn gallows stood here (1388–1783; see page 114) and condemned felons were allowed to make a final unexpurgated speech to the crowds before being hanged. Close by, in Park Lane, is the monument Animals in War, a reminder of the role played by millions of animals in warfare.

Kids enjoying the Serpentine Gallery.

BEST RESTAURANTS, PUBS AND BARS

PRICE CATEGORIES

Prices for a three-course dinner per person with a half bottle of house wine:
£ = under £25
££ = £25–35
£££ = £35–55
££££ = over £55

Restaurants

British

Geales
2 Farmer St, Notting Hill Gate, W8. Tel: 7727 7528. www.geales.com Open: L Tue–Sun, D daily. ££ [ p322, B3]
An up-market fish and chip restaurant which has been keeping locals happy for years.

Hereford Road
3 Hereford Rd, Notting Hill Gate, W2. Tel: 7727 1144. www.herefordroad.org Open: L & D daily. ££ [130 p322, B2]
Splendid British cooking enthusiastically served at this former butcher's. Try duck hearts, calf's brains and braised rabbits, or a

The Orangery, Kensington Gardens.

whole oxtail to share between two.

Maggie Jones's
6 Old Court Place, Kensington Church St, W8. Tel: 7937 6462. www.maggie-jones.co. uk Open: L & D daily. ££ [131 p322, C3]
Take a step into the courtyard and you become immersed in the ambience of a 19th-century country inn. Simple home cooking served by friendly staff. The pies and puddings are particularly recommended.

The Orangery
Kensington Gardens, W8. Tel: 0844 482 7777. Open: Mar–Sept daily 10am–6pm, Oct–Feb 10am–5pm. Occasionally closed for functions; check website. £££ [132 p322, A3 and p334, C3]
In a magnificent building designed for Queen Anne in 1704, this is the place to come for traditional afternoon tea. Light lunches also served.

French

Bibendum
Michelin House, 81 Fulham Rd, SW3. Tel: Restaurant: 7581 5817; Oyster Bar: 7589 1480. www.bibendum.co.uk L & D daily. ££££ (set lunch £££) [133 p318, C2]
Opened by Sir Terence Conran and Paul Hamlyn in 1987, Bibendum continues to thrive; there's an oyster bar on the ground floor and a restaurant on the first floor of this individual Art Deco-style building.

Racine
239 Brompton Rd, SW3. Tel: 7584 4477. www.racine-restaurant.com L & D daily. ££–£££ [134 p318, C1]
A real taste of France in the heart of London. The menu features classic French dishes like steak tartare, while indulgent desserts might include rich chocolate terrine.

Indian

Bombay Brasserie
Courtfield Rd, SW7. Tel: 7370 4040. www.bombaybrasserielondon.com L & D daily, last orders midnight. £££ (set lunch ££) [135 p318 B2]
This up-market Indian has rejuvenated its classic menu and deserves its reputation for good, if

expensive, food. Book a table in the conservatory.

Malabar
27 Uxbridge St, Notting Hill Gate, W8. Tel: 7727 8800. www.malabar-restaurant.co.uk Open: L & D daily. ££ [136 p322, B2]
Uses fresh herbs and whole spices and gives an innovative twist to traditional dishes. Good-value buffet lunch on Sundays.

Zaika
1 Kensington High St, W8. Tel: 7795 6533. www.zaika-restaurant.co.uk Open: L Tue–Sun, D daily. ££££ (set lunch ££) [137 p322, C2]
The name translates as 'sophisticated flavours' and this is what you get, with the menu mixing traditional favourites with 'new' Eastern dishes. Plenty of unusual vegetarian options too.

Italian

Osteria Basilico
29 Kensington Park Rd, Notting Hill, W11. Tel: 7727 9957. www.osteriabasilico.co.uk Open: L & D daily. £££ [138 p322, A1]
Established in 1992, this place buzzes with a Notting Hill crowd. Friendly staff serve classic Italian home cooking and pizzas. Booking is recommended.

San Lorenzo
22 Beauchamp Place, SW3. Tel: 7584 1074. www.sanlorenzo.com Open: L & D daily. ££££ [139 p318, D1]
A swanky Knightsbridge venue patronised by fashion, music and media moguls, as well as royals. The food is not as noteworthy as the clientele.

Modern European

Babylon
The Roof Gardens, 7th Floor, 99 Kensington High St, W8. Tel: 7368 3993. www.roof gardens.virgin.com Open: L daily, D Mon–Sat. ££££ (set lunch ££) [140 p322, C4]
This Richard Branson-owned modern restaurant overlooks 1.5 acres (0.6 hectares) of gardens, with great views of London. The food lives up to the spectacular setting.

Clarke's
122–4 Kensington Church St, W8. Tel: 7221 9225. www.sallyclarke.com Open: L daily, D Mon–Sat. **££££** (set menu **£££**) [141] p322, B3]
High-quality ingredients treated simply is key to this restaurant's success. Check the website for Sally's daily changing no choice menus. A bakery supplies divine fresh bread.

Fifth Floor
Harvey Nichols, 109–125 Knightsbridge, SW1. Tel: 7235 5250. Open: L daily, D Mon–Sat. **£££–££££** [142] p323, D4]
A postmodern space popular with media types and models offering an effective combination of big flavours and light dishes.

Kensington Place
201–9 Kensington Church St, W8. Tel: 7727 3184. www.kensingtonplace-restaurant. co.uk Open: L & D daily. **£££** (set lunch **£–££**) [143] p322, B2]
A trailblazer of the Modern European scene, this popular Notting Hill restaurant still serves simple yet inventive good food. Noise levels are high.

Marcus Wareing at The Berkeley
Wilton Place, Knightsbridge, SW1. Tel: 7235 6000. www.the-berkeley.co.uk Open: L Mon–Fri, D Mon–Sat, **££££** (set lunch **£££**) [144] p323, D4]
Chef Marcus Wareing has 2 Michelin stars for his cooking at this hotel restaurant. Serves plenty of British produce, such as Aberdeen Angus beef and Cornish seabass.

Ottolenghi
63 Ledbury Rd, Notting Hill W11. Tel: 7727 1121. Also at 1 Holland St, Kensington W8. Tel: 7937 0003. Open: Mon–Fri 8am–8pm, Sat 8am–7pm and Sun 8.30am–6pm. **££** [145] p322, B1]
Fabulous fresh food made on the premises – sit at the communal table or take away. The Kensington branch is takeaway only, perfect for a picnic.

The Terrace
33c Holland St, Kensington W8. Tel: 7937 9252; www.theterraceonhollandstreet.co.uk Open: L & D Tue–Sat. **£££** [146] p322, B3]
On fine days you can sit outside at this small restaurant. Serves main courses such as duck breast with spring onion mash and cabbage.

Pubs and Bars

Pubs

The Abingdon
54 Abingdon Rd; http://theabingdon.co.uk [82] p322, B4]
More a restaurant than a pub in this very swanky neighbourhood just off Kensington High Street.

Anglesea Arms
15 Selwood Terrace, South Kensington; www.capitalpubcompany.com/our-pubs/the-anglesea-arms/ [83] p318, B3]
Traditional pub in a pleasant setting offering good food and drink and some outdoor tables. Charles Dickens lived at number 11.

Churchill Arms
119 Kensington Church St; http://churchill armskensington.co.uk [84] p322, B3]
Classic old pub with a Thai restaurant at the back, in a pretty butterfly-themed conservatory.

Windsor Castle
114 Campden Hill Rd; www.thewindsor castlekensington.co.uk [85] p322, B3]
Dating from the 1830s, this popular west London pub has several separate cosy rooms and a lovely beer garden (although it does get crowded). Excellent roasts are served on Sundays, with a varied menu the rest of the week.

Bars
The best bars are found in the area's grand hotels where extravagant cocktails are mixed in the elegant and refined spaces of sumptuous living.

Beauchamp
43 Beauchamp Place; www.beauchampbar. com [86] p318, D1]
Expensive bar in Knightsbridge popular with celebrities.

The Blue Bar
Berkeley Hotel, Wilton Place; www.the-berkeley.co.uk [87] p312, D4]
Another Knightsbridge celebrity hang-out, this bar in the Berkeley Hotel serves cocktails, wines and over 50 different whiskies.

Library Bar
Lanesborough Hotel on Hyde Park Corner; www.lanesborough.com [88] p312, E4]
Very handsome bar furnished with deep leather chairs and lined with books. Exudes superiority, as do some of its clients.

Mandarin Bar
Mandarin Oriental in Knightsbridge; www.mandarinoriental.com [89] p312, D4]
An upmarket London nightspot, the Mandarin Bar is popular with the well-heeled.

Montgomery Place
31 Kensington Park Rd; www.montgomery place.co.uk [90] p322, A1]
Cosy cocktail bar near Portobello Road with low lighting and a nice vibe.

Salads in Ottolenghi.

THE SCIENCE MUSEUM

This museum is an astounding tribute to the ingenuity of human beings over the centuries.

With more than 10,000 exhibits, plus additional attractions such as an IMAX theatre and Launchpad, an interactive play area for children, this museum could take days to explore, so it is best to assign priorities before you start.

An important point to note is the distinction between the main wing, dating to 1928 and containing the classic steam engines and planes, and the Wellcome Wing, opened in 2000, concentrating on information technology. You can walk between the two wings at five of the museum's seven levels, but the ambience of the wings is quite different and it is more satisfying to explore one wing at a time.

The Making the Modern World gallery brings together many of the museum's most exciting exhibits. "Modern" is defined as post-1750 and the stars include the world's oldest surviving steam locomotive, the coal-hauling Puffing Billy (circa 1815), a Ford Model T (1916), a Lockheed Electra airliner hanging in silvery splendour from the ceiling (1935), a copy of Crick and Watson's DNA double helix model (1953) and the Apollo 10 command module (left, 1969).

Vintage car.

The first gallery you enter is the Energy Hall, dominated by a 1903 mill engine.

The Essentials

Address: Exhibition Road, SW7; www.science museum.org.uk
Tel: 0870 870 4868
Opening Hrs: daily 10am–6pm
Entrance Fee: free except exhibitions, IMAX cinema and simulators
Transport: South Kensington

The ever-popular Exploring Space gallery has been revamped to include a range of new exhibits, including the huge Spacelab 2 x-ray telescope – the actual instrument that was flown on the Space Shuttle – and full-size models of the Huygens Titan probe and Beagle 2 Mars Lander. The replica of the Apollo 11 lunar excursion module has been reconfigured to a new level of accuracy.

The Rocket, George Stephenson's 1829 passenger locomotive, is on display in the Making of the Modern World gallery.

OTHER HIGHLIGHTS

Wellcome Wing.

The Wellcome Wing looks to the future rather than the past. On the ground floor, Antenna is a series of changing exhibits based around current science news, while an IMAX film theatre conjures up dinosaurs or outer space. The theme of the first floor is 'Who am I?', asking such questions as 'How does your brain make you so special?' and 'Do we all come from Africa?'. In Future, on the third floor, is a series of large digital board games on which contestants are invited to vote on health, communications and lifestyle topics – for example, 'Should men be allowed to give birth?'.

The Flight Gallery (third floor) is a favourite with all ages; exhibits range from a seaplane to a Spitfire, from hot-air balloons to helicopters. The 1919 Vickers Vimy in which Alcock and Brown made the first non-stop transatlantic flight is here, as is Amy Johnson's *Gipsy Moth Jason*. There's also a replica of the Wright Flyer in which Wilbur and Orville Wright pioneered powered flight in 1903.

The Launchpad (third floor) for older kids is packed with experiments they can try out; 'explainers' help them understand what's going on. There are over 50 interactive exhibits from the world of physics, such as a thermal imaging camera.

The Secret Life of the Home (basement) displays domestic appliances and gadgets, with buttons to press and levers to pull, two of which show the internal workings of a flushing lavatory and a CD player.

VICTORIA AND ALBERT MUSEUM

The world's largest collection of decorative and applied arts covers everything from massive sculptures to knitting.

With 5 million objects and almost 8 miles (13km) of galleries, the Victoria and Albert Museum (founded in 1852) is colossal. Its exhibits range from exquisite Persian miniatures to a whole room designed by Frank Lloyd Wright. One minute one can be admiring Raphael's cartoons for the tapestries in the Sistine Chapel, and the next examining E.H. Shepard's illustrations for *Winnie-the-Pooh*.

The museum is undergoing a 10-year refurbishment. So far, the British Galleries have received a major overhaul and the Islamic Galleries have been redesigned with the superb Ardabil carpet, the oldest carpet in the world, as a centrepiece. The Ceramics galleries include porcelain animals crafted for Augustus the Strong, while highlights from the Gilbert collection (gold and silver objects, and enamel portrait miniatures), are in rooms 70–73.

The Paul and Jill Ruddock Gallery features Renaissance-era artworks.

The British Galleries document British taste, exploring "what was hot and what was new from the time of Henry VIII and the Tudors to William Morris". The exhibits include the Great Bed of Ware, a 16th-century four poster.

The Essentials

Address: Cromwell Road, SW7; www.vam. ac.uk
Tel: 7942 2000
Opening Hrs: daily 10am–5.45pm, Fri some galleries till 10pm
Entrance Fee: free except some exhibitions
Transport: South Kensington

The Iranian Ardabil carpet (1539–40) in the Jameel Gallery of Islamic arts.

A British Empire builder is savaged in Tippoo's Tiger (Mysore, 1793), in the South Asia Gallery.

An immense glass sculpture by the American glass artist Dale Chihuly hangs in the foyer of the Cromwell Road entrance.

Museum exterior detail.

OTHER HIGHLIGHTS

The Sculpture Courts. British and neoclassical works from the late 18th and early 19th centuries.
Plaster Casts. Fine copies, from Trajan's Column to Michelangelo's David.
Raphael Cartoons (1515–6). Templates for a series of tapestries in the Sistine Chapel.
Medieval and Renaissance. Renaissance pieces include Andrea Briosco's 16th-century Shouting Horseman.
The Fashion Galleries. Fashions through the ages from the 18th century to the present day.
The Ceramic Staircase. Completed in 1869, it symbolises the relationship between art and science.
The Hereford Screen. An intricate choir screen (1862) studded with semi-precious stones.
Henry Cole Wing. Prints, drawings, paintings and photographs ranging from John Constable's paintings to Beatrix Potter's watercolours. Don't miss the Frank Lloyd Wright Gallery.
Refreshment Rooms. Three fabulously ornate café interiors from the 19th century, interlinked and opening onto the courtyard garden.
The Museum Shop. Quite simply irresistible.

Platform shoes in stamped leather by Vivienne Westwood (1993). Recently re-opened after restoration, the Fashion Galleries display temporary exhibitions.

213

THE NATURAL HISTORY MUSEUM

This colossal collection has 75 million plants, animals, fossils, rocks and minerals – and it's growing by 50,000 new specimens a year.

Dinosaur skeleton.

In spite of the museum's vast size, the layout is easy to master due to colour coded zones: the Red Zone (entrance on Exhibition Road), which explores the forces that shape our planet; the Green Zone, which looks at Earth's ecology; the Blue Zone, which investigates earth's biodiversity; and the Orange Zone covering the wildlife garden and the Darwin Centre.

One of the museum's delights is the way it presents high-tech exhibits alongside lovely Victorian-style galleries filled with meticulously labelled cabinets. Many of the latter are found in quiet byways of the museum, but one vintage member of the collection is the wood and plaster model of a blue whale, which has been the centrepiece of the Mammals section since being built in 1938.

The Central Hall of the museum. The extravagant Gothic Romanesque building, by architect Alfred Waterhouse, was the first in Britain to be faced entirely in terracotta. Its soaring arches and rich ornamental detail bring to mind a cathedral, an effect intended by Sir Richard Owen, the superintendent of the collection. Owen wanted the building to be a temple of nature.

The Essentials

Address: Cromwell Road, SW7; www.nhm. ac.uk
Tel: 7942 5000
Opening Hrs: daily 10am–5.50pm
Entrance Fee: free except for some special exhibitions
Transport: South Kensington

The skeleton and dramatic full-size model of a blue whale is a big attraction. Many families also make a bee-line for the Dinosaurs section (Life Galleries), the highlight of which is a full-scale animatronic T-Rex that roars and twists convincingly, impressing most children.

A cross-section of a giant redwood.

OTHER HIGHLIGHTS

The Human Biology section.

Investigate (basement). Here children can touch, weigh, measure and examine under a microscope a range of specimens. A team of explainers is on hand to help. There is also an outdoor section where children can inspect pond life close up.

Human Biology. This section is packed with interactive exhibits: you can test your memory and senses or be tricked by optical illusions.

Mammals. As well as displaying an astonishing array of taxidermy, these galleries contain sobering statistics on the rapid rate at which species are becoming extinct.

Creepy Crawlies. Wander through a house and learn about the many uninvited housemates in an average home. Sit in a life-size model of a termite mound or watch a colony of leaf-cutter ants.

Earth's Treasury. This conveys the planet's beauty, displaying rocks, gems and minerals glittering in the gallery's semi-darkness.

The Jerwood Gallery. This houses a superb collection of watercolours, oils, prints and drawings, some of which are the original illustrations to books by 19th-century explorers.

The Darwin Centre. Opened in 2009, this cocoon-shaped centre for scientific study and repository for 20 million specimens gives visitors the opportunity to see scientists in action.

The Wildlife Garden *(enter via the Darwin Centre).* This lush spot is a refreshing way to end a visit (Apr–Oct 10am–5pm).

An escalator transports visitors into a vast globe, the entrance to the Earth Galleries, where Restless Surface covers earthquakes and volcanoes. The tremors of an earthquake are simulated in a mock-up of a Japanese mini-market.

Well-heeled cyclist crossing King's Road.

CHELSEA

Backing on to a secluded stretch of the Thames, Chelsea has a village feel, but also a strong bohemian side. Running through it is the King's Road, the centre of Swinging London in the 1960s and, later, of punk.

Sandwiched between Kensington and the Thames, Chelsea's tranquil enclaves still hint at the riverside hamlet it was until the late 18th century. Despite a modest character, by the 16th century Chelsea had become known as a 'Village of Palaces', with strong royal links – King Henry VIII among them – and was destined to be the site of Wren's Royal Hospital in 1682.

A reputation for art took root with the Chelsea Porcelain Works and the illustrations generated by the Chelsea Physic Garden's botanical publications. By the 19th century, a bohemian set had moved in wholesale, including the painters Rossetti, Whistler and Sargent and writers such as George Eliot (and later, T.S. Eliot).

BELGRAVIA TO SLOANE SQUARE

When the squares and terraces of **Belgravia** were built around 1824, these streets west of Hyde Park Corner were intended to rival Mayfair. From Knightsbridge, the best entrance to Belgravia is via **Wilton Place**. The stucco terraces were developed by architect Thomas Cubitt, who gave his name to the modern construction company known for

its motorway bridges. Like much of Mayfair, **Belgrave Square** is largely occupied by embassies and various societies and associations. The square usually has a heavy police presence.

Eaton Square, to the south, is more residential. However, many of its supposed residents live in other parts of the world and the houses are dark and obviously under-used. Chopin gave his first London recital here at No. 88.

In 1895 the playwright Oscar Wilde was arrested in the Cadogan

Main Attractions

Sloane Square
King's Road
Duke of York Square
Royal Hospital
National Army Museum
Chelsea Physic Garden
Cheyne Walk
Chelsea Old Church

Maps and Listings

Map, page 218
Shopping, page 10
Restaurant, page 224
Accommodation, page 285

Chelsea Physic Garden.

The Royal Court Theatre.

Hotel in Sloane Street, tried and sent to prison for his homosexual conduct. Sloane Street leads from Knightsbridge to **Sloane Square** ❶, where **Chelsea** proper begins. On the east side of the square is the **Royal Court Theatre**, where John Osborne's mould-breaking anti-establishment play *Look Back in Anger* was first staged in 1956. The company still has a robust reputation for shaping the classics of the future.

Sloane Square was named after a physician, Sir Hans Sloane (1660–1753), whose personal collection formed the basis of what is now the British Museum. He laid out much of this area and his name crops up often on street plans. He also unwittingly gave his name to a typical upper-class urbanite living in Chelsea in the 1980s: the Sloane Ranger, a lady in flat shoes, pearls, gathered skirt and a quilted jacket.

ALONG THE KING'S ROAD

Until 1829 the **King's Road** ❷, leading west from Sloane Square, was a private royal road leading from Hampton Court to the court of King James. It rose to

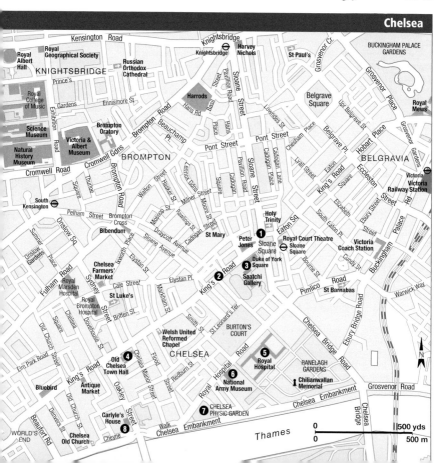

Chelsea

fame during the 1960s, and was later linked to punk fashions, after Vivienne Westwood and Malcolm McLaren opened their designer shop, Sex, at No. 430 in 1972. Westwood still sells her designs from these premises, renamed World's End, which is what this part of Chelsea is called. Sloane Square's GTC (General Trading Company), and Peter Jones department store are also long-established shops.

Duke of York Square ❸

Lately, the biggest innovation on the King's Road's retail front has been the redevelopment of the Duke of York's Headquarters, formerly a military campus. The main building with its Tuscan portico (1801), designed as a school for the orphans of soldiers, now houses the **Saatchi Gallery**, which moved here in 2007 (www.saatchi-gallery.co.uk). It contains the work of contemporary British artists assembled by former advertising mogul Charles Saatchi. In recent years the collection's bias has shifted towards paintings and away from works such as Damien Hirst's celebrated sheep in formaldehyde solution.

Old Chelsea Town Hall ❹

Prettily painted 18th- and 19th-century terraces leading off the King's Road have a tradition of housing artists and intellectuals. On the left-hand side of the road opposite Sydney Street stands the Old Chelsea Town Hall. The old borough of Royal Kensington, given its royal appellation by Queen Victoria in 1901, was merged much against its wishes with Chelsea in 1965, and took over the administration of both. The Old Chelsea Town Hall continues to provide a cultural and social focus for residents. The Register Office next door is well-known for society and celebrity weddings.

SYDNEY STREET

In 1836, Charles Dickens was married more conventionally – in **St Luke's**, a stunning Gothic church halfway up Sydney Street, running north of the King's Road. Eagle-eyed Disney fans may recognise it from the 1996 film version of *101 Dalmatians*. If the weather is fine its gardens are a lovely spot to unwind.

Sydney Street is also home to the popular Chelsea Gardener nursery and the **Chelsea Farmers' Market**, a small shopping enclave with a boho feel thanks to its organic supermarket and one-storey clapboard units where the emphasis is on natural remedies and ingredients.

At the top of Sydney Street is **Brompton Cross**, a network of streets containing up-market shops and restaurants, including Bibendum (see page 208), in the Art Deco-style former headquarters of the Michelin Tyre Company on Fulham Road.

ROYAL HOSPITAL ROAD

Among the leggy would-be models gliding along the King's Road are uniformed old gents with the initials

Old Chelsea Town Hall.

FACT

The telltale enormous windows looking out onto Tite Street (off Royal Hospital Road) betray the origins of these houses: in the 1870s, this street was crammed with artists' studios, including The Studios, at No. 33. These were once used by the American painter John Singer Sargent (1856–1925) who died at No. 31, while Oscar Wilde once occupied No. 34.

RH on their caps. These are Chelsea Pensioners, retired war veterans who live in the **Royal Hospital**, built by Christopher Wren in 1692 on Royal Hospital Road. From the King's Road, a practically uninterrupted vista is afforded down the length of **Royal Avenue**, the hospital perfectly framed in the distance. The gravelled boulevard now lined with 19th-century houses was laid out by Wren with the purpose of providing a direct route from the hospital to Kensington Palace. The scheme failed to materialise when Charles II, the sponsor, died, and this first and only section now stands as testimony to Wren's grand vision. Royal Avenue was the fictional home of James Bond.

Royal Hospital ⑤

Address: Royal Hospital Road, www.chelsea-pensioners.org.uk
Tel: 7881 5516
Opening Hrs: Mon–Sat 10am–noon, 2–4pm; grounds year round Mon–Sat 10am–sunset, Sun from 2pm
Entrance Fee: free
Transport: Sloane Square

Artwork at the Royal Hospital.

Dressed for summer on King's Road.

The idea behind this magnificent building housing the Chelsea Pensioners was inspired by the Hôtel des Invalides in Paris. The main buildings, two residential wings linked by the Great Hall and Chapel, were designed in English baroque style.

The wood-panelled Great Hall, the dining room, features a vast mural with Charles II on horseback, painted by Verrio. It was in this hall

in 1852 that Wellington lay in state. Decorated with regimental colours, the adjoining Chapel features *Christ Rising from the Tomb*, a fresco by Sebastiano Ricci. A huge painting of the Battle of Waterloo by George Jones hangs in the entrance to a small museum. It overlooks a 1:300 scale model that, with an audio presentation, illustrates the hospital and its massive grounds in the 18th century.

National Army Museum ❻

Address: Royal Hospital Road, www.nam.ac.uk
Tel: 7730 0717
Opening Hrs: daily 10am–5.30pm
Entrance Fee: free
Transport: Sloane Square

The permanent exhibition follows the history of the British Army from the defeat of the French at Agincourt in 1415 to the present day, although with much less emphasis on the latter. Massive flamboyant paintings, some as long as 20ft (6 metres), celebrate soldiers' greatest and worst moments, while portraits by Gainsborough, Reynolds and lesser artists crowd

other walls. There is also the skeleton of Napoleon's favourite horse, Marengo. You can feel the weight of a Tudor cannonball or try on a soldier's helmet, while the replica World War I trench is a place for quiet reflection. Three sections of the Berlin Wall stand outside the museum.

Chelsea Physic Garden ❼

Address: 66 Royal Hospital Road, www.chelseaphysicgarden.co.uk
Tel: 7352 5646
Opening Hrs: Apr–Oct Tue–Fri, Sun 11am–6pm, Sun noon–6pm; July–Aug until 10pm (last entry 8.30pm); closed Nov–Mar
Transport: Sloane Square

Behind a high wall is the Chelsea Physic Garden, founded in 1673 for the study of medicinal plants. The 3.5-acre (1.5-hectare) garden is divided into four contrasting sections: a Garden of World Medicine, a Pharmaceutical Garden, and systematic order beds in the two southern quadrants. The Pharmaceutical Garden displays plants according to their medical uses while the Garden of World Medicine details the use of

Chelsea Farmers' Market.

Pastel-coloured mews houses.

specific plants in different parts of the world.

You will also find a pond rockery, perfumery and aromatherapy borders, glasshouses, and herb and vegetable gardens. A woodland area has birds' nesting boxes, and there are themed trails for adults and children.

CHELSEA EMBANKMENT

At the foot of Royal Hospital Road, a fine row of Queen Anne houses make up **Cheyne Walk** (see page 223). Cheyne Walk sits back from the flagstoned, windblown sweep of **Chelsea Embankment**, roaring with traffic in the shadows of old plane trees but beautiful nonetheless. Flanked by greenery it is also known as Chelsea Gardens and opened to great fanfare in 1874. It retains its sculptural lampposts with their fat, milky globes, and its cast-iron benches with end supports shaped like sphinxes. The views stretch out across the Thames to the Battersea

There are blue plaques aplenty on Cheyne Walk.

Royal Hospital.

Park Peace Pagoda on the opposite bank, built by Japanese monks and nuns in 1985; east to the iconic chimneys of the Battersea Power Station – restoration of the Grade II listing building is due to be completed by 2016; and west to the pink-and-cream confection of the **Albert Bridge** (1873).

SHOPPING

Antiques

Chelsea has a large share of fine dealers. **Fulham Road** is excellent for period furniture and decorative items, as is the **King's Road**, with indoor markets such as **Antiquarius** housing a wide variety of artefacts.

Clothes

Agent Provocateur
16 Pont St, SW1
Tel: 7235; www.agentprovocateur.com
The place to go for decadently sexy lingerie.
Jimmy Choo
32 Sloane St, SW1
Tel: 7823 1051; www.jimmychoo.com
Footwear of choice for many celebrities and girls-about-town. Glamorous, vertiginous stilettos abound.

Department Stores

Peter Jones
Sloane Square, SW1
Tel: 7730 3434; www.johnlewis.com
This King's Road branch of John Lewis promises customers that its prices cannot be beaten and assures to refund the difference if you can prove otherwise. Stocks a variety of quality goods, most notably household furnishings and appliances.

Food and Drink

Rococo
321 King's Rd, SW3
Tel: 7352 5857; www.rococo chocolates.com
Gourmet chocolates. Unusual flavours are their key selling point.

Carlyle's House ❽

Transport: 24 Cheyne Row,
www.nationaltrust.org.uk
Tel: 7352 7087
Opening Hrs: mid-Mar–early Nov
Wed–Sun and bank holiday Mon
11am–5pm
Transport: Sloane Square

A statue of the Scottish essayist Thomas Carlyle (1795–1881) watches the traffic grind by further down the Embankment. The dour essayist lived here between 1834 and 1881. The house is preserved exactly as it was – to the point of not having electricity – and it is easy to imagine Mr and Mrs Carlyle sitting in their kitchen, although it may not have been a cosy scene. It was fortunate the Carlyles married each other, it was said, otherwise there would have been four miserable people in the world instead of two. Yet leading intellectuals, including Charles Dickens, John Ruskin and Alfred, Lord Tennyson, used to visit Carlyle here.

Sir Hans Sloane's tomb is outside **Chelsea Old Church** (All Saints) on Cheyne Walk. The church has several fine Tudor monuments and was painstakingly rebuilt after

Carlyle's House.

being destroyed by a landmine in 1941.

The site was formerly occupied by a 12th-century Norman church. Henry VIII, who had a large house on the river where Cheyne Walk now is, supposedly married Jane Seymour in secrecy here, several days before the official ceremony. Thomas More (1478–1535), author of *Utopia*, which sketched out an ideal commonwealth, had a farm here. His stormy relationship with Henry VIII, which resulted in his execution, was the subject of Robert Bolt's 1960 play *A Man For All Seasons*.

KIDS

The National Army Museum's Kid Zone is a free interactive learning and play space designed to unleash children's imaginations. There's a medieval castle to explore, life in a forest army camp to negotiate, and a variety of activity areas to challenge and entertain the under-10s. A soft play area for youngsters is also included. Entry is by timed ticket.

Chelsea Physic Garden.

THE ULTIMATE DES RES

Cheyne Walk has long been one of London's most exclusive streets. A host of famous people have lived in its fine, mainly 18th-century, properties, from writers George Eliot and Hilaire Belloc to the artist J.M.W. Turner and the engineer Isambard Kingdom Brunel. It is still a choice address today, with Paul Getty, Mick Jagger and Keith Richards having all been resident at one time.

The pre-Raphaelite artist Dante Gabriel Rossetti lived with the poet Swinburne in No. 16, and they kept peacocks in their back garden. The birds so disturbed the neighbours that nowadays every lease on the row prohibits tenants from keeping them.

BEST RESTAURANTS, PUBS AND BARS

Restaurants

British

Cadogan Arms
298 King's Rd, SW3. Tel: 7352 6500.
www.thecadoganarmschelsea.com Open: L &
D daily. **£££** [147 p318, C2]
Traditional Victorian pub turned
fashionable gastropub, offering
real ales along with good food.
Dishes might include rack of Welsh
lamb or pan-fried sea bass. Good
selection of British cheeses.

Tom's Kitchen
27 Cale St, SW3. Tel: 7349 0202. www.
tomskitchen.co.uk Open: B and L Mon–Fri,
brunch Sat–Sun, D daily. **££–£££** [148
p318, C3]

Tom Aikens' restaurant.

Relaxed brasserie run by award-
winning chef Tom Aikens. The
menu changes daily, but features
classic British dishes such as
Cumberland sausages and mash,
steak sandwiches, fish pie and
macaroni cheese.

Chinese

Eight Over Eight
392 King's Rd, SW3. Tel: 7349 9934.
www.rickerrestaurants.com Open: L & D
daily. **£££** [149 p318, B4]
This stylish restaurant offers Asian
dishes with a modern twist. Dim
sum, sushi, king prawn curry, and
chocolate pudding with green tea
ice cream are just some of the
delights on offer.

Ken Lo's Memories of China
65–9 Ebury St, SW1. Tel: 7730 7734.
www.atoz restaurants.com Open: L & D daily.
£££–££££ (set lunch available) [150
p320, A1]
Ken Lo's menus, skewed towards
Western tastes, have stood the
test of time, though the final bill

invariably comes as a costly sur-
prise.

French

Cheyne Walk Brasserie
50 Cheyne Walk, SW3. Tel: 7376 8787.
www.cheynewalkbrasserie.com Open: L
Tue–Sun, D daily (last booking 9pm on
Sun). **£££** (weekday lunch menu **££**) [151
p318, C4]
The flavours of Provence are
cooked up over the central grill of
this Belle Epoque dining room.
Also offers views of the Albert
Bridge and a sumptuous cocktail
lounge.

Poissonnerie de L'Avenue
82 Sloane Avenue, SW3. Tel: 7589 2457.
www.poissonnerie.co.uk Open: L & D daily.
£££ (set menu **££**) [152 p318, C2]
Run by the same family for over 40
years, it serves fresh fish and
seafood from the adjoining
fishmonger's. Dishes are old-
school French, although some
come with an Italian flourish.

La Poule au Pot
231 Ebury St, SW1. Tel: 7730 7763.
www.pouleaupot.co.uk Open: L & D daily.
£££ (set lunch **££**) [153 p318, E2]
The £19.75 fixed-price lunch
menu features dishes such as
mussels or tarte à l'oignon with
steak frites or cassoulet to follow.
In the evening, candlelight and
romantic nooks make it a hit with
couples.

Indian

Chutney Mary
535 King's Rd, SW10. Tel: 7351 3113.
www.chutneymary.com Open: L Sat–Sun, D
daily. **£££** (set lunch **££**) [154 p318, A4]
At the sister restaurant to Veeras-
wamy (the UK's oldest Indian eatery), take your pick of regional
dishes from Goa to Delhi, Kerala to
Bombay. The Sunday jazz brunch
is popular. Meat is halal.

Quilon
41 Buckingham Gate, SW1. Tel: 7821
1899. www.quilon.co.uk Open: L Mon–Fri
and Sun, D Mon–Sat. **£££** (set lunch **££**)

[155 p320, B1]

The lunch menu at this Michelin-starred, South Indian restaurant is good value, though an evening meal of, say, pepper shrimps followed by Manglorean chicken or duck roast, is pricier. Menu blends traditional and more progressive dishes.

Rasoi

10 Lincoln St, Sloane Square, SW1. Tel: 7225 1881. www.rasoi-uk.com Open: L Mon–Fri and Sun, D daily. £££ [156 p318, D2]

Run by celebrated chef Vineet Rasoi and holder of a Michelin star, this restaurant offers the ultimate Indian dining experience. It serves superb food in a traditional Chelsea townhouse.

Italian

Elistano

25–27 Elystan St, SW3. Tel: 7584 5248. www.elistano.com Open: L & D daily. £££ [157 p318, C2]

The menu varies with the seasons, but it might feature zucchini fritti (fried courgettes with mint), and saltimbocca romana. The pannacotta is delicious.

Japanese

Itsu

118 Draycott Ave, SW3. Tel: 7590 2400. www.itsu.com Open: Mon–Sat noon–11pm, Sun noon–10pm. £ [158 p318, C2]

Take away or eat-in at this brightly lit restaurant. If you don't fancy the incredibly fresh sushi or sashimi, try a dish from the hot grill such as chicken teriyaki. Bookings not accepted.

Modern European

Bluebird

350 King's Rd, SW3. Tel: 7559 1000. www.bluebird-restaurant.com Open: L & D daily. ££ [159 p318, C4]

The emphasis at this skylit restaurant, café and bar is on seasonal ingredients. It's a popular place for Sunday brunch, especially on sunny days when you can sit out in the courtyard.

Gordon Ramsay

68 Royal Hospital Rd, SW3. Tel: 7352 4441. www.gordonramsay.com Open: L & D

Mon–Fri. ££££ (lunch menu £££) [160 p318, D4]

This three Michelin-starred restaurant features the culinary talent of Chef Patron Clare Smyth,who has taken Gordon Ramsay's exquisite dishes and made them her own. The lunchtime set menu costs £55 for 3 courses. No jeans or trainers.

Others

Patara

181 Fulham Rd, SW3. Tel: 7351 5692. www.pataralondon.com Open: L & D daily. ££ [161 p318, C2]

Serves good Thai food at low prices considering the area. As a suggestion, try the prawn bisque scented with lemongrass and kaffir lime leaf or the DIY fresh spring rolls for starters.

Pubs and Bars

Pubs

Admiral Codrington

17 Mossop St; www.theadmiralcodrington. co.uk [91 p318, C2]

This pub off the beaten track attracts a smart-casual set, and does a popular line in fish and chips.

Chelsea Potter

119 King's Rd; www.taylor-walker.co.uk/pub/chelsea-potter-chelsea [92 p318, D3]

Traditional pub in the heart of what is still one of London's trendiest streets. Good classic British dishes such as shepherd's pie and bangers and mash are served.

The Cooper's Arms

87 Flood St; www.coopersarms.co.uk [93 p318, D3]

Popular Chelsea local serving real ales and good food.

The Fox and Hounds

29 Passmore St; www.youngs.co.uk [94 p318, E2]

With comfy armchairs and books lining the walls, this is a tiny pub which prides itself on being television- and music-free.

Grenadier

18 Wilton Row; www.taylor-walker.co.uk/pub/grenadier [95 p318, E4]

Tucked away on Belgrave Square, this historic pub was built in 1720. Serves typical pub food like fish

and chips and jacket potatoes.

Lots Road Pub and Dining Room

114 Lots Rd; www.foodandfuel.co.uk [96 p318, A1]

Beautiful pub where the staff are attentive and the food excellent.

Orange Brewery

37–9 Pimlico Rd; www.theorange.co.uk [97 p318, E3]

Recently restored gastropub with light and airy rooms.

Pig's Ear

35 Old Church St; www.thepigsear.info [98 p318, C4]

Somewhat lacking in authenticity after a continental-style refit, but with a fine real ale to its name.

Thomas Cubitt

44 Elizabeth St; www.thethomascubitt.co.uk [99 p318, E2]

Named after London's master builder, this is a very stylish, country-style gastropub.

Bars

606 Club

90 Lots Rd; www.606club.co.uk [100 p318, B4]

Popular live jazz venue and bar which celebrated its 25th anniversary in 2013.

Organic ice cream at Chelsea Farmers' Market.

Village London

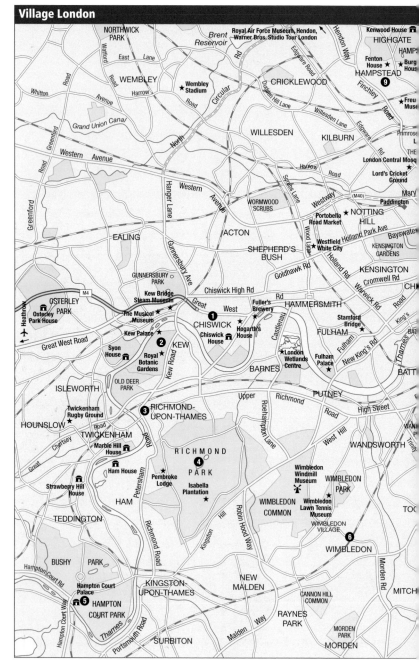

NORTHWICK PARK

Brent Reservoir

Royal Air Force Museum, Hendon, Warner Bros. Studio Tour London

Kenwood House 🏠

HIGHGATE

HAMPS

Fenton House ★ Burg Hous

HAMPSTEAD

❾

East Lane

WEMBLEY

CRICKLEWOOD

Freu Muse

★ Wembley Stadium

WILLESDEN

KILBURN

London Central Mosq

Lord's Cricket Ground

WORMWOOD SCRUBS

Paddington Mary

EALING

ACTON

SHEPHERD'S BUSH

Portobello Road Market ★ NOTTING HILL

Westfield White City

Holland Park Ave Bayswater

KENSINGTON GARDENS

KENSINGTON

Cromwell Rd CH

GUNNERSBURY PARK

Chiswick High Rd

Fuller's Brewery

HAMMERSMITH

OSTERLEY PARK

Osterley Park House 🏠

Kew Bridge Steam Museum

West

❶

CHISWICK

The Musical Museum ★

Kew Palace ★

❷

KEW

Chiswick House 🏠

Hogarth's House ★

Stamford Bridge ★

FULHAM

Syon House 🏠

Royal Botanic Gardens

London Wetlands Centre ★

Fulham Palace ★

ISLEWORTH

OLD DEER PARK

BARNES

PUTNEY

RICHMOND-UPON-THAMES

❸

Upper Richmond Road

High Street

WANDSWORTH

Twickenham Rugby Ground ★

HOUNSLOW

TWICKENHAM

RICHMOND PARK

❹

West Hill

WIMBLEDON PARK

Marble Hill House 🏠

Pembroke Lodge ★

Isabella Plantation ★

Wimbledon Windmill Museum

WIMBLEDON COMMON

Wimbledon Lawn Tennis Museum

TOO

Ham House 🏠

Strawberry Hill House 🏠

HAM

WIMBLEDON VILLAGE

❻

WIMBLEDON

TEDDINGTON

BUSHY PARK

Hampton Court Palace

🏠❺ HAMPTON COURT PARK

KINGSTON-UPON-THAMES

NEW MALDEN

CANNON HILL COMMON

MITCH

RAYNES PARK

MORDEN PARK

SURBITON

MORDEN

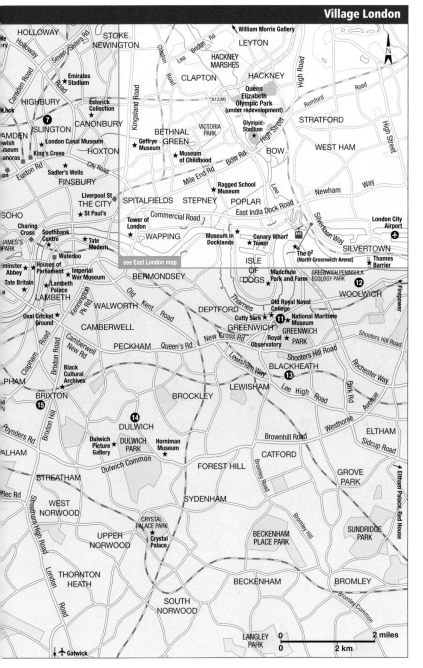

HOLLOWAY

Holloway

Seven Sisters Rd

Seven Sisters Rd

STOKE
NEWINGTON

Clapton

William Morris Gallery

LEYTON

HACKNEY
MARSHES

Lea Bridge Rd

Camden Road

Holloway
Road

Emirates
★ Stadium

HIGHBURY

Lock

7

ISLINGTON

CANONBURY

Estorick
Collection
★

AMDEN
ewish
useum
ancras

wish
useum

King's Cross

Euston Rd

London Canal Museum
★

HOXTON

Sadler's Wells
★

FINSBURY

on

Kingsland Road

BETHNAL
GREEN

CLAPTON

Geffrye ★
Museum

Museum
★ of Childhood

City Road

VICTORIA
PARK

Mile End Rd

Bow Rd

Olympic
Stadium
★

Queen
Elizabeth
Olympic Park
(under redevelopment)

HACKNEY

High Road

High Street

BOW

Romford

Road

STRATFORD

WEST HAM

High Street

A12(M)

SOHO

Charing
Cross

JAMES'S
PARK

Southbank
Centre
◆

Liverpool St
THE CITY
★ St Paul's

SPITALFIELDS

Ragged School
★ Museum

STEPNEY

Commercial Road

POPLAR

East India Dock Road

Newham

Way

★ Tate
Modern

Waterloo

minster
Abbey

Houses of
★ Parliament

Tate Britain

a

Imperial ★
War Museum

Lambeth
★ Palace

LAMBETH

Tower of
London
★

WAPPING

see East London map

Museum in
Docklands
★

Canary Wharf
★ Tower

ISLE
OF
DOGS

Silvertown Way

London City
Airport
◆

The O²
★ (North Greenwich Arena)

SILVERTOWN

Thames
★ Barrier

Firepower

Kennington
Pk Rd

WALWORTH

Old

Kent

Road

BERMONDSEY

Thames

DEPTFORD

Cutty Sark ★ ★

Mudchute
Park and Farm
★

Old Royal Naval
College

GREENWICH PENINSULA
ECOLOGY PARK

12

WOOLWICH

National Maritime
Museum

Oval Cricket ★
Ground

Camberwell
New Rd

CAMBERWELL

PECKHAM

Queen's Rd

New Cross Rd

GREENWICH
11 ★★

GREENWICH
PARK

Royal ★
Observatory

Shooters Hill Road

Brixton Road

Clapham
Road

Black
Cultural
Archives

PHAM

BRIXTON

15

Brixton Hill

oynders Rd

ALHAM

Lewisham Way

Shooters Hill Road

BLACKHEATH

13

LEWISHAM

Lee High Road

BROCKLEY

14

DULWICH

Dulwich
Picture ★
Gallery

DULWICH
PARK

Horniman
Museum
★

Dulwich Common

Brownhill Road

FOREST HILL

CATFORD

Bromley Road

Rochester Way

Park Rd

Shooters Hill Road

Westhorne

ELTHAM

Sidcup Road

GROVE
PARK

Avenue

Eltham Palace, Red House

STREATHAM

Bec Rd

WEST
NORWOOD

SYDENHAM

Streatham High Road

CRYSTAL
PALACE PARK

UPPER
NORWOOD

Crystal
Palace
★

BECKENHAM
PLACE PARK

Bromley Hill

SUNDRIDGE
PARK

THORNTON
HEATH

London
Road

SOUTH
NORWOOD

BECKENHAM

BROMLEY

Bromley Common

LANGLEY
PARK

↓ ✈ Gatwick

| 0 | | 2 miles |
| 0 | | 2 km |

VILLAGE LONDON

London grew by swallowing up surrounding villages. But many are still there in spirit, each with its own distinctive character. Here we explore them by the four points of the compass.

At its widest point, from South Croydon to Potter's Bar, the metropolis is nearly 60 miles (100km) from top to bottom, and London remains one of the world's most populous and multicultural cities. Perhaps because it is so big, many of those who live within its confines hardly think of it as a unified city at all, but as a collection of largely independent villages or communities. While Londoners may commute many miles to work, they are likely to do their shopping in their local high streets and build their social lives on their home patch.

The River Thames cuts through London, forming an effective physical and psychological block to free movement. While south Londoners stream across London Bridge to work in the City every day, they are more likely to go shopping in Croydon or Bromley than in the West End, and north Londoners will head further

Cows grazing on Petersham Meadows, Richmond.

north to such shopping citadels as Brent Cross. Many people born within the metropolis rarely move more than a few miles from their home, and would not dream of relocating to the other side of the river.

The 24-hour Shepherd Gate Clock at the Royal Observatory.

Where to go

While most visitors are busy with the tourist haunts of the West End and the City, those who go further afield are rewarded with a glimpse of what the locals call 'real London'. Head west to Kew for Kew Gardens and river walks at Chiswick and Richmond. Venture north to Islington and Camden for good shopping, nightlife, restaurants and Regent's Canal, or to Highgate and Hampstead for historic pubs and Hampstead Heath. Travel east of the centre to see high-rise Docklands, historic Spitalfields and the main 2012 Olympic site. In the southern suburbs are Greenwich, famous for its observatory and naval museum, Blackheath and Brixton.

All can be reached by public transport, using either the Tube, Docklands Light Railway, buses or, in the case of the southern suburbs, overground railway from London Bridge, Victoria or Charing Cross stations.

WEST LONDON

West London offers 18th-century mansions, magnificent parks and walks along the River Thames. To the southwest is Henry VIII's great palace, Hampton Court, and Wimbledon, home of the famous tennis championship.

Heading west out of London you can choose between grand riverside mansions, built as country retreats for royals and landed gentry, and wide-open spaces such as Richmond Park and Kew Gardens, the world renowned botanic gardens.

CHISWICK ❶

Although it accommodates the main artery to the M4 and Heathrow Airport, Chiswick has the feel of a small town, with its independent shops, flower stalls, fashionable restaurants and pretty terraces. Near the fragrant Fuller's Brewery (see page 232), off Hogarth roundabout, stands a hidden gem, much loved by locals and at last being given the attention it deserves.

Chiswick House

Address: Burlington Lane, www.chgt.org.uk
Tel: 8995 0508
Opening Hrs: Apr–Oct Sun–Wed and bank holidays 10am–5pm, Nov–Mar pre-booked appointments for groups only; gardens daily, all year round
Entrance Fee: gardens free
Transport: train from Waterloo to Chiswick, bus 190

This romantic 18th-century villa was designed by Lord Burlington (1694–1753), a renowned architect and patron of the arts, who was inspired by classical Rome. Burlington's Palladian house launched a new taste in architecture which was to spread throughout Britain and North America.

The gardens are historically important too, for it was here that the idea of the 'natural style' of gardening – one of England's main contributions to European culture – was conceived. Burlington brought in his friend William Kent to redesign the grounds; Kent broke from the rigid

Chiswick House.

Hogarth's House.

formality that had characterised gardens of the early 18th century and created a more natural landscape. Thus the English landscape movement was born. A £12 million project has recently restored the gardens, which include an abundance of statuary, a classical bridge, an Ionic temple, and a large conservatory.

Inside the house, the grand rooms are reserved for the first floor, which has a very unusual structure: in the centre is an octagonal room with a lavish domed ceiling – the tribune or saloon. This was the heart of the building and the setting for gatherings and *conversazioni*.

Amongst the celebrated guests welcomed here were Alexander Pope, Jonathan Swift, Handel and several crowned heads of state. The small scale and rounded edges of the rooms in the northern part of the house are intimate and sensual, with the overall symmetry heightened by framed views of the gardens through the doorways of the interconnected rooms. The most sumptuous of the Green, Red and Blue Velvet rooms, so-called because of their vivid wallpaper, is Lord Burlington's study, elegantly adorned in blue. The room's tiny dimensions and rich colours convey an impression of standing inside a jewel box, or inside a Fabergé egg.

Hogarth's House

Address: Hogarth Lane, Great West Road
Tel: 8994 6757
Opening Hrs: Tue–Sun and bank holiday Mon noon–5pm
Entrance Fee: free
Transport: train from Waterloo to Chiswick, bus 190

Not far from Chiswick House, sitting incongruously on the six-lane Great West Road, is Hogarth's House, the modest residence of the father of political cartoons, William Hogarth (1697–1764). Hogarth highlighted the ills of society in a series of witty engravings that became bestsellers. The house has recently been restored, and the collection of drawings, including *The Rake's Progress and Marriage à la Mode*, is worth seeking out. (Free parking for Chiswick House and Hogarth's House can be found a short distance from the Hogarth roundabout along the A4.)

Chiswick House gardens.

To see how a pint of fine English ale is made, take a tour around Fuller's Griffin Brewery on the Hogarth roundabout. Pre-booking is essential (tel: 8996 2063).

William Hogarth moved with his family to this three-storey house from busy Leicester Fields (now Leicester Square) in 1749. In a monstrous bit of irony that would not be lost on the satirist, this 'little country box by the Thames' now lies by the A4 to Heathrow, its owner immortalised in the thundering Hogarth roundabout. The traffic noise is muted in the house though, and a small garden at the back attempts a pastoral charm. The mulberry tree here is said to date from Hogarth's day, one of the few to survive from a time when the trees were brought to England in a vain attempt to get silkworms to breed.

Kew

Downriver from Chiswick is Kew, home to the Royal Botanic Gardens, known as Kew Gardens. The village green gives the place a rural feel, particularly when cricket matches are played here. On the green is St Anne's Church, where the painter Thomas Gainsborough is buried.

Royal Botanic Gardens ❷

Kew's Chinese Pagoda.

Address: Kew, Richmond, www.kew.org

Inside Kew's Palm House.

Tel: 8332 5655
Opening Hrs: Mon–Fri 9.30am–6.30pm, Sat–Sun and bank holidays 9.30am–7.30pm
Transport: Kew Gardens, or train from Waterloo to Kew Bridge

Kew Gardens, with 300 acres (120 hectares) of plants from all over the world, were first established in 1759 under the direction of Princess Augusta. In 1772, her son George III put Kew in the hands of the botanist Sir Joseph Banks, who had just returned from a round-the-world expedition to collect plant specimens with Captain Cook. Other explorers and amateur enthusiasts added to the collection over the centuries, so that today Kew is not only a vast botanical garden but also a formidable repository and research centre. In 2003 Kew was added to Unesco's list of World Heritage Sites.

The gardens present a mix of landscaped lawns, wooded areas, formal gardens and glasshouses. Make the most of the map you receive on entering, as it features seasonal highlights and where to find them.

The most famous of Kew's nursery buildings is the Grade I-listed **Palm**

House, built in 1844–8. The steamy warmth hits you as you enter this verdant tropical world, in which coconuts, bananas and coffee beans grow. Nearby, the **Waterlily House** (closed Nov–Apr) houses tropical aquatic plants. The **Temperate House**, closed for refurbishment, is the world's largest surviving Victorian glass structure.

In addition to the glasshouses there are various temples and other follies dating back to the period of royal ownership of the gardens in the 18th and early 19th centuries. The **Chinese pagoda**, built in 1762, reflects the fashion for chinoiserie in English garden design in the mid-18th century. A 650ft (200-metre) -high walkway allows you to walk above the lime, sweet chestnut and oak trees. The classically styled, Grade I-listed Orangery dating from 1761, too dark to house citrus trees as was intended, is now a pleasant café-restaurant.

Kew Palace

Built in 1631 for a Dutch merchant, **Kew Palace** (tel: 0844 482 7777; www.hrp.org.uk; daily 9.30am–5.30pm) was the country retreat of George III, Queen Charlotte and some of their children from 1801; the king came here during his bouts of supposed madness. The palace has been meticulously restored and brought back to life, revealing aspects of the original Georgian decor and architecture, and many of the family's treasures.

SYON PARK AND MUSEUMS

Across Kew Bridge is the **Kew Bridge Steam Museum** (Green Dragon Lane; tel: 8568 4757; www.kbsm.org; Tue–Sun 11am–4pm), whose original purpose was to supply London's water in the 19th century. It now houses the world's largest collection of steam-pumping engines and a steam railway, which you can ride (Sundays only Easter–Oct).

Further west along the high street is the **Musical Museum** (399 High Street, Brentford; Tue–Sun 11am–5.30pm; tel: 8560 8108; www.musicalmuseum.co.uk), which displays a large collection of automatic instruments, from clockwork music boxes to self-playing Wurlitzer organs.

Syon House

Address: Syon Park, Isleworth, www.syonpark.co.uk
Tel: 8560 0882
Opening Hrs: Syon House: Mar–Oct Wed–Thu, Sun and bank holidays 11am–5pm; gardens: Mar–Oct daily 10.30am–5pm/dusk

Syon House and its 200-acre (80-hectare) park is the London home of the Duke of Northumberland, whose family have lived here for over 400 years. Its 18th-century interior by Robert Adam is unsurpassed, celebrated as the architect's early English masterpiece. From the Long Gallery is a spectacular view over the last tidal water meadow on the Thames. The gardens were created by the great English landscape gardener Capability Brown in the mid-18th century.

Kew village green.

Xstrata treetop walkway, Kew Gardens.

Children are well catered for at Syon Park with Snakes and Ladders, a huge indoor play centre.

Further west is another grand house built as a country retreat: Osterley Park House (Jersey Road, Isleworth; tel: 8232 5050; www.nationaltrust.org.uk; house: Mar–Oct daily noon–4.30pm; garden: Mar–Oct Wed–Sun and bank holidays noon–4.30pm). This neoclassical mansion has fine interiors by Robert Adam, 18th-century gardens, and a large landscaped park.

Richmond-upon-Thames ❸

Richmond makes for a pleasant day out, easily reached by District Line Underground or by overground trains from Waterloo. Richmond Green is lined with 17th- and 18th-century buildings, while the town centre is good for shopping. Richmond Bridge is the oldest on the river, and the waterfront is always lively, with boats available for hire.

The walk up Richmond Hill to the park leads past views over the Thames and London; in the foreground you may see cows grazing on Petersham Meadows. This view is the only one in England to be protected by an Act of Parliament, passed in 1902.

Deer grazing in Richmond Park.

Richmond Park ❹

Address: Richmond, www.royalparks.gov.uk/parks/richmond_park
Tel: 8948 3209
Opening Hrs: daily May–Sep 7am–dusk, Oct–Apr 7.30am–dusk
Entrance Fee: free
Transport: Richmond, then No. 371 or 65 bus to Petersham Gate

At 2,500 acres (1,000 hectares), Richmond Park is the largest of all the royal parks. The pastoral landscape of hills, ponds, gardens and grasslands is popular with walkers, cyclists and horse riders. Since 1625, when Charles I brought his court to Richmond Palace (now demolished) to escape the plague, there have been herds of wild red and fallow deer in the park.

The 17th-century Kew Palace.

The **Isabella Plantation**, an ornamental woodland garden in the southwest corner, has been designed to be interesting all year round, though a favourite time to visit is from April, when the azaleas and rhododendrons bloom. At **Pembroke Lodge**, a Georgian mansion on the western edge of the park, there are fabulous views over west London. There's also a car park here, and refreshments.

Ham House

Address: Ham Street, Ham, Richmond, www.nationaltrust.org.uk
Tel: 8940 1950
Opening Hrs: house: mid-Mar–early Nov Sat–Thu noon–4pm; garden: all year Sat–Wed 11am–5pm
Transport: District Line to Richmond, then No. 371 bus

About a mile along the Thames Path from Richmond Hill is Ham House, built in 1610 with a sumptuous interior and important collections of textiles, furnishings and paintings. This Stuart mansion is also said to be one of the most haunted houses in the country. The formal garden is being restored to its former splendour.

Across the river is **Marble Hill House** (tel: 8892 5115; www.

english-heritage.org.uk; Apr–Oct Sat 10am–2pm, Sun and bank hols 10am–5pm), an elegant Palladian villa set in riverside parkland.

Intended as an Arcadian retreat, the house was built in 1724 for Henrietta Howard, mistress to King George II when he was Prince of Wales. It contains a fine collection of early Georgian paintings.

Hampton Court Palace ❺

Address: East Molesey, Surrey, http://hrp.org.uk/HamptonCourtPalace
Tel: 0844 482 7777
Opening Hrs: daily Apr–Sep10am–6pm, Oct–Mar until 4.30pm
Transport: train from Waterloo to Hampton Court

Surrounded by 60 acres (24 hectares) of magnificent gardens on the banks of the Thames, this vast palace, built to rival Versailles in France, dates from the reign of Henry VIII (reigned 1509–47). In the late 1600s many of the Tudor apartments were rebuilt by Sir Christopher Wren, but the Great Hall and Chapel Royal – the most striking rooms – survive.

Start at the introductory exhibition behind the colonnade in Clock Court; here you can decide on your

Kew Gardens.

Marble Hill House.

Starting at the Thames Barrier in the east and ending at the river's source in the Cotswolds 180 miles (290km) away, the Thames Path provides some of the best views of London. From Putney the path takes on a rural aspect, passing Barnes Wetland Centre, the grand riverside houses of Chiswick and the pretty cottages of Strand on the Green. After Kew Bridge, the path skirts round Kew Gardens, with Syon Park across the river. At Richmond, with Petersham Meadows on your left and a great sweep of the river ahead of you, it's hard to believe the city is in spitting distance. Along this stretch you'll see Marble Hill House and, a little further along, Ham House.

TIP

To visit Marble Hill House from the Richmond side of the river, take the Hammertons ferry, which runs between the riverbank outside Ham House in Richmond and Marble Hill Park in Twickenham (tel: 8892 9620; Apr–Oct Mon–Fri 10am–6pm, Sat–Sun 10am–6.30pm; Nov–Mar weekends only weather permitting).

route and find out about activities for children. Costumed guides give entertaining tours of some parts of the palace, including Henry VIII's **State Apartments**.

These you enter through the Great Hall, the last of its kind to be built, and the largest room in the palace. The hammer-beam roof and richly carved decoration are original. In the **Tudor Kitchens**, you can feel the heat of the massive kitchen fires and smell the meat simmering in the boiling pot, as if in preparation for a feast in Henry VIII's time.

Allow time to visit the riverside gardens, and get lost in the famous maze, planted in 1702 and nowadays enhanced with sound effects such as whispers of conversation and a dog barking.

Wimbledon ⑥

This suburb hosts one of the world's top tennis tournaments in June/July and its history is brought to life in the **Wimbledon Lawn Tennis Museum** (Church Road, Wimbledon; tel: 8946 6131; www.wimbledon.com; daily 10am–5pm). The Museum

Hampton Court Palace.

Ham House.

is closed to the public during the Championships.

On the edge of Wimbledon Common, a partly wooded expanse with nature trails, is the **Wimbledon Windmill Museum** (tel: 8947 2825; www.wimbledonwindmill.org.uk; Apr–Oct Sat 2–5pm, Sun and bank holiday Mons 11am–5pm), in a disused windmill. Displays illustrate the milling process, with hands-on milling for children.

BEST RESTAURANTS AND PUBS

PRICE CATEGORIES

Prices for a three-course dinner per person with a half-bottle of house wine:

£ = under £25
££ = £25–35
£££ = £35–55
££££ = over £55

Restaurants

Chiswick

High Road Brasserie
162–4 Chiswick High Rd, W4. Tel: 8742 7474. www.highroadhouse.co.uk Open: B, L & D daily. **££**
Located underneath the High Road House hotel, it attracts Chiswick's boho-chic crowd with its classic brasserie fare.

La Tarantella
4 Elliott Rd, W4. Tel: 8987 8877. www.la tarantella.co.uk Open: L & D daily. **££**
The restaurant owners are from Naples and are as passionate about their food as they are about their football. It's a bit of a tight squeeze, but the Italian home-cooking more than compensates for the lack of space.

La Trompette
5–7 Devonshire Rd, W4. Tel: 8747 1836. www.latrompette.co.uk Open: L & D daily. **£££**
Award-winning French country menu with mix of simple classics, such as côte de beouf, and more sophisticated offerings.

Sam's
Barley Mow Centre, 11 Barley Mow Passage, W4. Tel: 8987 0555. www.samsbrasserie. co.uk L & D daily. **£££** (set lunch **£**)
Excellent neighbourhood restaurant which will suit all moods and appetites. Brunch Sat–Sun.

Kew

The Glasshouse
14 Station Parade, Kew, TW9. Tel: 8940 6777. www.glasshouserestaurant.co.uk Open: L & D daily. **££££** (set lunch **££**)
In a pleasant location, this is one of southwest London's culinary

hotspots, with modern French-inspired cuisine.

The Orangery
Kew Gardens, TW9. Tel: 8332 5655. Open: 10am–1 hr before Gardens close. **£**
Enjoy coffee, lunch or afternoon tea in this elegant former hothouse.

Richmond

Chez Lindsay
11 Hill Rise, TW10. Tel: 8948 7473. www.chez-lindsay.co.uk Open: L & D daily. **££** (set lunch **£**)
Breton fishing village atmosphere, with superb fish, shellfish, galettes, crêpes and steak frites. Dishes change with the seasons, but the delicious galettes are a constant; try one with goats' cheese and spinach, or a casserole of red gurnard, sea bream and lobster.

Cote
24 Hill St, TW9. Tel: 8948 5971. www.cote-restaurants.co.uk Open: B, L & D daily. **££**
This bistro, one of a chain, serves classic French dishes such as moules marinières alongside more contemporary choices.

Petersham Nurseries
Off Petersham Rd, TW10. Tel: 8940 5230. www.petershamnurseries.com Open: L Tue–Sun noon–3pm. **£££**
An enchanting Michelin-starred café run by chef Skye Gyngell, with tables arranged around the greenhouse of a nursery. Seasonal produce features on the short but perfectly formed menu. Book in advance.

Pubs

Chiswick

Bell and Crown
11 Thames Rd
A pleasant riverside pub where you can eat out on the banks of the Thames.

City Barge
27 Strand on the Green; http://gkpubs.co.uk/pubs-in-london/city-barge-pub/
Another pub on the river in a very pretty location. This is where the Beatles filmed the video for Help.

Hammersmith

The Old Ship
25 Upper Mall
A smart pub overlooking the river which serves good food.

The Dove
19 Upper Mall
A pretty 17th-century pub with wooden beams and a terrace overlooking the river.

Kew

The Inn
292 Sandycombe Rd; www.theinnatkew gardens.com
A former coaching inn, at Kew Gardens Hotel, in the heart of Kew.

Richmond

The Cricketers
The Green; http://gkpubs.co.uk/pubs-in-richmond/cricketers-pub/
Picture postcard pub on the green.

The White Cross
Riverside Richmond; http://thewhitecross richmond.com
Historic Thames-side pub.

Wimbledon

Fox and Grapes
9 Camp Rd; http://foxandgrapeswimbledon. co.uk
This popular up-market pub offers a rural experience, with the Common on three sides.

The Cricketers pub, Richmond Green.

NORTH LONDON

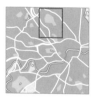

For centuries the well-to-do preferred to live in areas such as Islington, Hampstead and Highgate, away from the brothels and pollution south of the river. These areas still retain a distinct air of superiority.

I f you have time, there are several interesting areas to visit in north London, all of them most animated at weekends when they are a magnet for Londoners themselves. Choose between Islington with its vibrant eating and shopping scene, Camden with its canal and market, Hampstead with its famous heath, handsome period properties and museums, or Highgate with its overgrown Victorian cemetery containing the remains of many famous figures. They can all be reached on the Northern Line.

ISLINGTON ⑦

North of the City of London, City Road rises to the Angel, named after a long-gone coaching inn, marking the start of Islington. In the first half of the 20th century this was a poor and even dangerous area of London. Its once handsome properties were in deep decline, their buddleia-sprouting facades hiding slum conditions and multi-family occupancy.

But as London's Georgian and Victorian dwellings were refurbished in the 1970s, Islington rose phoenix-like from the ashes. It came to epitomise gentrification, and by the 1980s a popular stereotype portrayed it as the happy hunting ground of liberal-minded *bien pensants*. This is where Tony and Cherie Blair lived before moving to 10 Downing Street.

Place of entertainment

In the 18th and 19th centuries Islington was a place of entertainment. It remains a lively area, thronged with visitors both day and night. There are a vast number of restaurants and café-bars on Upper Street alone, a mile-long corridor of consumerism linking Angel Tube station with Highbury and Islington Tube station.

Arsenal's Emirates Stadium.

Interiors shop on Upper Street.

The area also has several theatres, most notably the Almeida Theatre in Almeida Street, one of London's most innovative small theatres, and, just around the corner, the **King's Head**, which is the best of several pub theatres. At the southern end of Islington on Rosebery Avenue, Sadler's **Wells** is one of London's principal dance venues.

Shopping

Near **Angel**, the crossroads at the top of Islington, the Angel Centre is a small mall of mainstream chain stores. More interesting for visitors is **Chapel Market**, a traditional London street market that retains its working-class character, and **Camden Passage** (off the other side of Islington High Street), whose elegant buildings and arcades have become a treasure trove of antiques shops, ranging from simple stalls to grand shops. There is also the **Mall Antiques Arcade** at 359 Upper Street.

For offbeat individual shops, seek out Cross Street and environs, near the Almeida Theatre halfway along Upper Street.

Islington's classic terraces

Prime examples of terraced houses can be found in **Gibson Square** and also **Canonbury Square**, where authors George Orwell and Evelyn Waugh once lived. At 39A Canonbury Square is the Estorick Collection (tel: 7704 9522; Wed–Sat 11am–6pm, Sun noon–5pm), a collection of Italian Futurist and figurative art in an elegant Georgian house, complete with bookshop.

Last, but to many minds by no means least, Islington is also the home of premier league **Arsenal Football Club**, which in 2006 moved to the new Emirates stadium. Although it is virtually impossible for non-members to obtain tickets for a game, you can take a tour of the stadium and visit the museum (www.arsenal.com).

CAMDEN ❽

It's Camden Market that attracts the crowds to Camden, though like Islington it also has many fine period terraces and squares, and a hip pub and club scene. The main market (Camden High Street, Thu–Sun 9am–5.30pm) has cheap clothes, and is still a place

Vintage fashion in Camden Passage.

You can take a 90-minute narrowboat trip from Camden (on the Jenny Wren, tel: 7485 4433; www.walkersquay. com). The boat cruises from Camden Town to Little Venice and back daily Apr–Oct, and at weekends in March.

for street style and cutting-edge fashion. **Camden Lock Market** (off Chalk Farm Road, outdoor stalls Sat–Sun 10am–6pm, indoor stalls Tue–Sun) focuses on crafts (also see page 53).

One of the delights of Camden is Camden Lock. A sequence of two locks and a bridge in quick succession, it is one of the most attractive stretches of **Regent's Canal**. From here the towpath, busy with cyclists (including bicycling commuters during the weekday rush hours), walkers and fishermen, heads west to Little Venice and east to Hackney (see page 53) and beyond. The last horse-drawn cargo passed along the canal in 1956.

The Jewish Museum

Address: 128–131 Albert Street, www.jewishmuseum.org.uk
Tel: 7284 7384
Opening Hrs: Mon–Thu, Sun 10am–5pm, Fri 10am–2pm
Transport: Camden Town

The Camden branch of the Jewish Museum (there is another one at 80 East End Road, Finchley, tel: 8349 1143) occupies an elegant early Victorian building but the interior is

Camden Lock Market.

modern with sophisticated displays, including an interactive map showing centres of Jewish population in different periods. There is a gallery devoted to Judaica, illustrating religious rituals as passed down the centuries, and exhibitions include the Holocaust Gallery and the story of the Jews in Britain.

HAMPSTEAD ❾

Hampstead has long been a desirable address and attracts a literary set. Open spaces predominate. The 3-sq-mile (8-sq-km) **Heath** leads down to **Parliament Hill**, which gives splendid views across London, as does the 112-acre (45-hectare) **Primrose Hill** overlooking Regent's Park. These are all welcome acres over which locals stride, walk dogs, fly kites, skate and swim in the bathing ponds. History-laden pubs near the heath include the **Spaniards Inn** and the congenial **Old Bull and Bush**.

Keats House

Address: Keats Grove, www.cityof london.gov.uk/keatshousehampstead
Tel: 7332 3868

REGENT'S CANAL

This 8.5-mile (14km) stretch of water running from Little Venice near Paddington in west London to Limehouse in Docklands was dug between 1812 and 1820 and drops 86ft (25 metres) through 12 locks beneath 57 bridges. The canal has some delightfully rural stretches and also passes through London Zoo. The stretch between Camden and Victoria Park in Hackney takes around a morning to complete (the towpath is interrupted in Islington, where the canal passes through a 0.75-mile (1.2km) tunnel, but can be picked up again close to Angel). To learn more about the history of the canal visit the Canal Museum at 12–13 New Wharf Road, King's Cross (see page 137).

Opening Hrs: Easter–Oct Tue–Sun
1–5pm, Nov–Easter Fri–Sun 1–5pm
Transport: Hampstead
The poet John Keats (1795–1821)
wrote much of his work, including
Ode to a Nightingale, during the two
years he lived in Hampstead. It was
here that he met and fell in love with
Fanny Brawne, the daughter of his next
door neighbour. His house-museum
contains memorabilia such as facsimi-
les of his letters, a lock of his hair and
Fanny Brawne's engagement ring. The
Regency-style garden is free to visit.

The Freud Museum

Address: 20 Maresfield Gardens,
www.freud.org.uk
Tel: 7435 2002
Opening Hrs: Wed–Sun noon–5pm
Transport: Finchley Road
Sigmund Freud, fleeing the Nazis
in 1938, moved from Vienna to this
house in Hampstead. He died just a
year later, but his daughter Anna, also
a psychoanalyst, looked after it until
her own death in 1982.

The museum preserves the house as
they left it, and includes many pieces
of furniture and other possessions
brought over from Vienna. Freud's
study on the ground floor includes the
couch on which his Viennese patients
free-associated, oriental rugs, books
and pictures, plus his prize collection of antiquities, including framed
Roman frescoes and Greek vases.

Kenwood House

Address: Hampstead Lane,
www.english-heritage.org.uk
Tel: 8348 1286
Opening Hrs: daily 11.30am–4pm
Entrance Fee: free
Transport: Archway or Highgate
Looking like a great wedding cake,
Kenwood House was remodelled in
1764–79 by Robert Adam and overlooks Hampstead Heath. Its beautifully maintained rooms reopened in
2013 after extensive refurbishment,
and showcase the **Iveagh Bequest**,
a major collection with works by
Rembrandt, Vermeer, Reynolds,
J.M.W. Turner and Gainsborough.
The first floor contains many family portraits, and items such as silver
tableware and fine furniture. The
house is also a backdrop for picnic
concerts held during the summer.

Keats House, where the poet lived between 1818 and 1820. In the winter of 1820 he was advised by his physician to leave England for the warmer climate of Italy. He never returned, dying in Rome in 1821, aged 25.

Boats on Regent's Canal.

Other grand houses

Hampstead has several other notable houses open to the public. On Windmill Hill, parallel to Heath Street, **Fenton House** (tel: 7435 3471; www.nationaltrust.org.uk; Mar–Oct Wed–Sun 11am–5pm) is a 17th-century mansion containing collections of harpsichords and ceramics. It is noted for its snowdrops in early spring.

Tucked away among the lanes is **Burgh House** (New End Square; tel: 7431 0144; www.burghhouse.org.uk; Wed–Fri, Sun noon–5pm, Sat ground floor gallery only; free), which has a fine music room and library and an award-winning garden. One of London's finest Queen Anne-style houses, it doubles as Hampstead Museum, which has a display on the landscape painter John Constable (1776–1837), a one-time local.

HIGHGATE ⑩

Neighbouring Highgate, a hilltop suburb built round a pretty square, contains London's grandest cemetery. **Highgate Cemetery** (tel: 8340 1834; www.highgate-cemetery. org) comprises two sections (see

Amy Winehouse exhibit at the Jewish Museum in Camden.

View from Parliament Hill.

page 242). The eastern cemetery (Mon–Fri 10am–4pm, weekends 11am–4pm) can be visited independently, though guided tours are available. The western section, across Swain's Lane, is more atmospheric but can only be visited on a one-hour guided tour (at weekends

tours are conducted hourly between 11am and 4.30pm; the weekday tour at 1.45pm should be booked). The cemetery is administered as a museum, with charges for taking photographs.

NORTHERN OUTPOSTS

Also worth highlighting are a couple of attractions in suburbs further north. Hendon is reached by the Northern Line.

Hendon

The main reason to visit this northern suburb is the **Royal Air Force Museum** (Grahame Park Way; tel: 8205 2266; www.rafmuseum.org.uk; daily 10am–6pm; free). It has a large array of bombers and fighter jets, plus flight simulators and a Battle of Britain Hall with tableaux of scenes from World War II. You can wander among some of the most famous aeroplanes in history.

Walthamstow

An outpost at the far end of the Tube's Victoria line, Walthamstow is not an obvious tourist attraction, but

Highgate Cemetery is full of elaborate memorials and statues, including plenty of weeping angels.

the **William Morris Gallery** (Lloyd Park, Forest Road, Walthamstow, E17; tel: 8496 4390; www.walthamforest.gov. uk; Wed–Sun 10am–5pm) is well worth the journey. Completely refurbished in 2012, the museum contains an outstanding collection of fabrics, rugs, wallpapers, furniture, glass and tiles, designed by Morris and members of the British Arts and Crafts movement.

The Royal Air Force Museum, Hendon.

BEST RESTAURANTS, BARS, PUBS AND CAFÉS

PRICE CATEGORIES

Prices for a three-course dinner per person with a half-bottle of house wine:

£ = under £25
££ = £25–35
£££ = £35–55
££££ = over £55

Restaurants

Islington

Afghan Kitchen
35 Islington Green, N1. Tel: 7359 8019.
Open: L & D Tue–Sat. **£–££**
A favourite of many Islingtonians, this tiny restaurant offers a small choice of delicately spiced, melt-in-the-mouth dishes such as chicken in yoghurt and lamb with spinach. One large table downstairs. Best to book. Cash only.

Almeida
30 Almeida St, N1. Tel: 7354 4777.
www.almeida-restaurant.co.uk Open: L & D daily. **£££** (set lunch **£**)
An ex-Conran restaurant specialis-

ing in modern French cuisine, with dishes such as red wine-braised beef and pan-fried salmon. Bang opposite the Almeida Theatre. Also offers a petits plats menu at the bar for those who only want a light dish.

Antepliler
139 Upper St, N1. Tel: 7226 5441.
www.anteplilerrestaurant.com Open: L & D daily. **£**
Serving cuisine from the Antep area of Turkey, this restaurant offers dishes such as spiced lentil koftes or diced lamb.

The Draper's Arms
44 Barnsbury St, N1. Tel: 7619 0348.
www.thedrapersarms.com Open: L Mon–Sat, D daily. **£££**
In a leafy residential street, this is one of the area's top gastropubs. Robust dishes include steak, Guinness and oyster pie. Has a patio garden.

Isarn
119 Upper St, N1. Tel: 7424 5153.
www.isarn.co.uk Open: L & D daily. **££**

Long and slender Thai restaurant with a few tables on the deck at the back. Well-prepared dishes range from simple green curries and stir-fries to lobster in tamarind sauce.

Ottolenghi
287 Upper St, N1. Tel: 7288 1454.
www.ottolenghi.co.uk Open: L & D daily. **£–££**
Stylish, with one long white table stretching down the centre of the restaurant. Great for breakfasts, light lunches (including inventive salads), savoury pastries, and divine cakes and tarts. They sell items on a takeaway basis too.

Pasha
301 Upper St, N1. Tel: 7226 1454.
www.pashaislington.co.uk Open: L & D daily. **££**
Upper Street has several inexpensive Turkish restaurants, but this one is a cut above the rest. It offers a sophisticated interior, good service and modern European food with a Turkish twist. The good-value meze is a great option for lunch.

Ottolenghi, Islington.

Camden

Bar Gansa
2 Inverness St, NW1. Tel: 7267 8909.
www.bargansa.co.uk Open: L & D daily. **££**
This popular Spanish bar and restaurant is a lively place to share some tapas with friends over a drink. Flamenco show Mon and Wed at 8pm.

Camden Brasserie
9–11 Jamestown Rd, NW1. Tel: 7482 2114.
www.camdenbrasserie.co.uk Open: L & D daily. **££–£££**
Still going strong after 30 years, this popular place appeals to celebrities and locals alike. The space is elegantly decorated and the grills, in particular, are recommended.

Cottons
55 Chalk Farm Rd, NW1. Tel: 7485 8388.
www.cottons-restaurant.co.uk Open: L Sat–Sun, D daily (until 1am on Fri). **££** (set menu **£££**)
Inspiring Caribbean restaurant with inventive options as well as firm favourites such as jerk chicken and roasted goat. A party atmosphere prevails on Friday and Saturday evenings.

Gilgamesh
The Stables Market, Chalk Farm Rd, NW1.
Tel: 7428 4922. www.gilgameshbar.com Open: L & D daily. **£££** (dim sum lunch **£**)
This glamorous pan-Asian restaurant, lounge, tea house and bar may have extravagant decor but this adds to its fun element. Food includes sushi, dim sum, and mains such as wagyu beef and Thai chicken curry.

Lemonia
89 Regents Park Rd, NW1. Tel: 7586 7454.
Open: L Mon–Fri, Sun, D Mon–Sat. **££** (set lunch **£**)
Long-established local serving tasty meze and Greek chargrills. A bona fide family restaurant.

Odette's
130 Regent's Park Rd, NW1. Tel: 7586 8569. www.odettesprimrosehill.com Open: L L Tue–Sun, D Tue–Sat. **£££** (set lunch **££**)
Primrose Hill restaurant where Oasis frontman Liam Gallagher proposed to Patsy Kensit in the 1990s. Fussy, over-the-top interior but good modern European food.

Hampstead

The Wells
30 Well Walk, NW3. Tel: 7794 3785.
www.thewellshampstead.co.uk Open: L & D daily. **£££**
Gastro-pub with discreet corners and pretty views from its upstairs restaurant. Dishes are seasonal but might include confit duck leg with braised cabbage, or pan-fried sea bass. The steaks are excellent.

Woodlands
102 Heath St, NW3. Tel: 7794 3080. Open: L Tue–Sun, D daily. **£**
Sophisticated setting for authentically spiced vegetarian dishes from southern India. Part of a global chain that began in India over 70 years ago.

Zara
11 South End Rd, NW3. Tel: 7794 5498.
www.zararestaurant.co.uk Open: L & D daily. **££**
Friendly Turkish place serving authentic Anatolian specialities. Ottoman rugs and cushions abound.

Pubs, Bars and Cafés

Islington

Canal 125
125 Caledonian Rd; www.canal125.co.uk [10] p310 B1]
Five minutes from Kings Cross, this is a laid-back local bar with two outdoor terraces looking onto Regents Canal.

The King's Head
115 Upper St; www.kingsheadtheatrepub.co.uk
Very lively traditional pub which pioneered pub theatre.

Patisserie Bliss
426 St John's St [10 p310 D2]
A tiny café just south of Angel which has possibly the best almond croissants in town.

Ottolenghi
(see main listings) is great for mid-morning or afternoon treats.

The Winchester
2 Essex Rd; http://thewinchesterbar [10] p310 D1]
Quirky Islington pub which does a good roast on Sundays.

Camden

Bar Vinyl
6 Inverness St; www.barvinyl.com
This hip bar was one of the first DJ wine bars in London. For nearly two decades it has provided edgy art and music to a happy crowd.

Camden Head
2 Camden Walk; www.camdenhead.com
One of Camden's oldest pubs, established in 1787. Live music, comedy and DJs, plus good food.

The Engineer
65 Gloucester Ave; http://theengineerprimrosehill.co,uk
A grandiose gastropub in uber-trendy Primrose Hill, with good but pricey food.

The Lord Stanley
51 Camden Park Rd; http://thelordstanley.co,uk
A fantastic, spacious gastropub with Mediterranean-inspired food and a walled garden. The menu changes frequently. Attracts everyone from students to retired folk.

Proud Galleries
The Horse Hospital, Stables Market, Chalk Farm Rd
A gallery, live music venue and club, this is where the cool people hang out in Camden.

Hampstead

The Flask
14 Flask Walk; www.theflaskhampstead.co.uk
A Victorian pub with a roaring fire in winter, where Karl Marx was a frequent visitor. There's a large outdoor space that can get very crowded on sunny days. Good pub food.

The Hill
94 Haverstock Hill; http://thehilllondon.com
This local bar and restaurant can get quite noisy, but the food is the main draw and with good reason.

The Holly Bush
22 Holly Mount; http://hollybushhampstead.co.uk
Traditional pub in the heart of Hampstead serving excellent food.

Spaniards Inn
Spaniards Rd
A 16th-century coaching inn (founded in 1585 as a tollgate inn – you can still see the tollgate opposite) with garden and summer barbecues. Dickens mentions it in The Pickwick Papers.

EAST LONDON

For centuries, waves of immigrants settled in parts of East London such as Bethnal Green and Spitalfields, often in slum conditions. Today, thanks in part to the 2012 Olympic Games held here, redevelopment is bringing considerable changes for the better.

East London was the first stop for many of the immigrants whose labour helped fuel the Industrial Revolution and build the docks through which much of the British Empire's trade passed. Poverty and overcrowding were endemic.

Today, this area is a mix of urban poverty and some of the hippest parts of London.

HOXTON

Hoxton, north of Old Street, first became fashionable when young artists such as Damien Hirst and Tracey Emin moved here, creating studios in redundant warehouses. As they became successful, art dealers and web designers followed and urban desolation became urban chic.

Commercial galleries radiate from **Hoxton Square**, the former location of Jay Jopling's White Cube gallery (it has now moved to Bermondsey Street). Café-bars and clothes shops line the streets around Curtain Road, and the area is one of London's most popular places for a night out. On Sundays Hoxton's **Columbia Road Market** (8am–3pm) specialises in flowers, plants and garden accessories (see page 52).

The Geffrye Museum Ⓐ

Address: 136 Kingsland Rd, www.geffrye-museum.org.uk
Tel: 7739 9893
Opening Hrs: Tue–Sat 10am–5pm, Sun noon–5pm
Entrance Fee: free except for special exhibitions
Transport: Old Street

This museum charts the interior decorating tastes of the urban middle classes from 1600 to the present day. Housed in a square of former almshouses, it was intended

Columbia Road Market.

to inspire workers in the East End furniture trade. The rooms – all of which are 'sitting' or 'living' rooms – are arranged chronologically from 1620 to 1990. Behind the buildings the museum's gardens comprise period and walled herb gardens (Apr–Oct), overlooked by a pleasant restaurant.

Hackney

East towards Hackney, Broadway Market (Saturdays only) is a great place to come for fabulous food stalls (spices, cheeses, breads, rare-breed meat, luscious cakes and olives), vintage clothes, hip cafés and indie music shops. Walk further east along the Regent's Canal to **Victoria Park**, a lovely big park with ponds, playgrounds, a deer enclosure and the Pavilion Café. In summer music festivals are held here.

BETHNAL GREEN

South of Victoria Park, Bethnal Green has two excellent museums focusing on childhood.

Museum of Childhood Ⓑ

Address: Cambridge Heath Rd,

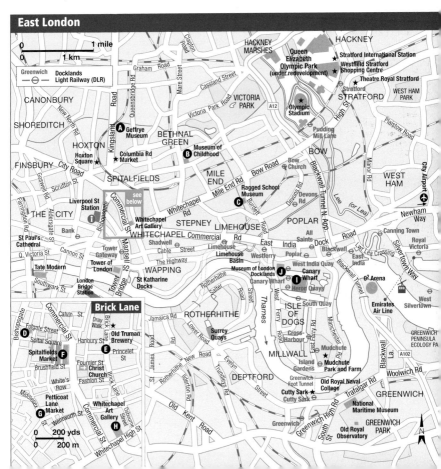

www.museumofchildhood.org.uk
Tel: 8983 5200
Opening Hrs: daily 10am–5.45pm
Entrance Fee: free
Transport: Bethnal Green

Displays in this outpost of the V&A Museum (see pages 212) range from classic children's toys to the development of nappies and the root of adolescent rebellion. There's much to appeal to children: a magnificent rocking horse can be ridden, the model railways can be activated, a dressing-up box can be rifled through, and an activity corner encourages learning through play. There are also some sobering facts to be learnt about childcare and health.

Less than a mile away, the **Ragged School Museum** ⓒ (46–50 Copperfield Road; tel: 8980 6405; www.raggedschoolmuseum.org.uk; Wed–Thu 10am–5pm, first Sun of month 2–5pm; free) has a reconstructed kitchen and classroom to show how life was once lived by London's indomitable East Enders. Children can sit at school desks and climb in the tin bath to get a taste of Victorian life.

SPITALFIELDS

Spitalfields contains several streets of fine 18th-century houses that were originally the homes of Huguenot silk weavers.

Dennis Severs' House ⓓ

Address: 18 Folgate St; www.dennis severshouse.co.uk
Tel: 7247 4013
Opening Hrs: every Mon 6–9pm (candlelit tours – booking required); Sun noon–4pm; Mon following the 1st and 3rd Sun of the month noon–2pm
Transport: Liverpool St

Among the 18th-century properties is this four-storey town house still lit only by gaslight. The late Dennis Severs, an American, laid out the 10 rooms as if they were still occupied by an 18th-century family, and your visit takes you on a sensory journey, room by room.

Markets

Successive waves of immigrants have left their mark on **Brick Lane** ⓔ. French Huguenots sought refuge here at the end of the 17th century, Jews fleeing the Russian pogroms

The Geffrye Museum.

arrived in the late 19th century and today the area has a large Bangladeshi community. Famous for its curry houses, it also has some of East London's best bars and nightclubs, most of which are within the Old Truman Brewery, the self-styled 'creative hub' of the East End. Also here is the Sunday UpMarket (Ely's Yard, Sun 10am–5pm), selling clothes from independent designers and gastronomic treats.

Dennis Severs' House.

The Museum of Childhood in Bethnal Green.

Legacy of the 2012 Olympics

London's 2012 Olympic Games not only exceeded expectations in the sports arenas and won universal plaudits for its organisation, but it also presented Britain as self-confident, forward-looking and fun.

UK Sport had set a minimum target of 48 medals for Great Britain's athletes and a top four finish in the medal table. After seven years of build-up, the level of international pressure on Britain was intense. By the end of the Games, Team GB had won a staggering 64 medals, 29 of them gold, coming third in the medal table, after the United States and China. But some of the most memorable moments came not in sporting triumph but in the taking part. The Paralympics were the most successful ever, and, for the first time, every one of the 204 countries sent a delegation that included female athletes. The Games have also boosted tourism, with a record-breaking 8 million visitors coming to London in the first six months of 2013 – a boom that mayor Boris Johnson described as 'a testament to the Olympic legacy'.

'Legacy' is the key word. One of the strengths of the London bid, which was led by former Olympic gold medallist Sebastian Coe, was the promise of large-scale redevelopment of some of the capital's most deprived areas, mainly in the East of the city. Once the events were over, the process began of turning the centrepiece of the Games, the Olympic Park in Stratford, into the Queen Elizabeth Olympic Park (www.noordinarypark.co.uk). The £292m project (completion date 2014) involves dismantling the temporary venues – such as the hockey and basketball arenas – and turning the site into an area of parkland, with walking and cycling routes and recreational facilities. The area will also have thousands of new homes, new businesses, schools, restaurants and shops – which should all generate thousands of new jobs.

There's a green legacy too. The area used to be a wasteland of derelict factories and polluted ground. As well as cleaning it all up, the authorities have refashioned the waterways into wildlife habitat, running between the upper Lee valley and the Thames. Hopefully birds and small mammals will be moving into the park as well as people.

Sculpture, shopping and cable car

Other major venues – the Olympic Stadium, the velodrome and swimming pool – continue to be used for sport. The stadium will also be hosting matches in the 2015 Rugby World Cup and the 2017 World Athletics Championships. Also open to the public will be the ArcelorMittal Orbit, the giant twisted sculpture at the heart of the Olympic area, designed by Anish Kapoor and Cecil Balmond. Westfield Stratford City, Europe's largest urban shopping centre, is the main gateway into the Park itself. For a spectacular aerial view of the whole Olympic site, take a trip on the cable car across the Thames from North Greenwich to the Royal Docks (www.emiratesairline.co.uk).

Patriotic attire in the Olympic Park during London 2012.

Spitalfields Market **F** (Commercial Street; Mon–Fri 10am–4pm, Sun 9am–5pm), once a wholesale fruit and vegetable market, now sells mainly clothes and crafts, as well as antiques on Thursdays. To the south, centring on Middlesex Street is **Petticoat Lane Market G**, packed on Sundays with dozens of stalls flogging cheap clothes.

WHITECHAPEL

To the east is the **Whitechapel Art Gallery H** (80–82 Whitechapel High Street; tel: 7522 7888; www. whitechapelgallery.org; Tue–Sat 11am–6pm, Thu until 9pm; free), founded by a local vicar and his wife in 1897. The gallery mounts highprofile exhibitions of modern and contemporary art by non-established artists. Guernica, by Picasso, was on display here in 1939.

DOCKLANDS

London's docks, made derelict by heavy World War II bombing and

Spitalfields Market.

rendered obsolete by new container ports to the east, were transformed in the 1990s. Their proximity to the financial institutions of the City made them an attractive location

KIDS

An incongruous attraction in this over-concreted part of Docklands (known as the Isle of Dogs) is the 35-acre (14-hectare) **Mudchute Park and Farm** (tel: 7515 5901; www.mudchute.org; park daily 9am–4.30pm, farm daily 8am–4pm; free) on Pier Street. As well as farm animals and rare breeds, it has llamas, a pets' corner and a riding centre.

At the end of Fournier Street, one of Spitalfields' finest streets, is Christ Church (1729), the greatest of Nicholas Hawksmoor's churches.

SHOPPING

Art

The Approach
47 Approach Rd, E2
Tel: 8983 3878; www.theapproach.co.uk
The gallery is situated above a pub in Bethnal Green. When it first opened in 1997 its aim was to offer solo exhibitions to emerging artists. Since then it has also expanded to represent established artists.

Flowers Gallery
82 Kingsland Rd, E2
Tel: 7920 7777; www.flowersgallery.com
The gallery was founded in 1970 in East London. It specializes in prints and contemporary international photography. It also has a branch in Mayfair.

Maureen Paley
21 Herald St, E2
Tel: 7729 4112; www.maureenpaley.com
The gallery's reputation was founded with the object of promoting contemporary and innovative art of all kinds. It was founded in 1984.

Clothes

All Saints
114 Commercial St, Spitalfields, E1
Tel: 7392 8098; www.allsaints.com
A UK fashion retail success story, All Saints was founded in 1994 and now has stores across the UK, Europe and the US. The store's name is taken from one of its founders, Stuart Trevor, whose initials, ST, are an abbreviation of Saint.

Canary Wharf.

for developments such as **Canary Wharf ❶**, whose main tower, One Canada Square, is one of Britain's highest buildings, at 800ft (244 metres). Several national newspapers are based here.

It's worth taking a ride through the area on the Docklands Light Railway (from Bank to Greenwich) to see how property developers turned the place into an architect's adventure playground.

The **Museum of London Docklands ❶** (No 1 Warehouse, West India Quay; tel: 7001 9844; www. museumoflondon.org.uk; daily 10am–6pm; free) recounts 2,000 years of history. It includes a 20ft (6-metre) model of Old London Bridge, an evocative reconstruction of the 19th-century Sailortown district, and a gallery on London, Sugar and Slavery, revealing the complexities of the city's involvement in the slave trade.

Model at the Museum of London Docklands.

BEST RESTAURANTS, PUBS AND BARS

Restaurants

Spitalfields

Canteen
2 Crispin Place, E1. Tel: 0845 686 1122. www.canteen.co.uk Open: B, L & D daily.
££
Down-to-earth restaurant serving modern British food made with seasonal ingredients.

Eyre Brothers Restaurant
70 Leonard St, EC2. Tel: 7613 5346. www.eyrebrothers.co.uk Open: L Mon–Fri, D Mon–Sat. **£££–££££**
Adventurous fusion of Iberian-influenced meat and vegetable dishes. Simple, distinct flavours. Tapas menu available.

Les Trois Garçons
1 Club Row, E1. Tel: 7613 1924. www.les troisgarcons.com Open: D only Mon–Sat. **££££** (set dinner **£££**)
Extravagantly decorated (stuffed tigers, etc) ex-pub with French food. The nearby Loungelover cocktail bar run by the same people is the perfect place for a pre- or post-dinner drink.

The Real Greek
6 Horner Square, E1. Tel: 7375 1364. www.therealgreek.com Open: L & D Mon–Sat, L only Sun. **££**
Serves delicious meze platters ideal for sharing, souvlaki and meat dishes cooked on a charcoal grill.

Docklands

Browns Restaurant & Bar
Hertsmere Rd, E14. Tel: 7987 9777. www.browns-restaurant.co.uk Open: L & D daily. **£££**
Traditional British atmosphere and classics such as salmon fishcakes. Sunday roasts are popular, with dishes such as rib of beef or pork loin served with vegetables and roast potatoes.

Royal China
30 West Ferry Circus, E14. Tel: 7719 0888. www.royalchinagroup.co.uk Open: L & D daily. **£££**
Up-market Chinese restaurant with a beautiful terrace overlooking the Thames. Serves up great Chinese specialities and fabulous dim sum (until 4.30pm only).

Pubs and Bars

Pubs

From classic East End pubs to trendy bars, there is no shortage of places to go drinking in east London.

The Pride of Spitalfields
3 Heneage St
The area is best known for its bars but this country-style pub makes the ideal escape from nearby Brick Lane.

Ten Bells
84 Commercial St
Most famous for being the pub where Jack the Ripper's last victim was allegedly sighted before she was murdered.

Bars

93 Feet East
150 Brick Lane; www.93feeteast.co.uk. A Brick Lane institution, this place has two bars, a large courtyard area and a main hall which plays host to a variety of gigs, DJs and film screenings.

Bar Kick
127 Shoreditch High St; www.cafe kick.co.uk
A laid-back place with a good food and drinks menu and table football.

The Big Chill Bar
Dray Walk (off Brick Lane); http://wearebig chill.com
In the heart of the Old Truman Brewery Arts and Media hub, this hip bar lives up to its name with comfy sofas and cool tunes.

Café 1001
Dray Walk (off Brick Lane); www.cafe1001. co.uk
In the Old Truman Brewery, this is a coffee shop, DJ bar and entertainment venue, putting on acts every night of the week.

Hoxton Square Bar and Kitchen
2-4 Hoxton Square; http://mamac olive.com
Here you can catch live music, sip cocktails or enjoy a tasty steak from their flame grill.

The Vibe Bar
91–95 Brick Lane; www.vibe-bar.co.uk
A buzzing venue spread over four rooms with DJs every night of the week.

Old Truman Brewery on Brick Lane.

SOUTH LONDON

South London's suburban 'villages' include Greenwich and Woolwich, with their distinguished naval and military heritage, historic Blackheath, leafy Dulwich and, in the southwest, vibrant Brixton.

Neighbourhoods and communities on the southern bank of the Thames offer parkland, museums, art galleries and great places to eat out. They are connected by a spaghetti of overground railway lines emanating from London Bridge and Charing Cross railway stations.

GREENWICH ⓫

A good way of getting to Greenwich is the time-honoured tradition of arriving at this maritime centre by water. Boats leave Westminster Pier daily from 10am (10.20am in winter) and take about 60 minutes. The best alternative is via the Docklands Light Railway.

Cutty Sark

Address: King William Walk; www.rmg.co.uk/cuttysark
Tel: 8312 6608
Opening Hrs: daily 10am–5pm
Transport: DLR Cutty Sark

Near the waterfront at Greenwich the *Cutty Sark* makes a handsome sight. The sailing ship from the great days of the 19th-century tea clippers, now a fascinating museum, has been beautifully restored (see page 255).

Built at a Dumbarton shipyard in 1869 the vessel was only expected to last about 30 years, but it has outlived its builders and crews. It opened as a museum in 1957 and was a popular London icon until old age began to show. The world's last tea clipper, the ship was named after one of the witches in Robert Burns' poem, *Tam O'Shanter*: 'she wore a short petticoat, a "cutty sark"'.

National Maritime Museum

Address: Park Row; www.rmg.co.uk
Tel: 8858 4422
Opening Hrs: daily 10am–5pm (some galleries open Thu until 8pm; check

View from Greenwich Park.

website)
Entrance Fee: free
Transport: DLR Cutty Sark

Located in Greenwich Royal Park, the National Maritime Museum displays an unrivalled collection of maritime art and artefacts, with its many galleries set around the Neptune Courtyard. The museum is going through a process of redevelopment, due to last until 2018.

Ground Floor

The Explorers Gallery looks at the history of sea exploration, covering early explorers such as the Vikings, Magellan's first circumnavigation of the earth, and the Europeans who sailed to America. The Maritime London gallery explores the city's naval heritage. Star item is the uniform coat worn by Admiral Horatio Nelson on HMS *Victory* during the Battle of Trafalgar. The fatal bullet hole at the shoulder is clearly visible.

In the new Sammy Ofer wing, visitors will find the Voyagers gallery, which looks at Britons and the sea. Focussing on the personal stories of this maritime nation, items on display include a letter from Nelson to Emma Hamilton, a sword and scabbard that belonged to Captain Bligh, and a watch worn by a passenger on the *Titanic*. This new wing also houses hi-tech exhibitions and a café.

First Floor

The new Traders gallery explores Britain's maritime trade with Asia, looking at the mighty East India Company and the tea trade. Artefacts on display include journals kept by sailors and a portrait of Robert Knox – the man said to have been the inspiration for Robinson Crusoe.

The Atlantic Worlds gallery deals with issues of trade and slavery, looking at the movement of people, goods and ideas across the Atlantic between the 17th and 19th centuries.

Cutty Sark.

Second Floor

The Navigators gallery looks at how maps were developed, the use of scientific instruments in sea voyages, underwater exploration, and the discovery of the polar regions. There are also interactive galleries aimed at children, one with a simulator allowing visitors to take the helm of a ship and steer it into port.

The Queen's House

Completed in 1637, the Queen's House, showcasing the museum's art collections, was designed as a

RESTORATION AND DEVASTATION

The *Cutty Sark* is the last ship of its kind in the world and for that reason the old tea clipper was made the subject of a £25 million restoration project in 2006. It was temporarily dismantled so that the hull and other valuable parts could be restored by a specialist team.

Then, in May 2007, midway through the project, there was a devastating early-morning fire at the site. The flames took two hours to contain. Although many sections of the ship, including the masts, were in safe storage at the time, the stern, considered too fragile to move, suffered acute damage, and about 50 percent of the hull's ironwork and timber were destroyed.

However, the Cutty Sark has been restored to her former glory, using only materials and techniques contemporary to the 19th century when she was built. She was officially reopened by the Queen in 2012. After the fire it was decided to raise the ship up 10ft (3 meters) on giant steel props, so you can now walk right beneath the iron hull, as well as exploring the cargo and lower decks, and trying out the cabins.

TIP

An alternative way to reach central London from Greenwich is to walk through a foot tunnel under the Thames and board a Docklands Light Railway train at Island Gardens. The 1,217ft (365-metre) -long tunnel, built in 1897–1902, enabled local workers to reach the West India Docks on the north bank of the river.

summer palace for Queen Anne of Denmark, the wife of James I. Designed by Inigo Jones, it was England's first classical Renaissance building.

Royal Observatory

Address: Greenwich Park, Blackheath Avenue, www.rmg.co.uk
Tel: 8858 4422
Opening Hrs: daily 10am–5pm (summer until 6pm)
Entrance Fee: free; charge for Flamsteed House and Meridian Courtyard
Transport: DLR Greenwich

It's a steep climb through the park – but worth it – to the **Royal Observatory**. Greenwich Mean Time was established here in 1884, and the observatory has Britain's largest refracting telescope. A brass rule on the ground marks the line between the Eastern and Western hemispheres.

Flamsteed House, designed by Sir Christopher Wren (himself a keen astronomer), contains exhibits tracing the history of astronomy from its earliest origins in the ancient civilisations of Sumeria and Egypt. Valuable items on display include a Chinese

National Maritime Museum exhibit.

sundial and a lodestone, an ore used for magnetising compass needles.

The *pièce de résistance* is a complete collection of John Harrison's ornate sea clocks, designed to remain accurate through the heat and cold, humidity and constant motion experienced on a ship at sea. They allowed

Looking across to Canary Wharf from the Greenwich foot tunnel.

mariners to determine their position east or west – an achievement chronicled in Dava Sobel's 1995 non-fiction bestseller Longitude.

A short distance from the main complex is the state-of-the-art **Peter Harrison Planetarium** (tel: 8312 6608; times of shows vary). It includes interactive exhibits and an education centre, and offers a variety of shows.

Old Royal Naval College

Address: 2 Cutty Sark Gardens, www.ornc.org
Tel: 8269 4747
Opening Hrs: daily 10am–5pm
Entrance Fee: free
Transport: DLR Greenwich

The Old Royal Naval College begun by Sir Christopher Wren in 1696 was built in two halves to preserve the view from Queen's House to the river. Originally a royal palace, it was given over to the training of naval officers in 1873. The chapel, where regular Sunday services are held, is full of decorative touches, and the ceiling of the Painted Hall, originally a sailors' dining room, displays a celebrated painting of William and Mary (who

The Painted Hall at the Old Royal Naval College.

SHOP

Greenwich Market (Tue–Sun) spreads out from Greenwich Church Street. Here clothes, crafts created by local artisans, books and antiques are on sale, and there are numerous stalls offering tempting snacks and produce.

reigned 1689–1702) handing Liberty and Peace to Europe.

In 2006, during routine maintenance work, Tudor brickwork was unearthed in the grounds. Subsequent excavations revealed the remains of the palace chapel and

The Old Royal Naval College.

There are excellent views of the Thames Barrier from a small urban park on the northern bank of the river. Thames Barrier Park on North Woolwich Road has a visitor café, a children's playground and paths lined with shrubs and flowers. Transport: Pontoon Dock DLR.

vestry. The Discover Greenwich visitor centre has exhibitions, a shop and brewery café.

Greenwich centre

The heart of Greenwich lies just to the west of the park. The town centre has interesting restaurants and shops, as well as **Greenwich Market** around Greenwich Church Street (see page 257). On the same street is St **Alfege's Church**, built in 1712–18 by Nicholas Hawksmoor to replace an earlier church in which Henry VIII had been baptised. It was restored in 1952 after being badly bombed during World War II.

In an elegant period house is the **Fan Museum** (12 Croom's Hill; tel: 8305 1441; www.thefanmuseum.org.uk; Tue–Sat 11am–5pm, Sun noon–5pm) displaying an unusual collection of hand-held fans from the worlds of fashion and the stage.

WOOLWICH ⑫

River trips continue downriver from Greenwich, sweeping back up the eastern side of the Isle of Dogs to **Blackwall Reach**, around the

The Thames Barrier.

O2, an exhibition arena built for the year 2000, and once known as the Millennium Dome (www.theo2.co.uk). It is now a venue hosting everything from comedy and music gigs to ballet and the tennis ATP World Tour Finals. This is also where the Emirates Air Line departs, London's only cable car (www.tfl.gov.uk). As it climbs high above the river you get fabulous views of the sweep of the Thames and beyond to the new Olympic Park.

THAMES BARRIER

Address: 1 Unity Way;
www.environment-agency.gov.uk
Tel: 8305 4188
Opening Hrs: Thu–Sun 10.30am–5pm
Entrance Fee: charge for information centre

Beyond the O2 is the massive **Thames Barrier**, which protects 45 sq miles (117 sq km) of London from the very real danger of flooding. In 1953, 300 people died in floods and the threat of tidal surges remains. The giant gates of the £435 million barrier, finished in 1982, can rise to 60ft (21 metres) high. The barrier has been closed 119 times in defence since its completion, and is raised once a month for tests (phone for times). You can reach the visitor centre on the south side by boat or bus from Greenwich.

Beyond is Woolwich, once the Royal Navy's dockyards and arsenal. The main attraction at the Royal Arsenal is **Firepower** (tel: 8855 7755; www.firepower.org.uk; Tue–Sat 10am–5pm;), also known as the Royal Artillery Museum.

The centrepiece of this military museum is the ground-shaking 'Field of Fire', which puts viewers in the midst of battle. Bombs and shells whizz overhead, guns roar and smoke fills the room. There is also a large two-level gunnery gallery which has an impressive display of artillery and 'have a go' simulator.

BLACKHEATH ⑬

A few miles south of Greenwich is **Blackheath**, one of London's neat middle-class villages. The windy heath is where Henry V was welcomed home after beating the French at Agincourt in 1415. Overlooking the heath is the Paragon, a crescent of colonnaded houses. St **Michael's Church** (1829) has a severely tapering spire known as 'the needle of Kent'.

DULWICH ⑭

With leafy streets, elegant houses and a spacious park, Dulwich is an oasis of calm. It is largely the creation of one man, Edward Alleyn, an Elizabethan actor-manager who bought land in the area in 1605 and established an estate to administer a chapel, almshouses and a school for the sons of the poor.

Today, the estate has more than 15,000 homes, Dulwich College, Alleyn's School and James Allen's Girls' School.

Dulwich Picture Gallery

Address: Gallery Road; www.dulwich picturegallery.org.uk
Tel: 8693 5254
Opening Hrs: Tue–Fri 10am–5pm, Sat–Sun 11am–5pm
Transport: mainline train from Victoria to West Dulwich or London Bridge to North Dulwich

Dulwich College, which schooled the writers P.G. Wodehouse and Raymond Chandler, spawned the **Dulwich Picture Gallery** by combining Edward Alleyn's collection with a bequest of paintings intended for a Polish National Gallery but diverted when the King of Poland was forced to abdicate.

The magnificent building, designed by Sir John Soane, opened in 1811 as the country's first major public art gallery. It contains 300 works by Rembrandt, Rubens, Van Dyck, Gainsborough and Murillo. A highlight is seven paintings by Poussin, including *The Roman Road*.

Horniman Museum

Address: 100 London Road; www.horniman.ac.uk
Tel: 8699 1872
Opening Hrs: daily 10.30am–5.30pm
Entrance Fee: free
Transport: mainline train from London

Dulwich Picture Gallery.

Horniman Museum.

Bridge to Forest Hill

A mile to the east of the gallery is the **Horniman Museum**, one of south London's unsung treasures. Combining rich collections of ethnography and natural history, it was founded in 1901 by a wealthy tea merchant, Frederick Horniman, and is set in 16 acres (6.5 hectares) of parkland.

Highlights include a spectacular collection of African masks, bronze plaques from Benin, a large aquarium and a reptiles area. There are also over 7,000 unusual and historical musical instruments.

BRIXTON ⑮

It's not the architecture but the people who give **Brixton** its character. The population is around 60 percent white, and the balance includes Vietnamese, Chinese, Africans and Caribbeans. Its laid-back attitude to recreational drugs gets it a bad press, but the area has been steadily gentrified, and attracts plenty of affluent young professionals.

Brixton Market (Mon–Sat 8am–6pm, Wed until 3pm), running from Electric Avenue to Brixton Station

Strolling through Brixton Village.

Road, mixes Caribbean produce with fruit, vegetables and fish, plus stalls of second-hand clothes, music and junk. Brixton Village Market in Coldharbour Lane, not so long ago a rundown arcade, is the new culinary and cultural hub of Brixton, with vintage shops, boutiques, live music and lots of great places to eat. It's open late Thursday and Fridays and gets very busy, with a real community buzz.

Nightlife is lively here too. The five-screen **Ritzy** cinema in Coldharbour Lane is popular, as are edgy dance clubs such as **Electric Brixton** (1 Town Hall Parade), and bars/clubs such as **Dogstar** (389 Coldharbour Lane).

Lively restaurants and bars line the high street of nearby Clapham.

THE SOUTHEAST

The National Trust-owned **Red House** (Red House Lane; tel: 8304 9878; www.nationaltrust.org.uk/red-house; Mar–mid-Nov Wed–Sun 11am–5pm; book a guided tour if you wish to visit 11am–1pm, unguided from 1.30pm) is the only house commissioned by William Morris and is a temple to the Arts and Crafts movement. Built in 1859 by his friend Philip Webb, it contains furniture by Morris and Webb, and paintings and stained glass by Burne-Jones. Morris lived here for five years and the house was central to the lives of many of the Pre-Raphaelites. Trains depart from Charing Cross to Bexleyheath.

Eltham Palace (off Court Road; tel: 8294 2548; www.english-heritage.org.uk; Apr–Oct Mon–Wed, Sun 10am–5pm, Nov–Mar check website) is a stunning Art Deco mansion. It was built in the 1930s for the Courtaulds, onto the existing Great Hall of the medieval palace (built for Edward IV in the 1470s). The lavish rooms include a bathroom with gold-plated taps, and a centrally heated area for the Courtaulds' pet ring-tailed lemur. Trains run from London Bridge to Eltham and Mottingham stations.

BEST RESTAURANTS, PUBS, BARS AND CAFÉS

PRICE CATEGORIES

Prices for a three-course dinner per person with a half-bottle of house wine:
£ = under £25
££ = £25–35
£££ = £35–55
££££ = over £55

Restaurants

Greenwich

Davy's Wine Vaults
159–161 Greenwich High Rd, SE10. Tel: 8858 7204. www.davy.co.uk Open: L daily, D Mon–Sat. **££** [162 p323, C3]
Informed wine list, and good food. Sunday lunch is served until 4pm.

Inside
19 Greenwich South St, SE10. Tel: 8265 5060. www.insiderestaurant.co.uk Open: Brunch Sat, L Tue–Sun, D Tue–Sat. **£££** (set menu **££**) [163 p323, C3]
Excellent, reliable local serving modern European dishes, such as pan-fried sea bass and barbary duck. Good-value set menus are available at breakfast and dinner.

North Pole Bar and Restaurant
131 Greenwich High Rd, SE10. Tel: 8853 3020. www.northpolegreenwich.com Open: L & D daily. **£££** (set menu **££**) [164 p323, C3]
Lively place with two bars and modern European cuisine served in the upstairs restaurant. Good roasts on Sundays.

The Spread Eagle
1–2 Stockwell St, SE10. Tel: 8853 2333. www.spreadeaglerestaurant.co.uk Open: L & D daily. **£££** [165 p323, D2]
French restaurant occupying a 17th-century coaching inn. Strong wine list.

Blackheath

Chapters
43–45 Montpelier Vale, SE3. Tel: 8333 2666. www.chaptersrestaurants.com Open: B Sat–Sun, L & D daily. **£££**
Eclectic menu (roast belly of pork; Sardinian couscous with seafood) and a range of excellent desserts.

Laicram
1 Blackheath Grove, SE3. Tel: 8852 4710. Open: L & D Tue–Sun. **££**
Friendly low-key Thai restaurant offering the standard satay, pad thai and green curry formula, but well executed.

Dulwich

Dulwich Gallery Café
College Rd, SE21. Tel: 8693 5244. Open: Tue–Fri 9am–5pm, Sat–Sun 10am–5pm **£**
Enjoy lunch or afternoon tea in a pastoral setting.

Franklins
157 Lordship Lane, SE22. Tel: 8299 9598. www.franklinsrestaurant.com Open: L & D daily. **£££** (set lunch **££**)
A little off the beaten track, this offers unfussy modern British dishes.

Brixton

Asmara
386 Coldharbour Lane, SW9. Tel: 7737 4144. Open: D daily. **££**
This quirky little Eritrean place offers a traditional Messob dinner, a 'royal feast' of injera (like sour pancakes) topped with stews and vegetable concoctions.

Brixton Village Market
This covered arcade is lined with great places to eat; try Honest Burger for top-quality British burgers, Elephant, a tiny Pakistani café, or Agile Rabbit, for thin and crispy pizzas.

Lisboa Grill
256a Brixton Hill, SW2. Tel: 8671 8311. Open: L Sat–Sun, D daily. **££**
No-frills Portuguese restaurant behind a takeaway. Hearty fish and meat dishes – the piri-piri chicken is popular.

The Satay Bar
447–455 Coldharbour Lane, SW9. Tel: 0844 474 6080. www.sataybar.co.uk Open: L & D daily. **£**
Round the corner from the Ritzy cinema. Offers cheap Indonesian rice and noodle dishes. Happy hour daily 5–8pm.

Pubs, Bars and Cafés

Greenwich

Cutty Sark
A fine riverside pub with great views and good food.

The Greenwich Union
56 Royal Hill; www.greenwichunion.com [104 p335, D3]
Popular local pub which offers over 60 beers. Good home-cooked food is also served.

The Trafalgar Tavern
Park Row; www.trafalgartavern.co.uk [105 p335, E1]
A traditional Thames-side pub with great views.

Blackheath

Hare & Billet
1a Hare and Billet Road; www.capitalpub company.com/
On the edge of the heath, this traditional pub has an excellent range of beers and serves good food.

Princess of Wales
1a Montpelier Row; www.princessofwales pub.co.uk
Very pretty pub where drinkers spill out onto the grass in summer.

Dulwich

The Crown and Greyhound
73 Dulwich Village; www.thecrownand greyhound.co.uk
A decorative Victorian pub which has a pleasant beer garden.

Brixton

Dogstar
389 Coldharbour Lane
A legendary three-floor street corner pub and dance venue.

Trinity Arms
45 Trinity Gardens; www.trinityarms.co.uk
In a lovely Georgian building, this is a classic local just off Brixton Road.

Clapham

Esca
160 Clapham High St; http://escadeli.co.uk
A café/deli serving terrific food made fresh daily.

Winchester Cathedral.

DAY TRIPS

Within striking distance of the capital is a
vast range of places to visit, from castles
to country houses, from theme parks to
seaside resorts. Bath, Oxford, Cambridge
and Canterbury are within reach, too.

The roads around the capital are as busy as any European city's and, unless you are following a complex itinerary, it is best to travel by train or coach. For directions on how to reach places in this chapter, see page 272.

WINDSOR

Just 25 miles (40km) from central London is **Windsor Castle ①** (tel: 01753 831118; www.royalcollection.org. uk; daily Mar–Oct 10am–5.15pm, Nov–Feb 9.45am–4.15pm, last admission one hour 15 mins before closing), still a favourite residence of the Royal Family. William the Conqueror began fortification here in 1066, immediately after defeating King Harold at the Battle of Hastings.

The present stone castle was started 100 years later by Henry II. Queen Victoria had a special love for Windsor and is buried, along with her husband, Albert, at Frogmore (limited opening times; www.royal.gov. uk/theroyalresidences/frogmore), a former royal residence, set among sweeping lawns and exotic trees, about a mile (1.6km) away.

Though overshadowed by its vast castle, Windsor is a pleasant town, with lovely walks among deer and ancient trees in Windsor Great Park,

which spreads south from the castle, and along the River Thames.

A great draw for children is **Legoland Windsor ②** (2 miles/3km from the town centre on the B3022 Bracknell/Ascot road; tel: 0871 222 2001; www.legoland.co.uk; daily Apr–Oct, closed selected weekdays in Apr, May, Sept and Oct). This theme park is based on the children's building blocks – in this case, millions of them. Its 150 acres (60 hectares) of wooded landscape has rides for all age groups, ranging from

Main Attractions
Windsor Castle
Blenheim Palace
Canterbury
Brighton
Bath
Cambridge
Oxford
Stratford-upon-Avon

Maps and Listings
Map, page 264
Restaurants, page 269
Accommodation, page 287

Changing the Guard, Windsor Castle.

KIDS

Harry Potter fans young and old will love the **Warner Bros. Studio Tour** (www.wbstudiotour.co.uk; you must book in advance). Here you can discover the magic behind the film franchise by exploring the sets and a fascinating collection of props and costumes. It's located 20 miles northwest of London near Watford; the nearest station is Watford Junction where a shuttle bus will take you to the tour.

roller-coasters for teenagers to gentle jaunts for toddlers.

More sedate, but also very popular with children, is **Bekonscot Model Village** and **Railway** (tel: 01494 672919; www.bekonscot.co.uk; Mar–Oct daily 10am–5pm), near Beaconsfield, a stone's throw north of the M40 (junction 2). This delightful attraction, rich in detail, has been expanding since 1929.

Six miles east of Windsor, on the other side of the river, is **Runnymede** (tel: National Trust 01784 432891; summer 8.30am–7pm, winter until 5pm; charge for car park). This riverside meadow is where King John signed the Magna Carta in 1215.

GREAT HOUSES AND GARDENS

The largest private house in England, **Blenheim Palace ❸** (tel: 0800 849 6500; www.blenheimpalace.com; mid-Feb–Oct daily 10.30am–4.45pm, Nov–early Dec Wed–Sun only) is

just outside the Oxfordshire village of Woodstock (8 miles/13km north of Oxford on the A44 Evesham Road).

The palace was built by John Vanbrugh for the first Duke of Marlborough as a reward for his victory over the French at the Battle of Blenheim (1704). Winston Churchill was born here in 1874. He is buried in the church at nearby Bladon, on the edge of the Blenheim estate.

One of the country's most popular gardens is in Kent. **Sissinghurst Castle ❹** (tel: 01580 710701; www.nationaltrust.org.uk; mid-Mar–Oct daily 11am–5pm) has the famous garden created in the 1930s by the English aristocrats Vita Sackville-West and her husband, Harold Nicolson.

Winston Churchill's country home at **Chartwell ❺** (tel: 01732 868381; www.nationaltrust.org.uk; Mar–Oct daily 11am–5pm; entry by timed ticket) at Westerham, close to the M25, has a water garden, rose garden

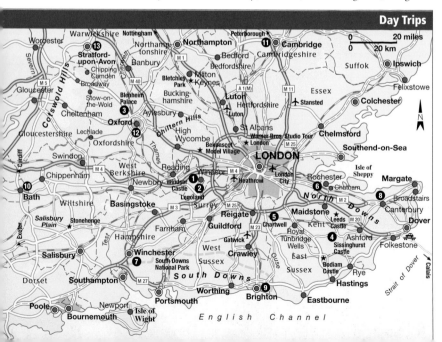

Day Trips

and stunning views, and you can visit Churchill's studio.

Cathedrals and Dickens

Rochester ❻ has a lovely Norman cathedral, and its huge castle, a gaunt ruin, stands brooding over the River Medway, 30 miles (48km) east of London. For many years the town was home to Charles Dickens, and in nearby Chatham is **Dickens World** (tel: 01634 890421; www.dickensworld.co.uk; daily 10am–5.30pm, last tour is at 3.30pm), a re-creation of Victorian London complete with Dickensian characters and an atmospheric boat ride.

Winchester ❼, a refined country town 66 miles (106km) southwest of London, was the capital of England in Saxon times. Its cathedral has a fine English Perpendicular interior.

Canterbury ❽, 62 miles (100km) southeast of London, is also famous for its cathedral, where Thomas à Becket was martyred in 1170.

SEASIDE EXCURSION

Brighton ❾, 59 miles (95km) south of London, is a perennially popular

Blenheim Palace, one of England's finest stately homes, was built in the early 18th century by John Vanbrugh and is the birthplace of Winston Churchill.

spot. The old-fashioned pedestrianised streets known as The Lanes are a maze of antiques shops, booksellers and souvenir stores, and much of the enjoyment to be had is in wandering. The jewel of Brighton is the exotic **Royal Pavilion** (tel: 03000 290900; www.brighton-hove-rpml.org.uk; daily Apr–Sept 9.30am–5pm, Oct–Mar 10am–4.30pm), built in the architectural style of Mughal India by Henry Holland and John Nash for the Prince Regent at the end of the

Brighton beach and pier.

TIP

You can sample Bath's spa facilities at Thermae Bath Spa, a luxurious and architecturally inspiring complex utilising two of the historic spa buildings. It offers an extensive range of pampering treatments to both men and women, and incorporates a rooftop pool with lovely views (tel: 01225 331234 or 0844 888 0844 from the UK; www.thermaebathspa.com).

18th century. The brilliant oriental interiors are decorated with golden dragons, chinoiserie, burnished palms and coloured glass.

ROMAN BATH

Bath 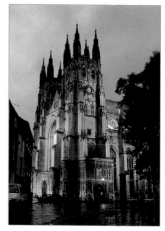, with its beautifully integrated crescents, squares and terraces, is a Georgian masterpiece and well worth making a special effort to visit. Although 116 miles (187km) from London, it can be reached in 80 minutes by fast train from Paddington. At its elegant heart are the impressive **Roman Baths** (tel: 01225 477785; www.romanbaths.co.uk; daily July–Aug 9am–9pm, Mar–June, Sep–Oct 9am–5pm, Nov–Feb 9.30am–4.30pm) to which has been added a new complex utilising the mineral-rich, soothing hot springs (see page 266).

The adjacent Pump Room was built in the 1790s as an elegant antechamber to the baths where visitors could sample the water, promenade and listen to musical entertainment. Today it is a restaurant and a lovely spot to have lunch or tea. You can still try the spa water, too.

Canterbury Cathedral.

Other architectural highlights of the city include the sweeping **Royal Crescent, Queen Square**, the Circus, the **Assembly Rooms** (which contain an excellent Museum of Costume) and pretty **Pulteney Bridge**, which is lined, like the Ponte Vecchio in Florence, with tiny shops.

UNIVERSITY TOWNS

Within easy reach of the capital are the UK's finest university towns, each of which offers tours around the historic colleges, a pleasant city centre and that quintessentially Oxbridge pastime, punting on the river Cam or Isis.

Cambridge ⓫, 61 miles (98km) from London is compact and best explored on foot. It gained its first college, Peterhouse, in 1284, but undoubtedly the finest of all the college buildings is **King's College Chapel**, which boasts magnificent fan vaulting, 16th-century stained-glass windows and Rubens' *Adoration of the Magi*.

The college is also famous for the King's College Choir, whose carol performance is broadcast live across the world on Christmas Eve.

The Bridge of Sighs, Hertford College, Oxford.

Among the other historic colleges, Sidney Sussex College in Sidney Street is remarkable for being the last resting place of the head of Oliver Cromwell, leader of the Roundheads in the English Civil War (1642–49), who had briefly been a student here.

Like Cambridge, **Oxford** ⑫, 56 miles (90km) from London, is also easily explored on foot. There's something about the light in Oxford, reflecting off the ancient stones, that gives the town a unique allure. Indeed, it was regarded by the poet John Keats as 'the finest city in the world'.

Coach-loads of tourists come to check, trooping respectfully round the university's three dozen colleges, a few of which have been centres of learning for up to seven centuries.

The best place to start a tour is Carfax, where the four main streets – Cornmarket, High Street, Queen Street and St Aldate's – meet. On St Aldate's is **Christ Church**, the grandest of Oxford's colleges, founded in 1525 by Cardinal Wolsey, Henry VIII's chancellor, on the site of an earlier priory.

For drivers, the Cotswolds to the west of Oxford beckon, their quaint showpiece villages seeming to grow out of the earth, so perfect is their relationship with the landscape. Tourism is intensive here, though it is possible to get off the beaten track with your own transport. Among the prettiest villages are Lechlade, Stow-on-the-Wold, Broadway and Chipping Campden.

To the northeast of Oxford, at Bletchley around 40 miles (64km) away, is a place that was once the best-kept secret in Britain. **Bletchley Park** (tel: 01908 640404; www.bletchley park.org; daily Mar–Oct 9.30am–5pm, Nov–Feb 9.30am–4pm) was a rambling country estate that became the heart of Britain's codebreaking operations in World War II. It was here that Germany's seemingly impenetrable Enigma code was broken, and here that the genius Alan Turing worked to build the Bombe, the machine that helped to crack it. You can see operational rebuilds of the Bombe, and the Colossus, the first semi-programmable electronic computer, built by the Post Office engineer Tommy Flowers

Trinity College fountain, Cambridge.

TIP

The RSC (Royal Shakespeare Company) presents a varied programme of Shakespeare and other plays at its venues in Stratford (the Royal Shakespeare Theatre and the Elizabethan-style Swan Theatre). Check its website for details: www.rsc.org.uk.

to break another German cipher. Many of the original huts are still standing. If travelling from London, you may reach Bletchley by direct train from Euston in 40 minutes.

SHAKESPEARE COUNTRY

Stratford-upon-Avon ⑬, birthplace of Shakespeare, is 40 miles (64km) north of Oxford. The Shakespeare Centre (tel: 01789 204016; www. shakespeare.org.uk) in Henley Street is the headquarters of The Shakespeare Birthplace Trust, which administers five properties associated with the Shakespeare family (each with its own opening times, check website for details; money-saving multi-house tickets available).

Shakespeare's Birthplace, adjacent to the centre, was the Shakespeare family home and business premises – his father was a glove maker, wool merchant and money-lender, and became mayor in 1568. Like the other period properties run by the Trust, it has been authentically restored and furnished.

Ann Hathaway's Cottage, the childhood home of Shakespeare's

Chipping Campden's main street.

wife, is in Shottery, about 1 mile (1.6km) west of town. It is an idyllic timber-framed thatched cottage with a pretty garden rather than the working farmyard it would have been in Shakespeare's day. The other properties are Mary Arden's Farm, Hall's Croft, and Nash's House and New Place.

Royal Crescent, Bath.

BEST RESTAURANTS AND CAFES

PRICE CATEGORIES

Prices for a three-course dinner per person with a half-bottle of house wine:

£ = under £25
££ = £25–35
£££ = £35–55
££££ = over £55

Windsor

Hungry Eye

1 Church Lane. Tel: 01753 830099. Open: L & D daily. **££**
Lovely warm welcome at this popular Nepalese place. Authentic dishes include Nepali thali and excellent tandooris.

Brighton

Food for Friends

17–18 Prince Albert St, The Lanes. Tel: 01273 202 310. www.foodforfriends.com Open: L & D daily. **£**
This vegetarian restaurant is highly rated.

The Gingerman

21a Norfolk Square. Tel: 01273 326688. www.gingermanrestaurant.com Open: L & D Tue–Sun. **££** (set menu **£**)
Modern European dishes incorporating best-quality ingredients.

The Regency

131 King's Rd. Tel: 01273 325014. www.theregencyrestaurant.co.uk Open: L & D daily. **£–££**
Old-fashioned and bustling fish restaurant on the seafront. Serves everything from fish and chips to mussels and sea bass. Some meat choices too.

Terre à Terre

71 East St. Tel: 01273 729051. www.terreaterre.co.uk Open: L & D daily. **££**
Busy café with innovative vegetarian menu. Just off the seafront.

Bath

Demuths

2 North Parade Passage. Tel: 01225 446059. www.demuths.co.uk Open: L & D daily. **£–££**
Terrific vegetarian restaurant near the Roman Baths. Sample dishes include a Middle Eastern platter.

The Hole in the Wall

16 George St. Tel: 01225 425242. www.theholeinthewall.co.uk Open: L & D daily. **££**
Long-established restaurant serving seasonal, modern European food in a period property. Good-value set lunches and pre-theatre menus. Log fires in winter.

The Moon & Sixpence

27 Milsom Place. Tel: 01225 320088. www.moonandsixpence.co.uk Open: L & D daily. **££**
Restaurant in the centre of town. British favourites are given an imaginative twist. Smart but casual ambience.

Rustico Bistro Italiano

2 Margaret's Buildings. Tel: 01225 310064. www.rusticobistroitaliano.co.uk Open: L & D daily. **££**
Authentic Italian home-cooking using only organic and locally farmed produce in a lovely setting in the heart of Bath.

Cambridge

Midsummer House

Midsummer Common. Tel: 01223 369299. www.midsummerhouse.co.uk Open: L & D Tue–Sat. **£££**
Modern European cuisine in stylish surroundings beside the River Cam.

Duck with cherries, Brasserie Blanc.

Three Horseshoes

High St, Madingley. Tel: 01954 210221. www.threehorseshoesmadingley.co.uk Open: L & D daily. **£££**
Thatched inn in a pretty village 2 miles (3km) from Cambridge. Modern Mediterranean food.

Oxford

Brasserie Blanc

71–2 Walton St. Tel: 01865 510999. www.brasserieblanc.com Open: L & D daily. **££–£££**
Member in a small chain of Raymond Blanc restaurants that provide quality French food at reasonable prices.

Browns

5–11 Woodstock Rd. Tel: 01865 511995. www.browns-restaurant.co.uk Open: B, L & D daily. **££**
This well-established restaurant combines classic British food with a relaxed atmosphere.

Stratford-upon-Avon

Bensons

4 Bard's Walk. Tel: 01789 261116. www.bensonsrestaurant.co.uk Open: B & L daily. **£**
Come here for a champagne breakfast of eggs and smoked salmon, a light lunch or a first-rate afternoon tea. Booking is advisable for tea.

Leadenhall Market pub.

INSIGHT GUIDES TRAVEL TIPS
LONDON

TRANSPORT

GETTING THERE AND GETTING AROUND

Note: London telephone numbers are shown as 8-digit numbers. If dialling from elsewhere in the UK, precede these with the code 020. If outside the UK, dial +44 20 and then the 8 digits.

GETTING THERE

By Air

London is served by two major international airports: Heathrow, 15 miles (24km) to the west (mainly scheduled flights); and Gatwick, 28 miles (45km) to the south (scheduled, charter and low-cost flights). The smaller airports of Stansted and Luton, both to the north of London, are used by many European low-cost airlines, but have some long-haul flights. The tiny London City Airport in Docklands is used by small aircraft connecting London with some European cities.

Heathrow Airport

Heathrow can be a daunting place in which to arrive, and it's important to plan how you'll get into central London. For further information on all airport services, see www.heathrowairport.com.
Train The fastest route is the **Heathrow Express** to Paddington

Station, which runs every 15 minutes and takes 15 minutes. Paddington connects with several Underground (Tube) lines (see map inside back cover). The fare is £20 single (£34 return) – perhaps the world's costliest rail ticket per mile. A cheaper option is the 25-minute **Heathrow Connect** service, which stops at several stations en route to Paddington, and costs £9.50.
Underground There is also a direct Tube route on the Piccadilly Line, which reaches the West End in around one hour. It goes directly to Kensington, Park Lane (Hyde Park Corner), Piccadilly, Covent Garden and King's Cross, and operates from 5am (6am on Sunday) until 12.30am daily. A single ticket to central London will cost £5.50; keep your ticket, as you need it to exit the system. Heathrow Terminals 1, 2 (currently closed) and 3 all connect to the same Tube station, but there are separate ones for Terminals 4 and 5.
Bus National Express runs

coaches from Heathrow to Victoria Coach Station; the journey takes between 45 and 80 minutes, depending on traffic, and the single fare is £6. The bus station is at Terminals 1, 2 and 3; from Terminals 4 and 5, take the free Heathrow Connect train to the bus station. For information, tel: 0871 781 8178; www.national express.com.
Taxis Heathrow is well-served by taxis. A ride into town in a London 'black cab' will cost £40–70 plus 10 percent tip, depending on destination.
Car Hire Heathrow offices of major car rental firms are:
Alamo, tel: 0871 384 1086; www.alamo.co.uk.
Avis, tel: 0844 581 0147; www.avis.co.uk.
Budget, tel: 0844 544 3439; www.budget.co.uk.
Hertz, tel: 0843 309 3099; www.hertz.co.uk.

Gatwick Airport

Gatwick airport, 28 miles (45km) from the city centre, isn't on the

FLIGHT INFORMATION

Heathrow Airport, tel: 0844 335 1801
Gatwick Airport, tel: 0844 892 0322
Luton Airport, tel: 01582

405100
Stansted Airport, tel: 0844 335 1803
London City Airport, tel: 7646 0088

COACH CONNECTIONS

National Express coach (long-distance bus) services connect Heathrow, Gatwick, Stansted and Luton airports with one another and with Victoria coach station. There are

also direct bus services from all the main airports and destinations around Britain. For details and bookings, tel: 0871 781 8181, www.national express.com.

the trip takes 35 minutes. Bookings are not essential, but advisable at peak times. Fares vary according to the time of travel: late at night or early morning are cheaper. Taking a car (with any number of passengers) through the tunnel costs from about £149 return, depending on availability. For information and reservations, tel: 0844 335 3535 (UK), or see www.eurotunnel.com.

Underground network, but trains and buses run to and from Victoria rail and coach stations. For further information, see www.gatwick airport.com.

The **Gatwick Express** train leaves every 15 minutes from 3.30am to 12.35am; it takes 30 minutes and for a single journey costs £17.75 online or £19.90 from the ticket office. Children under five travel free; children aged 5–15 travel for half the adult fare. For more details tel: 0845 850 1530 or see www. gatwickexpress.com.

First Capital Connect and Southern Railway also run services from Gatwick to Victoria, with stops en route: journey time is 30–40 minutes, and the fare £14.40.

easyBus (www.easybus.co.uk) run services from Gatwick to West London while National Express bus services (tel: 0871 781 8181) operate the 32-mile (51km) journey between Heathrow and Gatwick (£25 single), taking between 60 and 90 minutes.
Car Hire from Gatwick:
Alamo, tel: 01293 567790
Avis, tel: 0870 010 4068
Enterprise, tel: 01293 609090; www.enterprise.com.
Hertz, tel: 0870 846 0003.

Luton Airport

Luton is linked by First Capital Connect rail services with London St Pancras; some trains continue to Gatwick via Blackfriars. There is a shuttle bus between the airport and Luton train station. The journey to St Pancras takes about 40 minutes, and trains run every 7–15 minutes. Green Line buses (route 757) run to Victoria in London, and take about 90 minutes

(tel: 0844 801 7261, www.green line.co.uk).

Stansted Airport

Stansted Express trains run to Liverpool Street Station in London every 15 minutes; journey time is 45 minutes, and a single ticket is £23.40. Buses run from Stansted to several destinations in London, notably the A50 bus direct to Victoria. It runs every 30 minutes, and tickets cost £9.

London City Airport

London City Airport is mainly used by business travellers. The airport has its own station on the Docklands Light Railway (DLR), which connects with the Underground network at Bank station. For airport and flight enquiries, tel: 7646 0088; www.londoncityairport.com.

By Channel Tunnel

The London terminus for **Euro-star** passenger trains from Paris and Brussels is St Pancras International/King's Cross. Journey times are about 2 hours 15 minutes from Paris, or 1 hour 50 minutes from Brussels. For information and reservations, tel: 0843 218 6186 (UK) or 00 44 1233 617575 (from outside the UK), or check www.eurostar.com.

Vehicles are also carried by **Le Shuttle** trains through the tunnel between Folkestone in Kent and Calais in France. There are two to four departures each hour, and

By Ferry

Ferries operate between many British and Continental ports. Calais–Dover is the shortest crossing (75–90 minutes). Some of the main companies are:
Brittany Ferries, tel: 0871 244 0744 (UK), www.brittany-ferries. co.uk. Sail from Portsmouth to Caen, Le Havre, Cherbourg or St-Malo, Poole–Cherbourg and Plymouth–Roscoff.
Norfolk Line, tel: 0871 574 7235 (UK), www.norfolkline.com. Dover–Dunkirk.
P&O Ferries, tel: 0871 664 2121 (UK), 08 25 12 01 56 (France), www.poferries.com. Dover–Calais.
SeaFrance, tel: 0844 493 0651 (UK), www.seafrance.co.uk. Frequent sailings from Dover to Calais.

GETTING AROUND

Public Transport

The Tube

The Underground (known as the Tube, see map on the inside back cover) is the quickest way across town, but is often very busy. In rush hours (8am–9.30am and 5–7pm) every station is packed with commuters. Trains run from 5.30am to around midnight. If you're heading for the end of a line, the last train may leave closer to 11pm.

Make sure you have a valid ticket and keep hold of it after you

Docklands Light Railway.

have passed through the electronic barrier – you will need it to exit at your destination. If you have an Oyster card (see page 275), be sure to touch in on entry and on exit, or you will be charged the maximum fare for the line. Stations are divided into one of nine zones, spreading out from the centre; the minimum adult fare for a single ticket in zones 1–2 is £4.70, but much less with an Oyster card. A single ticket from Heathrow to the centre will cost £5.50.

It is illegal to smoke anywhere on the London transport system.

You can print out itineraries from www.tfl.gov.uk.

Docklands Light Railway

Known as the DLR, this is a fully automated railway that runs through redeveloped areas of east London and to Greenwich, and connects with the Tube network at Bank, Tower Gateway, Stratford and a few other stations. Tickets and fares are the same as for the Tube.

Buses

Bus routes run throughout the city day and night. The flat fare in central London is £2.40, but only £1.45 for Oyster card-holders. On several routes, if you do not have a Travel- or Oyster card, you must buy single tickets before boarding, from machines at the bus stops – you cannot pay by cash when you board.

A new breed of double decker buses has been introduced in London to replace the old hop-on hop-off Routemasters. Designed by Thomas Heatherwick, who designed the Olympic cauldron, these stylish driver-and-conductor buses feature an open back door and two sets of stairs. At the time of writing, they run on routes 11, 24 and 38, with more due to be introduced.

Several bus routes run 24 hours a day, and on others Night Buses (identified by an N before the number) run about every 30 minutes from midnight to 6am. Most Night Bus routes run through Trafalgar Square. A full bus route map is available from London's six Travel Information Centres.

Taxis

London's **taxis** ('black cabs') are licensed and display the regulated charges on a meter. They can be hailed in the street (an orange roof-light is displayed when they are free) or you will find them at railways stations, airports and taxi ranks. You can book a taxi in advance at www.tfl.gov.uk (comments and complaints can

RAILWAY STATION TERMINALS

Britain's rail services are run by a variety of private companies. These are the principal mainline stations, with the areas they serve:

Charing Cross Station. Services to south London and southeast England: Canterbury, Folkestone, Hastings, Dover Priory.

Euston Station. Services to northwest London and beyond to Birmingham and the northwest: Liverpool, Manchester, Glasgow.

King's Cross Station. Services to north London and beyond to the northeast: Leeds, York, Newcastle, Edinburgh and Aberdeen.

St Pancras Station. Points not quite so far north, such as Nottingham, Derby and Sheffield, plus the Eurostar terminal for trains from Paris and Brussels.

Liverpool Street Station and

Fenchurch Street. To east and northeast London, Cambridge and East Anglia.

Paddington Station. Services to west London and to Oxford, Bath, Bristol, the west, and South Wales.

Victoria Station. Services to south London and southeast England, including Gatwick airport, Brighton, Newhaven and Dover.

Waterloo Station. To southwest London, Southampton, and southern England as far as Exeter, including Richmond, Windsor and Ascot.

Other terminals, such as **Marylebone**, **London Bridge**, **Cannon Street** and **Blackfriars**, are mainly commuter stations, used for destinations around London.

For information on **train times**, tel: 0845 748 4950.

be registered here too), or by using the smart phone app Hailo.

Minicabs are cheaper than black cabs, but can only be hired by telephoning for one, as they're not allowed to pick up passengers on the street. Use minicabs with caution, particularly if travelling alone, and do not use any of the unlicensed cabs that tout for business on the street late at night in central London. To receive the telephone numbers of the two nearest minicabs and the nearest black cab number, text CAB to 60835 from your smartphone (charge).

Cable Car

London's newest addition to the public transport network is the Emirates Air Line, a cable car which runs between North Greenwich (near the O2) and the Royal Docks. It's a great way to get fabulous views of east London, including the new Olympic park and the sweep of the Thames as it heads out to sea. You can use your Oyster or buy tickets on site (more expensive). For more information, check www.tfl.gov.uk.

Coaches

Coach (long-distance bus) travel is generally cheaper than travelling by train. National Express runs services throughout the country from Victoria Coach Station on Buckingham Palace Road, tel: 0871 781 8181, www.nationalexpress.com.

Central London is a nightmare to drive in, with its web of one-way

To arrange for a licensed black cab by phone, call:
Call-a-Cab
Tel: 8901 4444
Minicab Companies
Addison Lee
Tel: 0844 800 6677
London Cabs
Tel: 7205 2677

Single tickets on London's transport networks are very expensive, so it's best to buy one of several multi-journey passes. **Travelcards** give unlimited travel on the Tube, buses, DLR and valid rail services. London is divided into nine fare zones, with zones 1–2 covering all of central London. A one-day Travelcard for zones 1 and 2 and off-peak (valid after 9.30am) costs £8.90 (£9 peak time, children aged 11–15 pay £2 each if an accompanying adult has a travelcard). You can also buy seven-day or one-month Travelcards.

Oyster cards are smart cards that you charge up with however much you wish to pay, then touch in on card readers at Tube and rail stations and on buses, so that an amount is deducted each time you use it. They are cheaper than Travelcards if you only travel a few times daily.

Cards and Oysters can be bought from Tube or DLR stations. Visitors can order them from www.visitbritainshop.com. Children aged 11–15 travel free on buses with an Oyster photocard, and under-11s travel free on the Tube and DLR at off-peak times provided they are with an adult.

streets, bad signposting, and impatient drivers (taxi drivers hate hesitation). Drive on the left and observe speed limits (police detection cameras proliferate). Do not drive in bus lanes at the hours signposted. There are heavy penalties for driving after drinking over the limit. Drivers and passengers (front and back) must use seat belts.

Parking

Meters are slightly cheaper than car parks, but only allow

Licensed taxis are reliable.

parking for a maximum of two or four hours. Wardens are unforgiving. Some meter parking is free after 6.30pm each evening, after 1.30pm in many areas on Saturday afternoons and all day Sunday. However, always check the details given on the meter. Many areas of central London operate 'pay by phone' parking only, for which you will need a credit card. Penalty tickets cost £80 or £130 and reclaiming your vehicle once it has been

towed away can set you back over £200.

Congestion Charge

Cars driving into a clearly marked Congestion Zone in inner London between 7am and 6pm Mon–Fri are filmed and their owners fined if a £10 payment is not made by 10pm the same day. You can pay at many small shops (newsagents, off licences/liquor stores) or by telephoning 0845 900 1234. See www.tfl.gov.uk for details.

Car Hire

To rent a car you must be over 21 years old and have held a full driving licence for more than a year. The cost usually includes insurance and unlimited mileage.
Alamo, tel: 0871 384 1086
Avis, tel: 0844 581 0147
Budget, tel: 0844 544 3939
Hertz, tel: 0843 309 3049 (Marble Arch branch)

Trips Out of London

This section details how to reach day-trip destinations.
Windsor
Either take the train from Paddington, journey time 30–50 minutes, or from Waterloo, journey time about 55 minutes.

CYCLING

Cycling in London can be intimidating, but a bike is often the quickest means of getting around the city. Extensive information on cycling in London can be found on the Transport for London website, www.tfl.gov.uk, which has information on the Barclays cycle hire scheme (also known as Boris Bikes, found all over the city). You can pay at docking stations with a credit or debit card. More information is available from the London Cycle Network (www.londoncyclenetwork.org.uk) and the London Cycling Campaign (www.lcc.org.uk).

Green Line coaches (tel: 0844 801 7261; www.greenline.co.uk) depart from Victoria approx. every hour, journey time about 1 hour.
Blenheim Palace
Trains from Paddington to Oxford, journey time 1 hour (see also under Oxford). Bus No. S3 from Oxford to Woodstock at approx. 30-minute intervals.
Sissinghurst Castle
Trains from Charing Cross to Staplehurst Station, journey time 1 hour. A bus link from Staplehurst to the castle runs Tue and Sun only from May (tel: 01580 710 700). Or take Arriva bus No. 5 Maidstone–Hastings alighting at Sissinghurst.
By road, it is 2 miles/3km northeast of Cranbrook, 1 mile/1.6km east of Sissinghurst village.
Chartwell
Take a train from Victoria to Bromley South, then take bus 246. Alternatively, catch trains from Charing Cross or London Bridge to Sevenoaks, then take bus 238.
By road, it is 2 miles/3km south of Westerham, fork left off B2026.
Rochester
Trains from Victoria, journey time 40 minutes–1 hour.
Winchester
Trains from Waterloo, journey

Hiring a Boris bike.

CYCLE HIRE

Velorution
tel: 7637 4004
www.velorution.com
18 Great Titchfield Street, W1.
London Bicycle Tour Company
tel: 7928 6838
www.londonbicycle.com

time 1 hour.
National Express coaches from Victoria, journey approx. 90 minutes–2 hours.
Canterbury
Trains from Victoria and Charing Cross, journey time 90–105 minutes.
National Express coaches depart from Victoria, journey time 110 minutes.
Brighton
Trains from Victoria or London Bridge, journey time 50 minutes–1 hour.
National Express coaches from Victoria stopping at Gatwick and elsewhere, journey time 2 hours.
Bath
Trains from Paddington, journey time 90 minutes.
National Express coaches from Victoria; direct-service journey time 3.25–3.75 hours.
Cambridge
Trains from King's Cross, journey time 50–80 minutes; a slower service runs from Liverpool Street Station.
National Express coaches from Victoria, journey time 2 hours.
Oxford
Trains from Paddington, journey time 60–100 minutes.
Two competing bus lines, Oxford Tube and Oxford Bus Company, run from Victoria bus station; they have services every 12 or 20 minutes.
Stratford-upon-Avon
Trains from Marylebone station, direct-service journey time 2–3 hours.
National Express coaches from Victoria: three services a day (approx. 3 hours).

ACCOMMODATION

SOME THINGS TO CONSIDER BEFORE YOU BOOK THE ROOM

Choosing a Hotel

London's hotels are famously expensive, and foreign visitors can be disappointed by the standard provided for the high rates charged. But fortunately, this is less true than it used to be. New hotels offering affordable accommodation in a central location, many belonging to mid-range chains, have sprung up in areas such as the South Bank and the City, and even top-end hotels offer special deals.

London has everything from grand hotels of international renown to family-run hotels, guesthouses, self-catering flats and youth hostels. If a clean room and a hot breakfast are all you ask, a small hotel may offer them for about a sixth of the price of a top hotel. The smaller hotels are often more friendly, making up in the welcome what they may lack in facilities. Just don't expect a lot of space – the cheaper rooms really are cell-like. If you are a light sleeper, bear in mind that central London is quite noisy, both by day and night. Enquire about noise levels and remember that in small hotels, rooms at the rear are often quieter.

Hotel Areas

There are hotels everywhere in London, but some areas have more than others. Don't necessarily expect to find a bargain two minutes' walk from Piccadilly Circus, though; the main concentrations tend to be around Victoria, Earl's Court/Kensington, the West End and Bayswater. SW1 is London's traditional hotel district. There are some delightfully old-fashioned hotels in Victoria, in most price brackets, and the streets close to Victoria Station are full of terraced bed-and-breakfast accommodation. There are also streets full of terraced (or rather town house, for this is Kensington) hotels in the second big hotel area of SW5 and SW7. This zone, around Kensington High Street, Earl's Court and Gloucester Road, is another major centre for medium-range hotels of dependable comfort.

The West End is the third area and the best-known zone. You'll pay more for budget or moderate accommodation here than you will in SW1 or SW5. W1 hotels at the bottom end of the price range can be very humble. WC1 is a clever choice: it's central and has reasonable prices, and there is still some dignity, even romance, in Bloomsbury (don't expect to find either quality in Oxford Street).

Bayswater, or at least the area between Edgware Road, Bayswater Road, Paddington and Queensway, is full of hotels. It does have a few large, expensive hotels on its fringes but has a greater concentration of moderate and budget accommodation. Quality and prices vary enormously but the area is convenient for the West End.

Budget Chains

Premier Inn is Britain's biggest budget hotel chain, with several outposts in central London, including County Hall (by Westminster Bridge), Euston, Kensington, Southwark and Tower Bridge. There are also branches close to Gatwick and Heathrow. They are clean, modern and cost between £80 and £100 per night. Central reservations: 0871 527 9222, www.premierinn.com.

The **Travelodge** chain does a similar job at similar prices; book early for good deals: www.travelodge.co.uk. Other reputable chains include **Best Western** (tel: 0845 776 7676; www.bestwestern.co.uk), Holiday Inn (tel: 0871 423 4896; www.holidayinn.com) and **Thistle** (tel: 0871 376 9099;

www.thistle.com), which often
have hotels in prime locations.

Prices and Booking

The following listings are organised alphabetically, with each hotel
given a price rating (£–££££)
based on the cost of one night's
accommodation in a double room,
exclusive of breakfast. Generally
you can get whatever your heart
desires in expensive hotels. In
budget accommodation, you're
not buying a view; if you get one it's
a bonus. Almost all hotels offer
special deals that are cheaper
than the published 'rack rate', particularly at weekends, so it is
always worth checking.

Book ahead. London fills up in
the summer months (May and
September are also crowded
because of conference traffic),
but if you arrive without a reservation, you can call **Visit London's**
telephone accommodation booking service on 3964 5657 and
book by credit card.

Among the numerous websites
worth consulting:
www.bhrc.co.uk
British Hotel Reservation Centre;
centres throughout London to
help you find somewhere to stay.
Tel: 7592 3055.
www.londontown.com
Hotel information and online reservations for moderate and luxury
accommodation in London. Special discounted rates for selected
hotels.
www.visitbritain.com
The national tourist agency.
www.visitlondon.com
The capital's tourist agency. Lists
all types of accommodation, all
bookable online.

Hotel bills usually include service and no extra tip is needed,
but if you wish to repay good service, 10 percent split between the
deserving is the custom. Equally,
you can insist that service be
deducted if you feel you've been
treated poorly.

Check when booking that the
price quoted is inclusive of VAT,
whether it includes breakfast and if

the price is per room or per person.
If you reserve in advance, you may
be asked for a deposit. Reservations made, whether in writing or
by phone, can be regarded as bind-
ing contracts, and you could be
prosecuted for breaching that con-
tract by not turning up on the day.
Rooms must usually be vacated by
midday on the day of departure.

Youth Hostels

English Youth Hostels tend to be
extremely basic but the price is
low, especially if you book reasonably far in advance or for several
nights; it will often include breakfast.

The **Youth Hostelling Association** (YHA) has eight London
locations, including St Paul's (36
Carter Lane, EC4V 5AB, tel: 0845
371 9012), Earl's Court (38 Bolton Gardens, SW5 0AQ, tel: 0845
371 9114) and Holland Park,
Kensington (Holland Walk, W8
7QU, tel: 0845 371 9122).

Accommodation prices for
members are about £20–25;
non-members pay slightly more.
To join, visit www.yha.org.uk.

Another popular choice is **Piccadilly Backpackers Hostel** (12
Sherwood Street, W1F 7BR, tel:
7434 9009, www.piccadillyhotel.
net), which has 700 beds, online
booking prices starting from
£12–15 per night, and a lively
location just off Piccadilly Circus.

Details of other student and
budget accommodation are free
from the **Tourist Information
Centre** (TIC) at 1 Regent Street,
Piccadilly Circus, SW1, or online
at www.visitlondon.com.

Bed and Breakfasts

Staying in a private home ensures
that you meet at least one London
family. The **London Bed & Breakfast Agency** specialises in such
accommodation, with prices from
£37–55 per person per night double occupancy, or £50–90 single
occupancy, depending on the area.
Tel: 7586 2768; www.londonbb.
com. Other bed and breakfast

options include: **At Home in London** (70 Black Lion Lane, W6 9BE,
tel: 8748 1943, www.athomeinlon-
don.co.uk) and **London Home-to-
Home** (42 Dahomey Road, London,
SW16 6ND, tel: 020 8769 3500,
www.londonhometohome.com)

A Place of Your Own

There's no shortage of agents and
private companies offering London
apartments, many of them luxurious, others basic and frankly, overpriced. Many holiday letting
agencies ask for a deposit which is
also to cover against cancellation.
Avoid agents who charge a fee for
finding you accommodation (such
a fee is chargeable only when you
have agreed to take a property).

Rental in the following apartments includes all bills excluding
the telephone:
Allen House, 8 Allen Street, W8.
Tel: 7938 1346; www.allenhouse.
co.uk. 42 Kensington flats, 1–3
beds. From £1,400–2,345 a week.
Apartment Services, 2 Sandwich Street, WC1H 9PL. Tel: 7388
3558; www.apartment-services.
co.uk. Sixty flats in central London, particularly Bloomsbury.
From £700–1,400 a week.
Holiday Serviced Apartments,
P.O. Box 226, Northwood, HA6
2ZJ. Tel: 0845 470 4477; www.
holidayapartments.co.uk. Have a
large number of serviced flats in
Greater London for £630–1,400
a week. Brochure available.
Kensgate House, 38 Emperor's
Gate, SW7 4HJ. Tel: 7370 1040.
Three Victorian houses split into
studios and 1-bed apartments in
Kensington and Victoria. From
£180–450 a week.

Halls of Residence

University halls of residence offer
some of the best value for money
accommodation in central London from mid-June to the end of
September. The **London School
of Economics** (LSE) for example,
has a number of residences that
are centrally situated. Tel: 7955
7676; www.lsevacations.co.uk.

WESTMINSTER AND VICTORIA

41
41 Buckingham Palace Rd, SW1W 0PS
Tel: 7300 0041
www.41hotel.com
££££ [① p320, A1]
You can't sleep closer to Buckingham Palace than in this posh
30-room boutique hotel with full
amenities and club-like atmosphere.

Airways Hotel
29–31 St George's Drive, SW1V 4DG
Tel: 7834 0205
www.airways-hotel.co.uk
£ [② p320, A2]
A pleasant hotel close to Buckingham Place and Westminster
Abbey. 40 en-suite rooms.

Berkeley Hotel
Wilton Place, SW1X 7RL
Tel: 7235 6000
www.the-berkeley.co.uk
££££ [③ p312, D4]
Many regular guests consider
the Berkeley to be the best
hotel in London. It's low-key,
seldom advertised, with a
comfortable country-house
atmosphere. Facilities include a
pool. Attracts a lot of British
customers.

Blair Victoria Hotel
78–84 Warwick Way, SW1V 1RZ
Tel: 7828 8603
www.blairvictoria.com
£ [④ p320, A2]

The Goring's garden.

Attractive period hotel close to
the train and bus stations. 48
rooms.

Dover Hotel
42–44 Belgrave Rd, SW1V 1RG
Tel: 7821 9085
www.dover-hotel.co.uk
£ [⑤ p320, A2]
Friendly B&B hotel three minutes'
walk from Victoria station. 13
rooms.

Georgian House Hotel
35 St George's Drive, SW1V 4DG
Tel: 7834 1438
www.georgianhousehotel.co.uk
££ [⑥ p320, A2]
Friendly and well-run bed and
breakfast hotel close to Victoria
station. 53 rooms.

Goring Hotel
15 Beeston Place, Grosvenor Gardens,
SW1W 0JW
Tel: 7396 9000
www.thegoring.com
££££ [⑦ p320, A1]
This is a family-owned, traditional
hotel not far from Buckingham
Palace. Kate Middleton spent the
night here before her wedding.

Grapevine Hotel
117 Warwick Way, SW1V 4HT
Tel: 7834 0134
www.grapevinehotel.com
£ [⑧ p320, A2]
Friendly family-run B&B in Victoria. English breakfast provided.

Halkin Hotel
5–6 Halkin St, SW1X 7DJ
Tel: 7333 1000
www.halkinhotel.net
££££ [⑨ p314, E4]
The style is very contemporary
and there's a first-class restaurant.

Hanover
32 St George's Drive, SW1V 4BN
Tel: 7834 0367
www.hanoverhotel.co.uk
£ [⑩ p320, A2]
Good hotel close to Victoria station and situated between two
garden squares. 42 compact
rooms.

Luna Simone Hotel,
47–49 Belgrave Road, SW1V 2BB
Tel: 7834 5897
www.lunasimonehotel.com
£ [⑪ p320, B2]
You'll receive a warm welcome in
this family-run hotel, with its por-
ticoed façade. The house has
vibrantly decorated bedrooms
with thoughtful extras and a well-
equipped computer room. 36
rooms.

The Rubens
39–41 Buckingham Palace Rd, SW1W
0PS
Tel: 7834 6600
www.rubenshotel.com
£££ [⑫ p320, A1]
Traditional hotel with a smart
location near the Royal Mews, but
also conveniently close to Victoria
station. Ten suites, 143 rooms,
and eight 'royal' rooms named
(and themed) after British monarchs.

Sanctuary House Hotel
33 Tothill St, SW1H 9LA
Tel: 7799 4044
www.sanctuaryhousehotel.co.uk
£££ [⑬ p320, B1]

PRICE CATEGORIES

Price categories are for a
double room without breakfast:
£ = under £110
££ = £110–180
£££ = £180–280
££££ = more than £280

Handy for St James's Park, but even handier for the Fullers pub underneath the hotel's 34 rooms.

Sidney Hotel
68–76 Belgrave Rd, SWIV 2BP
Tel: 7834 2738
www.sidneyhotel.com
£ [ 14] p320, B3]
Cosy hotel with bright, modern rooms situated near Victoria station and Buckingham Palace.

Tophams
24–32 Ebury St, SW1W 0LU
Tel: 7730 3313
www.tophamshotellondon.co.uk
£££ [15] p318, E2]
This luxury boutique hotel in Belgravia occupies five period houses and is very popular. Friendly and welcoming.

Victoria Inn
65 Belgrave Rd, SWIV 2BG
Tel: 7834 6721
www.victoriainn.co.uk
£ [16] p320, B2]
Popular, brightly furnished, 43-room hotel. Conveniently situated. Breakfast is included.

Victoria Park Plaza
239 Vauxhall Bridge Rd, SW1V 1EQ

W Hotel.

Tel: 0844 415 6750
www.parkplaza.com
££ [17] p320, A2]
Four-star hotel close to Victoria station, with all amenities. 287 rooms.

The Windermere Hotel
142–144 Warwick Way,

SW1V 4JE
Tel: 7834 5163
www.windermere-hotel.co.uk
£££ [18] p320, A1]
Small, friendly hotel a short walk from Victoria Station, Sloane Square and Chelsea. Serves a very good breakfast.

SOHO AND COVENT GARDEN

Charing Cross Hotel
The Strand, WC2N 5HX
Tel: 0871 376 9012
www.guoman.com
£££ [19] p306, D4 also p314, C3]
Comfortable and reliable, this hotel occupies a Grade II listed building in a busy location by Charing Cross station.

Hazlitt's
6 Frith St, W1D 3JA
Tel: 7434 1771
www.hazlittshotel.com
££££ [20] p306, C2 also p314, B1]
Named after the great English literary critic, Hazlitt's occupies one of London's oldest houses (built in 1718), in the heart of Soho. 23 rooms, all furnished with antiques.

One Aldwych
1 Aldwych, WC2B 4RH
Tel: 7300 1000
www.onealdwych.com

££££ [21] p306, E3 also p314, D2]
Smart and stylish, One Aldwych has an excellent location a stone's throw from theatreland and Covent Garden. This hotel is a showcase of modernity throughout with high-profile guests to match. 105 rooms, each with a minimum 6ft (2-metre) -wide bed, and television in the bathroom. Has a chlorine-free swimming pool.

St Martin's Lane
45 St Martin's Lane, WC2N 4HX
Tel: 7300 5500
www.stmartinslane.com
££££ [22] p306, D3 also p314, C2]
Designed by Phillippe Starck, and still the most fashionable hotel in London. Outlandish lighting, good if expensive food and 204 blindingly white bedrooms. Very well placed for West End theatres and Trafalgar Square.

The Savoy
Strand, WC2R 0EU
Tel: 7836 4343
www.fairmont.com/savoy
££££ [23] p306, E3 also p314, D2]
This classic London hotel has a reputation for comfort and personal service. A massive £220m refurbishment has restored its reputation as one of London's very best hotels. 268 rooms and suites.

Strand Palace Hotel
372 Strand, WC2R 0JJ
Tel: 7379 4737
www.strandpalacehotel.co.uk
£££ [24] p306, E3]
Good-value central hotel offering contemporary rooms near Covent Garden and the river. Two restaurants and three bars on-site. 786 rooms.

W Hotel
10 Wardour St, W1D 6QF

Tel: 7758 1000
www.wlondon.co.uk
££££ [25] p306, C3 also p314, B2]
This Soho hotel, opened in
2011, radiates an urban hip
vibe. A luxurious base with 192
rooms, all equipped with
everything you could want for an

utterly indulgent stay. Spa and
gym.
The Waldorf Hilton
Aldwych, WC2B 4DD
Tel: 7836 2400
www.hilton.co.uk/waldorf
££££ [26] p306, E2]
Renowned Edwardian hotel with

292 rooms. Modernised and
with a superb location, close to
Covent Garden and theatreland.
Rooms come with plasma TVs
and original Edwardian wash-
stands. Restaurant, patisserie,
bar, gym, sauna and swimming
pool all on site.

ST JAMES'S AND MAYFAIR

Claridge's.

Brown's Hotel
30 Albemarle St, W1S 4BP
Tel: 7493 6020
www.brownshotel.com
££££ [27] p306, A4 also p314, A3]
A distinguished, very British hotel
with 117 rooms and a smart Mayfair location.
Claridge's
Brook St, W1K 4HR
Tel: 7629 8860
www.claridges.co.uk
££££ [28] p312, E2]
Has long had a reputation for dignity and graciousness. The film
stars' favourite.
The Connaught
16 Carlos Place, W1K 2AL
Tel: 7499 7070
www.the-connaught.co.uk
££££ [29] p312, E2]
One of the best hotels in
London, and very popular with
British visitors. Discreet but
immaculate service, and a

restaurant with one Michelin
star. Only 90 rooms.
The Dorchester
Park Lane, W1K 1QA
Tel: 7629 8888
www.thedorchester.com
££££ [30] p312, E3]
This is one of the most expensive
hotels in London, owned by the
Sultan of Brunei. Lovely views
over Hyde Park.
Dukes Hotel
35 St James's Place, SW1A 1NY
Tel: 7491 4840
www.dukeshotel.com
££££ [31] p314, A3]
With 90 opulently furnished
rooms and suites, and home to
Dukes Bar, famous for its martinis. Health club with marble
steam room and beauty treatments.
The Four Seasons
Hamilton Place, Park Lane, W1J 7DR

A Lanesborough suite.

Tel: 7499 0888
www.fourseasons.com/london
££££ [32] p312, E4]
This is a temple of modern opulence overlooking Hyde Park.
Friendly and efficient service. Luxury spa.
The Lanesborough
1 Lanesborough Place, SW1X 7TA
Tel: 020 7259 5599
www.lanesborough.com
££££ [33] p312, E4]
Deluxe hotel overlooking Hyde
Park Corner. The stately neoclassical facade of the former St
George's hospital complements
the opulent Regency-style interior. Despite being a relative new-
comer this is one of London's
finest hotels.
London Hilton on Park Lane
22 Park Lane, W1K 1BE
Tel: 7493 8000
www.hilton.co.uk
££££ [34] p312, E4]
The more expensive rooms are on
the higher floors, and the
Michelin-starred restaurant on
the 28th floor has stunning views
of Hyde Park. Additional charge
for internet access.
**London Park Lane
InterContinental Hotel**
1 Hamilton Place, Hyde Park Corner, W1J
7QY
Tel: 7409 3131
www.ichotelsgroup.com

PRICE CATEGORIES

Price categories are for a
double room without breakfast:
£ = under £110
££ = £110–180
£££ = £180–280
££££ = more than £280

££££ [35 p312, E3]
Opulent, modern and well-equipped, with an Elemis spa and a fitness centre. Superb park views.
Metropolitan
19 Old Park Lane, W1K 1LB
Tel: 7447 1000
www.comohotels.com/metropolitanlondon
££££ [36 p312, E3]
Christina Ong's attempt to create a New York ambience. Home to the Michelin-starred, celebrity favourite, Japanese restaurant Nobu.
Millennium Hotel London Mayfair
44 Grosvenor Square, W1K 2HP
Tel: 7629 9400

www.millenniumhotels.co.uk
££££ [37 p312, E2]
In an 18th-century townhouse overlooking Grosvenor Square Gardens, this hotel is in a great location for shopping. Very friendly staff.
No. 5 Maddox Street
5 Maddox St, W1S 2QD
Tel: 7647 0200
www.no5maddoxsreet.com
££££ [38 p306, A2 also p314, A2]
A stylish range of suites with minimalist decor and full facilities including a kitchen.
The Ritz
150 Piccadilly, W1J 9BR
Tel: 7493 8181
www.theritzlondon.com

££££ [39 p306, A4 also p314, A3]
This is one of the most famous hotel names in the world. Not quite what it was, despite refurbishment, but it endeavours to keep up standards. Jackets and ties must be worn. Tea at the Ritz is an institution. 136 rooms.
Stafford Hotel
16 St James's Place, SW1A 1NJ
www.kempinski.com
££££ [40 p314, A3]
Beautifully located just minutes away from Piccadilly near Green Park. Three town houses converted into a characterful hotel, with 105 rooms and suites.

MARYLEBONE, BLOOMSBURY AND HOLBORN

Academy Hotel
21 Gower St, WC1E 6HG
Tel: 7631 4115
www.theacademyhotel.co.uk
£££ [41 p310, A4]
A small and welcoming Blooms-bury hotel created from five town houses, with 49 rooms.
Crescent Hotel
49–50 Cartwright Gardens, WC1H 9EL
Tel: 7387 1515
www.CrescentHotelofLondon.com
£££ [42 p310, A3]
Situated in a quiet Bloomsbury crescent, with private gardens, tennis courts and 27 rooms.
Cumberland Hotel
Great Cumberland Place, W1A 4RF
Tel: 0871 376 9014
www.guoman.com
££ [43 p312, D2]
Over 1,000 hi-tech designer rooms, each with individual works of art. Near Marble Arch.
Durrants Hotel
George St, W1H 5BJ
Tel: 7935 8131
www.durrantshotel.co.uk
£££ [44 p312, E1]
Period hotel in a Georgian ter-race, 200 years old and oozing graciousness.
Gower House Hotel
57 Gower St, WC1E 6HJ
Tel: 7636 4685

www.gowerhousehotel.co.uk
££ [45 p310, A4]
Pleasant bed-and-breakfast hotel near the British Museum.
Holiday Inn Bloomsbury
Coram St, WC1N 1HT
Tel: 0871 423 4901
www.holidayinn.com
£££ [46 p310, A3]
Modern, pleasant hotel with small indoor pool and leisure club. 313 rooms, all with private bath.
Landmark London
222 Marylebone Rd, NW1 6JQ
Tel: 7631 8000
www.landmarklondon.co.uk
£££ [47 p308, B4]
This modern eight-storey building with a glass-domed, palm tree-filled atrium has good-sized rooms and all facilities.
The Langham
1 Portland Place, Regent St, W1B 1JA
Tel: 7636 1000
http://london.langhamhotels.com
££££ [48 p314, A1]
Elegant and efficient hotel with 380 rooms, two bars and a res-taurant. The attractive fountain room is an ideal place for taking afternoon tea. A short walk from Oxford Circus.
Lincoln House Hotel
33 Gloucester Place, W1U 8HY

Tel: 7486 7630
www.lincoln-house-hotel.co.uk
£ [49 p312, D1]
Georgian-style bed-and-breakfast hotel, with well-equipped rooms.
Lonsdale Hotel
9–10 Bedford Place, WC1B 5JA
Tel: 8166 0990
www.lonsdalehotellondon.com
££ [50 p310, B4]
Long-established bed-and-breakfast hotel with real charac-ter. Over 40 rooms.
Marble Arch Inn
49–50 Upper Berkeley St, W1H 5QR
Tel: 7723 7888
www.marblearch-inn.co.uk
£ [51 p312, D1]
Convenient for Oxford Street and Hyde Park. 29 rooms.
Montague on the Gardens
15 Montague St, WC1 5BJ
Tel: 7958 7731
www.montaguehotel.com
£££ [52 p310, A4]

PRICE CATEGORIES

Price categories are for a
double room without breakfast:
£ = under £110
££ = £110–180
£££ = £180–280
££££ = more than £280

TRANSPORT

St Pancras Renaissance Hotel.

A pretty period property with a garden at the rear. Flamboyant decor.

Montagu House Hotel
2 Montagu Place, W1H 2ER
Tel: 7467 2777
www.montagu-place.co.uk
£££ [53 p308, C4 also p312, D1]
Well-equipped bed-and-breakfast hotel. The 16 rooms in this Georgian town house are graded 'comfy', 'fancy' and 'swanky'. All the stylishly designed rooms have good facilities. Has a bar and lounge.

Montcalm Hotel
34–40 Great Cumberland Place, W1H 7TW
Tel: 7958 3200
www.montcalm.co.uk
£££ [54 p312, D1]
Quiet and rather plush hotel integrated into an elegant Georgian crescent. 153 rooms.

No Ten Manchester Street
10 Manchester St, W14 4DG
Tel: 7317 5900
www.tenmanchesterstreethotel.com
£££ [55 p312, E1]
Comfortable Edwardian townhouse with just 45 bedrooms

and an 'all weather' cigar terrace, with a range of hand rolled Havanas. A lounge bar serves food all day.

The Regency Hotel
19 Nottingham Place, W1U 5LQ
Tel: 7486 5347
www.regencyhotelwestend.co.uk
£ [56 p308, C4]
An elegantly converted mansion in the heart of the West End close to Regent, Oxford and Harley streets. Just 20 comfortable rooms.

Hotel Russell
Russell Square, WC1B 5BE
Tel: 7837 6470
www.londonrussellhotel.co.uk
£££ [57 p310, A4]
Landmark building in the heart of Bloomsbury with 373 rooms, all en suite.

Thistle Marble Arch
Bryanston St, W1H 7EH
Tel: 0871 376 9027
www.thistle.com
£ [58 p312, D2]
A huge, Art Deco hotel with 692 rooms. Very central, overlooking Oxford Street and across from Hyde Park.

St Georges Hotel
Langham Place, Regent St, W1B 2QS
Tel: 7580 0111
www.saintgeorgeshotel.com
£££ [59 p318, A1 also p314, A1]
Close to the BBC and Oxford Street, with 92 rooms. Impressive views from its public rooms and restaurant.

St Pancras Renaissance Hotel
Euston Rd, NW1 2AR
Tel: 7841 3540
www.marriott.co.uk
££££ [60 p310, A2]
Stunning public areas at this restored hotel, originally designed by Sir George Gilbert Scott. There are 38 suites in the original building, and 207 in a new annexe. Right beside St Pancras Station.

Sanderson Hotel
50 Berners St, W1T 3NG
Tel: 7300 1400
www.sandersonlondon.com
££££ [61 p314, B1]
A surrealist ultra-chic hotel, restaurant and bar with modern sex appeal, just north of Soho. A good retreat from the bustle of the city. 150 rooms.

Sherlock Holmes Hotel
108 Baker St, W1U 6LJ
Tel: 7486 6161
www.parkplazasherlockholmes.com
£££ [62 p308, C4]
Handy for Oxford Street shopping and close to Regent's Park. Contemporary furnishings strive for a boutique feel.

Wyndham Hotel
20 Wyndham St, W1H 1ED
Tel: 7723 7204
www.wyndhamhotel.co.uk
£ [63 p308, B4]
Family-run hotel in period property on a quiet street. Small courtyard.

ACCOMMODATION

ACTIVITIES

THE CITY AND CANARY WHARF

A – Z

Apex City of London
1 Seething Lane,
EC3N 4AX
Tel: 7702 2020
www.apexhotels.co.uk
£££ [64 p316, C2]

A modern, medium-sized hotel near the Tower of London. The 179 rooms have good views of the City, walk-in power showers and widescreen TVs.

Crowne Plaza London Shoreditch
100 Shoreditch High St,
E1 6JQ
Tel: 0871 423 4901
www.ichotelsgroup.com

£££ [65 p316, C1]
Situated in the heart of the City, a few minutes' walk from Liverpool Street Station and Spitalfields Market. Has 264 rooms and a rooftop restaurant. Like many City hotels, weekend rates are considerably cheaper than weekday rates.

Grange City
8–14 Cooper's Row, EC3N 2BQ
Tel: 7863 3700
www.grangehotels.com

££££ [66 p316, D2]
This 5-star hotel is a member of a small well-run chain, and is close to the Tower of London with views of the City. Has excellent business facilities plus a pool.

Novotel Tower Bridge
10 Pepys St, EC3N 2NR
Tel: 7660 0675
www.novotel.com

£££ [67 p316, D2]
Overlooks the Tower of London and London Bridge. 203 light, well-equipped rooms. Full range of business facilities. Good rates available at weekends.

South Place Hotel
3 South Place, EC2M 2AF
Tel: 3503 0000

London Bridge Hotel.

www.southplacehotel.com
£££ [68 p310, E3]
This sleek boutique hotel is within walking distance of the Museum of London and Barbican Centre and includes a fitness centre and a spa. You can eat alfresco on the Rooftop Terrace.

West India Quay Marriott
22 Hartsmere Rd, Canary Wharf, E14 4ED
Tel: 7093 1000
www.marriott.co.uk

£££ [69 p316, E1]
This branch of the Marriott offers

particularly good weekend rates.
The Zetter
St John's Square
86–88 Clerkenwell Road EC1M 5RJ
Tel: 7324 4444.
www.thezetter.com.

£££ [70 p316, E3]
The Zetter is youthful and very much in the spirit of the area. Nice touches in rooms include old Penguin paperbacks and hot water bottles; free fresh coffee and tea is available all day. There's a Mediterranean restaurant downstairs. 59 rooms.

SOUTHWARK AND THE SOUTH BANK

London Bridge Hotel
8–18 London Bridge St, SE1 9SG
Tel: 7855 2200
www.londonbridgehotel.com

£££ [71 p316, B3]
Independent 4-star hotel in an efficient location for Bankside's attractions. Has 138 rooms, a gym, two restaurants and a bar.

Mad Hatter
3–7 Stamford St, SE1 9NY
Tel: 7401 9222
www.fullershotels.com

£ [72 p314, E3]
Thirty rooms above a Fullers pub. Just a short stroll from Tate Modern and other attractions on the South Bank.

Marriott London County Hall
County Hall, SE1 7PB
Tel: 7928 5200

www.marriott.co.uk
££££ [73 p314, D4]
Luxurious setting, with many of the 200 rooms facing the river at Westminster Bridge. Full-size indoor pool plus health centre.

Mercure London Bridge Hotel
75–79 Southwark St, SE1 0JA
Tel: 7660 0683
www.mercure.com

££ [74 p316, A3]
A French chain hotel close to Tate Modern and the Globe Theatre.

Novotel City South
53–61 Southwark Bridge Rd, SE1 9HH
Tel: 7660 0676
www.novotel.com

£ [75 p316, B3]

Close to Shakespeare's Globe and Tate Modern. Clean, modern rooms.

Park Plaza County Hall
1 Addington St, SE1 7RY
Tel: 0844 415 6760
www.parkplaza.com

£££ [76 p314, D4]
Sleek hotel convenient for the London Eye. 398 rooms, each with kitchenette equipped with fridge and microwave.

PRICE CATEGORIES

Price categories are for a double room without breakfast:
£ = under £110
££ = £110–180
£££ = £180–280
££££ = more than £280

KNIGHTSBRIDGE, KENSINGTON, NOTTING HILL AND CHELSEA

Abbey Court
20 Pembridge Gardens, W2 4DU
Tel: 7221 7518
www.abbeycourthotel.co.uk
££ [ p322, B2]
Beautifully restored Notting Hill town house, with the atmosphere of a private home. The 22 rooms have Italian marble bathrooms with whirlpool baths.

Aster House
3 Sumner Place, South Kensington, SW7 3EE
Tel: 7581 5888
www.asterhouse.com
£££ [p318, B2]
Victorian townhouse B&B, well located for the famous museums. The rooms have chintzy fabrics, Wi-fi and power showers in the bathrooms.

Bayswater Inn
8–16 Princes Sq, W2 4NT
Tel: 7727 8621
www.bayswaterinnhotel.com
££ [p322, C2]
Situated in a quiet residential square, close to Portobello Road Market, and handy for the Tube. 139 rooms, all en suite.

Blakes Hotel
33 Roland Gardens, SW7 3PF
Tel: 7370 6701
www.blakeshotels.com
££££ [p318, B2]
Very trendy and up-to-the-minute hotel which is popular with theatrical and media folk. Cosmopolitan, tolerant, laid-back in style. 51 rooms.

Cadogan Hotel
75 Sloane St, SW1X 9SG
Tel: 7235 7141
www.cadogan.com
££££ [p312, D4 also p318, D1]
Another 19th-century style hotel. Interesting position between Knightsbridge and Chelsea. Lily Langtry once lived in what is now the bar, and Oscar Wilde was arrested in room 118.

Capital Hotel
22 Basil St, SW3 1AT
Tel: 7589 5171

Draycott Hotel.

www.capitalhotel.co.uk
££££ [p318, D1]
Luxurious little hotel (50 rooms) in the heart of Knightsbridge. Restrained in style, with tasteful decor, and rooms in the country-house style of interior design. Friendly service.

Draycott Hotel
26 Cadogan Gardens, SW3 2RP
Tel: 7730 6466
www.draycotthotel.co.uk.
££££ [p318, D2]
This is country-house living, minutes away from Sloane Square and the King's Road. The charming Victorian house is set in a smart residential street and many of the luxuriously appointed bedrooms overlook a tranquil communal garden. 35 rooms.

easyHotel South Kensington
14 Lexham Gardens, Kensington, W8 5JE
www.easyhotel.com
£ [p318, A1]
Some of the cheapest rooms in London. No frills – some rooms don't even have a window – but great for budget travellers. There are other locations in London as well. Internet bookings only.

Enterprise Hotel
15–25 Hogarth Rd, SW5 0QJ
Tel: 7373 4502
www.enterprisehotel.co.uk
£ [p318, A2]
Good location close to Kensington High Street and Earl's Court Tube station. 100 small but func-

tional en suite rooms.

Garden Court Hotel
30–31 Kensington Gardens Sq, W2 4BG
Tel: 7229 2553
www.gardencourthotel.co.uk
££ [p322, C2]
Friendly, family-run 32-room bed-and-breakfast set in a traditional English garden square.

The Gore
190 Queen's Gate, SW7 5EX
Tel: 7584 6601
www.gorehotel.com
££££ [p312, B4]
This idiosyncratic Kensington hotel is close to the Royal Albert Hall. Every inch of the walls is covered in paintings and prints, and it attracts a lively, fashionable crowd. There are 50 individually themed rooms, some with four-poster beds.

Hotel Indigo
34–44 Barkston Gardens, SW5 0EW
Tel: 7373 7851
www.barkstongardens.com
££ [p318, A2]
Set in a quiet tree-lined street in a Victorian terrace, but close to the bustle of Earl's Court and the world-class museums of South Kensington. Meals available. 93 rooms, all with private bath.

Knightsbridge Green Hotel
159 Knightsbridge, SW1X 7PD
Tel: 7584 6274
www.knightsbridgegreenhotel.com
£££ [p312, D4]
This hotel is very good value for the location and is unusual in that

it consists mostly of suites, double and family-sized rooms. 30 rooms.

London House Hotel
81 Kensington Gardens Sq, W2 4DJ
Tel: 7243 1810
www.londonhousehotels.com
£ [98 p322, C1]
Friendly and stylish, in a pleasant location, and with 102 newly refurbished rooms. Extremely good value for money.

Mandarin Oriental Hyde Park
66 Knightsbridge, SW1X 7LA
Tel: 7235 2000
www.mandarinoriental.com/london
££££ [91 p312, D4]
A hotel of character (185 rooms), right on Knightsbridge and close to Harrods. Sumptuous in a Victorian marble-and-chandeliers style.

My Place Hotel
1–3 Trebovir Rd, SW5 9LS
Tel: 7373 0833
www.myplacehotel.co.uk
££ [92 p318, A2]
Modern amenities with Victorian ambience in Earl's Court area. 50 en suite rooms, bar and lounge.

Oliver Plaza Hotel
33 Trebovir Rd, SW5 9NF
Tel: 7373 7183
www.hoteloliverplaza.co.uk
£ [93 p318, A2]
Bed-and-breakfast hotel providing good, friendly service and comfortable rooms, all 46 of which have en suite bathrooms.

Royal Garden Hotel
2–24 Kensington High St, W8 4PT
Tel: 7937 8000
www.royalgardenhotel.co.uk
££££ [94 p312, A4]
Refurbished from top to bottom, this is now a 5-star hotel. Decorated throughout in a luxurious contemporary style, it has a health club and one of London's finest views over Kensington Gardens from the top-floor Min Jiang restaurant.

The Villa Kensington
10 Ashburn Gardens, SW7 4DG
Tel: 7370 6605
www.thevillakensington.co.uk
££ [95 p318, A2]
Located not far from Kensington High Street in a pleasant, rather old-fashioned hotel district. 38 en suite rooms.

West London

Cannizaro House
Wimbledon Common, SW19 4UD
Tel: 8879 1464
www.cannizarohouse.com
££££
Named after a Sicilian Duke, this 18th-century country house hotel is in as rural a setting as London can offer. The more interesting rooms lie in the original building.

Kingston Lodge Hotel
94 Kingston Hill, Kingston upon Thames, KT2 7NP
Tel: 8541 4481
www.brook-hotels.co.uk
££
Country-house hotel in a pretty location to the west of London. Close to Richmond Park, Hampton Court Palace, and Kingston shopping centre.

Hotel Orlando
83 Shepherd's Bush Rd, W6 7LR
Tel: 7603 4890
www.hotelorlando.co.uk
££
Family-run hotel with 14 rooms in Hammersmith, near the Tube.

The Petersham Hotel
Nightingale Lane, Richmond, Surrey, TW10 6UZ
Tel: 8940 7471
www.petershamhotel.co.uk
£££
Unspoilt views over parkland and the River Thames. Richmond train or Tube allow for an easy ride into London (20 mins). 60 rooms.

Richmond Hill Hotel
146–150 Richmond Hill, Richmond, Surrey TW10 6RW
Tel: 8940 2247
www.richmondhill-hotel.co.uk
£££
A 4-star, traditional English hotel with a friendly atmosphere and spectacular views over the Thames. Close to Kew Gardens, Richmond Park and Hampton Court Palace.

North London

Hampstead Britannia Hotel
Primrose Hill Rd, Hampstead, NW3 3NA
Tel: 0871 221 0191
www.britanniahotels.com
££
Near affluent and fashionable

Primrose Hill, this hotel has a relaxed atmosphere, 121 rooms, a restaurant and a bar.

Hampstead Guesthouse
2 Kemplay Rd, Hampstead, NW3 1SY
Tel: 7435 8679
www.hampsteadguesthouse.com £
This Victorian house with 9 rooms, close to Hampstead Heath, evokes images of writers and thinkers who have settled in the area. Not every room is en suite, but all are decorated with antiques.

Hendon Hall
Ashley Lane, Hendon, NW4 1HF
Tel: 8457 2500
www.handpickedhotels.co.uk
£££
An historic mansion with its own grounds, giving a country atmosphere in the middle of north London. Fully modernised kitchen and opulent dining room mean meals are available. 57 rooms.

La Gaffe
107–111 Heath St, NW3 6SS
Tel: 7435 8965
www.lagaffe.co.uk.
£
This small hotel (18 rooms) stands on the site of five former shepherds' cottages, and is only a short walk from Hampstead High Street. Ask for one of the bedrooms at the back overlooking a tranquil Georgian Square. The adjoining restaurant, also run by the owners, has a menu of traditional Italian cooking.

The York and Albany
127–129 Parkway, NW1 7PS
Tel: 7387 5700
www.gordonramsey.com/yorkandalbany
£££
This townhouse hotel, owned by Gordon Ramsey, has 10 rooms all individually designed with antiques and modern amenities. Located in Camden Town.

East London

Town Hall Hotel
Patriot Square, E2 9NF
Tel: 7871 0460
www.townhallhotel.com
£££
The former Town Hall in Bethnal Green has been converted into guest rooms and apartments. Crisp styling and a pool in the basement.

EXCURSIONS

Windsor

Oakley Court
Windsor Rd, Water Oakley SL4 5UR
Tel: 01753 609988
www.principal-hayley.com
£££
Victorian Gothic house with 118 rooms and extensive landscaped grounds.

Brighton

The George Inn
High St, Alfriston BN26 5SY
Tel: 01323 870319
www.thegeorge-alfriston.com
££
A 14th-century pub/hotel in a village 18 miles (29km) from Brighton. It has oak beamed rooms and the restaurant specialises in local fish.

The Grand
Kings Rd, BN1 2FW
Tel: 0871 222 4684
www.devere.co.uk
££££
Victorian grandeur and friendly service, with indoor pool. Overlooks beach.

Hotel Pelirocco
10 Regency Sq, BN1 2FG

The Royal Crescent hotel, Bath.

Tel: 01273 327055
www.hotelpelirocco.co.uk
££
Cheap but chic hotel in the best preserved Regency square in town.

Bath

Apsley House Hotel
141 Newbridge Hill, BA1 3PT
Tel: 01225 336966
www.apsley-house.co.uk
££
Georgian country house set in its own grounds, with 12 individually decorated rooms.

The Royal Crescent
16 Royal Crescent, BA1 2LS
Tel: 01225 823333
www.royalcrescent.co.uk
££££
Exclusive hotel in the centre of the splendid Royal Crescent. Traditional furnishings and every comfort.

Cambridge

Arundel House Hotel
53 Chesterton Rd,
CB4 3AN
Tel: 01223367701

www.arundelhousehotels.co.uk
£
A privately owned terraced hotel near the town centre that overlooks the River Cam.

Hilton Hotel Cambridge
Granta Place, Mill Lane CB2 1RT
Tel: 01223 259988
www.doubletreebyhilton.co.uk
££££
Modern Moat House by the river, in a convenient central location. Has its own punts and rowing boats.

Oxford

Bath Place Hotel
4–5 Bath Place, OX1 3SU
Tel: 01865 791812
www.bathplace.co.uk
££
Family-run, 15-room licensed hotel in the heart of Oxford that occupies a group of restored 17th-century cottages.

Le Manoir aux Quat' Saisons
Church Rd, Great Milton, near Oxford, OX44 7PD
Tel: 01844 278881
www.manoir.com
££££
The chef Raymond Blanc's renowned restaurant and hotel. Stunning gardens and luxurious rooms, some with a terrace.

Stratford-upon-Avon

Mercure Shakespeare
Chapel St, CV37 6ER
Tel: 02477 092807
www.mercure.com
£££
A 17th-century, half-timbered hotel next to the Town Hall.

PRICE CATEGORIES

Price categories are for a **double room without breakfast:**
£ = under £110
££ = £110–180
£££ = £180–280
££££ = more than £280

ACTIVITIES

THE ARTS, NIGHTLIFE, FESTIVALS, SPORT AND TOURS

The National Gallery.

THE ARTS

Museums & Art Galleries

A public lottery funded the British Museum's foundation in 1759 and fittingly it was lottery money released in the late 1990s to celebrate the new millennium that helped finance its spectacular Great Court. The same millennial largesse aided many of London's museums and galleries and the government decreed that the great national collections should abolish entrance fees.

Alongside the rejuvenation of the star attractions came a rash of specialist new museums. There are more than 130 museums and galleries worth a visit.

Money-saving Passes

Although national museums and galleries are free, most others have entrance charges. Energetic visitors will benefit from the London Pass, which allows free entry to several dozen attractions. Free travel on the Tube and buses is also included. At press time, prices ranged from £47 for a one-day pass to £102 for a six-day pass (children £30–72). For details tel: 0870 242 9988 or check www.londonpass.com.

Joining the Art Fund costs £53 a year and provides free admission to more than 200 museums, galleries and historic houses around the country, plus discounts on some exhibitions.

Details on 0844 415 4100 or from www.artfund.org.

Theatre

The only way to get a ticket at face value is to buy it from the theatre box office. Most open 10am–mid-evening. You can pay by credit card over the phone for most theatres, or reserve seats three days in advance before paying. A ticket booth (tkts) on the south side of Leicester Square offers unsold seats at half price or three-quarter price (plus booking fee) on the day of performance (Mon–Sat 9am–7pm, Sun 11am–4.30pm). There are booking agents throughout London (and quite a few unofficial kiosks around Leicester Square), but beware: some charge high fees. It's sensible to ask what the face value of a ticket is before parting with your money. Two reputable 24-hour agents are **Keith Prowse** at www.keithprowse.com and **Ticketmaster** at www.ticketmaster.co.uk.

Ignore ticket touts unless you're prepared to pay several times a ticket's face value for sell-out performances.

For further information see page 40. For West End theatre locations, see the map on the inside back cover.

Holland Park Open Air Theatre, Holland Park, W8. www.opera-

hollandpark.com or www.ohp.rbkc.gov.uk.
During the warm summer months, opera, dance and theatre performances are staged here in the semi-open air. Tube: Holland Park/High Street Kensington.

National Theatre, South Bank, SE1. Tel: 7452 3000; www.nationaltheatre.org.uk.
Three repertory theatres are housed within the National's concrete mass. They always provide a good and varied selection of plays. Tube: Waterloo/Embankment.

Open Air Theatre, Regent's Park. Tel: 0844 826 4242; http://openairtheatre.com.
With a 16-week summer season, this not-for-profit charity hosts a variety of plays, including Shakespeare. Tube: Baker Street.

Shakespeare's Globe Theatre, Bankside, SE1. Tel: 7401 9919; www.shakespeares-globe.com.
May–Sept season in a re-creation of the Tudor original. Tube: Southwark/London Bridge.

Ballet and Opera

Coliseum, St Martin's Lane, WC2. Tel: 7845 9300; www.eno.org.
This elegant Edwardian theatre is easily distinguished on London's skyline by the illuminated golden globe on its roof. Home to the English National Opera (ENO), this is where English-language operas are performed. Productions tend to be more theatrical than those of the Royal Opera. It also hosts performances of ballet in the summer months by the Royal Festival Ballet and visiting companies, particularly Russian ballets. Tube: Leicester Square.

Royal Opera House, Covent Garden Piazza, WC2E. Tel: 7304 4000; www.roh.org.uk.
Home to the Royal Ballet and the Royal Opera. Was extensively refurbished for the millennium. More traditional than the Coliseum, this theatre attracts the crème de la crème of the opera world. Operas are performed in

their original language and tickets are very expensive. Dressy affair. Backstage tours are available. Tube: Covent Garden.

Sadler's Wells Theatre, Rosebery Avenue EC1. Tel: 0844 412 4300; www.sadlerswells.com.
A flexible, state-of-the-art performance space that offers an exciting and innovative programme of dance and opera. London's leading venue for contemporary and classical dance. Tube: Angel.

Classical Music

Barbican arts centre, Silk Street, EC2. Tel: 7638 8891; www.barbican.org.uk.
Home to the London Symphony Orchestra and the English Chamber Orchestra. This huge concrete complex built for the arts is one of London's major classical-concert venues. Tube: Barbican.

The Royal Albert Hall, Kensington Gore, SW7. Tel: 0845 401 5045; www.royalalberthall.com.
This circular hall comes alive every summer for the Henry Wood Promenade Concerts, known simply as The Proms. Also hosts occasional comedians and indie bands. Tubes: Kensington High Street/South Kensington.

Royal Festival Hall, South Bank, Belvedere Road, SE1. Tel: 0844 875 0073; www.southbankcentre.co.uk.
London's premier classical music venue was built as part of the Festival of Britain of 1951. The exterior of this hall appears somewhat dated and arouses mixed public comment on its appearance. However, it is an excellent concert hall with space for large-scale performances. Next door is the Queen Elizabeth Hall, where chamber concerts and solos are performed. There is also the small Purcell Room for more intimate music. Tube: Waterloo/ Embankment.

Wigmore Hall, 36 Wigmore Street, W1. Tel: 7935 2141; www.wigmore-hall.org.uk.
Delightful intimate hall with seating for 550. It has a pleasant

Royal Opera House.

atmosphere and excellent acoustics and is most renowned for chamber recitals. Also hosts Sunday morning coffee concerts. Tube: Bond Street.

Churches

Many of London's historic churches also offer superb, and in some cases free, music. Three of the best are:

St John's, Smith Square, Westminster, SW1. Tel: 7222 2168; www.sjss.org.uk.
This church has been converted into a concert hall hosting chamber music and BBC lunch time concerts. Tube: Westminster.

St Martin-in-the-Fields, Trafalgar Square, WC2. Tel: 7766 1100; www.smitf.org.
Concerts are held at lunch times and evenings in this church. Tube: Charing Cross.

St Mary-le-Bow, Cheapside, EC2. Tel: 7248 5139.
Lunch time recitals most Thursdays (www.stmarylebow.co.uk has details). Home to the famous Bow bells. Tube: St Paul's/Mansion House/Bank.

NIGHTLIFE

Late Spots

If you're under 30 and believe the hype, London is one of the best

TRANSPORT

ACCOMMODATION

ACTIVITIES

A – Z

places to party in the world. It certainly has built a solid reputation as one of the great international clubbing centres. But not all nightlife is dance-till-dawn. Other nightlife options range from dinner dances to cocktail bars, comedy gigs to smart nightclubs.

Despite its reputation, and despite a relaxation of licensing laws in recent years, London is not an especially late city. Most restaurants, pubs and even bars have wound down by midnight, leaving just a few determined establishments to stagger on until the city awakes.

Jazz Clubs

Jazz Café, 5 Parkway, Camden NW1. Tel: 0844 847 2514 (tickets) or 7688 8899 (for a table). Intimate jazz club in Camden Town that attracts some top names. Tube: Camden.
Jazz@Pizza Express, 10 Dean Street, W1. Tel: 0845 602 7017. This Soho branch of the pizza chain has a high standard of performers. Tube: Leicester Square/ Piccadilly Circus/Tottenham Court Road.
Ronnie Scott's, 47 Frith Street, W1. Tel: 7439 0747. Scott, who died in 1996, had eclectic taste, and this is still reflected in this legendary Soho venue, which has hosted some of the biggest names in jazz since 1959. Very relaxed. Tube: Leicester Square/Piccadilly Circus/Tottenham Court Road.

Dance Clubs

Café de Paris, 3–4 Coventry Street, SW1. Tel: 7734 7700. Posh old dancehall attracts an older sophisticated crowd. Trendy/smart. Tube: Piccadilly Circus/Leicester Square.
Cargo, 83 Rivington Street, EC2. Tel: 7739 3440. This venue under the railway arches offers a variety of live line-ups. Tube: Old Street.
EGG, 200 York Way, N7. Tel: 7871 7111. Spacious venue with three dance floors. Fashionable gay nights. Tube: Caledonian Road.
Electric Ballroom, 184 Camden High Street, NW1. Tel: 7485 9006. This old dancehall has a huge main dance floor where on Saturday nights Shake plays hits of the 1970s, '80s and '90s, attracting a mixed crowd. Upstairs it's R&B and hip-hop. Smart casual. Tube: Camden.
Fabric, 77A Charterhouse Street, EC1. Tel: 7336 8898. Celebrated club that mixes big names (generally on Fridays), with top DJs (Saturdays) and new talent. Big on techo and electronica. Open until 6am (8am on Saturdays). Dress code: casual.

Tube: Farringdon.
Heaven, The Arches, Villiers Street, WC2. Tel: 7930 2020. Submerged beneath the Charing Cross development is this famous gay club, one of the best dance clubs in town. Party nights are Monday, Thursday, Friday and Saturday. Very casual dress code. Tube: Charing Cross/Embankment.
Koko, 1A Camden High Street, NW1. Tel: 0870 432 5527. Venue for club nights and gigs by some of the biggest names in rock and pop. Tube: Mornington Crescent.
Ministry of Sound, 103 Gaunt Street, SE1. Tel: 0870 060 0010. This renowned dance club is London's top house-music venue. Open until 7am Sat. Tube: Elephant & Castle/Borough.
Plan B, 418 Brixton Road, SW9. Tel: 7733 0926. Atmospheric Brixton venue with open warehouse-style interior. Talented house DJs and a buzzing crowd. Dress code: smart and sexy. Tube: Brixton.
Plastic People, 147–149 Curtain Road, EC2. Tel: 7739 6471. Deep, heavy sound system in a small but electric venue. Plays mainly dubstep but also hosts DJs who sway towards a more techno sound.
Roxx, Blagclub, 68 Notting Hill Gate, W11. Tel: 07762 104373. Trendy rock and roll club with modern house remixes and live entertainment. Great cocktails and good after-party vibe. Tube: Notting Hill Gate.
Salsa, 96 Charing Cross Road, WC2. Tel: 7379 3277. A good Latin venue in the heart of the West End. Lots of fun, very busy and a good place to practise your moves with regular dance classes. Casual. Tube: Charing Cross/Leicester Square.
333, 333 Old Street, EC1. Tel: 7739 5949. Hip club with a good drinking lounge upstairs and pounding dance music in the basement. Tube: Liverpool Street.

The plush interior of the Royal Opera House.

Comedy/Cabaret

Comedy Store, 1a Oxendon Street, SW1. Tel: 0844 871 7699 (tickets); www.thecomedystore. co.uk
A night at this well-established venue for stand-up comedians will remind you that comedy need not always be accompanied by canned laughter. Avoid sitting in the front row unless you want to become part of the show. Tube: Piccadilly Circus/Leicester Square.
Jongleurs, 61–65 Great Queen Street, WC2B. Also in Piccadilly. Tel: 08700 111 960.
Leading stand-up comedy club. Covent Garden venue attracts the best acts. Tube: Holborn.
Madame Jo Jo's, 8 Brewer Street, W1. Tel: 7734 3040; www. madamejojos.com
Ultra-camp transvestite revue bar popular for hen or stag nights. Lacking in the sleaze and daring associated with Soho's sometimes unsavoury past, Madame Jo Jo's still offers one of the best late-night outings in London with captivating cabaret shows. Closes 3am. Tube: Piccadilly Circus.
Stringfellow's, 16 Upper St Martin's Lane, WC2. Tel: 7240 5534.
This slightly tongue-in-cheek lap-dancing joint is strong on tacky glamour. Tube: Covent Garden/ Leicester Square.

Dinner Dance

Some of the best and most romantic dine and dance places are at the luxury hotels. The glamorous restaurant at The Ritz (Piccadilly, W1; tel: 7493 8181) holds traditional dinner dances on Friday and Saturday nights. A four-course meal is followed by dancing to a four-piece band. Dress is formal so ties for men and no jeans. Booking required.

Quick Bites

Takeaways

Beigel Bake, 159 Brick Lane, E1. Tel: 7729 0616.

Ku Bar, 30 Lisle Street, Soho. Tel: 7437 4303; www.ku-bar. co.uk
This lively drinking hole packs in a sexy international crowd over three floors, with the basement level home to energetic club nights; see website for details. Tube Leicester Square. (Also at 25 Frith Street, Soho).
G-A-Y Bar, 30 Old Compton Street, Soho. Tel: 7494 2756; www.g-a-y.co.uk
Although its crowd of screeching 18-year-olds might not be to everyone's taste, the fun never stops at the legendary club night's sister bar, where giant video screens blare out the latest hits across three floors. At closing, the party continues round the corner at **G-A-Y Late** (5 Goslett Yard, Soho; tel: 7734 9858) until 3am. Tube: Tottenham Court Road
The New Bloomsbury Set, 76

Join Londoners who ritually pile across to Brick Lane after a night out to stock up on freshly baked bagels filled with smoked salmon and cream or hot salt beef with lashings of mustard and gherkin. Open 24 hours. Tube: Shoreditch.
El Burrito, 5 Charlotte Place, W1. Tel: 7580 5048.
Mexican food to eat in or take away. Come for nachos, taco salad or burritos. Mon–Fri noon–3pm and 6–10pm. Tube: Goodge Street.
Paul Rothe & Son, 35 Marylebone Lane, W1. Tel: 7935 6783.
Historic café/greengrocers' shop offering imaginative sandwiches, bagels and hearty soups. Mon–Fri 8am–6pm, Sat 11am–5.30pm. Tube: Bond Street.

Coffee/Breakfast

Bar Italia, 22 Frith Street, W1. Tel: 7437 4520.
A piece of real Italy located in the centre of Soho. No matter what the hour, this family-run bar is always buzzing. Can be expensive

Marchmont Street, WC1N. Tel: 7383 3084.
Atmospheric and comfortable gay bar with celebrated cocktails. Great for a break from the usual wild Soho dance floor scene. Tube: Russell Square/Euston.
Heaven, under the arches, Villiers Street, WC2. Tel: 7930 2020; www.heavenlondon.com
Famous beyond these shores and still a good night out, even if it is a bit worn around the edges. There is generally plenty of flesh on show and a good range of music, and since 2008 it's been home to legendary cheese-fest G-A-Y club nights (www.g-a-y. co.uk; Thu–Sat). Tube: Charing Cross/Embankment.
XXL, 1 Invicta Plaza, SE1. Tel: 7261 0981. www.xxl-london. com. Iconic club night for bears and their admirers. There are two beer gardens, two bars and a range of DJs. Tube: Southwark.

but reputed to have the best coffee in London. Open 24 hours Mon–Sat, until 4am Sun (Mon morning). Tube: Leicester Square.
Full Stop, 202 Brick Lane, E1. Tel: 7739 7086. Home-made cakes and sandwiches available, and consistently good coffee.

London is a great place to shop. Whether you prefer to spend hours roaming around one of its grand department stores – Harrods, Liberty, Selfridges and Harvey Nichols are four of the best – or rummaging among the bargains of its many and diverse markets, there are retail opportunities to suit all budgets and tastes. The city is also known for its terrific end-of-season sales, especially after Christmas until the end of January and throughout July. There are shopping listings at the end of each chapter highlighting the most interesting shops.

Antiques

London has an enormous number of antique shops and markets. Advice and information on buying antiques in Britain as a whole can be obtained from: **London and Provincial Antique Dealers' Association (LAPADA)**, 535 King's Road, SW10. Tel: 7823 3511; www.lapada.org. They run an up-to-date online information service on auctions, specific items and antiques offerings throughout the country.

Markets

Camden Market, NW1. Hugely popular at the weekends, this sprawling market near Camden Lock sells clothes, jewellery, arts and crafts, food and antiques amongst other things.
Columbia Road Flower Market, E2. All kinds of cut flowers and houseplants are sold here at wholesale prices on Sundays, 8am–3pm. Other specialist shops on Columbia Road open to coincide with the market.
Petticoat Lane, Middlesex Street, E1. London's oldest market is so-named for the undergarments and lace once sold here by French Huguenots. Cheap clothes, fabrics and leather goods

are still sold here, on some of the 1,000 stalls.
Portobello Road, W11. Renowned for its antiques, this is also a good place to pick up fashionable and vintage clothing, art and general bric-a-brac. It gets very crowded on Saturdays.
Spitalfields, Commercial Street, E1. This historic covered market has been gentrified with cafés and boutiques, but remains a great place to spot new talent, as many young fashion and jewellery designers sell their wares here.

EVENTS CALENDAR

January

New Year's Day Parade from Parliament Square to Piccadilly.
London International Boat Show, ExCeL, Docklands. This is the world's largest exhibition of its kind. DLR: Custom House.
Charles I Commemoration (last Sunday). English Civil War Society dress up as Royalists from the King's army and make their way from Charles I's statue in Whitehall to his place of execution outside Banqueting House.

February

Chinese New Year (dates varia-

ble). Colourful Chinese celebrations centred around Gerrard Street in Chinatown, Soho. Tube: Leicester Square/Piccadilly Circus.
Great Spitalfields Pancake Day Race (Shrove Tuesday). Old Truman Brewery, Brick Lane, E1. Teams run along Dray Walk tossing pancakes. Musicians and jesters accompany them. Tube: Aldgate East/Shoreditch.

March

Ideal Home Show. Earl's Court. Exhibition of new ideas and products for the home. Tube: West Brompton/Earl's Court.
St Patrick's Day Parade. Parade of traditional music and Irish culture, with a festival in Trafalgar Square. Tube: Charing Cross.

April

London Marathon. One of the world's biggest runs, beginning at Blackheath and ending at Buckingham Palace a gruelling 26.2 miles (42km) later.
Queen's Birthday (21st). The Queen's real birthday (as opposed to her official one in June) is celebrated with a gun salute in Hyde Park and at the Tower of London.
The Boat Race Two teams from Oxford and Cambridge universities row down the Thames from Putney to Mortlake in a fiercely fought contest. This annual event (since 1856) in late March/early April is watched by around 250,000 cheering spectators lining the river banks.

May

Chelsea Flower Show, Royal Hospital, SW3. www.rhs.org.uk/chelseaflowershow. Major horticultural show, featuring spectacular displays, and social event in the fine grounds of the Chelsea Royal Hospital. Tube: Sloane Square.
Covent Garden May Fayre and Puppet Festival, Bedford Street, WC2E. A celebration of the art of

For reliably good jazz visit Ronnie Scott's on Frith Street.

puppetry, commemorating the first time Samuel Pepys recorded seeing a Punch and Judy Show. Puppeteers, folk music, workshops and maypole dancing. Tube: Covent Garden.

FA Cup Final, Wembley. The final of the nation's main football competition. Tube: Wembley Park/ Wembley Central.

Founder's Day, Chelsea Royal Hospital. Parade of the Chelsea Pensioners in memory of their founder, Charles II. Tube: Sloane Square.

The Comedy Store.

June

Beating Retreat, Horse Guards Parade, Whitehall. Annual ceremonial display of military bands on two successive evenings. Tube: Charing Cross/ Westminster.

City of London Festival (www. colf.org). Venues in the city host a range of artistic events, from concerts in St Paul's to swing bands in the Guildhall Yard.

Derby Day, Epsom Racecourse. Tel: 01372 726311. Famous flat race for three-year-old colts and fillies. Train: from Vauxhall or Victoria to Epsom, or Victoria to Tattenham Corner.

Greenwich & Docklands International Festival. Three-week festival beginning at the end of June, with free music, dance, theatre and spectacular firework displays. Various venues.

Pride, Marble Arch to Whitehall. London's annual gay pride parade is the biggest in Europe. Tube: Marble Arch.

Hard Rock Calling, Queen Elizabeth Olympic Park. Hard rock festival with some of the biggest names in the genre; moved from Hyde Park to the new Olympic Park due to curfew issues.

Royal Academy Summer Exhibition, Burlington House, Piccadilly. Tel: 7300 8000. Large exhibition of work by professional and amateur artists running until August. All works for sale. Tube: Piccadilly/Green Park.

Royal Ascot, Ascot Racecourse. Tel: 0844 346 3616. Elegant and dressy race meeting attended by royalty. Train: Waterloo to Ascot.

Trooping the Colour. Apply in writing for seats, details at www. royal.gov.uk. The Queen's official birthday celebrations, with a royal procession along the Mall to Horse Guards Parade for the ceremonial parade of regimental colours. Followed by the presence of the Royal Family on Buckingham Palace's balcony. Tube: Green Park/St James's Park.

Wimbledon Lawn Tennis Championships, All England Club. Tel: 8944 1066 (or 8971 2473 for tickets). World-famous fortnight of tennis on grass courts. Tube: Southfields.

July

BBC Proms, Royal Albert Hall. Tel: 0845 401 5045. Series of classical concerts (officially called the Henry Wood Promenade Concerts), culminating in the rumbustious Last Night which spills out into Hyde Park. Tube: South Kensington/High Street Kensington.

Doggett's Coat and Badge Race. Race for single-scull boats between London Bridge and Chelsea that has been a tradition since 1715.

Hampton Court Palace Flower Show. The world's largest flower show held in the stunning setting of the Palace grounds.

Henley Royal Regatta, Henley-on-Thames. Historic rowing

regatta – picnic by the Thames and watch the fun. Train: Paddington to Henley-on-Thames.

Lovebox Festival, Victoria Park, E3. Acclaimed as the best festival in London, Lovebox features up-and-coming DJs and well established live acts.

Swan Upping on the Thames. All the swans on the Thames belong to the Queen, the Vintners and the Dyers and for five days every year officials can be seen rowing on the river registering them.

August

London Riding Horse Parade, Rotten Row, Hyde Park. Elegant competition for best turned-out horse and rider. Tube: Hyde Park Corner/Knightsbridge/Lancaster Gate/Marble Arch.

Notting Hill Carnival, Ladbroke Grove (last weekend). Colourful and lively West Indian street carnival (Europe's largest) with exciting and imaginative costumes, live steel bands and reggae music. The streets can get extremely crowded. Tube: Notting Hill Gate.

September

Chelsea Antiques Fair, Old Town Hall, King's Road, SW3. Tel: 01825 744074. Wide range of antiques on sale. Tube: Sloane Square.

Horseman's Sunday, St John's Church, Hyde Park, W2. Morning service dedicated to the horse

The Puppini Sisters performing at the City of London Festival.

with mounted vicar and congregation. Followed by procession through Hyde Park. Tube: Paddington/Edgware Road.
Open House London, Hundreds of great buildings not usually open to the public open for one weekend, free of charge. Check tourist board for dates.
Thames Festival, from Westminster Bridge to Tower Bridge. Fanfare, river displays, face painting, craft and food stalls.

October

Costermongers' Pearly Harvest Festival (1st Sunday or last Sunday in September), St Martin-in-the-Fields, Trafalgar Square. Pearly Kings and Queens (street traders) attend a service in their traditional adorned with pearl buttons. Tube: Charing Cross.
Judges' Service marks the beginning of the legal year in Britain with a procession of judges in full attire from Westminster Abbey to the Houses of Parliament. Tube: Westminster.
Trafalgar Day Parade (21st). Commemorates Nelson's victory over the French and Spanish at Trafalgar. Tube: Charing Cross.

November

Christmas Lights switched on in Oxford and Regent streets. Tube: Oxford Circus/Piccadilly Circus.
Guy Fawkes Day (5th). Traditional firework celebration

of the failure to blow up the Houses of Parliament by Guy Fawkes in 1605. Bonfires and organised firework displays all over London.
London to Brighton Veteran Car Run (1st Sunday). Hundreds of immaculately preserved veteran cars and their proud owners start out from Hyde Park and make their way sedately to Brighton. Tube: Hyde Park Corner.
Lord Mayor's Show. Grand procession from the Guildhall in the City to the Royal Courts of Justice, celebrating the annual election of the Lord Mayor. Tube: Bank.
Remembrance Sunday (nearest the 11th). Commemorates those who have died in war since WWI while serving their country. Main wreath-laying service is at the Cenotaph. Tube: Westminster.
State Opening of Parliament, House of Lords, Westminster. Official re-opening of Parliament (following the summer recess) by the Queen, who travels down the Mall in a state coach. Tube: Westminster.

December

Christmas Carol Services, Trafalgar Square. Carols (Christmas hymns) are sung in the evenings beneath the giant tree which is presented each year by Norway. Tube: Charing Cross. Carol services are also held in many churches all over London.
London International Horse Show, Olympia. Tel: 0871 230

5580 (tickets). Major international show-jumping championships that attracts all the big names. Dog agility and Shetland pony Grand National included. Tube: Kensington (Olympia).
New Year's Eve. River Thames fireworks display at midnight around the London Eye. Thousands gather on the Embankment to watch.

SPORT

Spectator Sports

Football (Soccer)

The football season runs from August to May, with matches usually held Saturday 3pm, but also sometimes on Sundays, and Tuesday evenings. The top football clubs in London are Arsenal (Emirates Stadium, Drayton Park, N5, www.arsenal.com), Chelsea (Stamford Bridge, Fulham Road, SW6, www.chelseafc.com) and Tottenham Hotspur (White Hart Lane, 748 High Road, N17, www.tottenhamhotspur.com).

Rugby

This is played Sept–April/May. Top Rugby Union games are played at Twickenham Rugby Football Ground (Whitton Road, Twickenham, Middlesex, tel: 0871 222 2120; www.rfu.com/TwickenhamStadium). The Rugby League holds its cup final matches at Wembley Stadium (tel: 0844 980 8001; www.wembleystadium.com).

Cricket

The game is played in summer only, at the Oval (Kennington, SE11, tel: 0844 375 1845 (Surrey County Cricket Club; www.kia oval.com), or at Lord's Cricket Ground (St John's Wood, NW8, tel: 7432 1000 for tickets; www. lords.org). You should buy tickets well in advance for Test matches but there's generally less competition for seats for one-day internationals and Twenty20 games.

Tennis

Wimbledon, on the District line of the Underground (Southfields or Wimbledon), is the venue for the famous two-week tennis championship, which starts in the last week in June. Seats for the show courts (Centre Court and Courts 1 and 2) are allocated by ballot and should be applied for before mid-December the preceding year by writing to the All England Tennis Club, P.O. Box 98, Wimbledon, SW19 5AE, enclosing a self-addressed envelope (or an international reply coupon if applying from overseas). However, apart from Centre Court action on the last four days, you can queue on the day for tickets (cash only, to speed things up), though for popular games this can mean queueing all night under the watchful eye of supervisors. For information contact the ticket office on 8971 2473 or check www.wimbledon.com. Buses for the championships leave Victoria and Marble Arch every 30 minutes, while trains from Waterloo are met by a shuttle bus at Wimbledon station.

Horse Racing

The flat-racing season is March to November, while steeplechasing takes place virtually all year round. The nearest racecourses to London are: Ascot (tel: 0844 346 3616 for tickets; www.ascot. co.uk); Jockey Club Race Courses (Kempton Park, Epsom and Sandown Park, tel: 0844 579 3019 for tickets; www.jockeyclubrace-courses.com); and Windsor (tel:

SWIMMING

Few hotels have swimming pools and most municipal pools are indoors.

Outdoor pools include:

The Oasis, 32 Endell Street, WC2. Tel: 7831 1804. Between Covent Garden and Tottenham Court Road, this heated outdoor pool is a hidden gem and open year-round (steamy in winter). It isn't smart but it is clean and well-loved by regulars.

Brockwell Lido, Dulwich Road,

01753 498400; www.windsor-racecourse.co.uk).

Participant Sports

Golf

Contact the English Golf Union (tel: 01526 354500; www.english-golfunion.org) for details of courses. Many golf courses in London's suburbs offer 'pay and play' access, though booking is advisable at weekends. They include:

Beckenham Place Park, Beckenham Hill Road, Beckenham, BR3 (tel: 8650 2292), a parkland course with an imposing 18th-century mansion for a clubhouse.

Lee Valley, Lee Valley Leisure Complex, Picketts Lock Lane, Edmonton, N9 (tel: 8803 3611), an urban course built on reclaimed land.

Stockley Pines, Uxbridge, UB11 (tel: 8813 5700), a championship-length course in 240 acres (97 hectares) of pleasantly undulating parkland.

Horse Riding

Hyde Park Stables (tel: 7723 2813; www.hydeparkstables.com) arrange hacking in Hyde Park and lessons, and are approved by the British Horse Society (BHS). Wimbledon Village Stables (tel: 8946 8579; www.wvstables.com) are BHS- and ABRS-approved and offer hacking on Wimbledon Common and lessons.

SE24. Tel: 7274 3088; www. brockwelllido.com.

Very popular amenity open during the summer months only. Barbecues held on hot days. Other pools include the **Serpentine** in Hyde Park and the Bathing Ponds on **Hampstead Heath**. The latter comprise three pools – a men's, a women's and a mixed one, open 7am–7pm year-round for the single-sex pools and summer only for the mixed.

Tennis

Many local parks have bookable courts. The Lawn Tennis Association (tel: 8487 7000; www.lta.org. uk) has a leaflet on grass courts and you can locate a court in a park or leisure area near you by checking www.londontennis.co.uk.

TOURS

Guided Tours – Bus

A guided tour of London by bus is the best way for visitors to familiarise themselves with the city. All tours that are registered with the London Tourist Board use Blue Badge Guides, whose ranks number around 1,000.

Emirates football stadium.

The Big Bus Company, tel: 7233 9533; www.bigbustours.com. Open-top bus tours over a choice of two routes lasting 2.5 to 3.5 hours. You are free to hop on or hop off at any of the 70 stops. Buses run every 5–15 minutes. Tours have live commentary in English or recorded commentary in seven languages as well as English. Tickets are valid for 24 hours; buses operate 8.30am–8pm in the summer and until 6pm in the winter. Cost: £30 for adults and £12 for children.

Evan Evans, tel: 7950 1777; www.evanevanstours.co.uk. A variety of tours giving a comprehensive introduction to the city with emphasis on historic sites. Admittance to St Paul's Cathedral, the Royal Albert Hall and the Tower of London are part of some tours. Picks up from many hotels. Cost: £79 (£69 for children under 16) for a full day.

Golden Tours, tel: 7630 2028; www.goldentours.com. Various tours of the city in air-conditioned coaches accompanied by guides who hold the coveted Blue Badge. The London Experience full-day tour takes in major sights such as the Tower and St Paul's, and includes a Thames cruise and a London Eye ride. Cost: £92 (£82 for children).

The Original London Sightseeing Tour, tel: 8877 1722; www.theoriginaltour.com. A choice of three different tours in traditional red double-decker buses, some of which are open-top. The Original tour features live commentary in English; the other two have recorded commentary in a choice of seven languages. A unique feature is the recorded children's commentary – by kids for kids. Tours run from 9am approximately every 15–20 minutes and passengers can hop on and off at any of the 90 stops. Tickets cost £28 for adults and £14 for children under 16, and are valid for 24 hours. There are departure points throughout central London. A free river cruise from Embankment is included in the price.

River Tours

Bateaux London, tel: 7695 1800. Romantic dinner cruises along the Thames with cabaret and dancing. From £48–62 for a Sunday lunch jazz cruise, £78–155 per person for a dinner cruise (including wine).

Thames River Services, tel: 7930 4097. Trips between Westminster and Greenwich piers every 30 minutes (£15.50 return, child £7.75). Tours go beyond Greenwich to the O2 Arena and the Thames Flood Barrier.

Guided Tours – Walks

Some walking tour operators use London Tourist Board-trained **Blue Badge Guides** – a guarantee of quality. Walks generally last one or two hours. *Time Out* magazine lists a selection of weekly walks in its Visitors section.

City Walks, www.walklondon-uk.com. Tailor-made tours of London and the City.

Ghost Walk, tel: 8530 8443, www.london-ghost-walk.co.uk. Explores the graveyards, nooks and crannies of the City of London. Cost: from £29.

Jack the Ripper Tours, tel: 8530 8443, www.jack-the-ripper-walk.com. As the title suggests, a two-hour after dark tour which explores London's more murky past and shady courtyards. Cost: from £29.

Original London Walks, tel: 7624 3978; www.walks.com. More than 200 walks, including Along the Thames Pub Walk, Hidden London, Hampstead, Historic Westminster, Little Venice and Ghost walks. Adults £8, under 15s free with an adult.

Theatrical Tours

National Theatre, tel: 7452 3400. Daily tours and workshops. Up to five times a day (Mon–Sat), with each tour lasting 1.25 hours. Cost: £8.50.

Shakespeare's Globe Theatre, tel: 7902 1500. Daily (9.30am–5pm) 40-minute tours. Adults £13.50, children £8.

Royal Opera House, tel: 7304 4000. Tours (Mon–Fri) three times a day. Not suitable for children under 8. Cost: £12.

Theatreland Walking Tour, tel: 7557 6700; www.londontheatre.co.uk. Two-hour tours on Sunday, except during winter. Book in advance. Cost: £9.50.

BBC Television Tours, Broadcasting House, Portland Place, W1A, tel: 0370 901 1227; www.bbc.co.uk/tours. Tours of Broadcasting House, home to BBC Radio and all the BBC television news programmes. Pre-booking essential. Adults £13.50, children (over nine) £9.

See the city from a different angle on board a tourist boat.

A – Z

AN ALPHABETICAL SUMMARY OF PRACTICAL INFORMATION

A

Accidents

In the event of a serious accident or emergency, dial 999. In the case of minor accidents, your hotel will know where to find the nearest hospital with a casualty department. If you're outside, hail a taxi – cabbies know even more than hotel receptionists.

Admission Charges

Major state-owned museums in London are free of charge but a donation is appreciated. You usually have to pay for special exhibitions. Museums and galleries which do charge usually offer reductions for families, children, students, pensioners and the unemployed.

B

Budgeting for a Trip

London is a very expensive city. You'll be lucky to find a conveniently located double room for less than £100 a night and prices soar to well over £400. Breakfast is often included in the price, but if not, a full English will start at £6 and a Continental breakfast at £3. Expect to pay from £30 to £55 each for a three-course dinner, including a modest wine, at a reasonable restaurant. Most cinema tickets cost £8–15, and a good seat for a West End musical is about £50. Taxis aren't cheap, especially at night, but neither is the Underground, with a short Tube journey costing from £4.50 – check out the special passes available, see page 275.

C

Car Breakdown

The following organisations operate 24-hour breakdown assistance. Phone calls to these numbers are free, but the service is free only to members:
AA, tel: 08457 887 766
RAC, tel: 0800 828 282
Green Flag, tel: 0800 051 0636

Children

For ideas on museums and other attractions suitable for children of various ages, see page 8.

Accommodation. Some hotels do not accept children under a certain age, so be sure to check when you book. Most restaurants accept well-behaved children, but only those that want to encourage families have children's menus and nappy-changing facilities. Only pubs with a Children's Certificate can admit children, and even these will usually restrict the hours and areas open to them. Publicans, like restaurateurs, reserve the right to refuse entry.

Public transport. Up to four children aged 11 or under can travel free on the Tube if accompanied by a ticket-holding adult. Eleven- to 15-year-olds can get unlimited free travel on buses, and child rates on the Tube, DLR and London Overground, providing they have a photo Oyster card (this can take up to two weeks to obtain).

Buses are free for all children under 16, but those over 10 years need an Oyster photocard if unaccompanied. Buses can take up to two unfolded pushchairs (buggies) at one time (they must be parked in a special area halfway down the bus). Any further pushchairs must be folded. Visit www.tfl.gov.uk.

Supplies. Infant formula and nappies (diapers) can be found in chemists (pharmacies) and supermarkets.

Hospitals. In a medical emergency, take your child to the Accident & Emergency department of the nearest hospital. If you require over-the-counter medications such as Calpol (liquid paracetamol) late at night, Bliss Pharmacy (5 Marble Arch; tel: 7723 6116) is open until midnight every day.

Climate and Clothing

The climate in London is mild, with the warming effects of the city itself keeping off the worst of the cold in winter. Snow and temperatures below freezing are unusual, with January temperatures averaging 43°F/6°C. Consequently, if it does snow hard, London is unprepared. Temperatures in the summer months average 64°F/18°C, but they can soar, causing the city to become airlessly hot (air conditioning is not universal). Rainfall is unpredictable, and it's wise, even in summer, to keep a fold-up umbrella close by.

What to Wear

Between the stuffy Tube and often damp weather, it's best to dress in layers. A cool, rainy day can turn beautiful unexpectedly and vice versa. In general, short sleeves and a jacket are recommended for summer and a warm coat and woollens for winter.

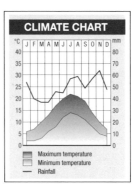

CLIMATE CHART

Maximum temperature
Minimum temperature
— Rainfall

While a few of the traditional restaurants retain a dress code, smart-casual is generally the norm for restaurants and theatres. In general, Londoners are quite style-conscious but also practical; most getting around will be on foot or via public transport, so wearing comfortable shoes is wise.

Crime

Serious crime is low for a city of this size, but the Dickensian tradition of pickpocketing is alive and well. Hold on tightly to purses and handbags, do not put wallets in back pockets, and do not place handbags on the floor in busy restaurants.

In a genuine emergency, dial 999 from any telephone (no cash required). Report routine thefts to a police station (address found under Police in a telephone directory). The threat of terrorism has led to an increase in police patrols, so don't hesitate to report any suspicious packages.

Customs Regulations

There are no official restrictions on the movement of goods within the European Union, provided those goods were purchased within the EU. However, British Customs have set the following personal-use 'guide levels'.
Tobacco 3,800 cigarettes or 400 cigarillos or 200 cigars or 1kg tobacco.
Alcohol 10 litres spirits, 20 litres fortified wines, 90 litres wine, 110 litres beer.
Those entering from a non-EU state are subject to these limits: Tobacco 200 cigarettes or 100 cigarillos or 50 cigars or 250g of tobacco are permitted.
Alcohol 1 litre of spirits, or 2 litres of fortified or sparkling wine, or 2 litres of table wine (an additional 2 litres of still wine allowed if no spirits are bought).
£390-worth of other goods, such as perfume, are also permitted.
Animals Cats and dogs may enter Britain from EU countries providing they have the appropriate documentation. All unauthorised pets are placed in quarantine upon arrival at the owner's expense. For further details, log on to www.gov.uk/defra.
The following are prohibited entry into the United Kingdon:
Plants and **perishable foods** such as meats and meat products, eggs, fruit; some drugs (check with your doctor if you need to carry strong medication. You may need to carry a letter from them).
Firearms and ammunition (without special arrangement).
Obscene film or written material.
There are no restrictions on the amount of currency you can bring into the country.

Posing with police officers outside Buckingham Palace.

D

Disabled Access

Venues. Artsline (www.artsline.org.uk), London's information and advice service on access to the arts and entertainment for disabled people, provides detailed access information for venues across London, including theatres, cinemas, museums, arts centres, tourist attractions, comedy and music venues, and selected restaurants.

Advice. William Forrester is a museum lecturer, co-author of Access in London, a trained guide and wheelchair user. He offers tailor-made tours of the city for chair users utilising accessible taxis, and arranges special visits to the Houses of Parliament, Westminster Abbey and the British Museum. He operates a telephone advice service for anyone planning to visit the UK in a wheelchair. Tel: 01483 575401.

Toilets. Britain has a system of keys to open many of the public toilets available for disabled people. To obtain a key, contact Disability Rights UK on 7250 3222; www.disabilityrights.org. There is a charge of £4 for the key and £4.99 for the smart phone app detailing their locations.

Public transport. Wheelchair-friendly buses have been progressively introduced across the network; almost all are accessible via low-floor vehicles or retractable ramps. Tubes are more difficult as entry is mainly by steps; for exceptions, look for the stations' 'step-free access' symbol on the tube maps. The Jubilee Line has lifts. Ticket offices can provide a free leaflet on Access to the Underground or alternatively call 7222 1234 for help planning an accessible route.

River cruises. Step-free access is available from most major piers and newer boats have designated wheelchair spaces. Mobility-impaired groups can obtain information and advice by telephoning London River Services on 7941 2400.

E

Electricity

230 volts. Square, three-pin plugs are used, and virtually all visitors will need to bring or buy adaptors if planning to plug in their own equipment.

Embassies

Australia Australia House, Strand, WC2B 4LA. Tel: 7379 4334
Canada Macdonald House, 1 Grosvenor Square, W1X 4AB. Tel: 7258 6600
India India House, Aldwych, WC2B 4NA. Tel: 7836 8484
Ireland 17 Grosvenor Place, SW1X 7HR. Tel: 7235 2171
Jamaica 1 Prince Consort Road, SW7 2BZ. Tel: 7823 9911
New Zealand 80 Haymarket, SW1Y 4TQ. Tel: 7930 8422
South Africa South Africa House, Trafalgar Square, WC2N 5DP. Tel: 7451 7299
United States 24 Grosvenor Square, W1K 6AH. Tel: 7499 9000.

Emergencies

Call 999 for all emergency services (no charge) and ask for fire, police or ambulance.

Entry Requirements

To enter Britain you need a valid passport (or any form of official identification if you are an EU citizen). Visas are not needed if you are from the USA, are a Commonwealth citizen or an EU national (or from most other European or South American countries). Health certificates are not required unless you have arrived from Asia, Africa or South America. If you wish to stay for a protracted period or apply for work, contact the Border and Immigration Agency after looking at the website www.ind.homeoffice.gov.uk. London's nearest Public Enquiry Office (PEO) is at Lunar House, 40 Wellesley Road, Croydon, CR9 2BY, tel: 0870 606 7766.

G

Gay and Lesbian

With Europe's largest gay and lesbian population, London has an abundance of bars, restaurants and clubs to cater for most tastes. Many of them will make space for one or more of London's free gay weekly magazines, Boyz, the Pink Paper, and QX. Monthly magazines on sale at newsstands include Gay Times, Diva and Attitude.

Two established websites for meeting other gay people in London are www.gaydar.co.uk and the female version, www.gaydargirls.com. Other websites reflecting the gay scene include www.lgbtlondon.com and www.londonfriend.org.uk.

Useful telephone contacts for advice and counselling include **London Lesbian and Gay Switchboard** (tel: 0300 330 0630) and London Friend (7.30–10pm, tel: 7837 3337).

Government

When people refer to London, they mean the county of Greater London. When they speak of the City of London, they generally mean the financial district, the historic square mile between St Paul's Cathedral and the Tower of London, governed by the Corporation of London and headed by the Lord Mayor, which even has its own police force. The rest of the metropolis is run by 12 inner boroughs and 20 outer boroughs, each of which is responsible for local services.

TRANSPORT

ACCOMMODATION

ACTIVITIES

A–Z

Newsstands abound, but free newspapers are also plentiful.

Health & Medical Care

If you fall ill and are a national of the European Union, you are entitled to free emergency medical treatment for illnesses arising while in the UK. Many other countries also have reciprocal arrangements for free treatment. However, most visitors will be liable for medical and dental treatment so will have to pay for any non-emergency treatment. They should ensure they have adequate health insurance.

Major hospitals include Charing Cross Hospital (Fulham Palace Road, W6, tel: 3311 1234), St Mary's Hospital (Praed Street, W2, tel: 3312 6666), and St Thomas's (Westminster Bridge Road, SE1, tel: 7188 7188).

Emergency dental treatment is available on weekdays 9am–5pm (queuing begins at 8am) at Guy's Hospital, St Thomas Street, SE1, tel: 7188 7188.

Chemists (pharmacists). Boots is a large chain of pharmacies with branches throughout London that will make up prescriptions. The branch at 114 Queensway, W2 is open until 10pm daily, whilst Bliss Chemist at 5 Marble Arch is open until midnight daily.

Accidents: in the case of an emergency, dial 999.

Internet

London has many internet cafés, and most coffee chains and restaurants have free Wi-fi, There is also Wi-fi available in some fast-food chains like McDonalds, many banks and the Apple store.

Left Luggage

Most of the main railway stations have left luggage departments where you can leave your suitcases on a short-term basis, although all are very sensitive to potential terrorist bombs. Left luggage offices are generally open 24 hours a day, but at Heathrow they close at 11pm.

Lost Property

If you can't find a policeman, dial directory enquiries (118 500 or 118 888 or 118 118) and ask for the number of the nearest police station. Don't call the emergency number 999 unless there has been a serious crime or accident. For non-emergencies, the Metropolitan Police number is 101. If your passport has been lost, let your embassy know as well.

For possessions lost on public transport or in taxis, contact Transport for London's central Lost Property (200 Baker Street, NW1 5RZ, tel: 0343 222 1234; www.tfl. gov.uk/lostproperty) Mon–Fri 8.30am–4pm, or fill in an enquiry form, available from any London Underground station or bus garage. It can take two to four days for items left on a Tube train or bus to reach the office and more than a week for items a taxi driver has handed in at a police station. It is therefore advisable to wait several

days before visiting or phoning the office, which can search for your property while you are on the phone. It can also post your property back to you for a fee. The office receives 600 items a day.

Maps

Insight Guides' *FlexiMap London* is laminated for durability and easy folding. For detailed exploration of the city centre and suburbs, the London A–Z books come in various formats. Free Tube maps are available at Underground stations. Map lovers should head for Stanford's flagship shop (12–14 Long Acre, Covent Garden), one of the world's top map and guidebook stores.

Money

The pound sterling (divided into 100 pence) is the currency, though many large London stores will accept euros.

Most **banks** open Mon–Fri 9.30am–5pm (or even later), with Saturday morning banking common in shopping areas. Major British banks tend to offer similar exchange rates; it's only worth shopping around if you have large amounts of money to change. There will be a charge for changing cash into another currency. The easiest way to get cash out is through a cash machine (ATM).

Some High Street travel agents, such as Thomas Cook, operate **bureaux de change** at comparable rates. There are also private bureaux de change (some are open 24 hours) where rates can be very low and commissions high. Chequepoint (www.chequepoint.com) is a reputable chain with branches at 222 Earl's Court, 71 Gloucester Road, 2 Queensway and 550 Oxford Circus.

International **credit cards** are almost universally accepted.

However, a few stores and restaurants do not accept them, so check for signs at the entrance first.

Tax refunds enable visitors from outside the European Union to reclaim the 20 percent value-added tax when spending over a certain amount. Stores can supply VAT refund forms which should be presented to Customs officials when leaving the country.

N

Newspapers

Politically speaking, the *Daily Telegraph* and *The Times* are on the right, *The Guardian* is on the left and *The Independent* has a liberal, international slant. To appeal to commuters, some are printed in a compact (tabloid) format rather than the traditional full-size broadsheet. On Sunday *The Observer* is more liberal than the *Sunday Times*, *Independent on Sunday* and *Sunday Telegraph*. The *Financial Times* is renowned for the clearest, most unslanted headlines in its general news pages (plus, of course, its financial coverage).

Among the mass-market tabloids, *The Sun* and *The Star* are traditionally on the right (and obsessed with royalty, soap operas and sex), and the *Daily Mirror* and *Sunday Mirror* are on the left, as is the *Sunday People*. The *Daily Mail* and *Mail on Sunday* are more up-market and right-wing equivalents of the politically eclectic Express.

Editions of the free, London-only *Evening Standard* come out Mon–Fri mid-morning and are good for London news, cinema and theatre listings. The free tabloid Metro can be picked up at stations in the morning from Mon–Fri. Both of these contain useful but not comprehensive listings sections.

Listings magazines. Supreme in this field is the long-established weekly Time Out.

Foreign newspapers and magazines can be found at many street newsstands, at mainline stations, and at these outlets:

A. Moroni & Son: 68 Old Compton Street, W1.
Compton News: 48 Old Compton Street, W1.
Selfridges: Oxford Street, W1.
Victoria Place Shopping Centre: Victoria Station, SW1.

O

Opening Hours

Most shops open Monday to Saturday between 9am and 10am and close around 5.30pm to 6pm. In commercial areas such as Oxford Street shops stay open until 8pm Monday to Saturday (until 9pm on Thursdays). On Sundays major shops are only allowed six hours of trading between 10am and 6pm. The large shopping centres such as Westfield Stratfield and Westfield White City have longer opening hours during the week, and open noon–6pm on Sundays.

For post office opening hours, see under Postal Services.

For bank opening hours, see under Money.

P

Population and Size

After decades of decline, London's population has increased since the mid-1980s to its present 8.3 million and forecasts show it surging to almost 9 million by 2021. More than 40 percent of residents are non-white, and around 300 languages are spoken (from Abem, a language of the Ivory Coast, to Zulu, from

South Africa).

Officially, London's area is 610 sq miles (1,580 sq km), but the urban sprawl around the capital makes it hard to know where to stop measuring.

Postal Services

Post offices open Mon–Fri 9am–5pm, Sat 9am–noon. Stamps are available from post offices and selected shops, usually newsagents, and from machines outside some post offices. There is a two-tier service within the UK: first class is supposed to reach a UK destination the next day, second class will take at least a day or two longer. London's main post office is at Trafalgar Square, behind the church of St Martin-in-the-Fields. It stays open until 6.30pm Mon–Fri.

The cost of sending a letter or parcel depends on weight as well as size. Queues tend to be long over the lunch period.

Postcodes

The first half of London postcodes indicates the general area (WC = West Central, SE = Southeast etc) and the second half, used only for mail, identifies the exact block. Here is a key to some of the more common codes:

W1 Mayfair, Marylebone, Soho; **W2** Bayswater; **W4** Chiswick; **W8** Kensington; **W11** Notting Hill; **WC1** Bloomsbury; **WC2** Covent Garden, Strand; **E1** Whitechapel; **EC1** Clerkenwell; **EC2** Bank, Barbican; **EC4** St Paul's, Blackfriars; **SW1** St James's, Belgravia; **SW3** Chelsea; **SW7** Knightsbridge, South Kensington; **SW19** Wimbledon; **SE1** Lambeth, Southwark; **SE10** Greenwich; **SE21** Dulwich; **N1** Hoxton, Islington; **N6** Highgate; **NW3** Hampstead.

Public Holidays

Compared to most European countries, the UK has few public

holidays:
January New Year's Day (1st)
March/April Good Friday, Easter
Monday
May May Day (first Monday of the
month), Spring Bank Holiday (last
Monday)
August Summer Bank Holiday
(last Monday)
December Christmas Day (25th),
Boxing Day (26th).

Radio Stations

You can receive national stations
as well as many targeted
specifically at London. A
selection:

Commercial Stations

Capital FM – 95.8FM, 24-hour
pop music.
Classic FM – 100.9FM, 24-hour
light classical music.
Choice FM – 96.9FM, soul
music.
Heart – 106.2FM, classic rock.
Kiss FM – 100FM, 24-hour
dance music.
LBC – 97.3FM, 24-hour chat,
showbiz, opinion, news.
Smooth FM – 102.2FM, bland
playlist of jazz, soul and blues and
middle-of-the-road.
Virgin – 105.8FM, adult-oriented
rock.

BBC Stations.

Radio 1 – 98.8FM, mainstream
pop.
Radio 2 – 89.2FM, easy-listening
music, chat shows.
Radio 3 – 91.3FM, 24-hour
classical music, plus drama and
serious talks.
Radio 4 – 93.5FM, heavyweight
news, current affairs, plays.
Radio Five Live – 909MW, rolling
news, sport.
BBC Radio London – 94.9FM,
London-oriented music, chat and
sports station.
BBC World Service – 648 kHz,
international news.

S

Smoking

In July 2007 England imposed a
ban on smoking in all enclosed
public spaces, including pubs,
clubs and bars (though not in outside beer gardens). This extends
to railway platforms.

Student Travellers

International students can obtain
various discounts at attractions,
on travel services (including Eurostar) and in some shops by showing a valid ISIC card. Visit www.
isiccard.com.

T

Telephones

Despite the ubiquity of mobile
phones (cellphones), London still
has an adequate number of public
kiosks and public phones in pubs.
It is cheaper to use a public phone
than one in your hotel as many
hotels still make an outrageous
charge for calls from your room.
    British Telecom (BT) is the main
telephone operating company. The
smallest coin accepted is 10p.
Most kiosks will also accept phone
cards, which are widely available
from post offices and newsagents
in varying amounts between £5
and £20. Credit card phones can
be found at major transport terminals and on busy streets.

Phoning Abroad

You can telephone abroad directly
from any phone. Dial 00 followed
by the international code for the
country you want, and then the
number. Some country codes:
Australia (61); **Hong Kong** (852);
Ireland (353); **New Zealand** (64);
Singapore (65); **South Africa**
(27); **US** and **Canada** (1).

    If you are using a US credit
phone card, first dial the compa-
ny's access number as follows:
Sprint, tel: 0800-890877
MCI, tel: 0800-279 5088
AT&T, tel: 0800-890011.

Useful Numbers

Emergency – police, fire, ambu-
lance: 999
Operator (for difficulties in get-
ting through): 100
International Operator: 155
Directory Enquiries (UK): 118
500 or 118 888 or 118 118
International Directory Enquiries
118 505 or 118 866 or 118 899
Transport for London 24-hour
information: 0843 222 1234
Rail information for all London
stations: 0845 748 4950.
Accommodation bookings: Visit
London on 3564 5657.

Television Stations

The BBC (British Broadcasting
Corporation) is financed by com-
pulsory annual television licences
and is advertising-free. The independent channels (ITV1, Channel
4 and Channel Five) are funded by
commercials.
    In recent years the choice of
channels has expanded exponen-
tially as cable, satellite and digital
channels have joined the small
number of terrestrial channels.
The BBC has several digital channels, including the round-the-
clock BBC News 24, the

*A British icon, sadly becoming less
common.*

youth-oriented BBC3, and the arts-oriented BBC4. In 2012, analogue television transmissions were shut down, and even BBC1, BBC2 and the terrestrial commercial channels are now only available through digital technology. All of the major UK independent channels have catch-up services available online: BBC iPlayer, 4OD, ITV Player and Demand 5.

Time

British Summer Time (one hour ahead of Greenwich Mean Time) operates from the last Sunday in March until the last Sunday in October. Greenwich Mean Time is 8 hours in front of Los Angeles, 5 hours in front of New York and Montreal, and 10 hours behind Sydney.

Tipping

Most hotels and many restaurants automatically add 10–15 percent service charge to your bill. It's your right to deduct it if you're not happy with the service. If you pay by chip and PIN, the machine will often require you to add or decline to add a tip before you insert your PIN number, which feels rather cheeky when the waitress or waiter is standing in front of you. If a service charge has already been included in the bill, you certainly shouldn't feel obliged to add anything extra.

It is not customary to tip in pubs, cinemas, theatres or elevators, but you should tip sightseeing guides (about 10 percent) and hotel porters. It is also usual to tip cab drivers if they've been particularly helpful or assisted with your bags.

Tour Operators

The Original Tour is the first and biggest London sightseeing operator. Hop-on and hop-off at over 90 different stops, with commentary in a wide choice of languages and a Kids' Club for 5- to 12-year-olds. Buy tickets on the bus or in advance. Operates year round.

Tel: 8877 1722; www.theoriginal tour.com.

Big Bus Company operates three routes of hop-on hop-off services. Tel: 7233 9533; www.bigbustours. com.

Duck Tours use World War II amphibious vehicles which drive past famous London landmarks before taking to the water. It's expensive, but great for children. Departure from County Hall. In late 2013 a partner operator were running the river leg of the tour following a fire on a vessel earlier in the year. Tel: 7928 3132; www. londonducktours.co.uk.

Tourist Offices

The offical tourist board maintains a website at www.visitlondon. com. It contains a huge amount of information on attractions, upcoming events and festivals, as well as practical information and a hotel booking service.

Personal enquires can be made at Britain and London Visitor Centre, 1 Regent Street, Piccadilly Circus, SW1Y 4ST. The office is open Mon 9.30am–6.30pm, Tue–Fri 9am–6.30pm, Sat–Sun 10am–4pm (June–Sept, Sat 9am–5pm). You can email BLVCenquiry@visit-london.org, or tel: 0870 156 6366. Other tourist information centres are located at:

City of London Information Centre, St Paul's Churchyard, EC4M 8BX. Tel: 7332 1456. Open Mon–Sat 9.30am–5.30pm, Sun 10am–4pm.

Greenwich TIC, Pepys House, 2 Cutty Sark Gardens, Greenwich SE10 9LW. Tel: 0870 608 2000. Open daily 10am–5pm. Email: tic@greenwich.gov.uk.

Visas and Passports

EU nationals will need their **passport** or **national ID card** to enter the UK. Non-EU nationals may

also require a **visa** in addition to their passport.

Loss or theft should be reported to the appropriate embassy or consulate and to the local police. It is sensible to photocopy the relevant pages of your passport and keep the photocopy separate from the passport itself.

A visa to visit the United Kingdom is not required by nationals of member states of the European Economic Area (EEA), the Commonwealth (including Australia, Canada, New Zealand and South Africa) and the USA. Nationals of other countries should check with the British Embassy and apply for a visa, if necessary, in good time.

Entry visas are required by Australian, New Zealand, Canadian and US nationals for a stay exceeding three months. All visitors from areas outside the EEA must apply for a visa before travelling if they plan to stay for more than six months.

For up-to-date official information on visas, visit www.ukvisas. gov.uk.

US citizens should view Tips for Traveling Abroad online (travel. state.gov) for general information on visa requirements, customs regulations and medical car.

Websites

www.visitlondon.com The official tourist board site, with lots of advice, listings and links. www.thisislondon.co.uk Run by the Evening Standard newspaper; has detailed listings of events. www.london-se1.co.uk has up-to-date coverage of the South Bank and Bankside. www.streetmap.co.uk locates the address you type in. www.culture24.org.uk has up-to-date information on what UK museums are exhibiting. www.bbc.co.uk is a gigantic site with lots on London.

TRANSPORT

ACCOMMODATION

ACTIVITIES

A – Z

FURTHER READING

Good Companions

London: A Literary Companion by Peter Vansittart. A journey around the capital with the literary luminaries.

Secret London by Andrew Duncan. Uncovers London's hidden landscape from abandoned tube stations to the gentlemen's club.

The London Blue Plaque Guide by Nick Rennison. Details the lives of more than 700 individuals who have been commemorated with a blue plaque on their houses.

A Literary Guide to London by Ed Glinet. A very detailed, street-by-street guide to literary lives.

London on Film by Colin Sorensen. How the cinema has portrayed the city.

History

The Concise Pepys by Samuel Pepys. Read a first-hand account of the Great Fire of London and find out about daily life in 17th-century England.

Dr Johnson's London by Liza Picard. Brings 18th-century London to life.

London: The Biography by Peter Ackroyd. Anecdotal and entertaining history.

London: A Social History by Roy Porter. Less quirky than Ackroyd but a telling account of how badly the capital has been governed over the centuries.

The Story of the British Museum by Marjorie Caygill. A fascinating tale, authoritatively told, featuring an astonishing variety of heroes and villains.

London Villages by John Wittich. A walker's notes on his travels through village London.

Thames: Sacred River by Peter Ackroyd. Social history of London's famous river.

Memoirs

The Shorter Pepys by Samuel Pepys. A distillation of 11 volumes of diaries describing London life, including the Great Fire and the plague, from 1660 to 1669.

84 Charing Cross Road by Helene Hanff. Touching booklover's correspondence with a London bookseller.

London Orbital by Iain Sinclair. A walk round the M25, exploring little-known parts of London's periphery.

The Oxford Book of London edited by Paul Bailey. A bran-dip of observations by famous visitors over eight centuries.

Art and Architecture

A Guide to London's Contemporary Architecture by Ken Allinson and Victoria Thornton. Covers buildings since the 1980s; black-and-white pictures.

London Under London by Richard Trench and Ellis Hillman. Traces the astonishing maze of railway lines, sewers and utilities that lies beneath the streets.

Other Insight Guides

Other titles covering London in the Insight Guides range include **Insight Explore London**. This book details 20 self-guided routes written by a local expert and designed to suit every interest and taste. Comes with a free pull-out map with street index.

Insight FlexiMap London is a fold-out laminated map that is easy to use and long-lasting.

LONDON STREET ATLAS

The key map shows the area of London covered by the atlas section. An index of street names and places of interest shown on the maps can be found on the following pages. For each entry there is a page number and grid reference.

Map Legend

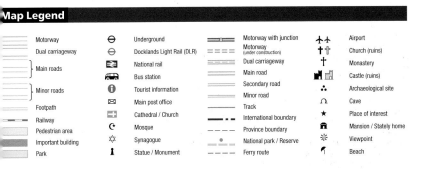

Motorway	⊖	Underground		Motorway with junction	✈✈	Airport
Dual carriageway	⊖	Docklands Light Rail (DLR)	====	Motorway (under construction)	†✝	Church (ruins)
Main roads	⊠	National rail		Dual carriageway	†	Monastery
	🚌	Bus station		Main road	🏰🏛	Castle (ruins)
Minor roads	❶	Tourist information		Secondary road	∴	Archaeological site
	✉	Main post office		Minor road	Ω	Cave
Footpath	➕	Cathedral / Church		Track	★	Place of interest
Railway	☾	Mosque		International boundary	🏠	Mansion / Stately home
Pedestrian area	✡	Synagogue		Province boundary	※	Viewpoint
Important building			●	National park / Reserve		
Park	⚊	Statue / Monument		Ferry route	⌐	Beach

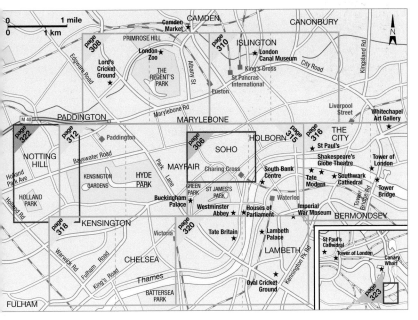

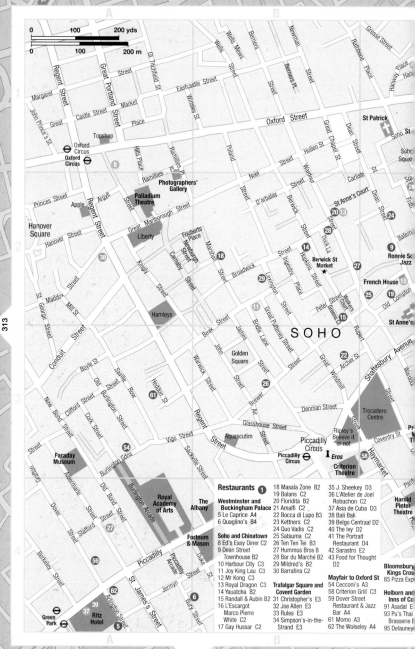

313

314

Map labels:

0 100 200 yds
0 100 200 m

Margaret Street · John Prince's St · Gt Titchfield St · Wells Mews · Wells Street · Berners Mews · Berners Pl. · Newman Street · Gresse Street · Rathbone Place · Hanway Place

Regent Street · Great Portland Street · Castle Street · Market Place · Eastcastle Street · Winsley St · Oxford Street · Dean Street · St Patrick · Soho St

Topshop · Princes Street · Hills Place · Ramillies Pl. · Ramillies Street · Poland Street · Noel Street · Hollen St · Wardour Street · Chapel St · Carlisle Street · Soho Square · Sq

Oxford Circus

Hanover Square · Hanover Street · Argyll Street · Palladium Theatre · Liberty · Great Marlborough Street · Foubert's Place · Newburgh Street · Marshall Street · Broadwick Street · D'arblay Street · Berwick Street · Ingestre Place · Hopkins St · Duck La. · St Anne's Court · Dean Street · Ronnie Sc Jazz

Photographers' Gallery

St George Street · Maddox Street · Mill St · Conduit Street · Regent Street · Apple · Kingly Street · Carnaby Street · Hamleys · Beak Street · Lexington Street · Great Pulteney Street · Peter Street · Walker's Court · Wardour Street · Rupert Street · Berwick St Market · French House · Old Compton · St Anne's

SOHO

Boyle St · Saville Row · Old Burlington Street · New Burlington St · Heddon St · Golden Square · James St · Bridle Lane · John St · Warwick Street · Brewer Street · Air St · Glasshouse Street · Denman Street · Archer St · Windmill Street · Shaftesbury Avenue · Trocadero Centre · Coventry St

New Bond Street · Clifford Street · Cork Street · Burlington Gdns · Vigo Street · Regent Street · Aquascutum · Piccadilly Circus · Ripley's Believe it or not · Pr

Faraday Museum · Burlington Arcade · Sackville Street · Eros · Criterion Theatre · Haymarket · Harold Pinter Theatre

Royal Academy of Arts · The Albany · Fortnum & Mason · Piccadilly

Dover Street · Albemarle Street · Old Bond Street · Stafford St · Berkeley Street · Piccadilly Arcade · Duke Street · Jermyn Street · St James's Street · Bury Street · King St

Green Park · Ritz Hotel · Arlington Street

Restaurants ①

Westminster and Buckingham Palace
5 Le Caprice A4
6 Quaglino's B4

Soho and Chinatown
8 Ed's Easy Diner C2
9 Dean Street Townhouse B2
10 Harbour City C3
11 Joy King Lau C3
12 Mr Kong C3
13 Royal Dragon C3
14 Yauatcha B2
15 Randall & Aubin B2
16 L'Escargot Marco Pierre White C2
17 Gay Hussar C2

18 Masala Zone B2
19 Balans C2
20 Floridita B2
21 Amalfi C2
22 Bocca di Lupo C2
23 Kettners C2
24 Quo Vadis C2
25 Satsuma C2
26 Ten Ten Tei B3
27 Hummus Bros B
28 Bar du Marché B2
29 Mildred's B2
30 Barrafina C2

Trafalgar Square and Covent Garden
31 Christopher's E3
32 Joe Allen E3
33 Rules E3
34 Simpson's-in-the-Strand E3

35 J. Sheekey D3
36 L'Atelier de Joel Robuchon C2
37 Asia de Cuba D3
38 Bali Bali
39 Belgo Centraal D2
40 The Ivy D2
41 The Portrait Restaurant D4
42 Sarastro E2
43 Food for Thought D2

Mayfair to Oxford St
54 Cecconi's A3
58 Criterion Grill C3
59 Dover Street Restaurant & Jazz Bar A4
61 Momo A3
62 The Wolseley A4

Bloomsbury Kings Cros
85 Pizza Exp

Holborn and Inns of Co
91 Asadal E
93 Pu's Thai Brasserie E
95 Delauney

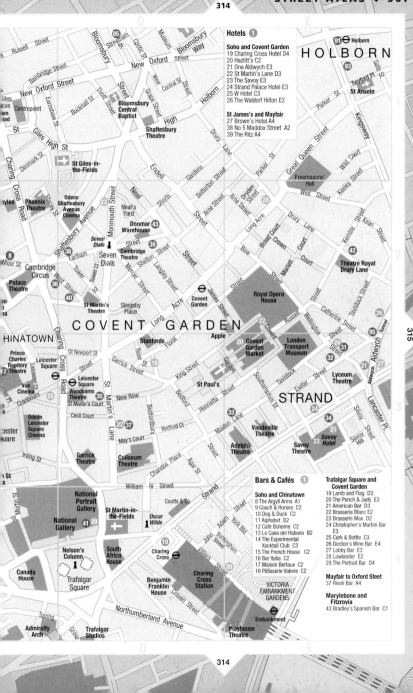

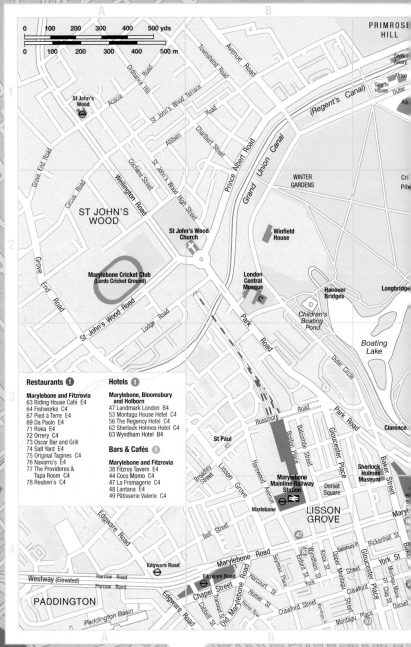

PRIMROSE HILL

| 0 | 100 | 200 | 300 | 400 | 500 yds |
| 0 | 100 | 200 | 300 | 400 | 500 m |

Townshend Road

Avenue Road

Snowd Aviary

Africa

Giraffe House

Outer

Aqu

Ordnance Hill

(Regent's Canal)

Cri Pit

St John's Wood

Acacia

St John's Wood Terrace

Road

Grand Union Canal

Circus Road

Grove End Road

Cochrane Street

Allitsen

Charlbert Street

Prince Albert Road

WINTER GARDENS

Wellington Road

St John's Wood High Street

Winfield House

ST JOHN'S WOOD

St John's Wood Church

London Central Mosque

Grove End Road

Marylebone Cricket Club (Lords Cricket Ground)

Lodge Road

Hanover Bridges

Longbridge

Children's Boating Pond

St John's Wood Road

Park Road

Boating Lake

Outer Circle

Restaurants ①

Marylebone and Fitzrovia
63 Riding House Café E4
64 Fishworks C4
67 Pied à Terre E4
69 Da Paolo E4
71 Roka E4
72 Orrery C4
73 Oscar Bar and Grill E4
74 Salt Yard E4
75 Original Tagines C4
76 Navarro's E4
77 The Providores &
    Tapa Room C4
78 Reuben's C4

Hotels ①

Marylebone, Bloomsbury and Holborn
47 Landmark London B4
53 Montagu House Hotel C4
56 The Regency Hotel C4
62 Sherlock Holmes Hotel C4
63 Wyndham Hotel B4

Bars & Cafés ①

Marylebone and Fitzrovia
38 Fitzroy Tavern E4
44 Coco Momo C4
47 La Fromagerie C4
48 Lantana E4
49 Pâtisserie Valerie C4

Rossmore

Road

Park Road

Clarence

St Paul

Balcombe Street

Gloucester Place

Sherlock Holmes Museum

Baker Street

Bradley Street

Lisson Grove

Harewood Avenue

Boston Place

Marylebone Mainline Railway Station

Dorset Square

Marlebone

LISSON GROVE

Maryl

Edgware Road

Bell Street

Westway (Elevated)

Harrow Road

Harrow Road

PADDINGTON

Paddington Basin

Edgware Road

Edgware Road

Chapel Street

Marylebone Road

Marylebone Road

Harcourt St

Homer St

Old Marylebone Road

Homer Row

Crawford Street

Seymour Place

Salisbury Pl

Wyndham St

Knox St

Enford St

Upper Montagu Street

York

York St

Crawford Place

Bickenhall St

Gloucester Place

St Clay St

Montagu Mans

Dorset

Montagu Place

47

53

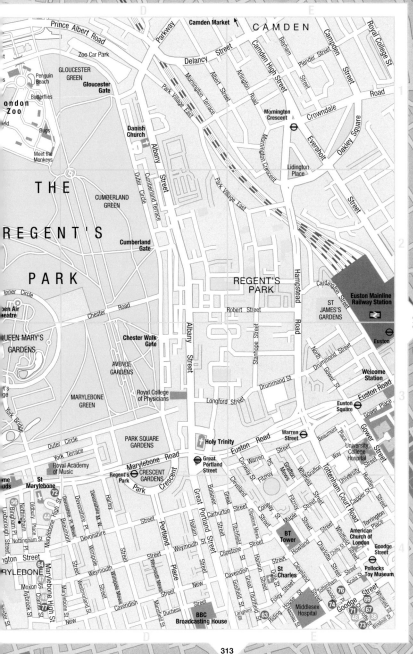

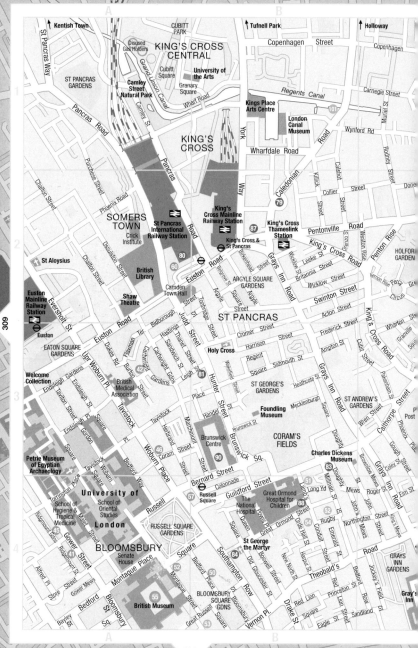

Highbury Theberton St

ISLINGTON
Celestial Church
of Christ

ISLINGTON
GREEN

Buisness
Design
Centre

St Mary's

Regents Canal
Noel Road
Vincent Terrace

Angel

0   100   200   300   400   500 yds
0   100   200   300   400   500 m

Arlington
Square

NTONVILLE

Angel ⊖

Road

City Road

City Road

Myddelton

Sadler's Wells
Theatre

FINSBURY

The City
University

Finsbury
Town Hall

CLERKENWELL

Moreland Street

Lever Street

Seward Street

Percival Street

Goswell Road

Old Street

St James

St John ⊖

70

Clerkenwell

Barts
Medical
College

Charterhouse

Farringdon
Station

Farringdon ⊖
Cross Street

98

Smithfield
Central Market

St
Etheldreda

94

Ben Johnson
House

Exhibition
Halls

Chiswell Street

Beech Street

Arts Centre

Defoe
House

BARBICAN

Barbican ⊖

109

Silk Street

Guildhall School
of Music & Drama

T. More
House

St Giles

Hotels ❶

Marylebone, Bloomsbury and Holborn
41 Academy Hotel A4
42 Crescent Hotel A3
45 Gower House Hotel A4
46 Holiday Inn Bloomsbury A3
50 Lonsdale Hotel B4
52 Montague on the Gardens A4
57 Hotel Russell A/B4
60 St Pancras Renaissance Hotel A2

St Paul's and The City
70 The Zetter D4

Restaurants ❶

Bloomsbury and King's Cross
79 Addis Restaurantxv
80 The Gilbert Scott A2
81 North Sea Fish Restaurant B3
83 Salaam Namaste B3
84 Cosmoba B4
87 Camino
88 Cigala B4
90 The Bruswick Centre B3

Holborn and The Inns of Court
94 Bleeding Heart Restaurant & Bistro D4

St Paul's and The City
98 Hix Oyster and Chop House D4
100 St John D4
102 Café du Marché D4
107 Eagle C3
108 Little Bay C3
109 Searcy's E4
110 Cicada D3
111 Moro C3

Bars & Cafés ❶

Bloomsbury and King's Cross
51 The Lamb B4
52 Perseverance B4
53 Truckles B4
54 Vats Wine Bar B4
55 Court Restaurant A4

St Paul's and The City
63 Jerusalem Tavern D4
69 Smiths of Smithfield D4
71 Vinoteca D4

North London
101 Canal 125 B1
102 Patisserie Bliss D2
103 The Winchester D1

315

Restaurants ❶

Mayfair to Oxford Street
45 Hard Rock Café E4
46 Kai E3
47 Princess Garden E2
48 Scotts E2
49 Alain Ducasse E3
50 Le Gavroche E2
51 Hélène Darroze E2
52 Truc Vert E3
56 Nobu E3
60 Maze E2

Marylebone and Fitzrovia
65 Golden Hinde E1
66 Galvin Bistrot de Luxe D1
68 Caffe Caldesi E1
70 Locanda Locatelli D1

**Knightsbridge, Kensington
and Notting Hill**
137 The Orangery
142 Fifth Floor Harvey Nichols D4
144 Marcus Wareing at The Berkeley D4

Bars & Cafés ❶

Mayfair to Oxford Street
30 Audley E2
33 Claridge's Bar E2
34 Coburg Bar at the Connaught E2
35 Dorchester Bar E3
36 Met Bar E3

Marylebone and Fitzrovia
39 Golden Eagle E1
50 The Wallace E1

**Knightsbridge, Kensington
and Notting Hill**
87 Blue Bar D4
88 Library Bar E4
89 Mandarin Bar D4

Chelsea
95 Grenadier E4

Hotels ❶

Westminster and Victoria
3 Berkeley Hotel D4
9 Halkin Hotel E4

St James's and Mayfair
28 Claridge's E2
29 The Connaught E2
30 The Dorchester E3
32 The Four Seasons E4
33 Lanesborough Hotel E4
34 London Hilton on Park
Lane E4
35 London InterContinental
Hotel E3
36 Metropolitan E3
37 Millennium Hotel London
Mayfair E2

**Marylebone, Bloomsbury
and Holborn**
43 Cumberland Hotel D2
44 Durrants Hotel E1
49 Lincoln House Hotel D1
51 Marble Arch Inn D1
54 Montcalm Hotel D1
55 No. Ten Manchester Street E1
58 Thistle Marble Arch D2

**Knightsbridge, Kensington
and Chelsea**
81 Cadogan Hotel D4
87 The Gore B4
89 Knightsbridge Green Hotel
91 Mandarin Oriental Hyde
Park D4
94 Royal Garden Hotel A4

PADDINGTON

Paddington Basin
Paddington Basin
South Wharf Road
Eastbourne Terrace
Praed Street
Norfolk Square
St Michael's Street
Star Street
Sussex
London Street
Chilworth Street
Gloucester

**Paddington
Mainline Railway
Station**

Paddington

Sussex Gardens
Gloucester
Sussex Square

Craven Road
Westbourne Ter
Gloucester Terrace
Westbourne St
Lancaster Ter

Craven Gate
Lancaster Gate
Marlborough Gate
Lancaster Gate
Lancaster Gate
Westbourne Gate
Victoria Gate
Bayswater

ITALIAN
GARDENS
The Fountains

West Carriage Drive

BUCKHILL

**Speke's
Monument**
Peter Pan

Longwater

Serpentine Sackler Gallery

Norwegian
British Monument

KENSINGTON

THE PADDOCK

The Broad Walk

**Sunken
Garden**

Kensington Palace 132

Round Pond

Temple Lodge
Physical Energy

Serpentine Gallery

Princess Diana Memorial Fountain

Rotton R

GARDENS

Kensington Palace Gardens
Palace Avenue

Bandstand

Tennis Courts

Bowling Green

West Carriage Drive

94
King's Arms Gate
Kensington High St
De Vere Gardens
Victoria Rd
Palace Gate
Palace Gate
Hyde Park Gate
Kensington Rd
Hyde Park Gate
Queen's Gate
Albert Memorial
Kensington Gore
Alexandra Gate
Prince of Wales Gate
Kensington Road

Queen's Gate Ter
67
Royal College of Art
Royal Albert Hall
Royal Geographical Society

Prince Consort Road
Exhibition Road
Princess Gardens

KNIGHTSBRIDGE

0 100 200 300 400 500 yds
0 100 200 300 400 500 m

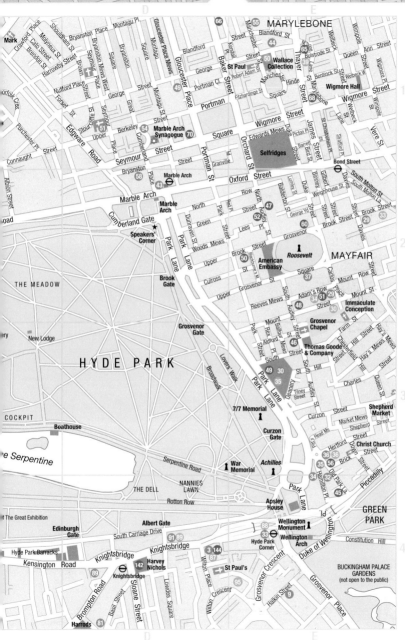

MARYLEBONE

St Paul

Wallace Collection

Wigmore Hall

Marble Arch Synagogue

Selfridges

Marble Arch

Speakers' Corner

Marble Arch

MAYFAIR

Brook Gate

American Embassy

Roosevelt

Grosvenor Gate

Immaculate Conception

Grosvenor Chapel

Thomas Goode & Company

THE MEADOW

HYDE PARK

7/7 Memorial

COCKPIT

Shepherd Market

Boathouse

Curzon Gate

Christ Church

New Lodge

War Memorial

Achilles

Serpentine

Apsley House

THE DELL

NANNIES LAWN

Rotton Row

GREEN PARK

f The Great Exhibition

Albert Gate

Edinburgh Gate

Wellington Monument

Wellington Arch

Hyde Park Corner

Hyde Park Barracks

Knightsbridge

Harvey Nichols

St Paul's

BUCKINGHAM PALACE GARDENS
(not open to the public)

Kensington Road

Knightsbridge

Harrods

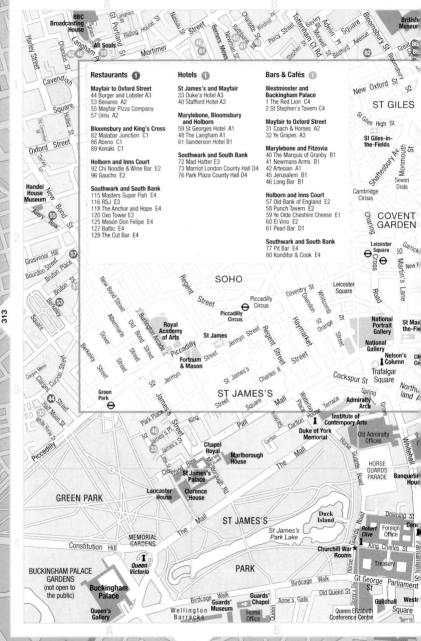

Restaurants ❶

Mayfair to Oxford Street
44 Burger and Lobster A3
53 Benares A2
55 Mayfair Pizza Company A3
57 Umu A2

Bloomsbury and King's Cross
82 Malabar Junction C1
86 Abeno C1
89 Konaki C1

Holborn and Inns Court
92 Chi Noodle & Wine Bar E2
96 Gaucho E2

Southwark and South Bank
115 Masters Super Fish E4
116 RSJ E3
118 The Anchor and Hope E4
120 Oxo Tower E3
125 Mesón Don Felipe E4
127 Baltic E4
128 The Cut Bar E4

Hotels ❶

St James's and Mayfair
33 Duke's Hotel A3
40 Stafford Hotel A3

Marylebone, Bloomsbury and Holborn
59 St Georges Hotel A1
48 The Langham A1
61 Sanderson Hotel B1

Southwark and South Bank
72 Mad Hatter E3
73 Marriot London County Hall D4
76 Park Plaza County Hall D4

Bars & Cafés ❶

Westminster and Buckingham Palace
1 The Red Lion C4
2 St Stephen's Tavern C4

Mayfair to Oxford Street
31 Coach & Horses A2
32 Ye Grapes A3

Marylebone and Fitzovia
40 The Marquis of Granby B1
41 Newmans Arms B1
42 Artesian A1
45 Jerusalem B1
46 Long Bar B1

Holborn and Inns Court
57 Old Bank of England E2
58 Punch Tavern E2
59 Ye Olde Cheshire Cheese E1
60 El Vino E2
61 Pearl Bar D1

Southwark and South Bank
77 Pit Bar E4
80 Konditor & Cook E4

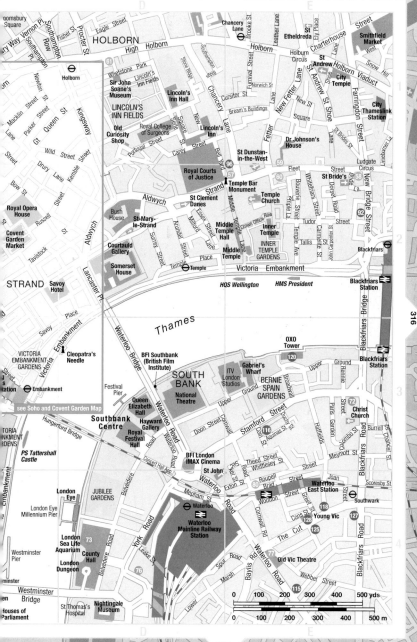

HOLBORN

Bloomsbury Square
Southampton Row
Vernon Place
Fisher St
Procter St
Eagle Street
Chancery Lane
Brooke St
Leather Lane
Ely Place
St Etheldreda
Charterhouse Street
Smithfield Market West
Smithfield Market

Southampton Row
Whetstone Park
Newton St
Macklin
Parker Street
Gt Queen St
Kingsway
High Holborn
Stone Bldgs
Southampton Bldgs
Furnival St
Holborn
Holborn Circus
St Andrew
Snow Hill
Holborn Viaduct
City Temple

Holborn

Sir John Soane's Museum
Lincoln's Inn Fields
Norwich St
New St
New Fetter Lane
Shoe Lane
City Thameslink Station

LINCOLN'S INN FIELDS
Lincoln's Inn Hall
Cursitor St
Bream's Buildings
Square
Fetter
St Bride's Street

Macklin
Lane
Old Curiosity Shop
Royal College of Surgeons
Portugal Street
Lincoln's Inn
Carey Street
Chancery Lane
New St Square
Dr Johnson's House

Wild Street
Drury Lane
Kemble Street
Bow St
Russell St
Tavistock

Royal Opera House
Covent Garden Market

Bush House
Aldwych
St Clement Danes
St-Mary-le-Strand
Royal Courts of Justice
Temple Bar Monument
Fleet
Street
Ludgate Circus
New Bridge Street

STRAND
Savoy Hotel
Lancaster Pl
Courtauld Gallery
Somerset House
Arundel Street
Surrey Street
Milford Lane
Essex Street
Temple Place
Middle Temple Hall
Middle Temple
Temple Church
Crown Office Row
Inner Temple
INNER TEMPLE GARDENS
Tudor Street
Tallis St
Carmelite St
Whitefriars Street
Bouverie Street
Temple Ave
Temple La
Blackfriars

Savoy Place
Victoria Embankment
Temple
Victoria Embankment
Blackfriars Bridge
Blackfriars Station

Cleopatra's Needle
VICTORIA EMBANKMENT GARDENS
Embankment
HQS Wellington
HMS President
Blackfriars Station

Thames

PS Tattershall Castle
Hungerford Bridge
Festival Pier
BFI Southbank (British Film Institute)
SOUTH BANK
ITV London Studios
Gabriel's Wharf
BERNIE SPAIN GARDENS
OXO Tower
120
Upper Ground
Ground
Rennie
Christ Church
Burrell St

National Theatre
Queen Elizabeth Hall
Hayward Gallery
Royal Festival Hall
Southbank Centre
Waterloo Bridge
Upper Ground
Doon Street
Cornwall
Stamford Street
Duchy St
Aquinas St
116
Hatfields
Paris Garden
Colombo St
Meymott St
72

London Eye
JUBILEE GARDENS
London Eye Millennium Pier
Belvedere Road
Concert Hall App
BFI London IMAX Cinema
St John
Theed Street
Whittlesey St
Roupell Street
Cornwall Rd
Waterloo
Exton St
80
Brad
Wootton
Great Suffolk St
Waterloo East Station
Southwark
118
127
Scoresby St

Westminster Pier
London Sea Life Aquarium
73
County Hall
London Dungeon
76
York Road
Leake St
Waterloo
Mepham St
Waterloo Mainline Railway Station
Cons St
128
Young Vic
The Cut
125
Blackfriars Road

Westminster Bridge
Houses of Parliament
St Thomas's Hospital
Nightingale Museum
Lower Marsh
Spur Road
Baylis Rd
Waterloo Road
Cornwall Rd
Old Vic Theatre
Webber Street
77
115

see Soho and Covent Garden Map

0	100	200	300	400	500 yds
0	100	200	300	400	500 m

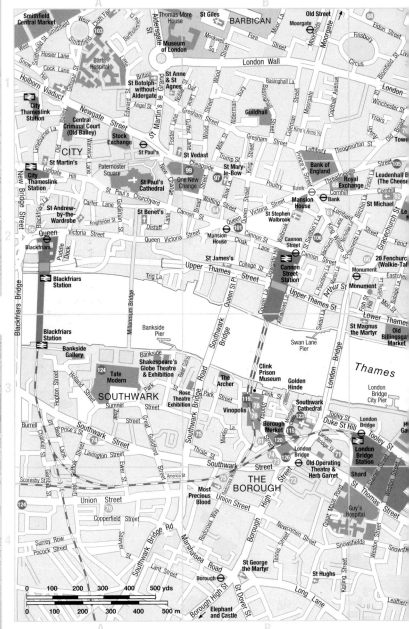

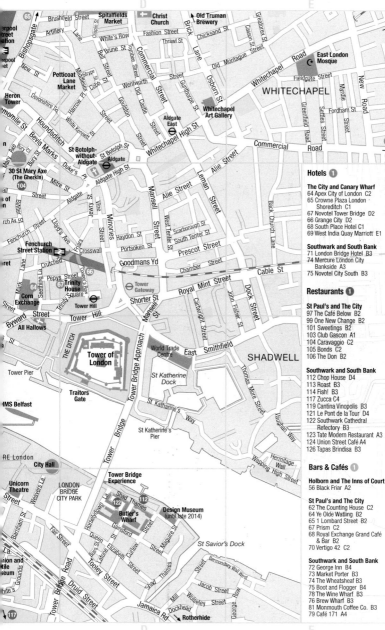

WHITECHAPEL

SHADWELL

Hotels ①

The City and Canary Wharf
64 Apex City of London C2
65 Crowne Plaza London
 Shoreditch C1
67 Novotel Tower Bridge D2
66 Grange City D2
68 South Place Hotel C1
69 West India Quay Marriott E1

Southwark and South Bank
71 London Bridge Hotel B3
74 Mercure London City
 Bankside A3
75 Novotel City South B3

Restaurants ①

St Paul's and The City
97 The Café Below B2
99 One New Change B2
101 Sweetings B2
103 Club Gascon A1
104 Caravaggio C2
105 Bonds C2
106 The Don B2

Southwark and South Bank
112 Chop House D4
113 Roast B3
114 Fish! B3
117 Zucca C4
119 Cantina Vinopolis B3
121 Le Pont de la Tour D4
122 Southwark Cathedral
 Refectory B3
123 Tate Modern Restaurant A3
124 Union Street Café A4
126 Tapas Brindisa B3

Bars & Cafés ①

Holborn and The Inns of Court
56 Black Friar A2

St Paul's and The City
62 The Counting House C2
64 Ye Olde Watling B2
65 1 Lombard Street B2
67 Prism C2
68 Royal Exchange Grand Café
 & Bar B2
70 Vertigo 42 C2

Southwark and South Bank
72 George Inn B4
73 Market Porter B3
74 The Wheatsheaf B3
75 Boot and Flogger B4
78 The Wine Wharf B3
76 Brew Wharf B3
81 Monmouth Coffee Co. B3
79 Café 171 A4

KENSINGTON

St Margarets Lane

Kensington Parish Park

Cornwall Gardens

Cornwall Gardens

Lexham Gardens

84

Stanford Road

Victoria Road

Launceston Place

Gloucester Road

Elvaston Place

Queen's Gate Gardens

Queen's Gdns

Queen's Gate Terrace

Royal College of Music

Imperial College

Imperial College Road

Science Museum

Natural History Museum

Victoria & A Museu

St Stephen

Cromwell Road

Cromwell Road

Cromwell Road

Cromwe

Thurloe Place

Thurloe Street

Lexham Gardens

Cromwell Road

Gloucester Road

135

Courtfield Road

Stanhope Gdns

SOUTH KENSINGTON

South Kensington

Pelham

Hammersmith

EARL'S COURT

85

88

Earl's Court

92
93

Courtfield Gdns

St Jude's

Collingham Road

Barkston Gardens

Laverton Place

Bramham Gdns

Bolton Gardens

Earl's Court Road

Courtfield Road

Harrington Gardens

Wetherby Gardens

Old Brompton Road

Harrington Road

Queen's Gate Mews

Gloucester Road

Onslow Gardens

Cranley Pl.

Summer

Onslow Square

Onslow

Square

78

St Paul

161

Four's Terrace

Neville St.

Selwood Terrace

Fulham Road

80

83

Old Brompton Road

Old Brompton Rd

Redcliffe Gardens

Finborough Road

Coleherne Road

The Little Boltons

Redcliffe Square

St Luke's

Hardcourt Terrace

The Boltons

Tregunter Road

Drayton Gardens

Roland Gardens

Cranley Gardens

St Yeghiche

Evelyn

Gardens

Drayton Gardens

Elm Park Gdns

Elm Park Gdns

Elm Park Road

Beaufort Street

Chelsea

Square

Old Church Street

Carlyle Square

King's R

147

WEST BROMPTON

Finborough Road

Ifield Road

Redcliffe Gardens

Cathcart Road

Hollywood Road

Redcliffe Road

Gilston Road

Fulham Road

Park Walk

BROMPTON CEMETERY

Cemetery Chapel

Edith Grove

Gunter Grove

Hortensia Road

Fulham Road

King's

WORLD'S END

149 159

Milman's Square

Pultons Square

Riley Road

Beaufort Road

Denyers Street

Che Old Chu

Cheyne Walk

Battersea Bridge

Stamford Bridge (Chelsea Football Club)

Fulham

96 154

100

Hotels ❶

Westminster and Victoria
15 Tophams E2

Knightsbridge, Kensington and Chelsea
78 Aster House B2
80 Blakes Hotel B2
82 Capital Hotel D1
83 Draycott Hotel D2
84 easyHotel
      South Kensington A1
85 Enterprise Hotel A2
88 Hotel Indigo A2
92 My Place Hotel A2
93 Oliver Plaza Hotel A2

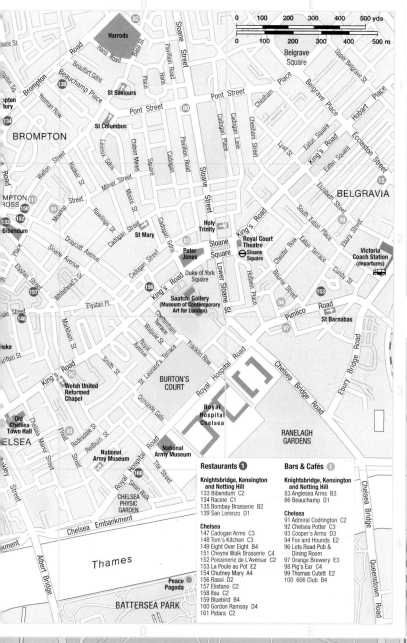

Restaurants ❶

Knightsbridge, Kensington and Notting Hill
133 Bibendum C2
134 Racine C1
135 Bombay Brasserie B2
139 San Lorenzo D1

Chelsea
147 Cadogan Arms C3
148 Tom's Kitchen C3
149 Eight Over Eight B4
151 Cheyne Walk Brasserie C4
152 Poissonerie de L'Avenue C2
153 La Poule au Pot E2
154 Chutney Mary A4
156 Rasoi D2
157 Elistano C2
158 Itsu C2
159 Bluebird B4
160 Gordon Ramsay D4
161 Patara C2

Bars & Cafés ❶

Knightsbridge, Kensington and Notting Hill
83 Anglesea Arms B3
86 Beauchamp D1

Chelsea
91 Admiral Codrington C2
92 Chelsea Potter C3
93 Cooper's Arms D3
94 Fox and Hounds E2
96 Lots Road Pub & Dining Room
97 Orange Brewery E3
98 Pig's Ear C4
99 Thomas Cubitt E2
100 606 Club B4

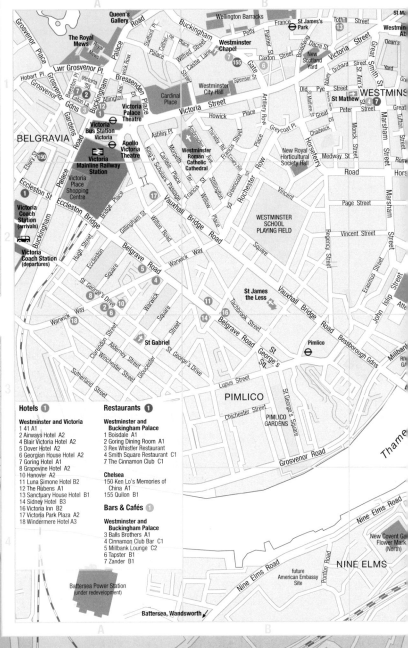

Hotels ❶

Westminster and Victoria
1 41 A1
2 Airways Hotel A2
4 Blair Victoria Hotel A2
5 Dover Hotel A2
6 Georgian House Hotel A2
7 Goring Hotel A1
8 Grapevine Hotel A2
10 Hanover A2
11 Luna Simone Hotel B2
12 The Rubens A1
13 Sanctuary House Hotel B1
14 Sidney Hotel B3
16 Victoria Inn B2
17 Victoria Park Plaza A2
18 Windermere Hotel A3

Restaurants ❶

**Westminster and
Buckingham Palace**
1 Boisdale A1
2 Goring Dining Room A1
3 Rex Whistler Restaurant
4 Smith Square Restaurant C1
7 The Cinnamon Club C1

Chelsea
150 Ken Lo's Memories of
China A1
155 Quilon B1

Bars & Cafés ❶

**Westminster and
Buckingham Palace**
3 Balls Brothers A1
4 Cinnamon Club Bar C1
5 Millbank Lounge C2
6 Tapster B1
7 Zander B1

Palace of
Westminster

Houses of
Parliament

VICTORIA
TOWER
GARDENS

's
rt Hall

Millbank

Millbank
Millennium
Pier

Embankment

Albert

ndsworth Rd

Glass House Walk

MI6
Headquarters

Vauxhall Cross

Vauxhall ⊖

Vauxhall
Station

rry Street

Street

South Lambert Rd

↓ Clapham

Lambeth Bridge

St Thomas's
Hospital

Road

Palace

ARCHBISHOP'S
PARK

Lambeth

Lambeth
Palace

Museum of
Garden History

Lambeth

Road

Lambeth High Street

Old Paradise St

Newport Street

Tyers Street

Black Prince Road

Vauxhall Walk

Vauxhall
Methodist
Church

SPRING
GARDENS

VAUXHALL

Tyers Street

Lane

Kennington

Harleyford Road

Durham St.

Lawn Lane

VAUXHALL
PARK

Fentiman Road

Kennington Oval

Carlisle Lane

Hercules Road

Lambeth Walk

Walnut Tree Walk

Fitzalan Street

LAMBETH
WALK

Newburn Street

Vauxhall Street

Sancroft Street

Kennington Lane

Vauxhall Street

Kennington Oval

The Oval
Cricket
Ground

Westminster

Bridge

Road

Baylis Rd

Lambeth
North ⊖

Kennington Road

Christ Church &
Upton Chapel

St Mary's

Road

Kennington

Road

Wincott Street

Chester Square

Kennington

Westminster Bridge Rd

St George's
Cathedral

St

George's

Road

Lambeth

GERALDINE MARY
HARMSWORTH
PARK

Imperial
War
Museum

Brook Drive

Gilbert Road

LAMBETH

Lane

Kennington

Kennington

Road

Kennington ⊖

Cleaver
Square

Kennington Park

Road

De Laune Street

Road

KENNINGTON

Clayton Street

Bowling Green St

Kennington Park Road

Kennington Park Pl

KENNINGTON
PARK

St Agnes Place

Oval ⊖

KENNINGTON
COMMON

| 0 | 100 | 200 | 300 | 400 | 500 yds |
| 0 | 100 | 200 | 300 | 400 | 500 m |

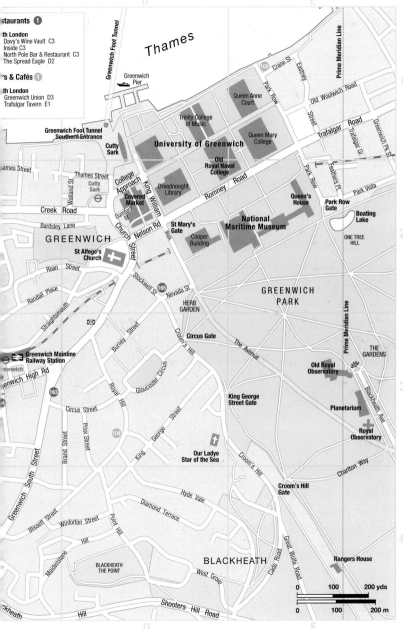

Thames

Greenwich Foot Tunnel

Greenwich Pier

Greenwich Foot Tunnel
Southern Entrance

Cutty Sark

hames Street

Thames Street

Cutty Sark

Creek Road

Bardsley Lane

GREENWICH

St Alfege's Church

Roan Street

Randall Place

Straightsmouth

Greenwich Mainline Railway Station

eenwich

enwich High Rd

Circus Street

Brand Street

Prior Street

Greenwich South Street

Blissett Street

Winforton Street

Maidenstone Hill

BLACKHEATH THE POINT

kheath

Hill

College Approach

King William Walk

Durnford St

Church Street

Walland St

Nelson Rd

Stockwell St

Nevada St

Burney Street

Royal Hill

Gloucester Circus

King George Street

Croom's Hill

Point Hill

Diamond Terrace

Hyde Vale

West Grove

Shooters Hill Road

Trinity College of Music

University of Greenwich

Dreadnought Library

Covered Market

St Mary's Gate

Cooper Building

HERB GARDEN

Circus Gate

Our Ladye Star of the Sea

Queen Anne Court

Old Royal Naval College

Romney Road

National Maritime Museum

GREENWICH PARK

The Avenue

King George Street Gate

Croom's Hill

Croom's Hill Gate

Crane St

Eastney

Park Row

Queen Mary College

Queen's House

Park Row Gate

ONE TREE HILL

Prime Meridian Line

Old Woolwich Road

Trafalgar Road

Feathers Pl

Park Vista

Park Row

Boating Lake

Prime Meridian Line

Old Royal Observatory

Planetarium

Royal Observatory

Charlton Way

Great Wolfe Road

Cade Road

Rangers House

BLACKHEATH

Greenwich Pk St

Trafalgar Gr

Park Vista

THE GARDENS

Blackheath Ave

0   100   200 yds

0   100   200 m

STREET INDEX

RESTAURANTS

PUBS, BARS AND CAFÉS

INSIGHT GUIDES

LONDON

Project Editor
Tom Stainer
Series Manager
Carine Tracanelli
Picture Editor/Art Editor
Tom Smyth/Shahid Mahmood
Map Production
original cartography Mapping based on OSM data, © OpenStreetMap contributors (CC BY-SA) Styled by Phoenix Mapping Ltd, updated by Apa Cartography Department
Production
Tynan Dean and Rebeka Davies

Distribution

UK
Dorling Kindersley Ltd
A Penguin Group company
80 Strand, London, WC2R 0RL
sales@uk.dk.com

United States
Ingram Publisher Services
1 Ingram Boulevard, PO Box 3006,
La Vergne, TN 37086-1986
ips@ingramcontent.com

Australia and New Zealand
Woodslane
10 Apollo St
Warriewood NSW 2102
Australia
info@woodslane.com.au

Worldwide
Apa Publications GmbH & Co. Verlag KG (Singapore branch)
7030 Ang Mo Kio Avenue 5
08-65 Northstar @ AMK
Singapore 569880
apasin@singnet.com.sg

Printing

CTPS-China
© 2014 Apa Publications (UK) Ltd
All Rights Reserved

First Edition 1989
Fourteenth Edition 2014

NO part of this book may be reproduced, stored in a retrieval system or transmitted in any form or means electronic, mechanical, photocopying, recording or otherwise, without prior written permission of Apa Publications. Brief text quotations with use of photographs are exempted for book review purposes only. Information has been obtained from sources believed to be reliable, but its accuracy and completeness, and the opinions based thereon, are not guaranteed.

www.insightguides.com

ABOUT THIS BOOK

What makes an Insight Guide different? Since our first book pioneered the use of creative full-colour photography in travel guides in 1970, we have aimed to provide not only reliable information but also the key to a real understanding of a destination and its people. To achieve this, our books rely on the authority of locally based writers and photographers.

The Contributors

This fully updated edition of *Insight Guide London* was commissioned and edited by **Tom Stainer** at Insight's London editorial office.

The entire book has been comprehensively updated by **Sian Lezard**, a travel editor who lives in west London.

The fourteenth edition of this book builds on previous editions produced by **Catherine Dreghorn**, **Rachel Lawrence**, **Dorothy Stannard**, **Brian Bell**, **Roger Williams** and **Andrew Eames**. Past contributors whose work is still evident here include **Roland Collins** (history), **Srinvasa Rao** (Who Lives in London?), **Rebecca Ford**, **Allison Lobbett** and **Tim Grimwade**. The design was created by **Klaus Geisler** and the principal photographer was **Lydia Evans**, a regular contributor to Insight Guides. **James Macdonald** was the cartography editor for this guide.

The book was copy-edited by **Stephanie Smith** and the index compiled by **Penny Phenix**.

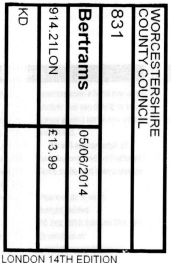

SEND US YOUR TH

We do our best to ensure the in
in our books is as accurate and
up-to-date as possible. The boo
updated on a regular basis usin
contacts, who painstakingly ad
and correct as required. Howev
details (such as telephone num
opening times) are liable to cha
we are ultimately reliant on our
to put us in the picture.

We welcome your feedback
especially your experience of u
book "on the road". Maybe we

WORCESTERSHIRE COUNTY COUNCIL
831
Bertrams 05/06/2014
914.21LON £13.99
KD
LONDON 14TH EDITION
London
962959/00064 - 1 of 1

West End Theatres and Cinemas

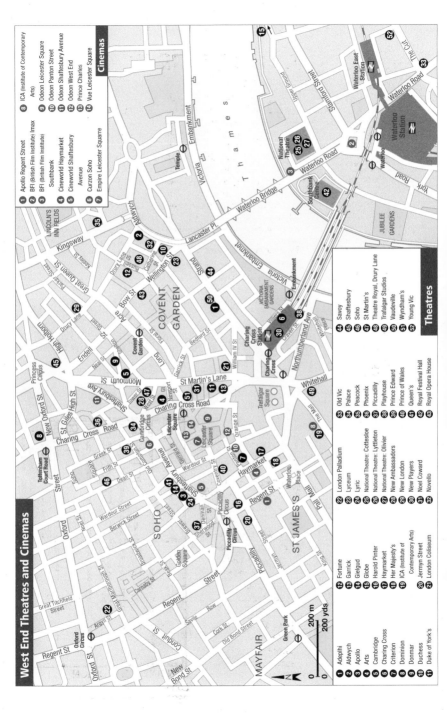

Theatres

① Adelphi
② Aldwych
③ Apollo
④ Arts
⑤ Cambridge
⑥ Charing Cross
⑦ Criterion
⑧ Dominion
⑨ Donmar
⑩ Duchess
⑪ Duke of York's

⑫ Fortune
⑬ Garrick
⑭ Gielgud
⑮ Globe
⑯ Harold Pinter
⑰ Haymarket
⑱ Her Majesty's
⑲ ICA (Institute of Contemporary Arts)
⑳ Jermyn Street
㉑ London Coliseum

㉒ London Palladium
㉓ Lyceum
㉔ Lyric
㉕ National Theatre: Cottesloe
㉖ National Theatre: Lyttleton
㉗ National Theatre: Olivier
㉘ New Ambassadors
㉙ New London
㉚ New Players
㉛ Noel Coward
㉜ Novello

㉝ Old Vic
㉞ Palace
㉟ Peacock
㊱ Phoenix
㊲ Piccadilly
㊳ Playhouse
㊴ Prince Edward
㊵ Prince of Wales
㊶ Queen's
㊷ Royal Festival Hall
㊸ Royal Opera House

㊹ Savoy
㊺ Shaftesbury
㊻ Soho
㊼ St Martin's
㊽ Theatre Royal, Drury Lane
㊾ Trafalgar Studios
㊿ Vaudeville
51 Wyndham's
52 Young Vic

Cinemas

① Apollo Regent Street
② BFI (British Film Institute) Imax
③ BFI (British Film Institute) Southbank
④ Cineworld Haymarket
⑤ Cineworld Shaftesbury Avenue
⑥ Curzon Soho
⑦ Empire Leicester Square

⑧ ICA (Institute of Contemporary Arts)
⑨ Odeon Leicester Square
⑩ Odeon Panton Street
⑪ Odeon Shaftesbury Avenue
⑫ Odeon West End
⑬ Prince Charles
⑭ Vue Leicester Square